CW00419541

An Inside Look at the
of the Ultra-Orthodox Society

One Above
and
Seven Below

A Consumer's Guide to Orthodox Judaism
from the Perspective of the Chareidim

by

Yechezkel Hirshman

 Mazo Publishers

Jerusalem, Israel

One Above and Seven Below

ISBN 978-965-7344-18-7 - Hard cover

ISBN 978-965-7344-38-5 - Soft cover

Published by:

Mazo Publishers

P.O. Box 36084 ~ Jerusalem 91360 Israel

Israel: 054-7294-565   USA: 1-815-301-3559

Website: www.mazopublishers.com

Email: cm@mazopublishers.com

Contact The Author
Yechezkel Hirshman
1a7b.author@gmail.com

Cover Photograph by Studio Fisch, Jerusalem
Cover Design by Moshe Handel
Edited by Zvi H. Starck

Printed in Israel

RABBI ZEV LEFF

Rabbi of Moshav Matityahu
Hayeshiva Yeshiva Gedola Matisyahu

modiin 71917 ד.נ. מודיעין   tel. 08-976-1138 טל׳   fax 08-976-5326 פקס

הרב זאב לף

מרא דאתרא מושב מתתיהו
ראש הישיבה ישיבה גדולה מתתיהו

בס״ד

Dear Friends,

I have read portions of the manuscript "One Above and Seven Below" by Yechezkel Hirshman.

Although I generally shun labeling Jews and so defining them, this book seeks to define chareidim not by any external or nonessential criteria but rather to define what a true serious Torah Jew is, transcending all grouping and labeling.

I recommend this book for all those who want to consider and examine what being a Torah Jew entails from a serious and essential perspective.

I commend the author on his bravery to tackle such a sensitive issue and for his insightful understanding of the essentials of true Torah Judaism. I have found the book inspiring, informative and entertaining – presenting at times very serious and biting mussar with a healthy sense of humor. May Hashem grant him the ability to continue to merit the community with further works.

With Torah blessings,

Rabbi Zev Leff

Moshav Shitufi   מושב שיתופי

d.n. modiin 71917   ד.נ. מודיעין
tel. 08-976-1016   טל׳
fax 08-976-1124   פקס

Excerpts of a letter to the author from Rabbi Mordechai D. Noigershall – (Translated from Hebrew):

Rabbi Mordechai Noigershall, Director
Judaism from a Different Angle, Ltd.
Public Relations and Publications
P.O. Box 50159 Jerusalem 91501
Tel/Fax +972-2-5816573

B"H Kislev 5767

To the Honor of R' Yechezkel Hirshman, N"Y

I have leafed through pages of your upcoming book, [One Above and Seven Below], which is geared to contend with sensitive questions that challenge the uniqueness of life within chareidi society.

There are numerous concepts that carry a need for clarification for, even among those who are believers of this way of life and who adhere to it, it is not always the case that they are sufficiently versed as to how to articulate them and, when they are flung into a dialogue concerning these and similar issues, they may at times come across to appear disoriented. Thus, you have done well in your approach to touch upon the heart of these issues based on the ideology of the Torah and with using an easygoing style. In the course of dealing with the issues themselves, you also point to an avenue of how to contend with them: with charm, with lightness, with a sense of humor, and with a small measure of sarcasm where it may be called for.

May Hashem grant that your work may achieve favor among all those for whom these matters are relevant, and may it increase forces for Torah and a proper ideology.

Blessing you with affection and with a full heart,

Mordechai Dovid Noigershall

FAQs About This Book

What is this book about?

This book is about the ideology of authentic Torah Judaism, otherwise known as chareidi Judaism, ultra-Orthodox Judaism, or Talmudic Judaism, although we think of it as just plain Judaism. It is what we call *hashkafa*. This book is unique in that it applies the principles of hashkafa to the cultural (what I call the socio-political) landscape of Orthodox Judaism and deals with many of the pertinent issues. As such, it is a blend of Torah hashkafa and socio-political debate.

Why did you write this book?

This question is addressed in detail in the Introduction. Nevertheless, the short answer is to help people deal with questions that I have heard again and again for years; questions that start with:

"Why don't yeshiva guys…?"
"Why can't chareidim be…?"
"Where is it written that…?"
"What could be wrong with…?"
"Isn't it a *chillul Hashem* (sacrilege) to…?"

What do you expect this book to achieve?

This book is meant to help people understand and come to terms with basic Torah hashkafa, based predominantly on Rashi's commentary of Chumash, and with those who endeavor to put it into practice.

The aims of this book are:

- To promote better understanding of the chareidi world in the eyes of Orthodox Jews who do not consider themselves to be chareidi. Hopefully, to build bridges.

- To help one who is searching for a clear religious ideology to see the benefits of being chareidi – I call this: Comparative shopping.

Important Note – The intention is to promote the conventions that the chareidim uphold. It is *not* meant to challenge the conventions of those who are not chareidi, although in some cases, it is an inevitable cause-and-effect. Although to some readers – who do not [yet] wish to identify themselves as chareidi – parts of this book may inadvertently seem patronizing or antagonistic, be assured that this is certainly not its purpose. I apologize in advance should this occur.

Who is this book for?

Anybody who can benefit from it.

Okay. So who can benefit from this book?

Lots of folks, such as:

- Mainstream chareidi yeshiva students who are fully knowledgeable in Torah *hashkafa* but need help in articulating the hashkafa and in presenting it to others.

- Seminary girls who need a concise guide (in plain English) to understand the hashkafot that they are being taught to embrace.

- Chareidim who are struggling with their sense of identity and/or may have been "turned off."

- *Baalei teshuva* (newly religious) and converts who are newly entering the Orthodox world and are confused and disparaged by the apparent discord within the various factions of Orthodoxy.

- Non-chareidi parents who have difficulty dealing with their offspring who have turned "black."

- My wife's cousins in Great Neck.

  And finally:

- Non-chareidi Orthodox Jews (NCOJs) who are sincerely interested in getting a clearer and more accurate understanding of the people who are closest to them, yet from whom they feel so distant.

Who is this book not for?

This book is definitely not for everyone!

I wrote earlier that this book is for anyone who may benefit from it. If you don't believe that you can benefit from it, *do not read it*.

- This book is for religious Jews who are chareidi and seek *chizuk* (encouragement) or who are non-chareidi and seek *hadracha* (guidance). While this book aims to help a chareidi who may be having "second thoughts" or a non-chareidi who is "undecided," it is not out to convert anyone who is "not interested." It is not targeted for "anti-chareidim." If you are one, don't read this book. It is not for you.

- This book is meant to reframe common perceptions of what constitutes a *chareidi* and will present a definition that may differ from your preconceived notions. If you are already certain about what constitutes a chareidi and are not open to new definitions, this book will not work for you.

- This book draws its premise from the writings of Rashi and the sages of the Talmud. This book will be of no benefit to one who does not consider Rashi and his sources to be authoritative and who, likewise, holds little regard for the perspectives of those who may actually consider these sources to be authoritative. If you meet this description, please read something else.

- As this particular volume places an emphasis on Torah ideology, it deals heavily with Jewish ethics, what is commonly called *mussar*. In some places, it emulates the techniques of some of the classical works of Jewish ethics. You might say that this volume is in part a "neo-mussar" book, albeit with a light touch. Readers who are not receptive to concepts of mussar will, very likely, not appreciate these parts of the book.

- This book must be read thoroughly, it cannot be skimmed through. If you are not a thorough reader, this book is not for you.

- This book presents ideas on intellectual, ideological, and academic (scriptural and textual) grounds. It makes no attempt to deal with issues on emotional grounds. If you are an overly sensitive or passionate person, do not read this book.

Can irreligious people benefit from this book?

This book is not meant to "convert" non-observant Jews and does not target the irreligious. Despite this, I purposely wrote the book in my best Queen's English (partly because my wife is from Queens) and used King James names for the books of Torah (Genesis, Exodus, etc.) and used the standard Modern Hebrew pronunciation for my transliterations so that the book should be accessible to those who are not so well versed in chareidi expressions and terminology. Many parts of the book will be of interest to irreligious people who are genuinely interested in the subject. Nevertheless, there are numerous intricate theological segments that can only be fully appreciated by those with a strong Talmudic background.

Can this book be taken into a restroom?

Absolutely not – too religious.

Can this book be taken into a Beit Midrash?

Absolutely not – too sacrilegious.

Please explain Book One and Book Two?

It is all clearly explained in the Introduction, but I will summarize it. This project follows the logical sequence of (1) state the theory and (2) apply the theory to real-time situations. In our case the theory is chareidi ideology (hashkafa) and its application is the basket of social issues. This volume covers the ideology segment and is sub-titled *Consumer Benefits*.

What is the sub-title of the volume that deals with the social issues?

Consumer Relations.

Why are you releasing the book in two installments?

It may certainly be preferable to put out the book in one complete publication but, as you probably suspect, the second segment is far from ready. In light of that, owing that this volume is in and of itself an independent unit and that it is ready for publication, I strongly felt that it is worthwhile to publish this volume by itself. I sincerely feel that this book can benefit many Jews and I would like to enable those who can benefit to do so. Besides, the expenses are half the price.

So what issues are slated for Book Two?

All the usual suspects – economy, national service, zealotry (those flying stones), stringencies and kashrut, technology (internet and cell phones), social interaction (*chillul Hashem*), Beit Din and *agunah* issues, deviancy, fallout (Children at Risk / Off the Derech), and more.

Sounds like quite a bit?!

It is.

So, when should that be coming out?

With G-d's help and if we don't yet merit the true redemption (which will render such books obsolete), some time in 5769 (2009).

I have never heard of you. Are you a Rabbi or educator?

No.

Are you somebody famous?

Not yet.

Are you a Baal Teshuva?

Also, not yet.

So, who made you the spokesman for all the chareidim?

Nobody in particular, so you are free to reject everything that I have written. Notwithstanding, I did write the Author's Foreword, which includes a concise autobiographical narrative, to establish my credentials as to what qualifies me to write such a book.

Having said this, I need to be very clear that I do not officially represent the chareidi community or any recognized body or organization that calls itself chareidi. Doubtless, there will be many of my co-religionists who may disagree with some of my views and certainly with my cavalier, candid, and oft-times cynical approach. I take full and sole responsibility for the contents of this book.

As long as you are already making disclaimers, what else do I need to know?

I am happy you asked. Yes, there are a few more things that I would like you to know:

- This book contains many discourses with exegeses (*drush*) of Scriptures and Talmudic passages. Most of the material is based on discourses that I have heard and read from renowned Jewish sages and thinkers, yet I have not shied away from embellishing these discourses with thoughts of my own. Since I do not rank among these renowned Jewish thinkers, the reader may evaluate these discourses at his or her own discretion.

- I am not qualified or ordained to issue Halachic rulings. Anything presented as a Halachic precept is a reflection of my (or my mentor's) personal understanding and interpretation of the Halacha and is subject to dissenting opinions, interpretations and errors. The reader is encouraged to verify all Halachic issues with their personal Halachic mentor.

- Many anecdotes that are presented for the purpose of characterizing a situation or delivering a message are word-of-mouth stories and folk legends. I cannot vouch for the accuracy of any such anecdotes nor, in many cases, can I be certain if they ever happened at all.

- This book may contain some scattered references to marital issues and is not recommended for readers below the age of 16.

- Two copyrighted articles are reproduced in full with permission: *Return of the Rambam* by Elliot Jager, © 2004 by the Jerusalem Post and *Handwriting on the Wall* by Naomi Ragen, © 1998 by Naomi Ragen, first printed in Jerusalem Report Sept. 14, 1998. The author is grateful to the Jerusalem Post and to Ms. Ragen for their permission.

All other copyrighted materials are excerpts of larger works and are printed for the exclusive purpose of criticism, comment, or review as allowed under the fair use law - Title 17 Chapter 1 Section 107 of the 1976 US Copyright Code.

Do you really expect me to buy this book?

Certainly. Plus some additional copies for your sister-in-law in Long Island and for that young guy who is working for your accountant.

How can I get answers to questions that you haven't raised?

I can be reached through my publisher or emailed at 1a7b.author@gmail.com

Table Of Contents

Acknowledgements

This book represents my first full featured writing project and, needless to say, it has been an exhilarating and enriching experience. For being privileged to be at the receiving end of something so valuable, I must say "Thank you."

One aspect of writing that has amazed me above all else is that when one sits down at his keyboard to write, regardless of what he intends to write when he starts, there is no telling what he will find on his screen when the session is done. Countless times I have reviewed passages and chapters that only I have written all but looking around to see who is truly formulating the ideas that seem to materialize out of nowhere. It may be blasphemous and narcissistic to claim that these insights are Divine inspiration yet I have no doubt that they are "divinely inspired". And with this, I must thank the *Chonen L'Adam Daat* – the "Bestower of Intellect to Man" – the true One Above who instilled within me the brains, the heart, and the courage to write this book.

I am likewise indebted to numerous Torah scholars, some of whom actually read all or part of the manuscript, who gave me either words of advice and encouragement or plain hard criticism. These include[1] HaRav G. Rabinowitz, Shlit"a, HaRav Asher Zelig Weiss, Shlit"a, HaRav Mordechai Noigershall, Shlit"a, HaRav S. Kamenetsky, Shlit"a, HaRav Zev Leff, Shlit"a, and, most notably Rabbi Berel Wein, Shlit"a, whose tapes and books on Jewish history served both as an influence and as reference material for many of the historical assertions that are presented in this book. In a similar vein, I wish to express a deep appreciation for the lectures of Rabbi Avigdor Miller, ZT"L. I maintain that there is much of his analytical and candid approach to the essence of Judaism reflected within these pages.

Many thanks to Rabbi Jonathan Rosenblum who lent me his annotated copy of *Real Jews* before I ordered a copy for myself and to Rabbi Moshe Grylak who provided me with a complimentary copy of his book,

---

[1] The appearance of one's name on this list is *not* to be construed as an endorsement for this book.

The Chareidim – Who are We Really? Likewise to Rabbi Lazer Berger who alerted me to the existence of Rabbi Noigershall's book before I actually met Rabbi Noigershall (and received a complimentary copy).

Much gratitude goes to my study partners Rabbi Michoel S. and Rabbi Yehoshua B. along with so many guests at my Shabbat table who served as the sounding board (or the soundly bored) for my obscure theories.

Many thanks to Rabbi Dovid Solomon for his assistance and expertise in locating Talmudic and Midrashic sources. On a like note, many thanks to Jeff Milgram of Torah Educational Software for providing me with his TES Tanach Plus program.

Navigation through the jungle of the world of Jewish book publishing would not be possible without the assistance of the experts. For this I am indebted to Rabbi Moshe Dombey, OB"M, and Mrs. Miriam Zakon of Targum Press, Rabbi Dovid Kahn of Feldheim Publishers, Yaacov Peterseil of Devora Publishing, Rabbi Moshe Kaufman of Israel Book Shop, and Rabbi Dovid Rossoff of Guardian Press, all of whom have given me direction even if they did not manage my project. Likewise, a note of thanks to fellow author and neighbor, Rabbi Don Roth for sharing his resources and experiences.

At last, we come to my publisher Chaim Mazo and his staff at Mazo Publishers. With the patience of Hillel the Elder, Chaim stood by me revision after revision (after revision…). He seemed to be always available and gave my work his personal attention.

Likewise, a note of thanks to Moshe Handel whose handiwork in graphic artistry adorns the cover of this book.

I am literally indebted to those people who cooperated to sponsor this project. At the head of the pack stand the officers of the Ezras Yisroel Charitable Fund whose generosity made this publication possible. They have taken a very personal interest in this project and their support goes far beyond the scope of this work. I likewise gratefully acknowledge the generous contributions of Mr. and Mrs. Heshy Schechter, Mr. and Mrs. Nissim Louzoun, Mr. and Mrs. Zvi Rosen, Rabbi and Mrs. Avraham Miller, and Mr. and Mrs. Allen Rubin.

Mere words of gratitude are never adequate for the truly important people. To my parents who have always known what is best for me and to my in-laws who know even better.

To my wife, my *bina yeteira*, who has kept the ship afloat through many a storm. If I have any sanity left, it is she who preserved it.

To my children for whom, thank G-d, I need more than two hands to tally them up. I cannot be assured that this book will sell a single copy, but it does not really matter – I wrote this book for them. A special note of recognition goes to my oldest son, Yaakov, who inspired me to the main premise of the One Above and Seven Below.

In the Author's Foreword I talk about a convoluted autobiography chapter, the surviving parts of which appear in an Appendix as an anthology of excerpts. The main purpose of that chapter was to explain how I got from point "A" (All-American Jewish boy) to point "B" (Black-hatter). It goes without saying that all of the people mentioned therein have played some significant role in the journey. As a result, every individual has in some way contributed to the insights that this book comprises and each one has earned my heart-felt gratitude.

Did I forget anybody? Oh, yes – many thanks to Zero Mostel.

Zero Mostel?

When I was a toddler, I used to love listening to musical phonograph records. So, to keep me occupied, my mother used to put a stack of phonograph records onto a record player and seat me in a wooden rocking chair to listen to them. Naturally, I soon knew the lyrics of all of the songs by heart. One of my favorite records was the sound track from the original Broadway version of *Fiddler on the Roof* starring Zero Mostel.

And so, many thanks to Zero Mostel who, in his role as the legendary Tevye, was the first to inspire me toward my two primary goals in life – "learning from the holy books seven hours every day" and "becoming a rich man". May at least the first one come to be. No, Zero Mostel wasn't a chareidi but at least he knew how to act like one.

Y.H.

My Three Uniforms

Over the course of this book, I consistently juggle three distinct roles. Or, as the cliché goes, I alternately don three hats – although, I prefer to say three uniforms.

The first uniform is the academic cap and gown of the university professor as I set out to deliver a series of lectures to the uninitiated about the sociological and ideological makeup of the chareidi entity. Yet, I am not a sociologist or anthropologist nor have I ever attended university. I do not hold any proper college degree.

The second, and most pretentious, uniform is the tall skull cap and black frock of the Rabbi and preacher as I expound on the words of the Scriptures and the sages and pretend to convey the "Word of G-d". Yet, I do not have *semicha* (Rabbinic ordination) and I have never served as a Rabbi or educator or an outreach professional.

The third uniform is the powdered wig and the black robes of the advocate, the defense attorney, in my efforts to fend off the criticisms and accusations against the chareidi community that I consider to be unjust. Yet, I have never attended law school.

So, in what way am I qualified to wear any of these three uniforms? (This question may not be nagging you, but it is definitely nagging me.)

To start with, there are two claims that I believe that I can assert with confidence:

- I am a chareidi – at the very least, based on the definitions that I present in the coming chapters which are my standards for determining chareidiness.

- I wrote this book.

So now, let me pose a new question:

Why did I write this book?

No-no. I am not asking "Why did I **write this book**?" After all, that question is fully addressed in the upcoming introductory chapter. The question I am asking is "Why did **I** write this book?"

I mean, shouldn't somebody else have done it – like, people who actually *are* qualified to wear these uniforms?

Obviously, the reason that I wrote this book is that I felt that a book such as this should be written for the English speaking Orthodox public and nobody else seemed to be doing it. Evidently, all of the more qualified people have other priorities. Moreover, it is not a simple task. A book such as this demands of its author a high level of motivation, perception, and idealism, not to mention adequate time flexibility, financial resources, perseverance, and writing and language skills, the sum total of which is what we call *siyatta d'shmaya* (Heavenly assistance). Being that, with regard to this work, I find myself a rare beneficiary of this comprehensive package of gifts, I can attest to having been granted an inordinate measure of Heavenly assistance over the duration of this project.

Is this sufficient to make me qualified?

I don't think that I can answer that (I am not qualified to).

This is a question for the reader to determine, and, in order to help the reader make an informed decision, I initially set out to write a succinct autobiography chapter and put it between the introduction and the pilot chapter. One purpose of the chapter would be to provide the reader with a bit of background information about myself to understand where I am "coming from." This much can be accomplished with a few dry paragraphs such as these:

> Both of my parents were raised in homes that can be characterized as chareidi. My father's family was Chassidic and my mother was enrolled in Bais Yaakov when Bais Yaakov was a novelty. Notwithstanding, circumstances led them to set up shop in an out-of-New York Orthodox community that did not promote chareidi ideals. As a result, not only did certain tenets of their chareidi'ish upbringing fall by the wayside in their own ideology but, in addition, they brought up their children to fit in with the prevailing local culture. Consequently, I was brought up with Religious Zionism in the foreground and chareidiism in the background. I grew up totally detached from my paternal grandparents as they were no longer living and predominantly detached from my maternal grandparents because they lived so far away. As such, they were unable to have much direct influence on my early development.
>
> Still, I always felt the background beckoning to me and I was inspired by my more chareidi East-coast relatives when I chanced to see them. After my bar-mitzvah, I eagerly forsook the comforts of home life to cast my lot in a prominent, high intensity, sleep-in, East-coast Yeshiva. After four years of high school I stayed on for three more years of post high school study and then moved on to the chareidi strongholds of Yeshivat Mir in Jerusalem (one year) and Lakewood, New Jersey (five years). I never went to college.

It was virtually on the final day of those five years in Lakewood Yeshiva that I chanced upon my wife and, by that time, I had already made a commitment toward the family business. As such, my dream of spending my newlywed years as a Kollel fellow never materialized. After two years of working in New York, we returned to my hometown where I officially joined the family business and assumed the status of a *yeshivishe baalabus* (working man who looks like a Rabbi). About nine years later, my wife finally prevailed upon me to make aliya to Eretz Israel which we accomplished with remarkable success.

Here in Eretz Israel, I succeeded in every aspect except in maintaining my status as a businessman. I attempted other occupational endeavors one of which was in the field of writing but even that was devastated in the high-tech upheaval of 2000 and 2001. In the absence of full time employment, I found myself spending more and more time in the study halls and, in effect, reclaimed the missing Kollel life that eluded me fifteen years earlier. Currently, I study in the mornings and evenings and am writing this book in the afternoons and I am sneaking in some schooling toward yet another mid-life career.

Now, this certainly brings us up to date but I was not convinced that it would suffice to establish my credentials. On one level, it does indeed point out that I "did time" in some of the most prominent Lithuanian-style yeshivot. But I really felt that I needed this chapter to do more. I needed it to explain not merely where I come from but what forces converged to qualify me and motivate me to write this book.

To accomplish this, I expounded on all of the elements that were touched upon in the above synopsis. I wrote all about my ancestry and upbringing to illustrate that nobody is truly born a chareidi, no matter what his family background may be; one must become chareidi. The narrative goes on to discuss my environs, yeshiva background and passage to adulthood, my courtship and marriage, my career(s) and our move to Eretz Israel in an effort to convey the way I perceive G-d's providence in becoming as "chareidi" as I have become and to proclaim how one who allows G-d to orchestrate his life can be blessed with the three most precious gifts that any truly Orthodox Jew could long for: the wisdom of Torah, a virtuous wife, and a portion of Eretz Israel. Hence, it comprises, in great detail, a growing up story and a *shidduch* (courtship) story and an *aliya* story which together serve as components of a *hashgacha pratis* (guiding hand of G-d) story geared to explain how I, of all people, come to be the one who is sitting here typing these words.

It was in too much detail. Before I knew it, it was upwards of 60 pages in 11 point book print – anything but succinct. This was no concise biographical blurb; it was almost its own book. I initially considered merely relocating the chapter and including the complete text as an Appendix to the book, but then I thought better of it. Clearly, it would be counterproductive for me to distract the reader with my entire life's story. After all, this book is not meant to be a storybook and, besides, are you really that interested?

My next inclination was to condense the chapter to a more palatable length while preserving it as a coherent narrative. This means to cut out most of what I wrote and to patch up what was left in a way that the reader could not discern that anything is missing. This turned out to be too daunting a task for me. Aside from a dearth of the required time and patience, it was like trying to make a car lighter by taking out parts of the engine – what parts can you do without and expect the same performance?

My final recourse was to take the lazy man's way out. That is, to extract a compilation of the most relevant and interesting segments and present them as an anthology of excerpts which basically meet my goals albeit at the expense of leaving numerous holes in the narrative. And so, the curious (and, perhaps, bored) reader can find some snippets of my memoirs tucked away in an Appendix at the back of this book.

Of course, this left me with a hole up front. I still needed to write something at the beginning of the book to serve the basic purpose of introducing myself and establishing my credentials. After all, I am single-handedly and voluntarily assuming the mantle of chareidi public relations in a format that – to my knowledge – nobody else has done (Jonathan Rosenblum notwithstanding) and that is a mighty broad-shouldered mantle to bear. Some of the Rabbanim that I consulted quaked in fear (as true chareidim do) when I proposed my project. Will I do the cause justice or make things worse?

To fill the hole, I wrote this foreword and cleverly snuck in that brief biographical blurb which you have already unsuspectingly read. Well, that's a start. At least I can boast a solid yeshiva background even if I didn't spend a day in Kollel. But what more can I say for myself? I even launched this chapter with a confession that I am not a sociologist, I am not a Rabbi, I am not a lawyer, or an educator, lecturer, journalist, or accomplished writer. I do not hold all that much in the way of higher education, titles, degrees, or positions.

While I was attending yeshiva, I undertook to study the renowned philosophical work, *Chovot HaLevavot* by Rabbi Bachya Ibn Pakuda. One spiritual advisor who took note of my endeavor urged me not to skip the author's introduction. I heeded this advice and have not regretted it. The introduction is no less inspirational as is the main body of the work.

In his introduction, Rabbi Bachya recounts his train of thought as to what motivated him to compose his magnum opus (I actually offer a brief summary of this account in Chapter 7). Essentially, what it boils down to is that he felt that a book such as this should be written for the Arabic speaking[1] Orthodox public and nobody else seemed to be doing it. (Okay, so call me a plagiarist!). After he tells us this, he writes that he engaged in a bit of soul-searching. Perhaps he shouldn't write the book after all – for "a man such as me is certainly not qualified to write such a book".

He concludes that he had to dismiss these thoughts as thoughts of indolence. He writes, "I said to myself, if every man who engages in a good work or wishing to teach the right and proper way were to hold his peace until his full desire [to perfect himself] will be fulfilled, not a word would be uttered by anyone after the Prophets…". In plain English, his message is that if everybody who sets out to do something constructive will say, "Who am I to do this?" not a whole lot will ever get done.

Spiritual guidance I get from spiritual giants such as Rabbi Bachya. Pragmatic guidance can come from some more mundane thinkers, even non-Jewish ones such as Thomas Edison. One of Thomas Edison's most famous quotes is: "Genius is one percent inspiration and ninety-nine percent perspiration." The problem with this formula is that, taken at its word, it is only meant to relate to geniuses. What does it say for the rest of us?

I, not being a genius, have to measure this work using a more primitive unit of measure: It is the result of two years of inspiration and more than forty years of perspiration. My hypotheses and conclusions are not the result of two or three years of intensive research but are actually the culmination of perspectives, insights, and experiences that have accumulated over decades.

All of my life, I have been, to myself, an observer and critic of the socio-political and socio-religious conventions of my environs. I have continually analyzed and meditated on the merits of the tenets of Torah Judaism (chareidiism) in relation to secular, non-Jewish, or non-Torah schools of thought and analyzed the observable ramifications of employing Torah precepts versus non-Torah ones in real life situations.[2]

Virtually all chareidim – especially, but not limited to, those like myself who hail from or circulate within non-chareidi circles – experience dialogues wherein they are called upon to explain or defend chareidi dogma. We all have friends, relatives and acquaintances who are either curious or critical (or both). No doubt, I have encountered my fair share.

---

[1] Chovot HaLevavot was originally written in Arabic. The Hebrew versions that we have are translations by the author's disciples.

[2] One notable example was the first of a short series of study sessions that I held when I was a youngster (about ten years old) with a local householder who I

One phenomenon is universal – all such acquaintances are uninformed or under informed with regard to basic Torah ideology. The sages tell us that we chareidim are all responsible to be proficient in public relations.[3] I have taken this charge very seriously and have resolved to be "up to the task".

It is argued that most human beings conceal a bit of a Walter Mitty[4] tendency – to imagine themselves as trailblazers when they are merely trailers. This can certainly apply to me. I have privately thought of myself as qualified to be an advocate or spokesman for the dissemination of chareidi ideals to the secular [minded] world. This is something that an authentic practitioner could manifest by becoming an educator, lecturer, *askan* (activist), journalist or outreach professional. We are blessed with capable models for all of these roles but I am none of them; G-d has not led me down that road. Yet, when the occasion has presented itself in a one-on-one setting, I have been able to debate the issues in a manner which appear to me to have been effective. In the aftermath of these isolated episodes, I have sometimes imagined myself presenting the same arguments to a large-scale audience. You might say that I have frequently imagined myself as a noted personality – a Yechezkel the Prophet – who champions the lost honor of Torah Judaism and who conveys its message to the masses. Whether this self-aggrandizement is realistic or grandiose may never be determined. Perhaps this book is the test.

Yechezkel Hirshman – Jerusalem, 5767

---

will call Mr. Gibber. Mr. Gibber could most likely be "categorized" as a sincere "modern Orthodox" (I disfavor the term "modern Orthodox" – you will not find it in the main body of this book) working class Jew. He is not noted as an accomplished Talmudic scholar but is, in fact, a brilliant criminal defense attorney. He introduced tractate Bava Metziah to me as the Jewish perspective of property law. We were discussing that, as an attorney, he is familiar with both the Western secular and Judaic legal systems. I asked him how he would rate the modern system against our ancient one. His immediate response was, "Oh, the Talmudic system is far superior, vastly superior." In my mind the logical extension was that if this worldly individual can assure me that the Talmudic legal system is far superior to the Western system, then the spiritual and philosophical aspects of Talmudic Judaism ought to be vastly superior, as well.

[3] Pirkei Avot 2:19; Talmud Bavli Kiddushin 30a

[4] Walter Mitty is the lead character of a James Thurber short story about a man with grandiose delusions.

One Above
and
Seven Below

A Consumer's Guide to Orthodox Judaism from the Perspective of the Chareidim

The Secret

L egend has it that the renowned Mark Twain had a great grandson who, upon reading his ancestor's writings concerning the Jews, was so greatly inspired, that he ultimately converted to Judaism.[1] Subsequently, he wrote this column in the *Jewish Wayward*[2]:

> If the statistics are right, the Hareidim constitute but five percent of the Jewish race. Properly, the Hareidi ought to be hardly heard of; but he is heard of, always has been heard of. He has made a marvelous fight in this world, in all ages; and has done it with his hands tied behind him. He could be vain of himself, and be excused for it. The Hellinist the Sadducee and the Karaite rose filled the planet with sound and splendor, then faded to dream stuff and passed away; the Maskil and the Yesvekzia followed, and made a vast noise, and they are gone; the Bundists, Reform, and Zionists have sprung up and held their torch high for a time, but it burned out, and they sit in twilight now, or have vanished. The Hareidi saw them all, beat them all, and is now what he always was, exhibiting no decadence, no infirmities of age, no weakening of his parts, no slowing of his energies, no dulling of his alert and aggressive mind. All Jews are mortal but the Hareidi; all other forces pass but he remains. What is the secret of his immortality?
>
> – *Shmuel Langbordt Cleminitz*

What is the secret of his immortality, indeed?

It is said[3] that David Ben Gurion made concessions to the chareidim because he fully expected that within fifty years, they would fade to dream stuff and pass away.

He didn't know the secret.

It is told that when Rabbi Yosef Kahaneman instituted a campaign to build a yeshiva for a thousand-plus students on a dusty desolate hilltop outside Tel Aviv, he was mocked and ridiculed, yet he prevailed. The

---

[1] I am totally making this up!

[2] The original text of these excerpts can be found in the Appendix at the end of this book (page 303)

[3] From here on in, I am not making anything up.

story goes that one potential benefactor admonished him, "You are dreaming!" He responded, "I am dreaming, but I am not sleeping."

That was merely a clever retort but it was not the truth. He was not dreaming. He knew the secret.

Rabbi Yochanan ben Zakai preserved the immortality of the chareidim by petitioning the Roman General Vespasian with a seemingly innocuous request.[4]

He knew the secret.

Vespasian granted the request.

He did not know the secret.

Every year more and more Jews come to identify with the chareidim.

They have discovered the secret.

A lesser number fall away from the society.

They have lost the secret.

It is an old secret and it has never been guarded, yet so very few know it.

Those who know it are eager to share it. They proclaim it loudly, yet so very few hear it.

It seems to have been very carefully hidden, but it is in plain sight, and so few see it.

I know the secret. I learned it from my great-great grandfather, Rabbi Shlomo Isaacson. He wrote it down for me. Not only for me, but for all his descendants and students. Almost a thousand years ago.

It is time to reveal the chareidi's secret of immortality.

Step into the Holy of Holies on the Day of Atonement and catch a glimpse of the secret:

> *"And he shall take from the blood of the bull and he shall sprinkle with his finger on the eastern surface of the covering; and before the covering, he shall sprinkle seven times of the blood in his finger."*[5]

Writes Rabbi Isaacson: "**And before the covering he shall sprinkle seven times** – Thus we have *one above and seven below*."

---

[4] Talmud Bavli Gittin 56b

[5] Leviticus 16:14

A Guide for the Consumer

Shimu d'var Hashem hachareidim el d'varo …

*Hear the word of G-d, those who are anxious (chareidim)
toward his word; your brethren, those who hate you, those who
shun you, have said, "It is for my name's sake that G-d finds
glory;" and we shall see in your rejoicing and they will be
ashamed.*

(Isaiah 66:5)

What should the chareidim hear? What is the word of G-d? Who are the brethren, haters, and shunners? Though we may prefer to assume that the haters and shunners are those who do not observe the commandments, the verse also states "brethren."[1] Malbim explains Brethren: *Brethren in commandments.*[2] This implies that even Orthodox Jews are the enemies of the chareidi.[3]

One thing is clear. Chareidim are hated and shunned – by their brethren!

Why?

---

[1] I did see one commentary (Abarbanel) that interprets the parties in the verse as non-Jews. "Haters" refers to the sons of Ishmael and "Shunners" refers to the sons of Esau. Both of whom can be called "Brethren" as Esau was a brother to Jacob and Ishmael was a brother to Isaac. In this sense, the "chareidim" can refer to the entire Jewish people. The standard commentators on Isaiah (Rashi, Radak, Malbim, Metzudot, etc.) as well as the Talmud Bava Metzia 33b do not concur with this interpretation.

[2] It can be argued that "brethren in commandments" may imply brethren who are commanded, yet do not observe the commandments, i.e., non-observant Jews. It must be noted that modern secularism did not exist in Biblical times. Although not all Jews were learned and righteous, virtually all Jews acknowledged the commandments in general and observed social commandments such as Shabbat, kashrut, and the tithes.

[3] See Talmud Bavli, Bava Metzia 33b

Who is a chareidi and who are their brethren?[4] What distinguishes them?

Numerous tomes have been written about the relationship between the secular and the ultra-Orthodox. This book is not meant to be another one. The secular authors of such books devote pages upon pages to analyze the ideological battle within a socio-political framework. As if the chareidi acts the way he does for political reasons and not for religious ones. They either miss or consciously overlook the point.

Although these books may not spell it out, the foundation of this struggle is in actuality the great chasm that divides the religious from the non-believer. The debate centers on the existential question: Did G-d create this world and Man? If so, is it not true that there must be a goal and a purpose for this creation, hence, Man is answerable to his Creator for his achievements and failures and is not free to do as he pleases?

In short, is G-d the boss or is Man the boss?

The religious choose G-d and accept these axioms as truth; the non-believers reject them and choose Man.[5]

The war of the secular against the chareidi is a war against [subservience to] G-d.[6] The secular do not wish to co-exist with the chareidi; they *cannot* co-exist with the chareidi. This is because the chareidi represents and, indeed, personifies the subservience of Man to a higher authority. This concept of subservience is anathema to the secular masses who are driven to define their responsibilities, privileges, and moral ethics as only they see fit. It is impossible to co-exist with such a concept. If G-d exists we must do His bidding. G-d impinges on our sovereignty. Consequently, they must eliminate the chareidi because they must eliminate G-d.

This principle is the root of the fierce animosity of the secular toward the chareidi. All else is window dressing. They cry out that the chareidi is to be hated and shunned because he does not serve his country in its army. To be sure, I intend to deal with this issue (and all similar issues) at length. Notwithstanding, this cry is a smokescreen, for it implies that if tomorrow 40,000 chareidim would report to the recruiting

---

[4] It has been noted that the initials of the consecutive words "*Acheichem, Sonaeichem, M'nadeichem, L'maan*" (Aleph-S'in-Mem-Lamed) when rearranged form the Hebrew word "Sma[o]l" (Left).

[5] Despite this, a substantial number of non-observant Jews fastidiously insist that they believe in G-d, thus creating a paradox. In some cases, G-d is redefined as an entity that makes no demands upon Man. In other (most?) cases, people internally acknowledge the reality of G-d and accountability but simply do not have the emotional or intellectual apparatus to deal with it in practice.

[6] See Rashi's commentary on Numbers 10:35 s.v. *Misanecha*

office with their beards and *peyot*, *tzitzit*, *tefillin* bags, and *Kitzur Shulchan Aruch*, love and harmony would descend upon the nation. No more hating and shunning.

Such is not the case, for it is not truly the chareidim that they hate and shun, but rather, the beards and *peyot*, *tzitzit*, *tefillin*, and *Kitzur Shulchan Aruch*.

There have arisen a number of spokesmen and defenders of the chareidi (read: *religious* or *Orthodox*) viewpoint in the face of the onslaught of denigration from the non-religious. Some have written books, some are activists and/or journalists who deal with the issues head on, others are outreach professionals and the like, whose comments and rebuttals have infiltrated into the secular press and bookstores. May their work and "those that acknowledge them be blessed."[7]

I, in a non-professional capacity, have likewise rebutted the denigration on numerous occasions, and I have an observation: as often as not (indeed, more often than not), to my great consternation, the party on the other side of the debate was not a non-observant Jew.

The roster of antagonists, it seems, is not confined to the non-believers. The hating and shunning is not limited to the non-observant and uneducated. They are even our brethren. Our brethren in commandments.

To what do I attribute this phenomenon?

For one thing, we must acknowledge the fact that the G-d who created us and commands us to serve Him instilled in Man a powerful craving for autonomy – to control our own lives and to determine our own morals. This applies to all of mankind. It is every man's challenge in life to banish this "demon" and nobody is totally successful. Even Noah, who personally heard the word of G-d and spent 120 years preaching morality – i.e., subservience to G-d – to his generation, is labeled as "from the minor believers."[8] Consequently, there are numerous Jews who adhere to belief in G-d and observing the commandments who cannot vanquish the serpent of autonomy.

But, what is more important, the religious community suffers from an acute affliction, something that I call *consumerist Judaism*.

For every commodity there are two parties, *providers* and *consumers*. The provider is responsible for the production of the commodity and for seeing to it that it reaches the market. The consumer demands that the commodity meets specific standards and delegates to the provider the headaches associated with meeting the demands.

---

[7] Ruth 2:19

[8] Bereishit Raba 32:6

In the realm of religion we are all consumers, primarily for the goods and services which must be *kosher* – kosher food, a kosher *eruv*, a kosher *mikveh*, kosher *tefillin*, *tzitzit*, *mezuzot*, a kosher marriage or divorce. For all these things, the religious consumer exercises his privilege of relaxing and leaving the responsibility of kashrut to the experts.

Consequently, the religious Jew loses sight of what is involved in getting the product to market. He or she fails to appreciate the depth of the subject matter which necessitates interminable study, interspersed with myriad intricacies that must be mastered and conflicts that must be resolved, coupled with the compulsory internships that include constant mentoral supervision which are the mandatory prerequisites for being more than a consumer.

In some religions there is a marked distinction between the providers and the consumers, a caste system of sorts. The providers are called *clergy* and the consumers are called *laymen*. Laymen are discouraged from encroaching into the domain of the clergy. Orthodox Judaism does not advocate such a schism between clergy and layman. Every Jew is encouraged to be as knowledgeable about his religion as he can be. We consider it *l'chatchila* (ideal situation or procedure; literally: *initial procedure*) for every Jew to be a provider. Consumerism is deemed *bidiavad* (not ideal but still acceptable; literally: *after the fact*).

Many Orthodox Jews are sufficiently content to remain consumers throughout their sojourn on Earth. They do not view this status as *bidiavad*. This stance carries with it numerous hazards, particularly:

- *Hazard #1* – A lack of faculties to deal with the situation when one suddenly finds oneself in a position where he must be a "provider."

- *Hazard #2* – A lack of intellectual capacity to discern between an authentic religious phenomenon and a semblance of one.

- *Hazard #3* – Vulnerability for allowing concepts (read: propaganda) from non-religious sources to influence one's position on religious issues.

- *Hazard #4* – Vulnerability to the erroneous impression that one need not buy all the items in the product line.[9]

- *Hazard #5* – A lack of knowledgeable conviction to inspire subsequent generations to remain within the fold.

---

[9] Some notable examples that I have observed are *Hilchot Yichud* (Laws of Seclusion) and some lesser known or understood kashrut issues such as *Bishulei Nochri* (foods prepared by non-Jews).

I wish to bring two case history examples to illustrate the first three of the aforementioned hazards (the fourth is relatively clear – see footnote 9; the fifth one, sadly, needs no example):

Example 1:

I was approximately 20 years old and, having just completed my final year of post high school study at a prominent East Coast yeshiva, I returned home for the summer. That summer, two of my siblings were attending a non-chareidi summer camp in a neighboring state. The coming Sunday would be visiting day and a group of parents from Natwich[10] devised the following plan:

Instead of undergoing a long exhausting drive on Sunday morning which would arrive in the later part of the day, the group would drive on Friday to a nearby motor inn and spend Shabbat there. Thereupon, on Sunday morning, the group would continue on to the camp and arrive bright and early. I was urged to come along and I felt compelled to comply despite my apprehension about spending Shabbat out in no-man's land. I was told that this was not the first year that this plan would be implemented and that the proper apparatus would be in place, i.e., there would be a Torah scroll and the motel would be enclosed by an *eruv* to ensure freedom of movement.

The eruv was necessary because the motor inn consisted of two buildings. One building housed the motel rooms and the other contained the lobby and the communal areas including the multi-purpose room where we would pray and eat. As each family had brought their own provisions, which they kept in their rooms, transport to the other building would be forbidden without an eruv.

I came up together with my parents and some siblings. No sooner did we arrive when one of the more learned members of the group approached me – the token chareidi – to discuss how to construct an eruv. At that stage I had not yet studied the laws of an eruv but, almost coincidentally, I had just finished studying the preliminary laws of the four domains.[11] As it turned out, the two buildings were joined by an awning that

---

[10] Acronym for: **N**orth **A**merican **T**own **W**ith **I**ntegrated **C**ommunity of **H**ebrews – a pseudonym for my hometown. See Appendix A.

[11] To spare the reader from a full halachic discourse on the laws of an eruv, I am relocating the discourse to this footnote. An open space that does not contain a substantial volume of human traffic is a *karmelit*. To permit transport in a karmelit, the karmelit must be transformed to a *reshut hayachid* – a private domain. To do this, the domain must be *mukaf l'dirah* – totally enclosed by solid partitions. When genuine solid partitions are not possible, the Halacha

constituted a valid "partition."[12] As one building was "L" shaped, the campus was well enclosed on 3½ sides; we only needed to contend with one unenclosed stretch (about 30 or 40 feet) from the unjoined edge of one building to the other.

This would be an ideal situation for a *tzurat hapetach* (see footnote 11) except that none present seemed to have any beams, nails, string, or tools.[13] As such, we (myself and two others) stood in the middle of the grounds discussing and weighing our alternatives.[14] Presently, one of the menfolk[15] notices us, strolls over and inquires as to what the conference is about. One of us responded that we are contemplating the most favorable method of constructing an eruv. At this, he pointed to the unattached walls and counseled with sagacious advice, "All you gotta do is tie a string from there to there!" and he strolled away.

How simple! Now, why didn't we think of that?!

Well, for good reason. It wouldn't help. I knew this and, to their

---

recognizes certain structural entities as if they are solid partitions. The most common of which is a *tzurat hapetach* – a semblance of a doorway. This is a structure comprising two uprights and a lintel. The lintel can be any material, even a string or wire, but it must conform to the standard design of a doorway in that (a) it must be straight and (b) the lintel (string or wire) must pass directly over the top of the uprights. It is not sufficient to tie a string from one pole or wall to another if it doesn't pass over the top of the pole or wall. A common practice is to take wooden beams as uprights and insert a nail to protrude from the end. Thereupon we can tie a string from nail to nail and this meets the requirements for the lintel of a *tzurat hapetach*.

[12] Employing the rule of *pi tikra yored v'sotem*.

[13] I haven't the foggiest idea what the organizers of this expedition expected. I had expected that the required halachic instructions and paraphernalia would have been obtained in advance, especially if this venture had been previously undertaken. I had not expected to find myself the (underqualified) halachic authority among people twice my age, but, I suppose that is the point of this whole story.

[14] Ultimately, upon my (chareidi) suggestion, we simply picked up a pay phone (no cell phones in those days) and contacted an authority in Natwich. He gave a suggestion using the *lechi* method. I do not remember all the details except that I had a hard time finding and erecting the necessary materials to the extent that I was highly uncertain that the lechi met the requirements. That evening it was announced – without my authority – that the organizers with the cooperation of "Rabbi" Hirshman have successfully erected a valid eruv. I did my utmost to avoid any carrying the entire Shabbat.

[15] This fellow was a late-thirty or forty-something gentleman, highly intelligent (an attorney), religious from birth, had some sort of yeshiva education, very devoted to and active in community institutions such as the synagogue, the schools, and HaPoel Mizrachi, and is descended from the family of a very illustrious and renowned 18th century sage.

credit, the other two gentlemen knew it. But this fellow didn't know it. This is because he is a consumer. And the handicaps of his consumerist status were evident. For hazard #1, there would have been a much slimmer chance of success if he was the one who had to determine how to accomplish the task. As for hazard #2, he understood the concept from what he saw, not from what he studied. When he saw an eruv, he saw a string. He did not see a tzurat hapetach. He was not trained to see a tzurat hapetach. To him a string is sufficient because it *resembles* an eruv. Evidently, it doesn't have to be an eruv as long as it looks like one. I wonder if he ever bought a diamond.

What impressed me so much about this is that when he approached the group to inquire the nature of the discussion he did not ask us why there are complications. He did not assume that if three people are conferring on an issue, it follows that there must be some depth to the issue. He had the "solution" in the palm of his hand, and graciously bestowed it upon us (no charge) and promptly went about his business. The consumer does not countenance complications. He does not need to know the details, like they say, "Don't confuse me with the facts."

Example 2:

This is not so much a story but a common occurrence that constantly recurs in typical discussions. This episode concerns my friend, "Morton." Morton grew up with me in Rainbow Beach, went to the same synagogue and school (one grade above me), Bnei Akiva, etc. I used to eat at his house on Shabbat and one Shavuot eve we attempted the "all nighter" at my place (we managed to wake up in time for the regular late minyan). In short, we were boyhood friends carved from the same mountain.

From Rainbow Beach we moved to different neighborhoods. I eventually attended an East Coast yeshiva and grew chareidi. He went to the local more modern yeshiva and remained Bnei Akiva. He later went to study in a *hesder* yeshiva in Israel (Kiryat Arba), took immigration status and did hesder army service.

After release, he returned to Natwich, married, and found his way into the diamond business. He finally made actual aliya and now lives a productive religious life in a religious Israeli settlement town. When he was blessed with a financial windfall, he displayed his gratitude to G-d by dedicating a Torah scroll. All in all, a fine Orthodox fellow.

Though I had never fully lost contact with him, I renewed a relationship with him as a fellow diamond merchant. We would see each other quite often at the diamond exchange in Ramat Gan.

On one such occasion we were having a *hashkafa* (ideology) conversation when he uttered the refrain that I had heard from others, "I don't understand how the chareidim justify not participating in the army – it's a *chillul Hashem* (desecration of the name of G-d; sacrilege)!"

Does this truly constitute a chillul Hashem? Let's check it out. What exactly is a chillul Hashem? To answer that, we consult our sources. The Talmud in Tractate Yuma (86a) defines chillul Hashem. This definition is quoted in Maimonides.[16] Does our situation typify this definition? I don't see how.[17] You don't have to take my word for it. We chareidim have, over the past 60 years (and for always), held the monopoly of erudite scholars fully versed in Talmud, Shulchan Aruch, and Maimonides, some of whom can quote full volumes by heart. Amazingly, none of these scholars have ever ruled that pursuing the lifestyle of a chareidi is a chillul Hashem.

Yet, Morton can rule that it is, indeed, a chillul Hashem. Does he know something that they don't? Au contraire, Morton is a consumer. Recall hazard #2 – a consumer has trouble discerning an authentic religious phenomenon from a look-alike. Morton thinks it is a chillul Hashem because it *resembles* a chillul Hashem (just like a string resembles an eruv). That is to a consumer's untrained eye. "Don't confuse me with the facts!" The facts, however, indicate otherwise.

And why does Morton think it is a chillul Hashem? Recall hazard #3 – the consumer shapes opinions from non-Judaic (read: secular) sources. Morton perceives a social injustice. Based on conventional thought (what is now called *politically correct*), a social injustice is immoral. Ergo, anything immoral perpetrated by a religious person constitutes a chillul Hashem. I intend to demonstrate that this is not the opinion of the sages of yore.

It would be reassuring if the two case history examples that I related above could be considered isolated incidents. If so, there would be no need for a book such as this. Unfortunately, they are all too common. They are actually banal, humdrum incidents and there is nothing dramatic about them, which is precisely the point – they occur all the time. The frightening fact is that my friend Morton is not alone. As I wrote, the viewpoint that he expressed reflects that of countless others of our brethren.

Morton has bought diamonds. Lots of them. And he profits from them. He can do that because he can discern an authentic one from a look-alike (which, in fact, barely look alike). When it comes to diamonds, Morton is

---

[16] Maimonides Yad Chazaka, Mada, Hilchot Yesodei Torah 5:10,11

[17] I am not going into detail here. I intend to devote a substantial amount of paper and ink to this subject in Book Two. I don't want to reveal the entire plot now and ruin the suspense.

not content to be a consumer. It wouldn't be profitable.

Chareidim maintain that it is not profitable to be a consumer for any religious issue. This does not mean that chareidim are not consumers. To some extent, many or even most of us are. It means that the chareidim understand that being a consumer is *bidiavad* and not *l'chatchila*. As Sy Syms always says, "An educated consumer is our best customer."

Alas, there is one department where we are not allowed to be consumers even *bidiavad* – being a kosher Jew. And for that I am writing this book.

Being a kosher Jew is no less contingent on the opinions of our sages and their writings than are the technical religious requirements of our foods, our religious articles and our rituals. But somehow, a great number of our brethren choose to overlook the philosophies of the sages in favor of the opinions of the Western world, of the secular and non-Jewish thinkers. These perspectives become so ingrained in the mind of the consumer that he loses sight of the fact that a more fundamentally "Jewish" ideology may actually exist. There are those brethren that have gone so far to reach a total state of denial. The pilot chapter of this book explains how this is possible (and, in some cases, inevitable).

The rules and regulations of being a kosher Jew are available for the asking, but the confirmed consumer does not ask – for he is content in his knowledge. "Everything I ever needed to know I learned in kindergarten." The typical consumer maintains that the most accurate source of information is by consensus of their fellow consumers. As such, someone who opposes the overwhelming consensus and presents a differing outlook based on more authoritative sources is swimming against the current and is consequentially branded as an outsider. And outsiders are hated and shunned.

I contend that many of our brethren would not automatically assume the role of haters and shunners were they not to fall prey to the hazards of consumerism. This is the conclusion that I have arrived at as the result of carrying out these copious futile debates. And so, the dedicated chareidi, among his many duties, must take on the task of combating consumerism.

This is not a simple task. As discussions, these debates usually occur during inadequate time frames. People operate under an assumption that a chareidi can explain his entire philosophy in ten minutes. This is never the case. Invariably, time does not suffice to adequately cover an issue especially if and when it requires a substantial backdrop. In order to understand the issues, it is necessary to understand the philosophies. Most often a conversation begins, escalates into a full-blown debate, and is sustained until the bus reaches the first one's stop. "Of course, we must continue this sometime – do lunch." But lunch never happens.

This book is meant to replace the dialog that there is never enough time to carry out.

But, it goes further. These debates are not confined to table talk. They also exist in the media. To be sure, the ostensive secular media, particularly in Israel, is inundated with news items, stories, features, documentaries, profiles, etc., ad nauseam, virtually none of it flattering, all of which serves one positive purpose – it confirms the prophesy of Isaiah that the chareidim are hated and shunned. Of course, chareidim do have their own journals and periodicals (and an occasional contraband radio station) to serve their constituents. These two forums exist to disseminate their "for" or "against" perspectives. I am not concerned with either of these.

What interests me is the "officially neutral" non-sectarian secular media whose main objective is simply to deliver the news and to sell papers to the widest possible audience – the general public. To that end, they allocate at least some token op-ed space to eloquent representatives of any rational faction of their readership.

As concerns the English-speaking Israeli public, the front runner for this distinction is the Jerusalem Post.[18] I believe that the Jerusalem Post holds a unique position in that it is (in my opinion) the only daily paper in English or Hebrew (I do not speak Russian) that endeavors to cater to readers from all shades of the spectrum.[19] Some people call it everybody's paper and some call it nobody's paper. Though it is by no means chareidi-friendly, by the same token, it does not champion an anti-chareidi vendetta. I confess to reading the Jerusalem Post regularly over the past seven years for the following reasons:

- I am a bit of a news junkie so I have to read something.

- It is very important to me to see news as it is presented to the general public.[20]

---

[18] I am obviously focusing on the printed media and, as the succeeding lines reveal, the Jerusalem Post is my main artery for secular news and, consequently, the primary source of media-based material for the thesis of this book. It goes without saying that this is not the sole source nor am I precluding other media forums (though I do not have nor watch television).

[19] I am not overlooking the fact that the Hebrew speaking population is substantially more polarized than the English speakers and such an endeavor is all but doomed from the outset.

[20] I likewise have one car radio station set on the BBC ("Brutish" Broadcasting Corporation). Despite the fact that the biased reporting is truly repulsive I do believe that there is some value to knowing how news is fed to the world at large. Besides that, for the most part, it's the only English speaking game in

- The true Jewish reason – it has always been free.[21]

Besides the news, I am interested in the opinion columns and the letters because they deliver a very accurate reflection of the feelings of the aforementioned "general public." Understandably, I have always taken a special interest in any news item, op-ed piece, or letter that displays an attitude regarding Orthodoxy and chareidim in particular.

I don't suppose that I am the only person who has made the following observation: in about 98% of the cases, unless the piece is authored by a chareidi, the attitude displayed is not favorable.[22]

It is not that chareidim are above criticism. There is always room for improvement. Indeed, "constructive" criticism is mandated by the Torah, subject to a host of stipulations as to the acceptable stature and earnestness of the critic,[23] the esteem and conscientiousness of the recipient and, equally important, the venue of the criticism. One common rule of criticism is: focus on the problem, not on the entity that bears the problem (this means: don't tell the guy that he's a schlemiel, tell him he's a super guy who just happens to consistently mess things up). Regarding what I see in the media, I do not consider this criticism to be constructive because:

- It does not meet the aforementioned criteria for constructive criticism.

- A "general public" newspaper is not the proper venue for constructive criticism as it is technically being delivered to the wrong address.

- It is not intended as *constructive* criticism.

---

town. I do try to listen to chareidi stations but they are always suddenly disappearing. I wonder why!

[21] When I first immigrated to Israel the AACI endowed all new immigrants with a free 6 month subscription which was automatically extended another 6 months after I refused to sign up. That's how I got on to it. Since then, it has been available at the local gas station for a fill-up, second hand from friends and neighbors and, more recently, on the internet (to be discussed later).

[22] One very noteworthy exception occurred in the aftermath of the Aug. 2003 bombing of the Jerusalem #2 bus in which 22 chareidi kedoshim perished, ZYA"A.

[23] Included in this are the laws of *loshon harah* (evil gossip). Of course the irreligious are not acquainted with the laws of loshon harah. What's more, it seems to be a universally acknowledged fact (though I have yet to locate it in any source) that *all* journalists, even Orthodox ones, are exempt from the laws of loshon harah (I suppose it is journalistic diplomatic immunity).

■ It is remarkably easy to controvert; which, by the way, is one of the main objectives of this book.

I want to dwell a moment on this last point. In general, the diatribes in the media are infected with numerous ailments. Among them are outright lies, distortions of facts, consciously or subconsciously omitted details, blatant double standards (i.e., the criticism is invalid by their own standards), imbalance (for example reporting that 50% of chareidim can't find Sri Lanka on a map but neglecting to mention a comparative figure for the general population which may be 60%), plain ignorance, misidentification (for lack of a consensus on what is the definition of a chareidi, people who are labeled as chareidi may actually not be chareidi), and misappropriation (blaming chareidim for a social problem that has nothing to do with the fact that they are chareidim).[24] I fully intend to elaborate on all these in a later chapter.

Of course, none of this should come as a shock to anyone who is familiar with the verse in Isaiah 66:5. The chareidim are hated and shunned, remember?

Now, this is all quite understandable as long as the article is authored by a secular Jew, a non-believer. We have already analyzed what it is that spurs the feelings of this faction. But, I am readily startled when I see disparaging articles written by people who are holding aloft the banner of [Orthodox] religious Judaism – in many cases with the express purpose of casting a negative impression of their co-religionists to a very impressionable public.

Two things astound me. One is that, in most cases, the aspersions are no less controvertible despite the religiosity of the author. Secondly, we would assume that one who promotes religious observance ought to be wary of casting aspersions on co-religionists in the public eye. Like, shouldn't the idea be to laud religious observance in an effort to interest the uncommitted? Why give a staunch secularist ammunition to reject observance by saying "Even their own kind think most of them are off their rockers?" Besides, if the writer is an Orthodox Jew, it would seem that an item that portrays other Orthodox Jews in a less than favorable light would be a form of self condemnation – *unless*...

---

[24] One example is litter. Litter is a childhood disease which sometimes lingers into adulthood. No one advocates it. It would be nice to program children not to litter but it is an uphill battle. To my knowledge, there is no evidence to suggest that chareidi children are worse litterers than any other children. Yet the chareidim have the lion's share of children, hence, the lion's share of litterers. Blaming chareidim for the universal byproducts of childhood immaturity is pointless.

...these writers do not consider chareidim to be co-religionists!

What does this say to me? It says that, in addition to the hazards of consumerism that I enumerated, there is yet another dimension, as there is yet another consumer hazard, heretofore omitted from the list:

- *Hazard #6* – A consumerist Jew is in danger of regarding himself to exist on a plane that is separate from other observant Jews whereas, and in many cases because, he does not comprehend their (his!) ideology.

In plain English, he considers other observant Jews as a distinct entity to which he has no association. There is an "us" and a "them." As the joke goes: There are two types of people – those who classify people into two types and those who don't.

Obviously, this means that, at least in the eyes of these consumers, not all Orthodox Jews are chareidim. Some are and some are not. Who is chareidi, and who isn't? Or, more accurately, *what* is a chareidi?

A consumer is one who knows "what" but does not know "why." In Hebrew, there are two words that express the English "why" – *lama* and *madua*. What is the distinction between these two terms?

The Malbim, in his book on synonyms, says that lama means, as the word structure indicates, "for what?" or, more accurately, "what for?" meaning: What is the purpose of this phenomenon? Madua is "*ma hadeah*?" meaning: What is the underlying knowledge? In other words, lama is "Why? For what purpose?" and madua is "Why? From what cause?"

The consumer who falls prey to the first three hazards is one who needs to ask "madua?" The consumer who falls prey to the sixth hazard is one who demands to know "lama?"

As a matter of course, the vast majority of anti-chareidi rhetoric in the press goes unchallenged. On occasion, the exception rather than the rule, a rebuttal appears, usually in the form of an op-ed piece or a letter to the editor. The topic comes, lingers briefly, and wafts away like a *sharav*, all but forgotten when the subject resurfaces all too soon.

I have trouble dealing with the lopsided score of anti-chareidi vs. pro-chareidi discourse in the media. The chareidi voice is relatively stifled in the public arena for numerous reasons. For one thing, whether due to self choice, prejudice, or relatively small numbers (all are true) they are not on the staff, and, therefore, are not players in the public media.[25] Secondly, their position is totally incomprehensible to one who has no substantial background understanding of Torah theology. As this is the

---

[25] As for the radio waves, it seems that the government has done everything in its

common situation among the secular and, to a lesser extent, among the consumerist religious Jews, it is almost impossible to present a clear response short of a full series of lectures. Thirdly, and most demoralizing, understanding the chareidi value system would automatically render their position on issues virtually self-explanatory. Indeed, many non-chareidi people are somewhat acquainted with chareidi philosophies and have no excuse not to be fully aware that these values have been in practice and promulgated unchanged for over 3,000 years and open to all for serious scrutiny. Yet, these detractors seem to consciously refuse to acknowledge the long-standing (and time tested) values and carry on as if either they do not exist at all or they were just formulated last week in some Bnei Brak *shtiebel*. No dialog can penetrate this shell.

Thus, this challenge cannot be met in the public media. It must be relegated to the second battlefront – the shelves of the bookstores. I recognize that I am not the first (and certainly not the most qualified) person to attempt to herald the chareidi message to non-chareidim with a full fledged book (though, possibly, the first in English). I am aware of two very excellent works that were recently released for the Hebrew speaking population. One is written by Rabbi Mordechai Noigershall[26] and the second by Rabbi Moshe Grylak.[27] Both of these works should be required reading for anybody involved with social intercourse and dialog. Aside from the obvious distinction that my book is written in English and targets the Anglo-Jewish population (though it would be a true honor if this book is deemed worthy to be translated into Hebrew), there is a more significant distinction. Their goal is to represent the chareidi from the perspective of the secularist. My objective is to represent the chareidi from the perspective of the religious consumer.

This book is for religious people. People who already believe that G-d created the world, consecrated the Jewish nation, and gave us the Torah. Religious people who wish to be more than merely a consumer but don't know where to start. Or for those who may think that a chareidi is a different class of Jew (or, perhaps, a different religion altogether!). It is not the purpose of this book to sell religion to the irreligious. It is to help elevate the religious from the status of consumer to a provider – a guide for the consumer.

---

power to ensure that the chareidim (as well as the political right) have little to no access to legal broadcasting.

[26] *Why are They Different? The Chareidim and the Israeli Society* – Noigershshall, Mordechai Hebrew, Undated, Yahadut Mizavit Shoneh, Pub., Jerusalem

[27] *The Chareidim: Who are we Really?* – Grylak, Moshe Hebrew, 2002, Keter Publishing House, Jerusalem

The purpose of this book is to offer a clear definition as to what "chareidi" means and to explain the Torah ideology that is the foundation of the chareidi perspective, lifestyle, and overall behavior. In this capacity it is a defense of chareidi ideas and actions in the face of critics and detractors both from within and without the Orthodox camp. It is, by no means, meant to be an attack or criticism on non-chareidi beliefs or practices per se. In many situations, however, it is simply unavoidable to present a defensive argument that is not critical and counteroffensive to the argument being addressed (and to those who are doing the arguing). The candid nature of this book makes it imperative to deal with sensitive issues. As such, sensibilities will be challenged. A work such as this is bound to offend the sensibilities of passionate people. This book is an intellectual discourse. It is not meant for sensitive or passionate people.

Although my main focus is to present the chareidi position in a dialog that is geared for religious people, it is not limited to religious dialog. Many of the issues and responses will be totally generic, i.e., they will confront complaints from the general [non-religious] population and respond with logical arguments, not necessarily theological ones. In this way, I hope to cover all the bases.

There are a number of reasons for this. Firstly, as previously elaborated, the main target of this book is the consumerist Jew. One symptom of this affliction that I noted (hazard #3) is that I have observed many religious people echo the complaints of the secular. This is partially due to the inordinate amount of anti-chareidi propaganda that is disseminated by the media. We are all exposed to it and influenced by it. Nevertheless, these complaints must be addressed on their terms. Secondly, an additional purpose of this book is to provide communicative chareidim such as myself with sophisticated expositions as to what is the chareidi position on these issues so that they can convey them to others in the course of a debate (*Dah mah l'hashiv*). In this capacity, it is worthwhile to be able to address the criticisms that emanate from all sectors of Jewish society.

There are a few parts to this book.

1. Who and what is a chareidi
2. What are the philosophies that govern their lifestyle
3. How these realities apply to the current issues
4. Responses to specific writings

Parts 1 and 2 constitute Book One, what I call *Consumer Benefits*. They are meant to answer those who ask: *Madua*?

Parts 3 and 4 constitute Book Two, what I call *Consumer Relations*.

They are meant to answer those who ask: *Lama*?

All the parts combined are meant to reduce the hating and shunning among our brethren.

Q. What should the chareidim hear?
A. The word of G-d.
Q. Is this book the word of G-d?
A. Only a Prophet can say that.

But, hopefully, it points in the right direction.

Behold the days are coming, says the L-rd who is G-d, and I will dispense a hunger upon the land. Not a hunger for bread, nor a thirst for water, only for to hear the words of Hashem.

(Amos 8:11)

Book One

Consumer Benefits

All of [the people of] Israel are entitled to a share in the World to Come as the verse says, (Isaiah 60:21) "And your nation, all of whom are righteous; they shall inherit the land for eternity. They are the branch of My planting, My handiwork in which to take pride."

(Babylonian Talmud Sanhedrin 90a)

One Above and Seven Below

Defining what is a chareidi

This book is about chareidim – I believe. I assume that it is being read by someone who is either a chareidi or not a chareidi (that pretty much covers all the possibilities). If you consider yourself to be chareidi, this book is about "us." If you do not, then this book is about "them."

This, then, begs the question: is this book about "us" or "them" – or neither? Are you chareidi? Am I chareidi? Are you a chareidi who does not think that I am a chareidi? Does Moses our Teacher qualify? How about Korach? Pinchas? Zimri ben Saleu? Is Elijah the Prophet chareidi? Will the Messiah be chareidi? What about Adam the First Man? Noah? Samson the Mighty? King Achab?[1] Your local Orthodox Rabbi? Your great grandfather? Do you think you qualify and actually do not? Is it possible that you would not prefer to be a chareidi but actually are? And, what about the man on the Quaker Oats cereal box?

In short, what exactly is a chareidi? (And, how do I know?)

I suppose that this is a fine setting for the classic cliché of three Jews and seventy-five opinions. These opinions will range from:

- Ultra-Orthodox Jews

- Followers of the Eida haChareidit

- Very traditional old-style Jews

- Ancient backward out-of-date Jews

---

[1] The Mishna in Sanhedrin (10:2) lists Achab as one of three kings who have no share in the World to Come. You are justified to ask, "By what measure is Achab even up for consideration for this list?" The answer is that the Scripture (Kings I 17:6) relates that when Elijah the Prophet hid from Achab alongside the Jordan River, he was provided with meat brought by ravens. The Talmud in tractate Chullin (5a) offers an opinion that the food was brought from the table of Achab. It seems that Achab was partial to mehadrin level kashrut.

- Jews with beards

- Jews with beards that aren't trimmed

- Jews with beards that aren't trimmed, funny black hats, long coats and long dresses, thick stockings, and wigs

- Jews with big families

- Jews who [say that they] don't watch television

- Jews who don't watch television, listen to the radio, read books, go to movies, nor to college and, therefore, haven't got a clue about what's going on

- Jews who don't work

- Jews who don't pay taxes even if they do work

- Jews who go around collecting money

- Jews who don't go to the Israeli army, who throw stones on Shabbat and burn Israeli flags

- Jews who are deeply committed to the laws of the Torah

- Jews who send all their boys to Yeshivot and girls to Bais Yaakovs

- Jews who won't eat in your house

- Chassidim

All of the above are true at least some of the time but none of them can constitute a real definition. Even the one that is most benevolent and altruistic – Jews that are deeply committed to the laws of the Torah – cannot be used as a definition as there are plenty of Jews who will identify themselves as such, and who truly are very committed to the laws of the Torah, who would be loathe to identify themselves as chareidi and indeed may not meet any of the other descriptions that are listed.

As a point of fact, let us try to apply the list of descriptions to one of the personages that are mentioned in the second paragraph of this chapter: Moses our Teacher. My assumption is that even non-chareidim would visualize Moses as a chareidi (especially if they consider Charlton Heston to be chareidi). But was he to be considered *ultra-Orthodox*?[2] I suppose

---

[2] The prefix "ultra" is defined in Webster's as: exceeding the norm; extreme. It is paradoxical for any person to call themselves "ultra-Orthodox" because, in the eyes of each individual, his personal level of observance personifies the norm and does not exceed it. It is only logical when expressed by someone whose

Korach thought so.[3] Did his people think he was traditional old-style? Ancient out of date? I wonder what was considered out of date in 2448.[4] Did he have a large family? Only two sons. Did he send them to yeshiva? Not the first one.[5] Did he not work? He was a shepherd, then a diplomat, a demagogue, a judge and a Head of State. Did he dress differently than any other Jews? He probably didn't watch TV or listen to radio. Was he clueless? Did he go around collecting money? Okay, he took those half shekels, but not for a living. Was he Chassidic? Ask any *mitnaged*.

So, again, what is a chareidi?

I actually saw an article focused on chareidim that defined chareidim as: "Hebrew for Quaker." My first impulse – actually, my first repulse – was that, aside from a strange similarity in habiliment, chareidim are the furthest thing on earth from the Quakers. On reflection, however, I had to appreciate the fact that the writer was technically correct; the precise translation of the word chareidi is indeed *Quaker*.[6] And the similarity in habiliment does project a comparable external image: that of a group of people who are traditional, simple, old fashioned, non-materialistic, devoutly religious, family oriented, self-contained, non-conformist, and, despite all the above, quite ostentatious.

And yet I maintain that chareidim are the furthest thing on earth from the Quakers.

So, after all this, what is a chareidi? And to whom does this accolade apply?

I think that if one really wants to know what a chareidi is, the first thing to do is to consult with the one who coined the term – the Prophet Isaiah. If I remember correctly from the Introduction, a chareidi is one who is anxious to hear the Word of G-d which, at first glance, would seem to indicate one who is anxious to do what G-d wants.

---

view of Orthodoxy is more subdued than that of the subject. It emerges that the expressor and the subject can never be in agreement as to this status.

[3] Moses, however, did not. G-d seems to have sided with Moses on this one. For more on this subject, see Chapter 8.

[4] Approximately 1312 BCE.

[5] This concurs with the Mechilta that states that Moses conceded to Jethro to expose his oldest son to idolatry. There are numerous interpretations of this Mechilta, many of which maintain that this is not to be understood literally.

[6] Most people follow a conventional translation for the word "charada" to mean trembling – or quaking – in fear. I have chosen to follow the commentary of Rashi and Metzudot Tzion in Isaiah 66:5. Rashi says "Those who rush with trepidation;" Metzudot merely says "Those who rush." These imply that the emphasis is on the *rushing,* which is due to fearfulness. The most succinct term for this (IMO) is to be *anxious.*

As simple as this may be, it doesn't really work in practice. This is because anybody and everybody who claims to be religious is convinced that they are doing precisely what G-d wants. Be it the Reform, Conservative, Reconstructionist, or Masorati Jew, any flavor of Orthodox Jew and even religious non-Jews; everybody is certain that everything he does is just hunky-dory with G-d.

But if we take a closer look at the words of the Prophet, we may notice something a bit more profound. It's not so much that we do what G-d wants as much as it is that we make it our business to know what it is that G-d wants us to do. The Prophet is talking about somebody who is anxious to hear what G-d has to say; somebody who is *listening* to what G-d wants.

These are the chareidim.

So now we have the Prophet Isaiah's definition of a chareidi:

A chareidi is somebody who is anxious to hear the "Word of G-d."

But, how do I apply this definition to the society of people who are known today as chareidi? And how are we to distinguish the chareidi from his "brethren"?

Well, since this is *my* book, I will give it my spin. Here is how I wish to adapt the Prophet's definition of what is chareidi (and what is not chareidi) and to apply it throughout this book:

A non-chareidi Orthodox Jew (NCOJ) knows the Chumash.
A chareidi knows the Chumash with Rashi's commentary.

What do I mean by that?

This statement can be understood on several levels.

The simplest and most superficial explanation is as it sounds. Chareidim collectively place a heavier emphasis on being knowledgeable about the Scriptures and religious texts. As such, they are not content with a bare bones superficial Sunday school level familiarity. Their study of the Scriptures is accompanied by Rashi's commentary as a matter of course.

This is essentially true. Nevertheless, such a distinction would likely be dismissed as "fuzzy". After all, are there not numerous non-chareidi Orthodox Jews who are well versed in the Scriptures including the principal commentaries? And are all chareidim so learned? Clearly, this is not my true intent.

On a deeper level, the implication is that the chareidim garnish their understanding of the Scriptures by imbuing them with the words and ideas of the great sages. So much so, that any interpretation of the Scriptures that is not supported by, or that blatantly contradicts, the meanings that are presented by the sages, Midrash, and the commentaries, is deemed invalid.

In this sense, when I say Rashi, I do not mean Rashi exclusively, but rather, Rashi as a representative of all the recognized Torah commentators including the sages of the Talmud, the Midrash, Rashi's contemporaries such as Nachmanides, Ibn Ezra, Rabbeinu Bachya, later commentators such as Abarbanel, Alshich, Ohr HaChaim, and relatively recent scholars such as Malbim and Rabbi S.R. Hirsch.

Similarly, in this sense, I am not referring to a level of scholarship but rather to a consensus on the perspective of the Scriptures that is shared by all the above and, consequently, shapes the religious philosophies of the camp of Jews that I am terming as the chareidim.

This is much closer to what I have in mind, though it is obvious that it falls short of giving a precise definition of what qualifies as chareidi and what does not qualify.

So, dear reader, what is the true meaning of my catchy definition?

Believe it or not, what I am really referring to is a specific passage in the Chumash along with Rashi's elaboration on that passage. It is one of the most fundamental passages of the Torah where, in all of eight words, G-d tells us precisely what He wants.

The Torah states (Leviticus 26:3-12):

> If you are to walk within my statutes and guard my commandments and perform them. And I shall give the rains in their time and the land will give forth its yield and the tree of the field will give its fruit. And the threshing will linger until the grape harvest… And I will give peace to the land… And you shall pursue your enemies… And I will devote my attention to you, and multiply you… And I shall put my sanctuary in your midst… And I shall walk in your midst and be your G-d and you shall be to me for a nation…

Here, G-d is clearly making a deal with us. Specifically, if we meet the requirements of verse 26:3, G-d promises to deliver all the benefits that are listed in verses 26:4-12. Quite an attractive offer, in my opinion. (Actually, we will soon see that it is an offer we can't refuse.)

So then, it pays (behooves us, actually) to fully understand what exactly are the requirements of verse 26:3.

Here is where the chareidim and NCOJs part company.

The NCOJ will say, "That's easy. All we have to do is 'walk within the statutes and guard the commandments and perform them.' Says so, right there."

Just tie a string from there to there.

The chareidi says, "Hmm. I'm not exactly sure. Let's see what my teacher says on this."

We know who that is.

The chareidi now examines the first Rashi on the verse (26:3):

If you are to walk within my statutes: I would assume that this is [merely] the fulfillment of the commandments, [however,] when the verse states "and guard my commandments" the fulfillment of the commandments is indicated. So, how am I to maintain "If you are to walk within my statutes?" That you must toil in [the study of] Torah.

"Aha!" says the chareidi. "Now I understand. I must toil in the study of Torah. This is not going to be as easy as it looks. It will require no small amount of toiling."

The chareidi takes the words of Rashi very seriously. There are a number of reasons for this. One being that Rashi is renowned throughout the entire Jewish nation as being a very wise and holy man and an exceptional scholar. He is believed to be a conduit of Divine inspiration. Secondly, there is scarcely a full-bred Ashkenazi Jew who cannot trace some path of ancestral lineage up to Rashi. He is our grandfather. But the third and most important reason is, like most of what Rashi writes on Chumash, *he did not make up this idea by himself.* Rashi is merely quoting what was written a millennium earlier in *Torat Kohanim.* Did I say written? Shame on me! I mean compiled. *Torat Kohanim* (a.k.a. *Sifra D'Bei Rav*) is the Halachic midrash on the book of Leviticus that was compiled from the teachings of the *Tanaim* by Rabbi Aba bar Ayvu (Rav) who was a disciple of Rabbi Yehuda HaNasi (compiler of the Mishna) and who bridged the generation between the *Tanaim* (Mishnaic scholars) and the *Amoraim* (Talmudic scholars).

As any student of *Pirkei Avot* is aware, any statement recorded by the *Tanaim* is a legacy of teachings that have traveled through an unbroken chain of sages originating with Moses our Teacher himself at Mt. Sinai.

Rashi has quite a hefty approbation for his commentary.

Let us review the passage (Leviticus 26:3-13) and understand – through the eyes of the chareidi – what it is saying to us:

G-d is giving us his exclusive recipe for successful living. He does not mince words. Like an itemized invoice, He details exactly what is included in the package. Though it is succinct, it leaves out nothing: economic stability, prosperity and wealth, peace and harmony, victory and international dominance, children, and best of all, a lasting relationship with G-d.

But wait! The goods are not for free. At the top of the invoice appears the price:

If you are to walk within my statutes and guard my

commandments and perform them.

And now (no, not *now*, but already for generations) comes Rashi and reminds us that the *Torat Kohanim* spells out exactly of what this currency consists – fulfilling the commandments *with* toil in Torah.

We now have a revised definition of a chareidi:

A chareidi is one who believes that success in life can only be achieved by observing the commandments and toiling in Torah.

Okay, are we done? Can I go home now?

Well, not just yet. Rashi – and, by extension, *Torat Kohanim* – is not quite finished.

The NCOJ may say, "Okay. I see the price quote for the full-blown premium package. I'm just not up to buying in to this plan with all the bells and whistles. How about I stick to just fulfilling the commandments like the verse says and leave out the 'toil in Torah' part and I'll take a scaled down version of the benefits? I can manage with a slower economy and a few dry spells and what's so bad if we need 10 guys to chase 100 of them instead of 5, and a six-day war every 30 years or so?"

I would think twice about that (at least).

Our Italian cousins (the children of Esau) pay respects to "the Godfather." We respect "G-d the Father." Our G-d the Father warns us that it is not healthy to turn down his offer.

The Torah continues (Leviticus 26:14-15):

And if you do not hearken to Me and you do not perform all of these commandments. And if in My statutes you will display loathing; and if your souls will repulse My judgments; to desist from performing all of My commandments for you to nullify My covenant.

After this passage begins another itemized list. It is a much longer and more detailed list. It is a list of chance misfortunes that are liable to accidentally befall people who think that it is not worthwhile to buy into G-d the Father's protection service. G-d the Father indicates that it would be a big shame to see such misfortunes occur to such righteous and deserving people as us, heaven forefend.

It would be a good idea to clearly understand exactly what modes of conduct are those to which G-d the Father disapproves.

Again Rashi:

And if you do not hearken to Me: To toil in Torah and to be knowledgeable of the exegeses of the sages. One might presume [that these words refer to failure] to fulfill the commandments. When the verse says "and you do not perform, etc." [failure of] fulfillment of the commandments is [already] indicated. So, how am I to maintain "And if you do not hearken to me"? To [abstain from] toil in Torah.

We now have a clear definition of a non-chareidi:

A non-chareidi [Orthodox Jew] is one who does not toil in Torah even though he observes the commandments.

Rashi says later in the verse – **And you do not perform**: Once one does not study, one does not perform. Here, there are two transgressions.

In geometry they say that two points determine a line.

Rashi continues:

And if in My statutes you will display loathing: Loathe others who perform.

And if your souls will repulse My judgments: Hate the sages.

To desist from performing: Prevent others from performing.

All of My commandments: Deny that I have commanded them.

For you to nullify My covenant: Deny the main concept [that G-d is Master of the world].

Rashi concludes:

Here there are seven transgressions, the first one draws in the second one, and so on until the seventh. And these are they: Does not study; does not perform; loathes others who perform; despises the sages; prevents others from performing; denounces the commandments; denounces the main concept.

In the original draft of this chapter I wrote the following – somewhat blasphemous – words:

G-d the Father has divided his people into two camps:

Camp A – the camp that is buying the benefits package.

Camp B – the camp that is rejecting the benefits package and exposing *themselves* to "chance" misfortune.

When I reviewed these lines I realized that they are wrong. G-d did not divide his people into two camps. Never did. Never will. We are and will remain one camp until the end of days.

What is more accurate is the analogy that the *Baalei Mussar* (Masters of Ethical Jewish thought) relate:

G-d the Father is offering us tickets to one of two destinations – the *Bracha* (Blessing) to the Port of Life and the *Kelala* (Curse) to the Port of Death. The tricky part is that *we are all on one boat*. The boat will dock at both ports. Every individual will disembark at his or her proper destination port. The question is: what kind of journey will be *collectively* endured by all of the passengers on the entire boat? Will it be a pleasant peaceful luxurious journey? Will it be a stormy, wavy, frightening experience fraught with trepidation and seasickness? Will they be attacked by pirates or held up at foreign ports by the authorities? Will it be a quick voyage or a long roundabout ordeal? Most important, to which port does it arrive first?

I suppose, since we are all in one boat, it would depend on how many people hold tickets to Port A versus how many to Port B.

I realize that I am getting a bit carried away. The purpose of this chapter (and, indeed, of this book) is not to preach to anybody, but to define what is a chareidi and what is not.

Let us return to the main discussion and rewrite the "blasphemous" lines.

We have divided *ourselves* into two camps:

Camp A (Camp Bracha) – the camp that is buying the benefits package, i.e., the *Bracha* ticket and encouraging the Captain to sail the *entire ship* on a straight course to "Paradise Island."

Camp B (Camp Kelala) – the camp that is rejecting the benefits package, i.e., buying the *Kelala* ticket, and exposing *all of us* to "chance" misfortune.[7]

It is Camp A, Camp Bracha, that I am calling the chareidi camp. Camp B, the non-chareidi camp.

From Rashi we understand that members of Camp Bracha meet a single (albeit multi-faceted) definition: *Those who perform the commandments along with toil in Torah [study].*

The members of Camp Kelala comprise seven levels:

1. Those that perform the commandments but do not toil in Torah.[8]
2. Those that do not perform the commandments.
3. Those who display loathing toward those who perform the commandments.
4. Those who despise the sages – i.e., Rabbis and teachers.
5. Those who prevent others from performing the commandments.
6. Those who denounce the veracity of the commandments.
7. Those who denounce the oneness, omnipotence, majesty, and sovereignty of G-d.

In other words, G-d has drawn a red line. Above the red line is a list of those who are in the category of "**If you are to walk within my stat-**

---

[7] See Rashi's commentary on Leviticus 26:37 s.v. *V'Kashlu.*

[8] Rashi qualifies this to mean "one who acknowledges his master and conspires to rebel." (Leviticus 26:14 s.v. *V'Im*) I am not sure what constitutes "one who acknowledges his master" but my assumption is that this would refer to anybody with an Orthodox education.

utes…" One entry. Below the red line is a list of those who are in the category of "**And if you do not hearken to me…**" Seven entries. *One above and seven below*.

The red line seems to be very thin. There is no twilight zone or no-man's land.[9] One must belong to one camp or the other.

This is to say that there are seven levels of non-chareidis. Only the first level (that does perform commandments) can be considered Orthodox. Granted that a Level 1 non-chareidi is not a Level 3 non-chareidi who is not a Level 5 non-chareidi who is not a Level 7 non-chareidi. (I know that I skipped a few.) It is also obvious from the Scriptures that the brunt of the *Tochacha*[10] is reserved for the sin of idol worship, i.e., the lowest extremes of the *seven below*. Nevertheless, it is clear from Rashi that one who stands at any of these levels is in danger of descending all the way down to Level 7. Though many individuals have the strength to resist deteriorating to lower levels, the danger passes to subsequent generations.[11] [12]

At this stage, I can present a more complete definition of a chareidi

---

[9] See Yalkut Shimoni Leviticus 26 Article 671: The Yalkut asks why the Torah must elaborate both sides of the contract, i.e., "if you hearken" and "if you do not hearken," is it not sufficient to state the positive side and we can deduce the inverse? The Yalkut continues that according to Rabbi Meir who consistently maintains that all contracts require duplex stipulations, this question is irrelevant. However, according to Rabbi Chanina ben Gamliel who maintains that for all contracts we can deduce the negative from the positive (and vice versa) the question stands. The Yalkut answers that according to Rabbi Chanina the negative side must be stipulated so that one will not say, "If I observe the commandments, I will be blessed and, if I do not observe them, I will not be blessed nor will I be cursed." Thus the Scripture must elaborate that to neglect to fulfill the stipulation for blessing is equivalent to fulfilling the stipulation for the curse. There is no neutral.

[10] Literally: Admonition. The colloquial term for the warnings and curses in Leviticus 26.

[11] This seems to be the message of the verse in Deuteronomy (30:19): "I am assigning as my witnesses in [regard to] you today the Heavens and the Earth [that they may attest to such that] the [gift of] life and the [punishment of] death I have placed before you, the blessing and the curse; and you shall choose in life, so that you may live, *you and your offspring*." See Klei Yakar ad loc.

[12] Although, for my purposes, the One Above and Seven Below is the most suitable model for portraying this factionalism in Judaism, there are yet other, more prevalent models. One of the most popular of which is that of the four sons that are discussed in the Haggadah of Passover. The conventional interpretation portrays them as four brothers of one household. I have seen a more profound interpretation that they are actually portraying the steady deterioration of succeeding generations. Thus, the grand patriarch is the *tzaddik* who performs the

(albeit, not the final one[13]):

> ***A chareidi is one who believes that success in life can only be achieved by observing the commandments and toiling in Torah. Any activities that do not concur with these are subject to happenstance and hold little chance of success.***

I am more than happy to assume all the credit – and the blame – for this definition; but I cannot. This is not really my definition. This is the Prophet Isaiah's definition. It must be so because it's what G-d wants. G-d tells us so Himself in Leviticus, Chapter 26. Am I sure this is what He means?

Sure I am.

Rashi says so.

Passover service meticulously. The son of the first generation is the *chacham*. He is wise but not a complete *tzaddik*. Though he strives to emulate his father and inquires sincerely as to the rituals and he fulfills them, this fulfillment is lacking in full conviction. The son of the *chacham* is the *rasha* (wicked son). He observes his father and grandfather performing the Passover service but he senses that his father, the *chacham*, is acting more out of tradition than faith. As one of even less faith, he refuses even to buy into the tradition. He is aware of the service but he doesn't bother to transmit the tradition down to his son, the *tam*, who consequently remains simple and unlearned. Still, the *tam* observes his grandfather, the *chacham*, performing the Passover service, thus he is aware that there is a tradition that was not taught to him, so he inquires, "What is this?" His son, the fourth generation, has no knowledge of any tradition as even his grandfather, the *rasha*, does not perform the service. Thereupon, the only remedy is for the community to indoctrinate him from scratch.

[13] We will not reach that plateau until the end of Chapter 2. Please bear with me.

Chapter Two

The Meaning of Toil

Defining the definition

The previous chapter was rather harsh. I expect to receive a lot of flak over it. (I can smell the scent of butane lighters flicking on.) Undoubtedly, it left many with the impression that I am trying to pigeonhole Jewish people, mitzvah observant ones, no less. It also would imply that, personally, I smugly feel safely ensconced in Camp A looking down at other Orthodox Jews that I am relegating to Camp B.

Don't flick those lighters just yet (or unleash those angry emails). This chapter is for damage control.

There is nothing subjective about the previous chapter. It is pure Chumash and Rashi. The only subjective aspect is that I take on the mantle of applying Rashi's interpretation of Leviticus 26:3 as the fundamental ideology of those known as chareidim. It is certainly the fundamental ideology to which I, along with my mentors and the like-minded people with whom I associate, subscribe. And we do think of ourselves as chareidim. I therefore consider this ideology as the most appropriate definition. Nobody needs to agree with this definition and I do not pretend to speak for anyone who does not wish to identify with my definition or with the ideological arguments that I present in this book. I welcome anybody to present a more appropriate definition (and to write his own book).[1] Still, I made certain to end the chapter before expounding on the idea using subjective interpretations. You may not burn that chapter; it requires *geniza*. The subjective bit starts here. You can now get your lighters and emails ready.

It is important for me to clearly stress that I am *not* categorizing people.[2] I am not relegating anybody to one camp or another. My purpose is to define *what* is a chareidi – not to define *who* is a chareidi. (Though I think it is safe to say that Moses our Teacher is in and the Quaker Oats

---

[1] Kudos to Noah Efron and to Rabbi Moshe Grylak for doing just that.

[2] I will defer that task to the Orthodox internet dating services.

man is out. Tommy Lapid and Korach are definitely out. Pinchas is in, but I'm still not sure about Zimri.) In fact, I have not yet arrived at the final revision of my definition of a chareidi. Once we arrive at a resolute definition, the reader can determine for him or herself to whom the definition can be applied.

So let us review our definition and try to comprehend its meaning.

A chareidi is one who believes that success in life can only be achieved by observing the commandments and toiling in Torah.

It is time to deal with the $64,000.00 question: Precisely what is "toil in Torah" (and how do I justify wasting my time writing this book)?

Oh, how I wish I knew! I also hope that I qualify. Since I also have a big stake in this, I will give it my best (highly subjective) shot.

At first glance, it appears that the Torah is compelling every single individual[3] to engage in nothing other than Torah study for the duration of his active life – *Kollel über alles*. I am not so sure. This is because there is no indication that the verse is speaking to an individual.

One difficulty with translating Scriptures into English is that much is lost in the translation. Though not discernible in English, the Scriptures in Leviticus are all in the plural. This means that when the verse instructs us "to walk within my statutes and guard my commandments" it means, "if you (plural), *as a collective group*, walk within my statutes and guard my commandments...." As Rashi interprets this to mean to toil in Torah, then the verse is demanding that you (we) should be a collective group, i.e., a society, that toils in Torah.

In other words, it may not be essential that each individual personally toils in Torah to maintain a society that collectively toils in Torah. No, I am not letting any individual off the hook (as if it's up to me). After all, what is a society [that toils in Torah study] if not a community of individuals [that toil in Torah study]? Furthermore, Maimonides[4] and the Shulchan Aruch[5] do not mince words as they articulate the profundity of each individual's obligation toward Torah study. In one voice and in identical terminology they impress the following three principles:

- The obligation is universal. i.e., it applies to every Jewish male in

---

[3] Here, and for the duration of this discourse, I am obviously referring to individuals of the male persuasion. Women have no obligation to actively participate in Torah study though they are expected to undertake a supporting role as indicated in Talmud Bavli Berachot 17a.

[4] Maimonides Yad Chazaka, Mada, Hilchot Talmud Torah 1:8-10

[5] Shulchan Aruch Yoreh Deah 246:1-3

accordance to his ability. Even if he, for whatever reason (time constraint or physical constraint), cannot study at all, he must assist others who can. In short, *nobody is exempt from some form of involvement*.

- The obligation is constant. It is in effect at all times, every day, night and day.

- The obligation is life-long. One cannot go into retirement as long as one lives.

It is not my place or purpose to preach to anybody about their obligations and I have come just about as far as I am qualified to go (one need not be an extraordinary scholar or saint to quote Maimonides and Shulchan Aruch). Additionally, I must stress that this book is not intended to be a treatise on the obligation, value, merits, and overall importance of Torah study (despite all the pages I devote to this topic in the upcoming chapter). For this, there are libraries stocked floor to ceiling with works of philosophy, ethics, and Halacha both in the Holy Tongue and in the vernacular of all walks of Orthodox Jewry. To these, I have nothing to add. Indeed, in my humble opinion, there is no need to study anything more than Pirkei Avot (Ethics of the Fathers) to gain an appreciation on how much to revere Torah study. There is no subsequent work of substance that does not draw upon the fundamentals enumerated in Pirkei Avot to build its structure.

The point that I wish to make is that the role of the individual is far from clear, both from the vantage point of Orthodox Jewish society as well as from the vantage point of the individual himself. There are soul searching theological questions that must be addressed: What is considered enough? What, if applicable, is considered too much? How do I reconcile my personal agenda to the needs of my friends and family who rely on me? How much study should be for my advancement and how much for others? If G-d expects me to toil so much, why am I so beset with personal needs? Why does He send me so many distractions? Why am I not more intellectually endowed? What can I accomplish when I had that terrible toothache the first half of last week, a must attend wedding the next night, after which the water pump on my 12-year-old Subaru went, and last night I spent five hours in the emergency room with my 7-year-old, and, the rest of the time, I can't keep my eyes open after ten minutes at the Talmud?[6] Passover is in two weeks and my wife expects me to do the garage and the basement and I still didn't do my taxes because I'm trying to hold on to that study session, for Heaven's sake! What

---

[6] A description of one of the better weeks.

does G-d expect me to achieve? Am I supposed to study like the Gaon of Vilna? Did he have to do taxes and the garage? Anyway, he was a mathematical genius!

I sure hope that you're not looking for the answers here. I do not pretend to have them. Besides, my objective in this chapter is to define the meaning of chareidi, remember? These issues are clearly beyond the scope of this book as I noted a few paragraphs back. Every individual Jew is on his own in cracking this one. I suppose that it qualifies as part of the toil.

What is, indeed, clear is that "the Torah was not given to the attending angels."[7] We are human and we must conduct our lives as such. There is no shortage of indications from the Scriptures[8] themselves and from the words of the sages[9] that we are not all expected to be "learning machines."[10] As one example, this very passage in Leviticus[11] includes among the benefits "And the time of threshing will extend for you until the time of the grape harvest; and the time of the grape harvest will extend until the planting." Rashi explains, **"And the time of threshing will extend for you until the time of the grape harvest** – that the threshing will be plentiful and *you are busy with it* until the grape harvest and with the grape harvest *you are busy* until the planting." This leaves us with the impression that the Torah expects at least some of its subjects to thresh and harvest and plant.[12] Likewise, "And you shall pursue your enemies, and they shall fall before you to the sword."[13] It seems that there will be time and manpower for pursuing enemies.[14] Yet, we shan't lose sight of the fact that these benefits are the payoff for observing the commandments *with* toil in Torah.

The fact is that this very issue is a subject of an intense debate between two Tannaic scholars, Rabbi Yishmael ben Alisha and Rabbi Shi-

---

[7] Talmud Bavli Berachot 25b

[8] One of the most classic examples is the much celebrated work/study partnership of Yissachar and Zevulun as indicated in Deuteronomy 33:18

[9] Pirkei Avot 2:2; Talmud Bavli Kiddushin 82a

[10] See Rashi Kohelet 7:28 s.v. *Adam*

[11] Leviticus 26:5

[12] According to the viewpoint of Rabbi Shimon ben Yochai, this can be understood that the prolonged chores will be carried out by non-Jewish workers. Nevertheless, the simple connotation of the Scripture and the precise terminology of Rashi "and you are busy" implies personal involvement.

[13] Leviticus 26:7

[14] See Ohr HaChaim (ad loc.) that this cannot refer to a defensive war as protection from the threat of attack has been previously assured. It therefore refers to a voluntary offensive war.

mon ben Yochai as recorded in the Talmud[15]:

> The Rabbis taught: **And you shall gather your grain harvest**.[16] What does this teach us? In accordance to the verse, "This Torah scroll shall not budge from your mouth,"[17] I would assume these words to be accepted [literally] as written. This teaching (verse) tells us: "And you shall gather your grain harvest," behave in the manner that is the way of the earth (i.e., engage in lucrative occupations for sustenance). Such are the words of Rabbi Yishmael.
>
> Rabbi Shimon ben Yochai says: It is possible for a man to [be ceaselessly occupied, to] plow at the plowing time, to plant at the planting time, to reap at the reaping time, to thresh at the threshing time, to winnow at the winnowing time[, etc. If so,] what will be with [his study of] Torah? Rather, at a time when [the nation of] Israel fulfills the will of G-d, their tasks are performed by others as it states, "And foreigners will stand and graze your flocks…"[18] and at a time when [the nation of] Israel does not fulfill the will of G-d, they perform their own tasks as it states "And you shall gather your grain harvest." What's more, the tasks of others will be performed by them as it states, "And you shall serve your enemies…"[19]

This debate is one of the most central themes of chareidi ideology as it illustrates the opinions of two of the foremost Talmudic sages as to how to prioritize our lives. Our problem is that, at this point, we face conflicting opinions. Rabbi Shimon ben Yochai maintains that the individual is enjoined to devote all of his energies toward Torah study and to forsake any other endeavor. Rabbi Yishmael maintains that it is expected for the individual to look after his personal needs at the inevitable expense of full-time uninterrupted study – akin to the well known adage, "*Yaffa Torah im derech eretz* (Torah study is enhanced in conjunction with worldly endeavors)." And we are torn – what's a body to do?

Thankfully, three Amoraic scholars step in to referee[20]:

> Abaye says: Many have attempted to do as Rabbi Yishmael and have succeeded, [and many have attempted to do] as Rabbi Shimon ben Yochai and have not succeeded.[21]

---

[15] Talmud Bavli Berachot 35b

[16] Deuteronomy 11:14

[17] Joshua 1:8

[18] Isaiah 61:5

[19] Deuteronomy 28:48

[20] Talmud Bavli (Ibid.)

[21] For those readers who are psychology students and may be familiar with the MBTI (Myers-Briggs Type Indicator) system of personality typing, it may be of

Rava said to his disciples: I beg of you on the ordinary days of Nissan and the ordinary days of Tishrei not to appear before me so that you should not be distracted throughout the year by your needs for sustenance.[22]

Rabba bar bar Chana said that Rabbi Yochanan said in the name of Rabbi Yehuda bar Rav Iloyi: Come and observe that the earlier generations are not like the later generations. The earlier generations made their Torah study regular and their tasks erratic. [As a result] both endeavors flourished. The later generations who made their tasks regular and their Torah study erratic, both endeavors failed to flourish.

The common denominator seems to be that all these sages concur that while Rabbi Shimon ben Yochai may be *idealistically* correct, the common man is not capable of attaining such perfection. What remains is a spiritually weaker level of man for whom the primary pursuit in life is Torah study, however, due to his chronic affliction of "physical need," this pursuit must be supplemented with regular doses of *derech eretz* – "the way of the land" (what I call "occupational therapy") – once every six months or as needed.

The conclusion to draw from all this is to establish that, in conjunction with performing the commandments, every Jewish individual, man and woman, has a fundamental obligation to promote and advance the study of Torah in accordance with his or her station in life. Beyond this fundamental obligation, any male individual must endeavor to *actively* engage in Torah study to the maximum intensity of which he is capable. It is up to him to determine (through the assistance of his spiritual advisor[s]) what that level of intensity is, based on his strengths and weaknesses (and not to sell himself short).

This, then, brings me to the final updated version of what I believe is the definition of a chareidi:

A chareidi is a Jew who defines Orthodoxy as a society whose

---

interest to note that in order to be successful in the style of Rabbi Shimon ben Yochai it is all but imperative that one must be predisposed to the N (Intuitive) characteristic versus the S (Sensory) characteristic. Statistical analysis has shown that the percentage of the general population that favors the N type is only 24% versus 76% for the S type – less than 1 out of 4. In the broader picture, it would seem that the Rabbi Shimon ben Yochai personality would call for an (E or I)NTJ typology which further reduces the percentage to under 10%.

[22] Nissan was the time of the early grain harvest and Tishrei was the time for pressing grapes and olives. As such, the producers of these commodities needed additional manpower for these seasonal tasks. It was customary for the scholars to hire themselves for these temporary jobs and the earnings would provide for them during the remaining months so they would be free to study.

primary function is to actively advance the observance of the commandments and the study of Torah and who identifies him or herself with this society.

Makes sense to you? Yes? Read on! No? Close this book and donate it to Ohr Somayach – even this chapter requires *geniza*.

Chapter Three

Everything You Always Wanted to Ask About The Chareidim (But Were Afraid to Know)

More FAQs about what is a chareidi.

As I reflect upon the two previous chapters in which I boldly and fearlessly (read: blindly and foolishly) rush headlong into the chaotic void of esoteric semantics to show the skeptics of the world that I can define the ethereal essence of the mystical entity known as the chareidi (and, that I know how to use a thesaurus), it dawns on me that there are yet many unanswered questions. So, as a public service, I shall attempt to answer them. To that end, this chapter will take on the format of a FAQ (Frequently Asked Questions) form that is so ubiquitous in today's high-tech world.[1]

What am I trying to avoid with this definition?

By now, it should be clear that I am defining a chareidi as an ideology-driven subject of socio-religious identity. With this definition, we can sidestep the following aspects as not being germane to the essence of a chareidi:

Clothes and external appearance

My definition is *entirely ideological* and not based on externalities. This means that one who fits the definition is a chareidi in my book (literally and figuratively) regardless of how he dresses. It doesn't matter if he does or does not wear dark clothes and white shirts exclusively, *tzitzit* on top, *tzitzit* underneath, with or without *t'chelet*, *peyot* or not, and the type of kipa is (literally) immaterial. As long as the garb conforms with Halacha (which, at the minimum, means that it does not violate Halacha) and is *shatnez*-free. I am not splitting hairs (i.e., I am not getting involved in electric shavers). Same goes for the ladies – wigs, snoods, kerchiefs, or hats (individually or all together) all count.

This can be somewhat paradoxical as there seem to be numerous

---

[1] Don't bother asking who has been asking these questions and how frequently.

[sects of] devoutly religious Jews who purposely eschew the more traditional "Quaker Oats" garb because they do not wish to identify themselves nor be identified as "chareidi." They may actually be repulsed by the association. Nevertheless, if external appearance is the only factor that distinguishes them and nothing else, they may have to "bite the bullet" and face up to the dark reality. I have friends in Kochav HaShachar like that. You know who you are!

It does go without saying that people who subscribe to a given ideology will have, by default, a like-minded approach as to what form of attire fits the ideology. One who exhibits liberal[2] or outlandish tastes in clothing, hairstyle, or even in the style and application of religious articles, is, in effect, advertising that he or she does not truly subscribe to the ideology.

The obligations of any individual

With this aspect, I am repeating what I wrote in the previous chapter. My definition for chareidi is not intended to delineate any individual's personal religious obligations. I consider a definition for chareidi such as, "one who studies Torah all the time" or, "one who believes everyone should study Torah all the time" to be inadequate as it implies that one who does not is not chareidi. Though this may be roughly true, it is far from clear cut. More importantly, since there is bound to be some degree of disagreement as to what are the obligations of individuals (note the dispute between Rabbi Yishmael and Rabbi Shimon ben Yochai), any definition so founded is subject to the same divergence of opinion. I, for one, am not trying to leave anybody out.

The performance of an individual or even of the collective society

My definition, likewise, makes no assessment as to the performance record of any individual or group. This means that a chareidi who, by all accounts, should be engaged in his fair share of toiling and appears to be

---

[2] Though this is digressing from the subject of this chapter, and my intentions are not to preach, I must use this opportunity to register a complaint to Orthodox Jews – even many who in most other ways fit the definition of chareidi – who, at casual times, see no problem coming to synagogue services wearing caps and T-shirts that display sports emblems, bright logos, catchy slogans, humorous quips, and tourist memorabilia. All these items distract other worshipers (put me on the top of the list) and cause them (Okay, us) to think about the advertised phenomenon, sometimes straining to make out the fine print on someone's T-shirt between "Shma koleinu" and "Hashem Elokenu." This is a serious obstacle. See Yalkut Me'Am Loez (Torah Anthology) Genesis 41:13 and Shulchan Aruch Orach Chaim 91.

falling short of his objective is no less a chareidi, provided he meets the stated definition. In fact, this disclaimer is geared to protect not only chareidim who are falling short, but also chareidim who are falling out. This is a chareidi issue that receives an inordinate amount of media attention and I do not intend to leave this issue unattended.

What am I trying to accomplish with this definition?

The main purpose is to illustrate that chareidi ideology is a value system that is derived from and mandated by the Torah and dates back to the point in history when the Torah and the Jewish people were initially unified. Consequently, the mannerisms and socio-political perspectives of the chareidim are a direct outgrowth of that value system and not the other way around – as the social scientists would have us believe.

It also serves to illustrate that even if one does not walk like a chareidi, talk like a chareidi, look like a chareidi, or act like a chareidi (or write books like a chareidi), he may still be one. As the previous chapter and some of the upcoming FAQs in this chapter point out, one who is already mitzvah observant does not need to quit his job, replenish his wardrobe, or drastically alter his lifestyle to secure a spot in Camp Bracha (i.e., you can still play tennis though you may have to give up mixed doubles). All one needs to do is to *ideologically* support the "program" and contribute to it in the way that he is most capable. You might say that I am trying to make some [self proclaimed non-chareidi Orthodox] readers realize that they may not be as removed from this society as they [would like to] believe.

Do I always mean this definition when I say chareidi?

Yes and no.

When *I* say chareidi for the purpose of my analyses and arguments regarding chareidim and their lifestyle, this is certainly what I mean. That's why I wrote all this. It seems that the true meaning of chareidi has hitherto been one of the world's best kept secrets. The Prophet Isaiah knew it, I know it, my editor knows it, and now you know it; but the masses and mass media that seem to know so much about chareidim do not yet know it. Therefore, when I say chareidi in regard to news items, common table talk, urban legends, and the like, I am referring to what *they* think is a chareidi.

Which is what?

Though I am never sure, as it is undefined, I assume it is one who walks like a chareidi, talks like a chareidi, looks like a chareidi, and acts like a chareidi – though the media seems to have a field day when it comes to discussing how a chareidi is expected to act. For this reason, I like to refer to the legendary chareidi as the Quaker Oats/Fagin (QOF) chareidi.

Why QOF?

Because the chareidi portrayed in the media is the quaint, conservative, aloof, steadfastly unchanging character who is at the same time (or from one minute or news item to the next) a puritanical saint (the Quaker Oats man) and a heartless, sinister, conniving, pocket-picking fiend (Fagin).

What about the writings of Heilman and Efron?

My innovation is that I present a comprehensive definition of "chareidi" from the perspective of a chareidi. I have yet to see this done in any English language work. What I have seen are descriptions, though not what I could call definitions, in some secular academic works. I am specifically referring to the entry for *Haredim* in the CD-ROM edition of Encylopaedia Judaica authored by Samuel C. Heilman as well as his full scale account, *Defenders of the Faith* and the superb study on Secular vs. Ultra-Orthodox relations portrayed by Noah J. Efron in his book, *Real Jews*. My basic impression is that it is quite a challenge for a secular academician to capture the essence of a chareidi. It takes one to know one.

I believe that the focal points that are stressed and the limitations that are evident from these descriptions are quite revealing as to how even an "objective" secular scholar perceives our society. It is well worth studying these descriptions and analyzing why they are expressed so. Such study calls for a full chapter which is forthcoming (Chapter 5).

Why have I, thus far, made no mention of the passage in Talmud Bavli Bava Metzia?

I have been avoiding it, that's why. This is because the thesis of this book centers on the passage in Leviticus 26 and not the verse in Isaiah 66. My true goal is to find a definition that most clearly distinguishes – *in today's Jewish socio-political environment* – what (or who) is and what is not a chareidi as an initial step to clear the air of prejudices and misguided criticisms and, ultimately, to "sell the product." Consequently, I am not sure how much currency it contributes to my hypothesis, although I do consider it to be a valuable ally.

However, now that you brought it up, we may as well discuss it. The Talmud Bavli in Bava Metzia 33b states:

> Rabbi Yehuda bar Rav Iloyi expounded: What is the meaning of the verse: "Hear the word of G-d, *you who are anxious toward his word*

(chareidim)…" these are the scholars[3]; "…*your brethren*…" these are those who mastered the Scriptures; "…*those who hate you*…" these are those who mastered the Mishna; "…*those who shun you*…" these are the uneducated. Perhaps you will say that they [the brethren, haters, and shunners] have lost their logic and forfeited their possibilities [for refinement]? The teaching says, "…and we shall [all] see their rejoicing…." Perhaps you will say that the Jews will be ashamed? The teaching says, "…and *they* (the non-Jews) will be ashamed." The idolators will be ashamed and the Jews will rejoice.

Tosefot[4] explains[5] that the "masters of Scriptures" are those who are familiar *only* with Scripture and nothing more and cannot determine laws and rulings without the "brotherly" help of the masters of Gemara (Talmudic scholars). Similarly, the "masters of Mishna" are those who are familiar only with the obscure memorandum that is the Mishna and yet they mistakenly maintain that their knowledge is sufficient to understand the intricacies of Torah and Halacha.[6] After that, there are the uneducated who hate the scholars to the point of shunning them totally. The Talmud seems to be saying that although these three groups are not "on the same page" as the Talmudic scholar, they are, nevertheless, inside the loop and will merit to share in the rejoicing of Israel and be spared from shame as opposed to the idolators.[7]

In effect, my definition does borrow from this idea[8] and applies it to the concept of "toil in Torah." I suppose we can say that I am fusing these two concepts together.

Is there but one kind of chareidi?

I'm happy you asked. Many people refer to a marked difference between native Israeli chareidim and Diaspora (i.e., Anglo) chareidim; or

---

[3] The Talmud is trying to make a point that to be considered a scholar, one must specifically be proficient in the Gemara which comprises Talmudic exegeses of the Scriptures and of the Mishna.

[4] A consortium of French and German Talmudists, many of whom were students and colleagues of Rashi.

[5] Ibid. s.v. *Acheichem*

[6] This actually corroborates my characterization of the consumerist Jew.

[7] The Talmud is rather magnanimous as some of the commentaries on the Scriptures in Isaiah are not so kindly disposed toward these three entities; in other words, they maintain that the word "they" at the end of the verse – "they will be ashamed" – refers to these three entities and not to the non-Jewish idolators.

[8] In fairness to myself, I came up with the catch line "The NCOJ knows Chumash; the chareidi knows Chumash with Rashi" before I came across the passage in Talmud Bava Metzia.

Eastern chareidim and Western chareidim[9]; or chareidim from community X vs. chareidim from community Y. In all cases, it seems that one group is reputed to be more unyielding and hard-lined than the other.[10]

On one hand, my definition provides a common denominator to unify all of us into the single society which we truly are. Yet, there does indeed seem to be two varieties of chareidim which can be characterized as *hard* and *soft*. How is this to be understood?

The answer lies in the classic dispute between Rabbi Yishmael and Rabbi Shimon ben Yochai that was discussed in the previous chapter.

As you recall, Rabbi Shimon ben Yochai maintains that a person should forsake all worldly involvement and devote himself entirely to Torah study. Assuming he is worthy, G-d will assign non-Jews to carry out the mundane tasks that are required to meet his physical needs. This complete devotion is what Rabbi Shimon understands to be "fulfilling the will of G-d."

Rabbi Yishmael maintains that a Jew is considered to be in fulfillment of the will of G-d even when his spiritual existence is supplemented with the prescribed measure of worldly intercourse. Taken in stride, he will be blessed with material success, which in turn, will enable him to reach higher spiritual levels. As we noted, it seems that all agree that Rabbi Shimon's description is the ideal toward which we should strive but that it is beyond the grasp of the common man. Ultimately, Rabbi Yishmael's description is the practical objective to which all men can relate.

These two viewpoints foment conflicting opinions as to how much involvement in non-spiritual matters can and should be tolerated. The debate has never truly been resolved. It has raged on through the generations and remains in full force to this very day. Actually, over the past century and a half, the debate has taken on new dynamics as the industrial age and Western democratic ideals have given us access to a slew of modern day "wheat fields, vineyards, and olive groves"[11] that have never existed in previous generations.

---

[9] Here, I am merely employing a different terminology for the same phenomenon. I absolutely do not mean to refer to Ashkenazim and Sephardim by these terms. Actually, unless specifically stated, I am not distinguishing between Ashkenazim and Sephardim in any discourse.

[10] Even to the extent that such a distinction exists, it is certainly not absolute. The terms are mere generalities. In practice, many diaspora chareidim meet the hard-line definition and many native Israeli ones meet the soft-line definition, etc. I am just parroting the common terms.

[11] A reference to the *"dagan, tirosh, v'yitzhar"* mentioned in Deuteronomy 11:14 the source verse of the classic dispute.

The inevitable result is the emergence of two main categories of chareidim – the [Rabbi] Shimonists and the [Rabbi] Yishmaelists. These two strains co-exist within every chareidi community and often within chareidi households. In most aspects, there are no substantial adverse effects to this phenomenon. The Yishmaelists admire the Shimonists for maintaining a higher standard and the Shimonists appreciate that the Yishmaelists are "doing their job." Essentially, they carry out a teamwork program (in the spirit of the Yissachar – Zevulun partnership) as, typically, both groups gain from the achievements of the other.

Problems do arise when Rabbi Shimonist chareidim expect or demand other chareidim who may lean toward the Yishmaelist school of thought to maintain their stricter standards. These problems tend to flair up in relation to community issues which collectively affect all of the chareidim in a community and where a common policy must be adopted. In this situation, these two conflicting schools of thought make it difficult to determine a single policy to serve the entire spectrum. In some cases, a rift within the community is unavoidable. This occurs mostly within the education system as that is one crux of the initial debate – should young chareidim be educated exclusively toward the higher Shimonist standard or not? Does the presence of the Yishmaelists make those standards harder to achieve? On occasion this disparity comes to the fore in family relations, mostly between fathers and sons (though sometimes even between husbands and wives or in-laws), sometimes with tragic consequences. This issue demands further study which I hope to provide.

What about the consumerist Jews from the Introduction?

Although this concept may aptly define non-chareidim, it certainly cannot be used as a distinguishing characteristic. This is because, as I wrote in that chapter, being chareidi does not preclude being a consumer. In fact, I contend that we are all consumers at some level. Even a chareidi can say, "Just tie a string from there to there" or be misled to think that their position on army service constitutes a *chillul Hashem*.

Still, as I wrote, the chareidi views his consumerist status as a shortcoming that ought to be overcome. As such, he is much less vulnerable to succumb to the hazards of consumerism, particularly hazards 3, 4, 5, and 6.

All of the Chareidim are like that?

Okay, I know what's troubling you.

Yes, of course, any institution or society that comprises a value system or bylaws includes loafers, shleppers, fakers, and dissenters and, to this, the chareidim are no exception. Indeed Rabbi Moshe Grylak in his book *The Hareidim: Who are we really?*[12] sets out to subdivide the chareidim into three levels of devotion:

1ˢᵗ Degree – *Hot:* the genuine, truly devoted article. He is the one that would more closely fit my description as a provider. I would like to make an analogy of three people riding a three-man bicycle. The devoted chareidi is in front. He is constantly pedaling and coasts only to catch his breath or when the going is exceptionally smooth. Rabbi Grylak contends that most chareidim fall into this group and I agree with him on this.

2ⁿᵈ Degree – *Lukewarm*: the habitual chareidi. He is the "I am a chareidi because I was born a chareidi" chareidi. He is one that I would classify as a consumer of chareidiism in the same way as I have classified the NCOJ as a consumer of Judaism in general. In both cases they go about their lifestyle as a matter of duty rather than as a matter of conviction. He is the man in the middle seat who is always coasting unless he absolutely has to pedal. Nevertheless, while we consider this the standard state of affairs for the NCOJ, we would like to think that, for chareidim, this is the minority.

3ʳᵈ Degree – *Cold*: the reluctant, artificial chareidi. What we would call an empty shell or the "F" in the QOF. He is the guy in the back seat who never does any pedaling, always asks "Are we there, yet?" and is in a hurry to get off. He is the darling of the media. Although we consider this category as the rare exception (the white sheep of the family), it deserves its own chapter.

Did I say something about sheep? That brings to mind another analogy about these three levels; in line with the kindergarten fable of the three little pigs. But, to make the analogy more "kosher," I will substitute sheep for the pigs.

The first degree chareidi is like the sheep who builds his house of bricks. No matter how many wolves come huffing and puffing, it doesn't fall down. The second degree chareidi is like the sheep who builds his house of sticks. The house will stand as long as no wolves come and challenge its durability with huffing and puffing. Should that happen, he will either have to reinforce the house with some bricks (or take refuge by his brother) or risk being eaten up alive. The third degree chareidi is like the sheep who builds his house of straw. Odds are the house will fall down even without any wolves huffing and puffing. One thing to keep in mind is that even the third level is a sheep.[13] He is not a dog or a cat but a

---

[12] *The Hareidim: Who are we really?*   Rabbi M. Grylak, Keter Press Jerusalem pp. 24-27

[13] It is because of this line that I was careful to describe sheep in place of pigs.

sheep even if his house is not in good shape.

To repeat my opening statement, this classification applies just as much to Judaism in general and, for that matter, to just about any "ism" that exists.

Is it possible for somebody to be "neutral" – like, have a foot in both camps?

An Orthodox agnostic, huh? Well, it won't work for us.

When a chareidi is defined based on external appearance and his comportment (read: QOF), as the masses and the media are wont to do, then, such a possibility exists. When we define a chareidi as one who believes in an explicit doctrine, as we are doing, it becomes clear that there can be no such thing as a partial chareidi.

This is because either one is an adherent of Leviticus 26:3 or he is not. Rabbi Noah Weinberg has often stated, in connection to belief in accountability to G-d, "I have never met a true agnostic." This is because true belief does not entail merely faith but also a lifestyle commitment. If one says, "I am neutral about the existence of G-d and reward and punishment in the afterlife" and conducts himself autonomously, he is not being neutral. He is rejecting. How can one smugly act without fear of accountability if he concedes a 50% chance that he is indeed accountable?

One cannot be "agnostic" about Leviticus 26:3 as it likewise entails a lifestyle commitment. It is much like doing business. I have spent many years in the diamond business and here is how things work: When you are sitting across the table from a merchant he will show you numerous parcels one after the next. For each parcel, you must decide if you want to buy it. Either you buy it or you don't. If you didn't buy it, you rejected it.

What's that you say? – "Hey, come on! I know something about the diamond business. You don't always have to buy the goods; you can usually take some *on memo* (consignment), where you can do business with the goods without committing yourself to purchase."

Fair enough, but that is only a temporary fix. Sooner or later the owner is going to contact you and call you to account and you will have to either return the goods or pay their price.

Imagine if I didn't, then critics of this book would say, "Get this, here is a book where a chareidi guy says all of the chareidim are like pigs" and, consequently, I would sell a ton more copies. Further proof that I am not writing this for money.

Don't we see many Jews who seem to be perfectly at home in either camp?

Of course we do. And we see it in two spheres:

Religious practice – We may see people who, for example, are very strict on their Kashrut (i.e., insist on *cholov yisrael*, mehadrin supervision, etc.) and they designate time periods for Torah study, yet at the same time, appear to be conspicuously materialistic or maintain incongruent leniencies (e.g., television and movies).

Religious politics – There are those whose religious comportment may be 100% chareidi, yet they are at odds with many of the political views, or the educational standards that the chareidim espouse (or vice versa).

We actually touched upon both of these spheres in some of the previous FAQs, but here's where it comes together.

Let's talk about religious practice first. I present a mild (and common) example:

My brother-in-law's brother is a fellowship student and *musmach* (ordained Rabbi) of Yeshivat Mercaz HaRav Kook. He is quite sincere and scholarly. Before he was married I would literally see him one day sporting a black velvet kipa and the next with a white knitted kipa.[14] He proudly called himself *kilayim* (hybrid). Is he truly?

What do we make of this? Can one be both a chareidi and NCOJ at the same time?

We must recognize that there are basically two concepts:

- Being a chareidi

- Doing what a chareidi does (this includes not doing what he doesn't)

In the previous FAQ, I wrote that according to my definition, to be a chareidi one has to comply with the prescription in Leviticus 26:3. Period! It follows that any hybrid is either *(a)* a chareidi who takes liberties or has weaknesses or *(b)* he is an NCOJ who maintains some chareidi values. You cannot determine which one he is simply by observing his comportment; and, many times, even by what he tells you openly. As I wrote, some Jews will emphatically disavow any connection to the chareidi community or be genuinely bewildered (or amused) by the mere suggestion (and not dress the part), yet they meet the criteria of my definition. They do not think that they are chareidi because they define a chareidi according to the media's QOF standards, certainly not by mine.

---

[14] Currently he seems to have settled on the black velvet. Obviously, as I have previously maintained, the choice of headgear is among the most ineffectual indicators of "chareidiness," though it is indeed symbolic.

If I understand my brother-in-law's brother correctly, he is fully aware and compliant with the Scripture and Rashi in Leviticus 26:3; (and, besides, he is not guilty of any of the above mentioned incongruences); hence, I would certainly consider him to be chareidi, *although he may not*!

Undoubtedly, I can make this determination only because I know him; otherwise, if we set out to identify a chareidi based solely on how an individual comports himself, we are bound to be caught looking at strike three, not only because it is hard to see the pitch, but also because some people are very good at throwing curve balls. What I mean to say is that many people do tend to be inconsistent and may truly live up to chareidi ideals (even by my definition) at a given time, location, or social setting but not at another time, another place or when confronted with a different set of circumstances.

What emerges is that although many Jews would prefer to claim neutrality and to say "I am *neither* chareidi nor non-chareidi," in fact, the opposite is true – such an individual is *both* chareidi and non-chareidi. He is chareidi when he chooses to live up to chareidi ideals and stand within Camp Bracha and he is non-chareidi when he chooses to fall short of the ideals and step out of Camp Bracha into [the first level of] Camp Kelala. He is always one or the other, never neither.

Where do we find a source for this concept?

The Mishna in Tractate Bava Kamma[15] deals with the following phenomenon:

> An ox that is cautioned[16] for its species but is not cautioned for what is not its species; cautioned for man but not cautioned for beast; cautioned for children (or small animals) but not cautioned for adults; for damages to the cautioned victims liability is full payment, for damages to non-cautioned victims liability is half payment. They said before Rabbi Yehuda, "Behold here is one that is cautioned to damage on the Sabbath but not cautioned to damage during the week." He said to them, "For damages that occur on Sabbaths it is liable for full payment; for damages that occur during the week it is liable for half payment."

The Mishna is telling us that the psyche of an ox can be in one state during one specific set of circumstances and in another state during an-

---

[15] Mishna Baba Kamma 4:2

[16] There are two classifications of a domesticated animal in regard to liability for wanton damage – plain and cautioned. A plain animal has no history of repetitive wanton damage and is only liable for half payment in the event of damage. If the animal has repeated its behavior three times the owner is "cautioned" to guard the animal. From then on it is liable for full payment.

other set of circumstances. It need not be classified as a "cautioned ox" under all circumstances if that is not truly the case. Nevertheless, when it is, it is, and when it isn't, it isn't.

Human beings are at least as complex as an ox.

Despite all this, I stand behind my assertion that, in an *ideological sense*, we cannot effectively vacillate between two camps. There are always some areas of life when one's true colors stand out, most notably when he displays his feelings about how *others* that he cares about or that he can influence should conduct their lives. The most relevant examples of this would be:

- How one educates his children

- If and when does one display negative feelings toward accepted chareidi conventions carried out by others

This last point leads me into what I referred to as the second sphere of ambivalent behavior: Religious politics.

Despite the fact that the underlying Torah ideology unites all chareidim toward one primary agenda there is yet much room for subjectivity as to exactly how to apply these principles in practice. In other words, all chareidim may agree that our ultimate goal is the quest to conquer Mt. Neverest,[17] but there may be conflicting ideas of exactly how to do it. As a result, there is bound to be some amount of discord among the various factions, or even within them, as to what policies to pursue. The policy that prevails will be that which is supported either by the majority or by the most dynamic Rabbinic personalities involved.

An observer may deceive himself into thinking that because one school of thought is dominant, this represents the unequivocal chareidi viewpoint. This is not necessarily the case. Dissenting viewpoints may be fully legitimate from the perspective of chareidi dogma. I'm sure there is more than one way to get to the top of Mount Neverest (all roads lead to the *Ma*-Rome) though there may be only one "best way" to do it. Therefore, when we see an individual that doesn't fully toe the conventional party line, it should not automatically undermine his standing as a chareidi.

This assumes, of course, that his vision is focused on the same peak. If somebody is really barking up the wrong mountain, he is not a member of our expedition.

What about the "Groupings" in the Encyclopaedia Judaica entry on "Haredim?"

---

[17] See footnote 24 and Glossary.

To fill you in, what the questioner means is that the Encylopaedia Judaica article on chareidim discusses two primary groups, *Hasidim* and *Benei Yeshiva* (Lithuanian influence). Unbeknownst to that author, it doesn't end there.

Comes Rabbi Moshe Grylak and he adds a third "group" – *Sephardim*.

Since then, the Israeli contingent has added another group, *Charda"lim* (officially, it means **Char**eidi **Da**ti Leumi – Religious Nationalist Chareidim – a hybrid of sorts between the chareidi and the national religious camps. Others interpret it to mean *chareidi dal*, meaning *chareidi lite*).

Enter Yechezkel Hirshman (my favorite) and throws in *CharBalim* – *baalebatishe* (working class) chareidim (predominately Anglo-chareidim). And don't forget that each group comprises *FFB's* (*frum* from birth, i.e., born Orthodox) and *Baalei Teshuva* (newly religious).[18]

I have come to put an end to all this *mishugoss* (nonsense). Again, I repeat my "what is a chareidi" mantra: **Leviticus 26:3** – take it or leave it! In other words, a true chareidi is a specific identifiable product although it can be marketed in different flavors – analogous to ice cream. Ice cream is not mashed potatoes and is not meatloaf and there are few people who cannot tell the difference.[19] It can come hard or soft, plain or mixed with other confections, and in countless flavors but everyone (who speaks English) calls it "ice cream." As such, the "57 Varieties" have no relevance to the definition of *chareidi* in this book.[20] As I annotated in the previous chapter, I am forwarding this matter to the domains of the online Orthodox dating services.

Do I really mean that as opposed to seven levels of Non-Chareidi there is but one level of Chareidi?

Absolutely not. Would that it should be so simple! Alas, our work has just begun. If my figures are right there are actually not less than twelve levels of chareidi, of which toil in Torah is the most rudimentary.[21] That means that it is the simplest and most elementary level – i.e.,

---

[18] For a fuller picture of this diversity, see *Boychiks in the Hood* by Robert Eisenberg, Harper Collins.

[19] All of my kids could identify ice cream before they were ready for Size 2 diapers.

[20] Even as Rabbi Grylak presented his "groupings" in the beginning of his book, there was no further reference to group distinctions throughout the remainder of the book.

[21] I sometimes think of this as the twelve-step program of CS – "Chareidi Synonymous."

bare minimum – that is required to qualify as a chareidi and lay claim to G-d the Father's benefits package. I suppose it is like being at the foot of Mount Everest as opposed to being situated below sea level. There is still a long climb ahead of us and we are expected to undertake it as far as it brings us.

"And what are the ensuing eleven levels?" I hear you ask.

For this, we do not need Rashi. This list appears in Talmud Bavli[22] and is attributed to Rabbi Pinchas ben Yair:[23]

> From this Rabbi Pinchas ben Yair states: (1) Torah brings one toward (2) vigilance; vigilance brings one toward (3) alacrity; alacrity brings one toward (4) innocence; innocence brings one toward (5) abstinence; abstinence brings one toward (6) purity; purity brings one toward (7) piety; piety brings one toward (8) humility; humility brings one toward (9) fear of sin; fear of sin brings one toward (10) holiness; holiness brings one toward (11) the Divine spirit; the Divine spirit brings one toward (12) revival of the dead.

To sum up, we have 12 stations in our quest to conquer "Mount Everest"[24]:

1 ~ Toil in Torah	*7* ~ Piety
2 ~ Vigilance	*8* ~ Humility
3 ~ Alacrity	*9* ~ Fear of Sin
4 ~ Innocence	*10* ~ Holiness
5 ~ Abstinence	*11* ~ Divine Spirit
6 ~ Purity	*12* ~ [Power of] Revival of the Dead

What a challenge! After all this, toil in Torah is merely a training camp for the long climb. It seems we chareidim truly have our work cut out for us.[25]

So why didn't I name the book "Twelve Above and Seven Below"?

---

[22] Talmud Bavli Avoda Zara 20b

[23] Rabbi Pinchas ben Yair was a student and son-in-law of Rabbi Shimon ben Yochai. He was known to be a great saint and mystic. He is buried in an unmarked grave in the ancient cemetery of Safed.

[24] Since the summit of the mountain is "Revival of the dead," I prefer to call it "Mount End-of-Rest" or, better yet, "Mount Neverest."

[25] These twelve stations are explored in great detail in my previous book written under my pen-name "Rabbi M. C. Luzzato" (okay, just kidding, I didn't write that book – not in this life, anyway). More on this book later.

Wise guy, huh? Anyhow, the real answer is that this book focuses on the demarcation line between chareidim and non-chareidim which is based on the passage in Leviticus 26 and Rashi's commentary. At that venue, nothing more is inferred by the Scriptures beyond the *"one above and seven below."* Incidentally, the title of this book is based on a passage from the Talmud that Rashi quotes in Leviticus 16:14 in conjunction with the commentary of the Chizkuni (*ad loc*).

So who is in and who is out? What about the Biblical personalities in the beginning of Chapter 1?

It is certainly sacrilegious for any of us contemporary plebeians to characterize the great saints of the Biblical era. Still, the Scriptures and the sages have revealed some details concerning the ancients to enable us to relate to them at some obscure level.

We Western-minded folk are used to "cut and dried" stereotypes; there are good guys and bad guys. The cowboys are the good guys and the Indians are the bad guys. The good guys wear the white hats and the bad guys wear the black hats. Indeed, times have changed. We have gone from "black-and-white" TV to high resolution color "Reality" TV. Much more colors and even harder to determine who is "good" and who is "bad." (At least the chareidim have it down pat – the good guys wear the black hats and the bad guys wear no hats at all.)

Of course, we have no idea what they wore in the real old days so we must rely on other symbols. Besides, I already wrote that, even today, mode of dress is not an accurate indicator of chareidiness.

The Biblical dignitaries that are listed in Chapter 1 were purposely selected to illustrate that without a precise definition, there is no clear cut system to determine who is who. One member of the list maintained the highest standards of *kashrut* and was heralded for honoring the Torah and for endowing scholars from his wealth. Yet, I cannot characterize him as a chareidi. Another was guilty of insulting his mentor and of licentiousness, and yet, I find grounds to classify him as a chareidi. This irony is one of two reasons that prompted me to devise this list.

The second reason is to reinforce my conviction that the chareidi of today is simply today's version of the chareidi of yesterday. One major aspect of being a chareidi is to strive to emulate those ancient ancestors who formed the Jewish nation that we are determined to perpetuate. Because of this, I felt that it is vital to compose a definition that is impervious to the passage of time.

Now, a Jew who suffers from consumerist hazard #6 – one who fervently maintains an "us" and a "them" – may find this concept a bit disconcerting. This concept is bound to make an NCOJ a bit uncomfortable.

If the seven loyal shepherds[26] and the twelve tribes were all chareidim – as they truly were by my definition (and, most likely, by many alternative definitions) – it would seem to indicate that the chareidi is the paradigm Jew. What is that common refrain that I hear? – "There were no chareidim in those days!" I am not sure that Isaiah would agree with that. "Yes, of course, they were all chareidim in the sense intended by Isaiah but not chareidim in the sense of what we today call chareidim." Is there a difference? What might that be?

I suppose it all depends on how we define a chareidi, doesn't it?

I believe that if we apply our definition to what we do know about some of those that I listed, we – chareidim and NCOJs alike – can learn a great deal about what makes us who we are. Such an analysis calls for a complete chapter, and I (G-d willing) will not let you down.

In the previous chapter, I set out to explain the "meaning of toil." Yet, aside from the three principles that were quoted from Maimonides and Shulchan Aruch, all I did was to describe what toil doesn't mean. Didn't I forget something?

Guilty! Here are some details that I omitted.

Like almost any commodity, toil can be measured by two attributes: quantity and quality. The three principles listed above provide a quantitative perspective. We have still not, as of yet, defined toil in Torah from the qualitative perspective.

Thankfully, we can always rely on our dedicated teacher. Rashi does not leave us totally in the lurch.

On the phrase "And my commandments you shall guard"[27] Rashi explains, "You shall toil in Torah for the purpose of observing and fulfilling [the commandments] as it states 'and you will study them and you will observe them to perform them.'" There is an end purpose to our Torah study – that we observe the commandments and incorporate Torah principles in all our daily activities.

Why is Torah study referred to as "toil?"

For many of us, it is a struggle to merely dedicate a serious block of time for this endeavor and to discipline ourselves to utilize the time efficiently.

As for the more disciplined, Rabbi Chaim ben Attar, the *Ohr HaChaim*,

---

[26] Abraham, Isaac, Jacob, Joseph, Moses, Aaron, and David. See Talmud Bavli Yuma 28b and Eruvin 53a.

[27] Leviticus 26:3

explains that it was decreed from Above that a man will forget what he learns and it will be necessary to review the material again and again. This serves to make the task much more cumbersome and slows down the rate of progress. Every man is enjoined to do his utmost to preserve what he has learned[28] and therefore the obligation to study will be non-ending. The need to redo work that is already done definitely constitutes toil.

Is there a minimum to qualify?

This book is not meant to be a Halacha book but it seems that in chareidi Judaism, Halacha and theology are hopelessly intertwined. We don't believe in separation of "church" and "state-of-mind." In an upcoming chapter (Chapter 7), we will discuss the chareidi perception of our overall goal and purpose in this world. (In short, it's to reach the top of Mount Neverest.) With this in mind, it is evident (to the chareidi, at least) that the Halacha is geared to the purpose of enabling one to achieve this goal.

The Halacha states that an Orthodox Jew must recite the *Shema* at least twice daily.[29] The commandment to recite Shema actually appears in two sections of Shulchan Aruch – in Orach Chaim where it discusses the laws of daily [prayer] service to G-d and in Yoreh Deah where it discusses the laws of Torah study. The Rema states there[30] that one who recites the Shema day and night is in compliance of the verse, "[my words] will not be budged from your mouth."[31] This says to us that the Shema is not merely a commandment but, additionally, is the minimal manifestation of toil in Torah.

How do we know that and why is that so?

This is a question that, most likely, if presented to ten different scholars, would generate ten different answers, all of them valid. I happen to be partial to those mentioned by Rashi in Chumash (if you hadn't noticed) and, to this end, I shall direct the questioner to Rashi in Deuteronomy 20:2. This verse details the pep talk that the Priestly Minister of War charges the troops at the brink of battle. The priest announces, "*Shema Yisrael* (Hear O Israel), you are approaching on this day to war against

---

[28] Avot 3:10; see also Maimonides Mada: Hilchot Talmud Torah 3:12

[29] See Kitzur Shulchan Aruch 45:23 concerning a quorum for Birkat HaMazon.

[30] Shulchan Aruch Yoreh Deah 246:1

[31] This verse is in Isaiah 59:21. Some say the more appropriate verse is the one in Joshua 1:8 "This Torah scroll shall not budge from your mouth and you shall delve into it day and night."

your foes." Rashi explains, "**Shema Yisrael** – Even if you have no more merit other than the recital of Shema alone, you are worthy of salvation."

Now, how do you like that? After all this talk of observing commandments with toil in Torah, just two doses[32] of Shema per day (as directed) and you are granted admission within the protective cloud.

The average Orthodox Jew knows that he is required to pray three times a day, of these prayer sessions, two involve reciting the Shema. If he is of a consumerist bent, he performs his chore dutifully, but is not necessarily catching the drift. The chareidi understands that the Shema is the secret password that all members of the fraternity exchange to demonstrate their loyalty to the club's charter. It is meant to be an expression of, "Even if I can't bring myself to actually perform any real toil in Torah, I am with the movement and want in on the action." And apparently it counts as a fulfillment of the basic membership requirements, as long as you mean it.

So do I mean to say that one needs this minimum fulfillment of toil in Torah to be protected in battle even if he performs the commandments?

That is how I understand Rashi's (actually, Rashbi's[33]) statement. Incidentally, I would like to suggest that this is the meaning of the much heralded verse in Psalms 20:8 – "These are with chariots and these are with horses; and we, in the name of *the Lord our G-d* (Hashem Elokenu), do call out."

The words "the Lord our G-d (Hashem Elokenu)" is a direct reference to the declaration of *Shema Yisrael* **Hashem Elokenu** (Hear O Israel, the Lord our G-d…). Our weapon in battle is to recite the Shema and proclaim "*Hashem Elokenu!*"

And what is the result?

"They kneeled and fell and we rose up and were heartened. G-d is the savior, the King will answer us on the day that we call out." (Ibid 20:9)

Why am I so sure they refer to the Torah aspect of the recital of Shema and not the commandment aspect?

---

[32] This commentary of Rashi is attributed to the Talmud Bavli Sota 42a. There, the terminology is slightly different: "The Holy One Blessed Be He says to Israel 'Even if you have not fulfilled anything other than the recital of Shema *morning and evening* you will not be delivered into their hands.'" And who, pray tell, is the author of this easy-going encouraging exegesis? None other than the hard-lined Rabbi Shimon ben Yochai.

[33] Acronym for Rabbi Shimon ben Yochai as per the previous footnote.

There are numerous indications that the merit of Torah study is vital for success and salvation, even when there is full observance of commandments. This point is emphasized in the Talmud with particular regard to battle against our enemies and to earning life in the World to Come.

With regard to battle I present the following examples:

For one thing, as for the verse in Deuteronomy 20:2 and Rashi's commentary, it can be assumed that all the soldiers are circumcised and therefore have a minimal fulfillment of commandments, yet, this merit does not seem to be sufficient.[34]

Secondly, The Talmud in Tractate Sanhedrin[35] discusses the encounter of Joshua with the War Lord of G-d on the eve of his assault on Jericho. The War Lord appeared as a man standing opposite him with a drawn sword in hand. When he asked the man his intentions he said, "I come now."

The Talmud explains:

> He (the man) said to him (Joshua), "Last night you cancelled the evening Tamid service and now you are quashing the study of Torah." [Joshua inquired,] "For which of these infractions do you come?"[36] "I come now (for the latter infraction)." It immediately follows: *And he retired in the valley.* And Rabbi Yochanan explains: "This teaches that he retired for the night in the depths of [the study of] Halacha." Says Samuel bar Onia in the name of Rav: "Study of Torah is greater than the offering of the daily Tamid sacrifice as it states 'I come now (for the latter infraction, i.e., the quashing of Torah study).'"

The above passage states explicitly that the "Study of Torah is greater than the offering of the daily Tamid sacrifice." It is needless to elaborate.

Thirdly, the Talmud in Tractate Sanhedrin[37] discusses the encounter of Jerusalem and King Hezekia with Sancherib and the Assyrian army. The Talmud explains this verse:

> *And it will be on that day his burden shall be removed from upon your shoulders and his yoke from upon your neck and a yoke is destroyed in the face of (due to) oil.* Says Rabbi Isaac Naphcha: "The yoke of

---

[34] Arguably, circumcision is a one time event that does not indicate continuous observance. Still, it is a great merit and if the point is to portray that the most minimum of merits is sufficient, then you can't get more minimum than this.

[35] Talmud Bavli Sanhedrin 44b. This passage is repeated two other places in Talmud Bavli.

[36] This being came from the celestial world. As it is quite a long journey, Joshua understood that only the gravest of issues would instigate it.

[37] Talmud Bavli Sanhedrin 94b

Sancherib is destroyed due to the oil of Hezekia that was burning in the synagogues and study halls." What did he do? He impaled a sword at the entrance of the house of study and declared, "All those who do not busy themselves with [the study of] Torah shall be stabbed by this sword." They checked from Dan to Beer Sheba and they did not find an ignoramus; from Gebath until Antiparis and they did not find a small boy or small girl, man or woman who was not fluent in the laws of the impure and pure.

We can be certain that the Jews of that time were observant of commandments, yet, they did not merit salvation from Sancherib until they committed themselves to Torah study.

Likewise, this concept applies to general merit for the World to Come. One source of this contention is a passage in Talmud Bavli Tractate Berakhot which states:

Rav said to Rabbi Chiya: How are women virtuous? By sending their sons to learn Scripture in the synagogues and by sending their husbands to study Mishna in the Rabbinic seminaries and by waiting for their husbands to return from the seminaries.

Here, the question is obvious. What is the uncertainty as to how women can be virtuous? Are there not countless commandments and acts of kindness which they can perform? The simple answer is that the merit of Torah is on a separate plane from commandments and is too vital to be lacking. The inquiry is, that in light of the fact that women are exempt from Torah study, how can they also earn this special and crucial merit? For this, Rabbi Chiya suggests that they can earn the vital merits by means of overt support, encouragement, and sacrifice.

Another source is indicated at the opening passage of Tractate Avoda Zara which states:

Rabbi Chanina bar Papa – and some say, Rabbi Semalai – expounds: In the future to come, the Holy One shall bring a Torah scroll and set it in His lap and proclaim, "For each one who occupied himself with it, let him come and receive his reward." Immediately all the nations of the world will gather and come in pandemonium…the kingdom of Rome will enter before Him first…The Holy One says to them, "In what way have you involved yourselves?" They will say before Him, "Master of the World! We installed many markets, we made many bathhouses, we amassed much silver and gold, and all this we did for no purpose other than to enable [the people of] Israel to busy themselves in Torah." The Holy One says to them, "Fools of the world! All that you did, you did for your own purposes."…The kingdom of Persia enters after them. The Holy One says to them, "In what way have you involved yourselves?" They will say before Him, "Master of the World! We built many bridges, we conquered many metropolises, we waged many wars, and all this we did for no purpose other than to enable [the people of] Israel to busy themselves in Torah." The Holy One says to them, "Fools of the world! All that you did, you did for your own purposes."...

The Talmud here indicates that for involvement in Torah study there will be a reward so enticing that all of mankind will resort to making pretentious and fallacious claims in the vain hope of receiving any amount. A gentile may be deemed virtuous and worthy of reward merely for observing the seven Noahide laws and has no obligations for Torah study. Doubtless, there will be numerous gentiles who so qualify. Despite this, this passage implies that the reward for Torah study is much more appealing than that of observing commandments and that a gentile could actually merit a portion of it if he were to support it with sincerity.

Do I view all this as corroborating evidence to my thesis based on Rashi in Leviticus 26 that this connection to toil is a vital necessity even if one performs the commandments?

Now you are catching on.

Why[38] is performance of the commandments not sufficient?

To begin, I need to make a disclaimer on some of the previous statements. Though I have presented ample sources that the merit of toil in Torah far exceeds that of performance of commandments,[39] I have no grounds to (nor do I) maintain that the performance of commandments does not have substantial merit. Commandments carry enormous merits, but with a proviso – they must be understood.[40] Understanding the commandments requires study; hence, a commandment properly performed may actually be an exemplary fulfillment of Torah study. All this notwithstanding, it still holds true that pure Torah study outweighs any indi-

---

[38] For everything that I have written up to this point – the "what" and "how" – I have quoted and relied upon open texts in the Scriptures and Talmud. Even so, I anticipate that some readers will challenge my views. The matter of "why" is not so blatantly divulged and is the domain of scholars who are much more erudite than I. In other words, I am out of my league and am straying way beyond the scope of this book. Still, because I am a non-entity and have nothing at stake, I will "take a stab" at it.

[39] See Maimonides Mada: Hilchot Talmud Torah 3:3,4 and Shulchan Aruch Yoreh Deah 246:18 both of whom state unequivocally that Torah study outweighs the performance of any other commandment and if one is faced with the option of engaging in Torah study or participating in a commandment that can be performed by others, Torah study takes precedence.

[40] I would like to suggest that this is akin to the basic requirement of *mitzvot*

vidual commandment as presented in footnote 39 above. Likewise, the merit of Torah study is apparently nevertheless superior based on the passages that I quoted in the preceding FAQs.[41]

Thus, the performance of commandments exists on two levels; the more advanced being what I just now described. At the more simple level, we have the "standalone" performance of commandments, without the requisite study and understanding – what the Prophet Isaiah[42] calls *mitzvot anashim melumada* (the regimen of trained people), or, once again, consumerist observance.[43] Needless to say, it is this simple level of performance that, in my thesis, represents the first level of the *seven below*. It does not require much introspection to understand why this status is insufficient. All of the commandments carry some objective in terms of refinement of character and declaration of one's subservience to G-d. Pure logic dictates that mechanical habitual performance that is devoid of conviction does not succeed in achieving this objective. Add to that the words of Rashi in Leviticus 26:15 – "Here there are seven transgressions, the first one tows in the second one and so on until the seventh." – and we have an open and shut case.

The larger question is why this applies even where the commandments are performed at the advanced level. Note that here I don't mean to intimate that the merit of commandments that are properly performed are not sufficient to protect one in battle or to earn one a share in the World to Come. There is no question that there is limitless reward for any commandment that is performed with conviction.[44] But we have seen that the merit of Torah is so potent that merely reciting the Shema is sufficient and that it outweighs the merit of the daily Tamid sacrifices. Why is that?

I can only guess the answer, but it shall be an educated guess. The Talmud Bavli in Tractate Shabbat[45] states:

---

tzrichot kavana (commandments require intent) although it is not fully the same idea. The true meaning of that term is that for a commandment to be considered valid the subject must be conscious (i.e., not asleep or comatose) and aware that he is performing a commandment. What I am saying here is that for one to reap the full benefits and merits of the act, one must understand the essence of the commandments as they are explained by scholars such as the Minchat Chinuch. Of course, one must also study the laws of the commandment to ensure that the act is actually validly performed.

[41] This seems to generate some kind of a paradox which is beyond the scope of our discussion.

[42] Isaiah 29:13

[43] That's right! The same fellow who introduces the Chareidim also introduces the consumers.

[44] See Avot 2:1

[45] Talmud Bavli Shabbat 88a

For Resh Lakish says: What is meant by the verse, "And it was evening, and it was morning, the sixth day."[46] Why is there an added [letter] 'heh' (the definite article 'the')? This teaches us that the Holy One made a stipulation with the works of creation and said to them, "If Israel accepts the Torah you will be sustained, if not, I will return you to void and chaos."

At first glance, this looks like a naked threat; as if it is not truly necessary to destroy the world if the Torah is not received but that G-d would destroy it nevertheless, simply because Israel has "let Him down." Of course, this is not so. G-d knew that the first Man would not withstand the test of the Tree of Knowledge. Henceforth, without the Torah (the Tree of Life), society would inevitably deteriorate toward the lowest levels of impurity and self destruction. Once Man reaches the threshold of the fiftieth level of impurity there are but two courses of treatment: to deliver the Torah or to deliver the Great Flood.[47]

The Mishna states: "There were ten generations from Adam until Noah. To inform us as to how much patience is before Him; that all the generations were angering Him and proceeding until He brought upon them the waters of the flood."[48] Here one may ask why was it necessary to destroy the world? Why was it that G-d could not simply hand down the Torah to mankind?

Although I can only speculate the reasons, it is evident that that particular generation or society could not accept the Torah.[49] There was only one alternative – to destroy mankind and begin again.

Approximately one thousand years later, the Children of Israel came to be. Initially they preserved the legacy of their forefathers and lived by the teachings of Shem and Eber. When they were forced to dwell among the Egyptians, who had already reached the 50th level of impurity, the

---

[46] Genesis 1:31

[47] This idea may be alluded to in the Talmud Berachot 8a. The Talmud sets out to interpret the meaning of the mysterious phrase "time of finding" that is mentioned in the verse "For this all pious ones pray to You at the *time of finding*; only for a flood of copious waters, may they not reach him." (Psalms 32:6). The Talmud offers five interpretations of the phrase. The second suggestion is: "Time of finding" means [study of] Torah, as it states "One who finds me has found life" (Proverbs 8:35). Although the Talmud does not explain how the phrase relates to the total verse, according to our discussion the meaning is clear – if not for Torah study, the world would be susceptible to a great flood.

[48] Avot 5:2

[49] One theory is that there is ample evidence that the Torah can only be sustained by a society that practices circumcision (see the section Adam the First Man in Chapter 4). It is brought down that circumcision weakens the sex drive. That

forces of decadence threatened to overwhelm them as well. This time, G-d foresaw that they would respond to the more positive course of treatment. He hastily withdrew them from Egypt and brought them to Mt. Sinai for the "procedure." The Talmud relates the following vignette:

> When the Torah was given to Israel, the sound carried from one end of the world to the other... They (the kings of the nations) all gathered beside Bilaam the Wicked and said, "What is this sound of confusion that we are hearing? Perhaps a flood is coming to the world? 'Is G-d returning to the flood?'"[50] He said to them, "'G-d will dwell as the King of the world'[51] the Holy One has already sworn that he will not bring a flood upon the Earth." They said to him, "A flood of water he will not bring, a flood of fire he may yet bring..." He (Bilaam) said to them, "He has already sworn that He will not destroy all flesh." "And [if so] what is this sound of confusion that we have heard?" He said to them, "There is a fine article of longing that He has in His storage house that has been stored with Him for 974 generations prior to the creation of the world. And He seeks to endow this to His sons." This is as it states, "G-d is giving boldness (the Torah) to His nation."[52] Immediately they all exclaimed, "May G-d bless His nation with peace!"[53]

We can surmise from this the following: The nations of the world understood that the world was in a wretched, seemingly incorrigible state. They assumed that the tremendous racket indicated that G-d was resorting to the same "drastic measures" as had happened previously. Even when they were assured that G-d swore off such extreme measures, they were not at ease. Perhaps this form of flood He won't bring but that form He will bring, etc. Only when Bilaam explained to them the true cause of the commotion – that G-d is handing down the Torah – did they realize that there is a substitute remedy that averts the need to destroy the world. At that point they wished only the best for this nation and blessed them with peace as their own welfare depends on their success.[54]

The upshot of this discourse is that maintaining the Torah is the sole

---

generation was steeped in licentiousness and it is highly unlikely that they could accept upon themselves the practice of circumcision. Alternatively, Maharsha in tractate Zebachim 116a s.v. *Hashem Oz* indicates that only the Jewish people have the fortitude to boldly oppose idolatry and only they were capable of accepting the Torah.

[50] Psalms 29:10

[51] Ibid

[52] Ibid 29:11

[53] Ibid

[54] It seems that this blessful attitude was rather short lived.

prerequisite for the perpetuation of the world. As such, engaging in Torah study, more than any other endeavor, *serves all of mankind collectively*. Arguably, any individual commandment primarily benefits the individual or individuals who perform it. Hence we learn that even the minimal Torah study that is performed *even by an individual* is more beneficial to the masses of the world than an individual commandment even if *performed by the masses* such as the Tamid offering.

I have other guesses which may come to light in a subsequent chapter, but this will suffice for now.

So, do I mean to say that anyone who recites the Shema twice a day is a chareidi?

I knew somebody was going to ask that.

I can certainly brush off the question with the classic "Just because any eagle is a bird doesn't mean any bird is an eagle" response. A minimum requirement is not the same as a definition and for the definition of a chareidi, I stand behind the definition I provided at the end of Chapter 2.

The real question is, if I stated that our aim is to be worthy of G-d the Father's benefits package in Leviticus 26:3 and that to recite the Shema twice a day is the minimum price to pay, WHY PAY MORE?

I believe the answer lies in a well known anecdote. The story goes that a working class Jew approached his Rabbi and said, "Rabbi, I have only a half hour per day to study. Is it preferable to use the time to study Talmud, Halacha, or *Mussar* (Jewish ethics)?" Without hesitation the Rabbi responded, "There is no question that you should devote the time to Jewish ethics. The study of ethics will lead you to discover that you can actually devote more than a half hour per day for study."

If you recall, when I first discussed this minimum requirement of reciting the Shema, I mentioned one stipulation: as long as you mean it. That means that you fully intend to follow what it says.

So here we have a catch (catch-22), for, if you notice, within the text of the Shema lies the fundamental requirement of Torah study, and it is not subtle. "And you shall teach them *diligently* (alternative translation: *repeatedly*) to your sons and speak in those [words] (i.e., words of Torah) when you dwell in your home and when you sojourn on the road..."[55] This passage is understood to include the general requirement to study and teach Torah as well as the specific requirement to recite this passage (Shema) at least twice daily and it continues with the commandments to don *tefillin* and to place *mezuzot* on the doorposts. Additionally, the Shema

---

[55] Deuteronomy 6:7

is referred to as, and requires, *kabbalat ohl malchut shamayim* (acceptance of the yoke of the Kingdom of Heaven – i.e., subservience to G-d). Quite a package.

As our anecdote illustrates, the minimum requirement of reciting Shema serves to alert the "recitor" that his personal minimum requirements involve substantially more than merely reciting Shema. (I think this is what they call a pandora's box.)[56]

One who recites Shema fully committed to its content is most likely a chareidi.[57] As to one who recites Shema sans such commitment, I am uncertain if it is considered a valid recital of Shema.

Why did I present the analogy of all of the Jews being transported on one boat?

From the title of this book and all that I have written until now it may appear as if I am trying to delegitimize a major portion of the Jewish people and, thus, exacerbate the standing schism that exists therein. The impression is that I am heralding the chareidim as an elitist club and surrounding them with guard dogs and barbed wire to keep out the undesirable elements. Or, in sociological terms, I am seeing to it that every Jew can be labeled and put in their place. The analogy was presented to reassure the reader that this cannot be my objective by pointing out that there is nothing to be gained thereby.

The analogy indicates that when there are enough subscribers to the benefits package and it gets delivered, even non-subscribers can enjoy the benefits. Similarly, when there are enough subscribers to the booby prize and it gets delivered, even non-subscribers suffer.[58] Consequently, chareidim are not interested in forming an exclusive club. It is in our interest that *all Jews* buy into the benefits package. So much so, that the "spiritually wealthier" chareidim are willing to "subsidize" the product to make it more affordable for everyone. (Remember the Shema principle. Even G-d the Father is offering a reduced price for new customers.) Some call this salesmanship, others call it coercion – we call it *outreach.*

I did not create the term chareidi nor have I ever advocated the socio-

---

[56] See the commentary of Ra"N (Rabbeinu Nissim ben Reuven) on tractate Nedarim 8a s.v. *D'Kivan.*

[57] I could accept this as another valid definition.

[58] We should not forget that in the perspective of the chareidim, this deal is not optional. This means that the obligations of Leviticus 26:3 apply to all Jews, even the secular ones. This point will come to light when we discuss current issues in Book Two.

political connotation (of being isolated, elitist and counterfeit) that it carries today.[59] My goal is to expose the fallacy of this perception and to show that the ideology is genuine, accessible, healthy, and mutually beneficial. As I wrote in the introduction, the true purpose of this work is to help people who are unfamiliar with chareidi (read: Torah) ideology begin to understand it properly so that they can identify with it, appreciate it, and, ultimately, gain from it. I am attempting to dispense with the guard dogs and barbed wire.

How does G-d steer the boat when some people bought tickets to this destination and others bought tickets to that destination?

To rehash the conundrum, we noted that the Scripture is in the plural and refers to many communal issues such as rainfall, peace, and dominance over other nations. It is clearly speaking to the collective society. This implies that either the entire community benefits with the *seven below* reaping unearned gains or the entire community suffers including those who toil in Torah. How is this "fair?"

Obviously, I cannot really answer this question, nor do I believe that anybody can. Furthermore, the purpose of this book is to help us understand chareidim (for which I can pretend to be qualified), not to help us understand G-d (certainly out of my league).[60]

What I [hope that I] can say is that, in the long run, we are much better off this way. Rashi tells us[61] that the value of virtue is reckoned 500 times that of a similar measure of retribution. We are also told that for a virtuous act, even an unrealized intention is rewarded, but for a sinful act, mere intent is not punishable.[62] The Talmud tells us that if one observes a fellow Jew engaging in a sinful act and does not rebuke him, he is caught up in the culpability for the sin.[63] It follows that when an individual performs a virtuous deed, his fellows are "caught up" in the benefits of the deed to a degree 500 times greater. What emerges is that, in theory at least, the benefits of those who subscribe to the package will benefit the non-subscribers to a much greater degree than will the shortcomings of the *seven below* harm the subscribers.

---

[59] For a complete overview on this topic, see Chapter 9.

[60] This is "A Guide for the Consumer" not "A Guide for the Perplexed."

[61] Exodus 20:6

[62] Talmud Bavli Kiddushin 40a

[63] Talmud Bavli Shabbat 54b

Still, G-d does not let anybody totally off the hook.[64] He has his "tricks." Our Sages give us a glimpse of G-dly justice as the Mishna in Avot states:[65]

> If some people parcel the tithes and some people do not parcel the tithes, a famine of scarcity occurs; *some people are hungry and some people are satisfied.* If the tithing is completely abolished, a famine of invaders and of scarcity occurs.

We actually see this lesson in the Scriptures themselves as the story is related in Kings II Chapter 7. There was a terrible famine in the days of the Prophet Elisha and the King Jehoram dispatched an emissary to beseech Elisha to intervene with G-d on behalf of the nation. Elisha told the emissary to convey to the king that on the very next day the price of barley will fall to two *seah* per shekel and wheat to one *seah* per shekel. The skeptical emissary scoffed at Elisha and exclaimed, "And if G-d should make hatches from the heavens, can such a thing occur?" Elisha replied, "Here now, you shall see it with your eyes and from there you will not eat."

Scripture relates that four lepers attempted to surrender themselves to the Aramaic camp and discovered it to be abandoned. The camp was looted and the food supply was found to be so abundant that the price of barley fell to two *seah* per shekel and wheat to one *seah* per shekel. This very emissary was appointed by the king to distribute the food, but amidst the frenzy of the starving masses, he was trampled to death.

It is important to note that the emissary did not suffer a heart attack. Rather the very advent that was the salvation of the masses was the instrument of his demise.

What we understand is that G-d can send a blessing to the community and this blessing can be a curse to some. Conversely, He can send a curse to the community which can be a blessing to some.[66] Chareidim maintain that it certainly pays to follow the advice of G-d the Father.

Are there no other Rashis or such that shape the character of the chareidim?

You must have noticed by now that there are quite a few Rashis that influence our perspective of what the Torah is telling us. To repeat what I wrote earlier, we know that it is not really Rashi. Very little of Rashi's commentary is of his own device. Throughout his commentary he is usu-

---

[64] See Talmud Bavli Baba Kamma 50a

[65] Avot 5:8

[66] Just listen to the stories of those who survived the Holocaust.

ally quoting passages from the Talmud or from the Aggadic or Halachic Midrash. The Talmudic sages impart to us the interpretations of the Scriptures as they received them from their mentors in an unbroken tradition that originated with Moses at Mount Sinai. Rashi merely opens our eyes to these interpretations to enable us to understand the Scriptures the way that Moses (the first true chareidi) understood them.

There are a number of Rashis on the Torah which seem relatively trivial but are really quite profound. They tend to be overlooked. When Rashi's words are overlooked, the words of the sages are overlooked. Consequently, the true essence of the verse is overlooked.

An uncomfortably large percentage of Jews either are not aware, or simply ignore the messages of the Scriptures that Rashi wanted us to know. This is the consumerist predicament. The chareidim do not ignore them. This is what differentiates them. Hence, my initial definition – *The NCOJ knows the Chumash, the chareidi knows the Chumash with Rashi.*

Aside from the Rashis in Leviticus 26, there are others that tend to be overlooked by the masses, but the chareidim notice them. Some of these were mentioned in previous discussions such as his commentary in Deuteronomy 20:3 that the recital of *Shema* is sufficient to protect one in battle.

A few more examples of Rashis that only the chareidim seem to notice:

Leviticus 19:2 – **You shall be holy**. Says Rashi: *You must be isolated from promiscuity and from sin; for, wherever one finds a barrier to promiscuity, one can find holiness.*[67]

Leviticus 19:3 – **And my Sabbaths you shall guard**. Says Rashi: *Guarding the Sabbath is juxtaposed to the fear of one's father to indicate that although I have cautioned you on [the obligation of] obedience toward your father, if he shall instruct you to violate the Sabbath, you must not obey him; and likewise with [the observance of] the remaining commandments.* In other words, one's direct obligations to G-d supersede one's subservience to any man, even where G-d Himself mandated this subservience.

Deuteronomy 32:47 – **For it is not a thing that is empty (futile) from you**. Says Rashi: *Another explanation – there is nothing meaning-*

---

[67] My focus on Rashi is certainly not meant to exclude any of the great Torah scholars of his era. The chareidim are well acquainted with the commentary of the Ramban (Nachmanides) on this verse and adhere to his interpretation with a reverence equal to that of Rashi. Nachmanides states:

"And the issue is that the Torah forbade illicit relations and forbidden foods but it permits cohabitation between a man and wife and the consumption of meat *less in the Torah that if you expound on it that will not yield reward.*

Deuteronomy 14:21 – **For you are a sacred nation to G-d**. Says Rashi: *You must sanctify yourself with what is permissible to you.*[68] In other words, it is a Torah-ordained value to distance one's self from unnecessary luxuries even if they are technically permissible.

Notwithstanding, I consider the Rashis in Leviticus 26 to be of exceptional importance because this is where G-d is whispering to us the secret of immortality. Rashi is amplifying the sound so we can hear it. Still, not everybody is listening.

If there are any more questions, please see me after class...[69]

---

and wine. If so, a lusty person will find room to be engulfed in pleasure seeking with his wife or numerous wives, and lushful in drink and gluttoness in food, and he will speak profanities at will, as the Torah does not explicitly mention this prohibition, and behold he is a vile person within the bounds of the Torah. Therefore, this verse comes, after the Torah detailed the matters that are unequivocally forbidden, and it commands in a general fashion that we are to be isolated from the excesses..."

[68] This should be understood somewhat differently than the commentary of Nachmanides in the previous note. Nachmanides was referring to people abusing the permissible indulgences of the material world to the point of being profane. This is presented as a mandatory prohibition, that one must avoid excessive indulgence. Rashi is advocating that holiness entails that one should abstain from even moderate levels of earthly pleasures and is presenting it as a desirable, yet voluntary, quality. This concept originates in Talmud Bavli Yebamot 20a.

[69] Or email me at 1a7b.author@gmail.com

Chapter Four

The Chareidim – and NCOJs – of Yore

The founding fathers of the chareidim

I once overheard the tail end of a conversation between a chareidi and a not-as-chareidi Orthodox Jew. Evidently, the chareidi had been criticizing the "NCOJ" for his exceedingly casual attire (he was wearing plaid shorts and a fishing cap[1]). In response, the NCOJ was pooh-poohing the Chassidic-style garb. He remarked, "Moshe Rabbeinu didn't go around with no *shtreimel* (fur hat) and those knee-length knickers."

A few thoughts occurred to me. Firstly, how does he know?

In fact, when I still lived in the U.S., I sent my boys to a Chassidic day school. When they brought home mimeographed sheets with illustrations of bible events from the weekly Torah portion, all of the Jewish Biblical figures were dressed in Chassidic garb.[2] Now that I live in Jerusalem, my boys attend the more Lithuanian-style schools. They bring home similar illustrations wherein the ancients sport the more Cecil B. DeMille-style garb.

Which was it? Does it matter? What can be safely assumed is that whatever they wore, it was the most conservative and reverent mode of dress that was in vogue at the time.

Which leads to my ensuing thought: Was his point that because Moses may not have dressed like today's chareidi that it is therefore acceptable to dress like one is headed for the beach or the country club?

But the most beguiling thought was: What would Moses wear if he was here today? It's anybody's guess but it would most likely resemble either that of a Lithuanian Rosh Yeshiva, a Chassidic Rebbe, a Sephardic

---

[1] This event actually took place during summer in the Appalachian or Pocono Mountains and it was not out of place to be dressed casually. I myself dress more casually in such a setting. My critique here is based more on the conversation – to which I was a detached eavesdropper – than on the event.

[2] For example, one illustration of Jacob blessing his grandsons Menashe and Ephraim depicted Jacob as a Chassidic Rebbe in full regalia (shtreimel and all), Joseph looking on as a Chassidic disciple, and the two boys (currently ages 22 and 25) as two small Chassidic cheder kids.

Chacham, or a Yemenite Elder. Certainly not like what this fellow was wearing. But is he not conceding that if Moses would be dressed in a particular fashion that this would set the standard? If so, what are the grounds to criticize people who emulate the dress of the Moses that they envision?

Getting more to the point, how about emulating the *behavior* of the Moses that one envisions?

I mentioned in Chapter 3 that we are expected to view the ancient ancestors as role models and chareidim certainly do so. A great portion of the Talmud is the Aggada (not to mention the entire Aggadic Midrash) where the depictions of the Biblical accounts are thoroughly scrutinized so that we can learn morals and ethics from the activities, successes, and failures of the ancients. Chareidim are committed to studying all of this for the purpose of putting those morals and ethics into practice. The bulk of our ethical conduct is based on it.[3] We, as chareidim, validate our demeanor as the inherent continuity of the ethics and mannerisms of the "heroes" of the Torah and Talmud, our ancestors. In other words, we are chareidim because they were chareidim. Is this not so? Obviously, much rides upon how we define chareidim. If you wish to define "chareidi" differently than how it has been defined thus far, then the message of this chapter (and indeed, this entire book) is irrelevant. But if this definition strikes a truthful note, we can pretend to understand how this timeless accolade applies to their characters.

First, let's review our final definition from Chapter 2:

A chareidi is a Jew who defines Orthodoxy as a society whose primary function is to actively advance the observance of the commandments and the study of Torah and who identifies him or herself with this society.

And let us not lose sight that this is based on Rashi's commentary of Leviticus 26:3 that prescribes performance of commandments *with* toil in Torah.

We can now take the plunge.

Moses our Teacher

I consider Moses to be the first modern chareidi. After all, he did spend forty days and forty nights toiling in Torah (without any recess) –

---

[3] One typical example is the Mishna in Avot 5:19 "All those who have these three attributes are among the disciples of the Patriarch Abraham; and [those who have] three different (opposite) attributes are among the disciples of Bilaam the Wicked."

on three consecutive occasions! Furthermore, he personally transcribed the very Scriptures that I am using to base my case. You might say "he wrote the book" on chareidi ideology (I do). Rashi in Numbers (9:6 and 27:2) indicates that Moses' regular venue for receiving the public was the House of Study. Succinctly, if he does not personify a chareidi, who does?

It is not only because he meets the core definition that I am so certain, but he also embodied another trait distinctive of chareidim: he had his share of detractors – the brethren who were haters and shunners. Not too many, but just enough.[4] No chareidi worth his salt should be without them. Aside from the perpetual antics of Dathan and Abiram, and the mutiny of Korach, the Talmud in tractate Moed Katan states[5] that *everyone* suspected Moses of adulterous liaisons.[6] The Talmud in tractate Bava Kamma[7] says the same regarding the Prophet Jeremiah. Maharsha in Bava Kamma[8] says that "everyone" refers to the *leitzanei hador*, the scoffers of the generation. That's one thing that they still make like they used to.

Hirshman's vote: Chareidi par excellence (Jeremiah, too[9]).

Korach

Korach was Moses' kith and kin, a first cousin and fellow Levite. The Midrash says that the Levites were exempt from the Egyptian servitude and spent their time engrossed in Torah study. As the written Torah was not yet given to the Jewish nation, we understand that the "Torah" consisted of oral traditions that were passed down from the Patriarch

---

[4] See Rashi's commentary on Deuteronomy 1:12 s.v. *U'Masaachem*. Also see Midrash Tanchuma on Exodus 33:8 (referenced by Rashi in Talmud Bavli tractate Kiddushin 33b s.v. *K'd'ita*) that the nation would look at Moses when his back was turned and comment, "See how thick are his calves, how fat is his neck. All of his [indulgences] are from our [personal assets]."

[5] Talmud Bavli Moed Katan 18b and Sanhedrin 110a

[6] It is unclear from the text if this suspicion was limited to Korach and his entourage or to a larger following. Read on.

[7] Talmud Bavli Bava Kamma 16b

[8] Ad loc. The Maharsha explains that both Moses and Jeremiah were Prophets who were constantly "on call" to receive the Divine spirit. As such, they abstained from marital relations. The skeptics of their generations could not accept that they could maintain celibacy on a permanent basis and, therefore, suspected them of illicit relations. Being a Prophet is a tough job, but someone's gotta do it.

[9] See Rashi's commentary on Exodus 16:32 s.v. *L'Doroteichem*.

Jacob. Korach was wise and learned and, after the Exodus, was a disciple of Moses. Initially, he looked chareidi, walked chareidi, talked chareidi, et al.

But a chareidi he wasn't. Korach fell down, fell out, and finally, fell through (in grand style).

I consider Korach to be the archetypical *anti-chareidi,* just as I consider Moses the archetypical chareidi.[10] I would also suggest that the dispute between Moses and Korach was the first political dispute between chareidim and non-chareidim in the history of the Jewish nation and that it serves as a progenitor for all those that follow. That means to say that every new entity[11] that arises to challenge the chareidim is another incarnation of Korach and his faction.[12]

How am I sure that he is not chareidi?

My answer is that if G-d Himself personally singled out this fellow as one *not* to emulate – as the verse states, "And he shall not become like Korach and his company"[13] – it's a pretty safe bet that he doesn't pass muster as a chareidi.

The point of including him is that, even during his rebellion, he *looked* like a chareidi. He was extremely pious – pious to a fault[14] (a bit like Esau).[15] So much so that 250 heads of Sanhedrin held that he out-pioused Moses. Moreover, as I wrote, in contrast to the typical non-chareidi, he was exceptionally learned (I suppose that even today we have our fair share of those). My impression is that the media certainly viewed him as a chareidi. I imagine the headlines reading: "Ultra-Orthodox Rebel Challenges Moses" and "Chareidi Family Buried Alive." Hence, the first QOF chareidi.

We will take a deeper look at Korach's antics in Chapter 8.

Hirshman's vote: Not a chareidi   **Maariv's vote:** Haredi

---

[10] I did not say the *first* anti-chareidi because one can argue that Dathan and Abiram previously earned that distinction. Nevertheless, Korach is more prominent because he is the first *turncoat* anti-chareidi. For all we know, Dathan and Abiram were never inside the "camp."

[11] For example: The Hellenists, Sadducees, Karaites, Shabbateans, and Maskilim.

[12] And is ultimately headed to the same destination.

[13] Numbers 17:5

[14] Pun is intended. The bigger they are, the deeper they fall.

[15] The Midrash says that Esau would shoot an arrow across the throat of his game in a manner that constituted a valid slaughter and that he consulted his father as to how to tithe salt and straw.

Adam the First Man and Noah

It is difficult (read: impossible) for us to comprehend the stature of the pre-nationhood righteous ancestors. Though the written Torah was not yet formally handed down to the world, Torah based oral traditions were instilled in the consciousness of mankind and upheld by the righteous. The sources for this are too numerous to list but a few random examples won't hurt (ready for more Rashi?):

- The Talmud states in Tractate Yuma[16]:

  > Rav said: Our father Abraham fulfilled the entire Torah as is written, "Ensuing that Abraham hearkened to my voice, and he observed my watches, my commandments, my statutes, and my Torahs."[17] Rav Shimi bar Chiya said to Rav: Perhaps it is merely the seven Noahide laws? Said Rav: But there is also circumcision. He said: Perhaps they are merely the seven Noahide laws and circumcision? He said: If so, why does the Scripture say, "My commandments *and* my Torahs?" Rav – and some say Rav Ashi – said: Abraham fulfilled even the laws of Eruv Tavshilin[18] as it states, "…my Torahs (plural)" implying also the written Torah and also the oral Torah.

- Both Abraham[19] and Lot served *matzot* to their celestial guests. Rashi confirms that their visit occurred on Passover.[20]

- When Judah suspected his daughter-in-law of illicit relations, he sentenced her to burning. Rashi explains that the Midrash maintains that Tamar was the daughter of Shem and that Shem had the status of a Kohen (Jewish priest); thus, Tamar was the daughter of a Kohen. Therefore her proper sentence was burning as prescribed in Leviticus 21:9.

It is safe to assume that these traditions originated with Adam the

---

[16] Talmud Bavli Yuma 28b

[17] Genesis 26:5

[18] A Rabbinic ordinance to set aside a portion of food before a holiday and thus enable one to prepare food on the holiday for an immediate successive Shabbat on the pretext that he is merely adding to the existing food.

[19] Abraham instructed Sarah to make cakes – *ugot* (Genesis 18:6). We know that this means matzot because matzot are called *ugot matzot* in Exodus 12:39. Some say that the episode with Abraham took place on Passover eve after midday when both matzoh and leaven are forbidden. The cakes in the verse refer to egg matzot.

[20] Genesis 19:3

First Man. As is the plight of mankind, most of mankind forsook these traditions but the righteous few held fast.

What made these few different?

It seems that Torah can only be sustained in a body that is circumcised in the Jewish manner.[21] From Abraham through Isaac[22] and on down, the Jewish nation has steadfastly observed the covenant of circumcision. As a result, the tribes and their descendents could sustain the oral law. During the servitude of Egypt, circumcision was disallowed[23] – the Torah traditions were forsaken and the nation sank to the 49th level of impurity. All of the Israelites were required to circumcise in order to partake in the Passover offering and to merit redemption. They were thus able to rise out of their impurities and to accept the written Torah. The *Eruv Rav* (Mixed Multitudes) joined in at the foot of Mount Sinai.[24] Only then could they receive the Torah.

So we see that in order for the Torah traditions to be sustained prior to the revelation at Mount Sinai, it was imperative that there be some righteous people who were circumcised. The Midrash[25] says that Heaven ordained that seven people were born circumcised: Adam the First Man, Seth son of Adam, Noah, Job, Jacob, Joseph, and Moses.

Ergo, I would feel honored to consider all of the above as the true

---

[21] This obviously excludes the Muhammedans that do not circumcise fully as we do.

[22] See Daat Zkeinim M'Baalei Tosafot in Genesis 25:25 that brings an opinion from the Midrash that Esau was never circumcised.

[23] The tribe of Levi was exempt from the servitude and were able to circumcise. Therefore they were capable of studying Torah. See Maimonides, Yad Chazaka, Kedusha, Hilchot Issurei Biah 13:2.

[24] See Rashi Exodus 24:6 who indicates that there was a mass circumcision at Mount Sinai. It is difficult to say that this refers to the primary Jews as they would not have been permitted to partake in the Passover offering if they were not already circumcised back in Egypt (Exodus 12:48). It therefore makes sense to say that this refers to the *Eruv Rav* despite the usage of the term "our fathers." An alternative explanation is that even though Rashi notes circumcision at this event (Revelation at Sinai), he is actually referring to the circumcision that took place in Egypt immediately prior to the Exodus. This seems to be the position of the Talmud Bavli Keritut 9a.

[25] Midrash Tanchuma Noah 5. Avot of Rabbi Nathan (2:5) lists thirteen people born circumcised. They are the aforementioned seven plus: Shem son of Noah, the Prophet Samuel, King David, the Prophet Jeremiah, King Zerubavel ben Shealtiel, and (believe it or not) the wicked Bilaam. Bilaam's inclusion enforces the position that circumcision is essential to sustain Torah or, in his case, prophesy. Rashi's commentary in Numbers 24:4 states that Bilaam was uncircumcised. Neither of these sources include Gad son of Jacob, although Rashi in Genesis 30:11 confers to him this attribute based on a Midrash.

founders of the chareidi camp.

Hirshman's vote: Chareidi across the board.

Pinchas

The Torah depicts Pinchas as a great hero. One who risked his life to defend G-d's honor and who succeeded to curtail a deadly plague in the process. G-d the Father blesses him with His personal pledge of friendship; and a friend of G-d's is a friend of the chareidim. Pinchas is in some ways the mirror image of Korach. He has all the trappings of the quintessential chareidi – top of the line ancestry, religious zealotry, deep conviction, unwavering loyalty to the *Gadol Hador* (recognized leader of the generation), and is ridiculed by the general population.

Hirshman's vote: Chareidi with a vengeance.

Zimri son of Saleu

Why is Zimri on this list?

After all, not only the basic text of the Scriptures but most of the related Talmudic passages and Midrashic accounts of the incident portray Zimri as the most depraved of people. There is no question that he castigated Moses in public and that, as for moral impropriety, he was literally caught in the act. The Talmud in tractate Sanhedrin (82b) refers to him as "that wicked one" and the Talmud in tractate Nazir (23b) seems to confirm the sentiment. Yes, he was a prince of a very dignified tribe, but was he any more pious and learned than Korach whom we have already discredited? Is it not undisputed that Pinchas was a true Jewish hero and that Zimri was the unequivocal villain? Indeed, the Talmud in tractate Sota[26] relates that King Jannus said to his wife: "Do not have any fear of those who are Pharisees[27] nor of those who are not Pharisees, but only of the hypocrites that appear as Pharisees who commit the deeds of Zimri and seek recompense as [if they are] Pinchas." The basic implication is that the authentic Pharisees (chareidim) personify the character of Pinchas the saint and that the blatant non-Pharisees (non-chareidim) personify Zimri the infamous sinner; one need only beware the hypocrites that try to play the game both ways.

---

[26] Talmud Bavli Sota 22b

[27] The Pharisees (literally: those who abstain or ascetics) were the Torah scholars at the time of the second Temple and are understood to be the societal equivalent of the chareidim of our times.

The NCOJ who knows Chumash without Rashi, and even most chareidim who haven't toiled at studying this obscure episode will most certainly reach this conclusion. But to the serious Talmudic scholar who reviews this topic, this position is far from conclusive. That is because an often overlooked (or underappreciated) passage tells us that our villain is someone far more complex than would appear on the surface.

The Talmud in Sanhedrin[28] tells us that Zimri son of Saleu was not just a prince from the tribe of Shimon, but that he was *the* prince of the tribe of Shimon. He was actually none other than Shlumiel ben Tzurishadai who brought the special offering with the other tribal princes at the inauguration of the Tabernacle. But it doesn't end – I mean begin – there. The Talmud also says that he is Shaul ben haCanaanite, a direct son of the tribal patriarch Shimon. Commentators[29] point out that this indicates that our Zimri was no less than 250 years old. Thus, he was most likely the most senior member of the entire Jewish nation, one who had known Jacob, Joseph, et al, and who had endured the entire Egyptian servitude. A number of these commentaries[30] point out that it is untenable that a person of such noble heritage and such a lofty position should suddenly and for no good reason, at the venerable age of 250-plus years, fall prey to the seductive charms of a loose woman. It is therefore put forth that he may actually have had "a good reason" for his behavior and these commentaries endeavor to discern what such "good reason" might be. I actually wrote an essay on this quandary which is independent of this book. There is no clear conclusion; based on the variety of opinions, the jury is still out.

So, now, why did I include Zimri in my list?

One reason is to highlight this very point – that the chareidi is trained to perceive the people of the Scriptures, as well as all of the aspects of the Scriptures, to a degree that goes beyond that which meets the eye. A second reason is that I wish to assert that chareidiness is not necessarily equivalent to, nor contingent upon, being impeccably righteous. And there is even a third reason – it is because we haven't heard the last of Pinchas and Zimri. We will visit them again in a later chapter when we discuss the concept of *Kanaot* (Zealotry). At that juncture, a clearer insight as to the

---

[28] Talmud Bavli Sanhedrin 82b

[29] E.g., Maharsha ad loc.

[30] See Pri Tzaddik and Shem M'Shmuel on the incident in Numbers 25. Also, Rabbi Yehonatan Eibishitz in Tiferet Yehonatan (Numbers 25:14) notes that the Torah refers to Zimri as a "Man of Israel" even after the event. This indicates that with his death at the hand of Pinchas, Zimri merited a portion in the World to Come.

motives of the people who are involved may prove to be very beneficial.

Hirshman's vote (and Pri Tzaddik, Shem M'Shmuel and Tiferet Yonatan): Misguided chareidi.

King Jannus's vote (and Rashi and most everyone else): Not a chareidi.

Samson the Mighty

If you are American and as old as I am, you are likely also a victim of Western imagery. Samson, like Moses our Teacher, has suffered the defilement of Hollywood, courtesy of Cecil B. DeMille and Victor Mature. We cannot blame them as, for one thing, these folks are high drama and adventure moguls of the mighty American entertainment industry which subsequently brought us Rambo. Secondly, we must concede that the ostensible textual account of Samson's adventures as presented in the book of Judges does indeed lend itself to this image. Samson is the militant activist, the prototype Irgunist, and a ladies' man, to boot. Consequently, he is idolized in the Jewish mind as the *yiddishe* Rambo. He is the hero of Jewish might, Jewish pride, Jewish chivalry and Jewish martyrdom. Conspicuously absent from this list is Jewish scholarship and piety. With such a full schedule as is packed into three chapters in Judges, it would seem that he hadn't a spare moment for toil in Torah.

Is this so?

Undoubtedly, Samson is one of the most enigmatic personalities of Biblical times (after Zimri son of Saleu). Hailed as a miracle baby whose parents were visited by a Heavenly angel (twice) and a nazirite from birth, there is no question that he was raised in an atmosphere of sublime holiness. The Talmud relates that he was the judge of Israel for about twenty years and he never asked any litigant to so much as carry a stick for him.

The Talmud[31] does indeed castigate him for "following after his eyes" and even states that "with his eyes he rebelled." The Talmud goes on to say that "the beginning of his ruination was in Gaza" (no surprise) which seems to imply that he was a fine wine that went sour. A little further on the same folio, the Talmud states that Delilah finally believed Samson's explanation as to the source of his strength because she knew that "that *saint* would not utter the name of G-d in vain" so that when he called himself "a nazirite of the L-rd" he is to be believed. Hence, the Talmud indicates that even at that stage, he is considered to be righteous.

---

[31] Talmud Bavli Sota 9b

So was he a saint or a sinner?

No question, he must have been one of the most accomplished boys in his yeshiva, from a fine family, and certainly had an admirable physique (a real *chatich* as they say here), though he had trouble finding himself a nice Jewish girl. The Talmud acknowledges that his initial forays with the members of the "opposition" were pre-ordained in Heaven, but goes on to say that as much as his parents didn't know that this match came from G-d, Samson didn't know it, either. He was "following after his eyes," and for that he was punished with blindness.

The commentators[32] struggle as to why such a holy person "fell in" with the wrong crowd.

Some opinions maintain that initially he did not sin at all. Some contend that the first non-Jewish woman that he married was converted[33] and others contend that it was deemed permissible as a *horaat shaah* (a one-time dispensationary ruling).[34] Yet, this experience weakened his repulsion for Philistine women so that when Delilah arrived on the scene, he took her without Halachic justification.

Another approach is that Samson was conceived with a special mission to wreak G-d's vengeance against the Philistines. This helps us understand why Samson was directed from Heaven to be a nazirite. One opinion on this is that, as a nazirite that abstains from wine and frivolity, Samson's demeanor would be the exact opposite of that of the Philistines who would eat any impure thing and guzzle wine from large mugs. The intent was that he should be so repulsed by their excesses that he would harbor an absolute abhorrence toward them and thus be motivated to avenge their atrocities. A second reason is that G-d knew that Samson would be tempted by women. The restrictions of the nazirite are designed to enable the subject to overcome his lusts as the sages declared "One who sees a *sotah* (adulterous wife) in her disgrace should isolate himself from wine."[35]

The initial intent – "Plan A" – was that he would certainly not consort with non-Jewish women, but rather, he would be a Jewish warrior (marry a nice Jewish girl) and attack the Philistines from within the Jewish camp. Yet once Samson exercised his propensity to noticing the women – despite his nazirite status – G-d capitalized on this situation to activate

---

[32] See Yalkut Meam Loez Judges 14:4

[33] Maharsha on Talmud Bavli Sota 9b s.v. *T'chilat Kilkulo*; also see Yalkut Meam Loez, ibid.

[34] See Encyclopedia Talmudit Vol. 8 Col. 518 on the topic of *Horaat Shaah*. This again seems to relate to the first wife but not to Delilah.

[35] Talmud Bavli Sota 2a (also tractate Nazir 2a and Berachot 63a)

"Plan B" – to enable Samson to strike at the Philistines from the inside. Much more effective. Thus, even his relationship with his first wife, though pre-ordained, is not to be considered strictly kosher.

It is true that Samson's "errors" had dire consequences, yet all indications seem to maintain that this weakness was his sole shortcoming. From Samson's final entreaty to G-d[36] we do know one thing – despite his blindness, he never for a moment lost sight of the source of all his strength.

Hirshman's vote: A mighty chareidi who was weak at times (undoubtedly, not the only one).

King Achab

The Talmud in Tractate Sanhedrin lists King Achab as one of three kings who have forfeited their share in the World to Come for the sin of proliferating idolatry to the extreme. The other two are Jerabaam, son of Nevat, and Menashe, the son of King Hezekiah. The point that I am trying to impress apply to all three so we may as well bunch them together. The reason that I focused on Achab in Chapter 1 is because of his status as arch nemesis of Elijah the Prophet who is likewise on the list. Also, the Talmud insinuates that his wickedness outdid that of the other two.[37]

Achab is characterized as one of the most wicked people of his era. He made a career out of idolatry and murder (I am sure we would be able to add promiscuity to the list except that the Talmud relates that he was frigid[38]). It's more or less the same for his two colleagues. My guess is – not a chareidi.

Nevertheless, the sages have one or two praiseworthy comments regarding Achab. The Talmud relates[39] that Achab merited to rule for 22 years because he honored the Torah that was written in 22 letters. Also, that Achab was forgiven for half of his iniquity regarding the murder of Navot because he was generous with his money and he enriched Torah scholars from his wealth. Evidently, as the chief proliferator of idolatry, toil in Torah still meant something to him (I suppose he had a status quo agreement). Additionally, I wrote in a footnote in Chapter 1 that one

---

[36] "Oh L-rd, the A-lmighty, please remember me and please strengthen me just this time, A-lmighty, and I may avenge one vengeance from my two eyes from the Philistines." – Judges 16:28.

[37] See Talmud Bavli Sanhedrin 102b. "The lightest transgressions of Achab were as the most serious of Jerabaam"

[38] Talmud Bavli Sanhedrin 39b

[39] Ibid

Midrash maintains that the food that Elijah the Prophet ate while hiding from Achab during the famine was plucked from Achab's table. Glatt kosher! You can eat in his house, just don't pray there.

These issues are puzzling enough, but the fascinating thing is that these three wicked kings were all scholars beyond our capabilities. The Talmud states:[40]

> Our Rabbis taught – [King] Menashe could teach 55 facets in Torat Kohanim to correspond to the years of his rule. Achab could teach 85 [facets in Torat Kohanim] and Jerabaam could teach 103.

Concerning Jerabaam, the Talmud states[41] that the Holy One grabbed Jerabaam by his clothes and said to him, "Repent and I, you, and [David] son of Jesse will stroll in paradise." G-d doesn't make such a personal entreaty to just anybody (I'm still waiting to feel a tug at my clothes); you gotta be a real somebody. Doesn't look like too bad a deal. Still, Jerabaam turned it down.[42]

Concerning Menashe, the Talmud relates as follows:[43]

> In Rav Ashi's academy they were holding at the subject of the three kings [that lost their share in the World to Come]. He (Rav Ashi) said, "Tomorrow we will open on the subject of our 'colleagues.'" [King] Menashe came and appeared to him in his dream. He said, "A 'colleague' and a 'colleague of your father' did you call us? From what point [on the loaf] must we slice the *Hamotzee?*" He (Rav Ashi) said to him, "I do not know." He (Menashe) said to him, "From where to slice *Hamotzee* you have not studied and yet you call us 'colleagues?'" He said, "If you will teach it to me, tomorrow I will relate it in the lecture in your name." He said, "From where it begins to form a crust when baking." He (Rav Ashi) said to him, "Now that it is apparent that you are quite learned [in Halacha], why did you serve foreign gods?" He said to him, "Would you have been there [in my era], you would have raised the hem of your cassock and pursued after me [to idol worship]." The next day, Rav Ashi said to his students, "We will now open on the subject of our *masters* [who lost their share, etc.]."

It is impossible for us to relate to all this. I cannot approach the stature of the sages of this generation, who in turn cannot approach the stature of the sages of previous generations (such as Rav Ashi) who in turn

---

[40] Ibid. 103b

[41] Ibid. 102a

[42] We must acknowledge that if he was capable of refusing this offer, so are we. I don't prefer to think about it much.

[43] Ibid. 102b

cannot approach the stature of the *sinners* of the early generations!

If the sinners of today knew a fraction of what the sinners of yesterday knew, we would all be in much better shape.

Hirshman's vote: Not chareidi but, oh, what they could have been!

Elijah the Prophet

I can only assume that by now my point is being overplayed. I cannot imagine that anybody would question the saintliness and piety of the only human being[44] who ascended to Heaven alive. The fascinating fact about Elijah is that as much as, or even more than, the "seven loyal shepherds"[45] and King Solomon, he is recognized by multitudes of *non-Orthodox* Jews as an integral figurehead in Jewish tradition. We know that the Jewish people were redeemed from Egypt by the merit of two commandments – circumcision and the Passover service (now the Passover Seder) – and that these two commandments, above all, have been upheld by the bulk of the Jewish people throughout the generations, even by those who observe absolutely no other Jewish ritual. These are two commandments that we can fulfill even if we are totally devoid of Torah scholarship as was the generation of the Exodus. And guess what?! We invite Elijah the Prophet to both of these rituals – all of us, every single time. And Elijah doesn't forget it. He keeps tabs, who performed the rituals and who did not. Our tradition is that Elijah the Prophet will travel through the world to announce the arrival of the Messiah. And on whose door will he knock? On the doors of all his old friends that invited him to their Passover and circumcision celebrations, whether chareidi or not, Orthodox or not. Yep, this fellow is every Jew's friend.

But is he chareidi?

Well, what else do we know about Elijah the Prophet?

Actually, his origins are shrouded in mystery and the sages have (as usual) varying opinions. One opinion maintains that he was from the tribe of Benjamin and another opinion maintains that he was from the tribe of Gad. But the most popular opinion is that he was actually the very Pinchas[46] mentioned earlier who was blessed by G-d with everlast-

---

[44] There is one opinion quoted in Yalkut Meam Loez, Kings I, 17:1, that Elijah the Prophet was never a genuine human being but rather an angel of G-d.

[45] The patriarchs Abraham, Isaac, and Jacob, Moses and Aaron, Joseph and King David.

[46] This is explicit in Yalkut Shimoni, Numbers 25, Article 771, in the name of Rabbi Shimon ben Lakish. It is alluded to in Talmud Bavli Bava Metziah 114b according to the commentary of Rashi s.v. *Lahv Kohen Mar*.

ing peace and that sometime after the reign of King David he "retired" from the Temple service and assumed a new identity. Supporters of this opinion point out that both Pinchas and Elijah were described as "Zealots of G-d." Pinchas single-handedly avenged the honor of G-d in Shitim, and Elijah, in his generation, likewise single-handedly fought the forces of idolatry that prevailed to zealously defend G-d's honor and the ubiquitous transgression of *Lo yihiyeh lecha elohim acheirim*, the chareidi significance of which is discussed at length in Chapter 6. Accordingly, it is fair to assume that Elijah is as much a chareidi as is Pinchas. Additionally, the Talmud in tractate Sota (13a) refers to Elijah as a disciple of Moses, the prototype chareidi.[47]

I want to add one more significant tidbit concerning Elijah, regardless of the various opinions. And that is that he is designated as the one who will eventually clarify all of our Halachic uncertainties at the time of our redemption, may it be speedily in our days.

My feeling is that when all Jews, Orthodox or not, host Elijah at their circumcision or Passover table, they are hosting a passionate chareidi.

Hirshman's vote: Eternal chareidi.

The Messiah

Yes, this is the one that we have all been waiting for.

All Orthodox Jews are familiar with the twelfth principle of Maimonides' Thirteen Principles of Faith – *Ani maamin b'emunah shelaimah b'biat hamashiach* (I believe with complete faith in the coming of the Messiah) – probably with a collection of melodious accompaniments from various recordings. Some of us say it with more conviction than others, but we all know it. It is well known that this and similar declarations were uttered by our ancestors at the doorstep of death during the Holocaust and other tragedies, with plenty of conviction.

But who is this Messiah and what is he coming to achieve?

Firstly, we all refer to the Messiah as the *goell tzedek*, the righteous redeemer who will redeem us from the oppressions of the gentiles.

Fair enough.

Still, I suspect that many Jews would be pleased to be redeemed and to leave it at that. But no, this is not his main job, it is just a prerequisite. He is to be our king – for the long haul. Judging by the Knesset elections over the past 50-some-odd years it seems that most Jews are not interested in having a chareidi as the Head of State. But, in my opinion, those

---

[47] I know, I know – so was Korach.

of us who anticipate the Messiah are anticipating a chareidi.

What makes me so certain?

It is because the Messiah has a surname. We call him Messiah ben David. He is certainly a descendant of the House of David and most of us envision him as a reincarnation, or at least a replica, of King David himself.

The greatest legacy that we received from King David is the Book of Psalms. And what did King David see fit as to be the opening message of his magnum opus?

> Fortunate is the man who has not walked in the counsel of the wicked, and in the path of sinners he has not stood and in a session of scoffers he has not sat; but rather has made the Torah of G-d his desire and in His Torah he will articulate daily and nightly. And he shall be as a tree firmly planted along the tributaries of water, that yields its fruit in its season and its leaves shall not wither, and all that he shall do will succeed.[48]

What am I reading? Toil in Torah day and night as the key to longevity, health, fruitfulness, and success – and this at the top of the agenda? Sounds a lot like Leviticus 26:3-13 to me.

Hirshman's vote: Royally chareidi.

Maimonides

Looks like we have a surprise entry.

I pretty much seem to have covered all the prominent figures on the initial list of examples that I presented in the beginning of Chapter 1 and even threw in some extras. Certainly, the list could go on indefinitely. It is quite obvious that the purpose of this whole discussion is to validate the status of being chareidi – by my definition[49] – by illustrating that this definition can be aptly applied to all of the righteous Biblical personages and ancestors that are looked upon by the entire Jewish people as our forebears and role models. I have ceaselessly repeated this idea throughout this and previous chapters of the book and there is nothing more to add. The reader may either accept or reject this concept.

Furthermore, this discussion serves the purpose of dating chareidiness, meaning, that if I can demonstrate that Biblical figures that go back 3,000 to 5,000 years can be construed to be chareidim, it goes without saying

---

[48] Psalms 1:1-3

[49] In the course of discussing this project with friends (including some very learned ones), I have heard some definitions that slightly vary from mine. I believe that if the same exercise was to be performed using any of these definitions, the results would be basically the same.

that we can apply this status to more recent Jewish leaders such as those of the eras of the Talmud,[50] the *Geonim*,[51] *Rishonim*,[52] *Poskim*,[53] etc. So, why do I wish to throw in a discussion about Maimonides?

Here is where I begin to take on the opinions of contemporary analysts in the centrist Israeli press.

Many non-Orthodox or non-chareidi Jews who never read and never will read this book are nevertheless conscious of this realization that the Jews from Biblical and Talmudic times were more in sync with today's chareidim than with themselves. They rationalize this disparity by maintaining that that specific style of Judaism fit that particular era but was never meant to be compatible with the modern secular age. Sure enough, over the past few centuries, the world has recognized many illustrious and enlightened Jews – Spinoza, Disraeli, Marx, Geiger, Heine, Mahler, Herzl, Ben-Gurion, Weitzman, Einstein, Barenboim, Bronfman, the list goes on. All great thinkers, intellectuals, culture-setters, achievers; none of whom were even observant, let alone chareidi. But go back more than 400 years and one is hard pressed to identify any prominent or accomplished Jew outside of the annals of the chareidim. In order to legitimize their position, non-chareidim must make a case that some notable, accomplished, illustrious Jew from the middle ages was "enlightened" and ahead of his time, and wouldn't coalesce with today's chareidi culture. As an added bonus, it can serve to disrupt the historical continuum of chareidi culture that I am trying to establish.

To that end, I took note of a December 26, 2004 Jerusalem Post op-ed piece entitled *Return of the Rambam*[54] by Elliot Jager.[55] For your convenience, I have included the entire column in the Appendix at the end of the book. This is the part that interested me, interspersed with my comments:

> Still, each stream of Judaism claims him. Within Orthodoxy he's appropriated by everyone from the Lithuanian mitnagdim to Lubavitch.

---

[50] Approx. 250 B.C.E. to 300 C.E.

[51] This would cover the post-Talmudic era until about 950 C.E. This is the era that secular history calls the Dark Ages about which we know very little.

[52] Approx. 950-1450 C.E.

[53] Approx. 1450-1600 C.E. also called the era of early Achronim.

[54] RaMBaM is an acronym for Rabbi Moses ben Maimon, a.k.a. Maimonides. Recently, Maimonides was accorded a lot of fan fare because this past year (5765) has marked the 800th anniversary of his passing.

[55] I emailed Mr. Jager in 2005 to ask him how he would describe his religious leanings. His response was Masorati/observant (traditional). What makes his article significant is that he quotes a number of respected Orthodox personages.

If the Rambam were alive today, I pressed Rabbi Wein, where would he feel most comfortable?

"He'd be hardal – ultra-Orthodox national-religious."

Comment: Objection, your honor! It appears to me that Rabbi Wein's response does not fit the question. What Mr. Jager asked is where would the Rambam feel more comfortable if he were *alive today* – meaning if he was born and raised and living in our generation. Rabbi Wein's response would better fit an inquiry of "If the Rambam came to us in a time capsule for a five-day visit, where would he most likely spend Shabbat?" To this, Rabbi Wein responds that he would be *hardal,* meaning that he would most likely be the guest of Rabbi Mordechai Eliyahu or of the Sephardic Chief Rabbi (currently Rabbi Shlomo Amar). My instincts tell me otherwise. He would most likely be in Har Nof as a guest of Rabbi Ovadia Yosef (and I would be in the crowd listening to his afternoon discourse).

As for Mr. Jager's *stated* question, the answer should be that Maimonides wouldn't need to feel comfortable with anyone. His scholarship, now as then, would pervade religious Jewry and set the standards for his following.[56] This question is largely moot. The true litmus test question is, "If the Rambam were alive today, *who would feel most comfortable with him?*" Again I don't think, as Rabbi Wein infers, that it would be a predominantly national-religious crowd such as would come to hear a lecture by Rabbi Eliyahu, but a very mixed crowd such as those who come to hear Rabbi Amnon Yitzchak when he is in mixed communities such as Jerusalem or those of the Diaspora (typically at least 50% "black-hat" chareidi).

Jager continues:

Perhaps. What's clear is that the Rambam would be uncomfortable with the more insular Orthodox sects because he argued that to better understand God, one has to study science and philosophy.

Comment: Far from clear. Let's initially accept Mr. Jager's contention at face value – the Rambam maintains that science and philosophy are necessary components of "better" understanding G-d. As far as philosophy is concerned, it has always been an integral part of chareidi curriculum. The Mitnagdim may call it *mussar* and the Chassidim may call it *Chassidus* (and they follow separate styles) but it's part of the package and there's more of it by us insular Orthodox sects than anywhere else.

---

[56] Indeed, this seems the opinion presented by Prof. Avi Ravitsky at the end of the column.

As for science, there is no argument, even by the insular Orthodox, that studying the sciences can help one to better understand G-d. There are numerous topics in the Talmud that delve into the realms of science such as in tractates Rosh HaShana (astronomy) and Nidah (biology). Likewise, much of Maimonides' personal views on scientific issues are incorporated in his writings in Yad HaChazaka and his commentary on Mishna (special emphasis on his introduction to Seder Zerayim). This *integrated* scientific knowledge can certainly enhance one's appreciation for Torah ideals and is welcome fare for the educational systems of the insular Orthodox sects.

When we consider sciences isolated as subjects unto themselves, however, there is a danger. If the sciences are not integrated into a theological framework, they serve no other purpose than to understand the sciences. Very few people who study sciences do so to better understand G-d. I have yet to meet the person who undertook four years of medical school to better understand G-d. Thousands of Jews have filtered through the Technion, Weitzman Institute, and all kinds of universities and know volumes about the sciences and very little about G-d. As for the chareidim, the main reason why the insular Orthodox do not study the sciences in depth is that there is a need to remain insular. I don't think that I need to elaborate on this.

But let's get down to the basic statement – "he argued...one has to study..." I don't know who he was arguing with or where this argument is found. I never studied *Guide for the Perplexed* as did Mr. Jager. I study Yad HaChazaka and the only curriculum that I am aware of is presented in Maimonides, Yad HaChazaka, Ahava, Hilchot Talmud Torah Chapter 1, Article 11: "And a person is required to divide into three his time for study; one third for written law, one third for oral law (Mishna), and one third to scrutinize and analyze how the [Halachic] result is derived from its source, to derive one issue from another, to compare one issue to another... and this matter is known as *Gemara*." No faction follows this prescription more closely than the more insular Orthodox sects. It is hard to imagine that Maimonides would be uncomfortable with the select few who heed his advice.

> The Reform movement claims the Rambam because he rejected Scriptural literalism, embraced rationalism, championed religious liberalism, and repudiated superstition.

Comment: It seems that the Reform like to glean through English translations of *Guide for the Perplexed* to piece together a Rambam who matches their philosophies, but not his own. They somehow miss the line in his introduction where he states, "But rather, the goal of this declara-

tion (the Guide) is to arouse the *religious person for whom the truth of our Torah is already established in his heart and perceived in his mind and who is complete in his observance of its laws and commandments…*"
Moreover, they somehow overlook that Maimonides spent fifteen years codifying the entire Talmud and hailed it as a mandatory code of conduct for all Jews.

Maimonides took every single Scripture that legislates Halacha very literally,[57] considered Talmudic law the standard for rational social conduct, was no more religiously liberal[58] than Hillel and Rabbi Akiva, Rav and Shmuel, Rava and Abaye, and, yes, he echoes the Torah's prohibition against superstition. If only the Reform were as religiously liberal (and rational) as Maimonides! Come now, if Maimonides was here giving a lecture on anything he wrote in Yad HaChazaka, let's say in Hilchot Shabbat, Hilchot Maachalot Assurot (forbidden foods) or Hilchot Issurei Biah (forbidden relations), how many Reform would come to listen?

> For its part, the Masorti movement values the Rambam for his cautious halachic innovations.

Comment: All of Maimonides "halachic innovations" appear nowhere else but in his treatise on Halacha, the Yad HaChazaka, also called Mishna Torah (Sequel to the Torah). Maimonides codified all of the Halachic conclusions and rulings of the entire Talmud that was sealed 900 years earlier, adhering to the Talmud to the letter, most often using identical terminology and case examples. The code may have been an innovation, but the Halacha was not. It was then well over 900 years old. Again I must ask, if Maimonides was here giving a lecture on anything he wrote in Hilchot Shabbat or Hilchot Taharat HaMishpacha or the Yichud laws, how many Masorti would come to hear all of those lovely cautious

---

[57] "All activities of work you shall not do [on Shabbat]" means literally all activities of work you shall not do. He even describes all of them. "Thou shalt not eat all that is unclean" means thou shalt literally not eat all that is unclean and "With a male thou shall not lie in the manner of women" means with a male thou shall not lie in the manner of women. Literally.

[58] I wonder if Mr. Jager is referring to the same Rambam who wrote (Yad HaChazaka, Shoftim, Hilchot Melachim 1:5): *We are not to instate a woman to be king as it states "…upon you a king" and not a queen. **And similarly for all positions in Israel** (author's note – presumably, this includes the Rabbinate) **we are not to appoint any but men.*** Bear in mind that this edict is not sourced in the Talmud but rather from the Halachic Midrash, *Sifri*. There, it merely says, "A king but not a queen." The application of this law to all appointments is Maimonides' own opinion and is not elaborated in the source. I have a hunch that if this "religiously liberal" scholar was with us today, he would vote Republican.

innovations?

> Rabbi Louis Jacobs wrote approvingly that "Maimonides' struggle for a rational approach to Judaism is evident on practically every page of his writings."

Comment: I am not convinced that Rabbi Jacobs saw every page of his writings. There is some truth to this statement in regard to the *Guide for the Perplexed* as one purpose of the Guide was to present a rational perspective of esoteric concepts. Here *rational* is not meant as an antonym for *irrational*, but as an antonym for *esoteric, mystical,* or *supernatural*. As I noted, I am much more familiar with Yad HaChazaka. Actually, I have examined quite a corpus of this work and have found no signs of struggle on the corpus. This is for obvious reasons. The Yad HaChazaka is, for the most part, a codified version of the Talmud, and the Talmudic scholars themselves already undertook the arduous chore of rational analysis 900-1450 years earlier. Sure made Maimonides' job quite a bit easier. Anyway, I'm glad he approves.

> But Rambam's rigid "Thirteen Principles of the Faith" – albeit written at the start of his career and open to interpretation – are nevertheless problematic for Conservatives.

Comment: For example, let's try "I believe with complete faith that this Torah will never be replaced and there will never be any other Torah from the Creator, may His name be a blessing." How many ways are there to interpret that? (This is the Torah that he has in mind when he spent the prime of his career writing the Mishna Torah.) How about, "I believe with complete faith that the Creator knows all of a man's actions and all his thoughts…" followed by "I believe with complete faith that the Creator lavishes good (reward) to those who observe his commandments and punishes those transgress his commandments"? I, myself, harbor a hope that the "punish" or at least the "transgress" parts are open to interpretation, but somehow, I am not so optimistic.

> Jacobs: "In matters of faith, the more correct approach is not to ask what Maimonides said 800 years ago, but what a teacher with his intellectual integrity would say if he were alive today."

Comment: Something doesn't flow here. First Jacobs says "what a teacher of his intellectual integrity," i.e., not Maimonides himself, but a nameless teacher with his intellectual integrity. Who might that be? "If he were alive today." Do you mean that there is no nameless teacher alive today with the intellectual integrity of Maimonides? What a shame! Incidentally, what is "intellectual" integrity? I suppose that it is something different than behavioral integrity. How many kinds of integrity are there?

Let's not beat around the bush; here is what Jacobs means: As the Aristotelian dictum goes, "Do as I say, not as I do," we now have a new Jacobian dictum, "Do as I say or as I *would* do, but if it doesn't meet your fancy, you can date me into ancient history and make believe that today I would say – and do – something else." This means to imply that if in the year 1200, Maimonides confirms a belief system that he himself claims to be 2500 years old,[59] we can safely determine that somewhere over the course of the next 800 years, he would undoubtedly abandon all of his principles. And this is because he has "integrity."

There are other portions of Mr. Jager's column that are worthy of comment, but this much is sufficient for our discussion.

The bottom line is that among all serious scholars and objective historians there doesn't seem to be much question that Maimonides dedicated his life to the advancement of observing the commandments along with toil in Torah study.

Hirshman's vote: From Moses to Moses there was none more chareidi than Moses.

So, one last time: What do we learn from all this?

That being a chareidi is nothing new.

And what is the significance of understanding this fact?

The answer lies (I mean, the lies are answered) in the following chapter.

---

[59] Recall the eighth principle, "I believe… that the entire Torah that is currently with us is the Torah that was given to Moses our teacher…" which occurred in the year 2448 (approx. 1312 B.C.E. or 2500 years before 1200 C.E.).

Chapter Five

The Theory of [Chareidi] Evolution

An historical and scientific perspective

It's been a bit more than a year since I last held what could be termed as a "real day-job." Over the course of this interval, I have been toiling at a new line of work – answering questions. The most common one is: "So, what is it that you do?"

To this, I usually answer, "I study part of the day, I take some courses in anticipation of some future respectable calling, and, in the afternoons, I am writing a book."

The next question always is (without fail), "Oh, what kind of a book?"

"It's a book about chareidim, or, more precisely, the relationship between chareidim and non-chareidim within the Orthodox community…" I explain that the purpose of the book is to enable people, particularly Orthodox Jewish people who do not consider themselves to be chareidi and who may even view the chareidim as a distinct and disconnected species of Orthodox Jew, to better understand who the chareidim are and what influences our conduct. I often add that, in order to do this, I must designate a significant block of chapters to the sole purpose of defining what exactly is a chareidi.

Sometimes I am asked, "Hasn't anybody else already done something like that?"

The answer is: Not really.

As part of the research for this project, I made it my business to track down and obtain as many pre-existing books on the subject that I could get my hands on and to read them through. To date, this immense bibliography consists primarily of four books, two of which were written in Hebrew by chareidi writers (Rabbi Moshe Grylak, editor of the popular *Mishpacha* magazine, and well known educator and lecturer Rabbi Mordechai Noigershall). The purpose of their works is to validate the chareidi position in the eyes of the secular Israeli Jewish world. The two books that I read in English are quite different. These books are written by accredited college professors who, quite obviously, are not chareidim and, accordingly, neither of which is geared to validating our position.

The first, and earlier, of the two books is *Defenders of the Faith*: Inside Ultra-Orthodox Jewry by Prof. Samuel C. Heilman, a professor of sociology at Queens College and at the Graduate Center of the City University of New York. This book is a sociological study of the behaviors and lifestyle of the chareidim in Israel. The entire book critiques the rituals and institutions of the chareidim. Heilman does not devote any part of his book to examining the underlying ideology of our belief system, save for an occasional mention in passing in relation to the specific ritual or institution that he is observing. In his prologue, he establishes the premise of his book: to determine, "Who are these people who appear to belong more to yesterday than today, *and why are they still around?*"[1] This question – why are we still here? – is the question that I address in the Preface of my book.

It is worthwhile to note that, in addition to this elaborate study, Prof. Heilman is the author of the entry on *Haredim* that was inserted into the 1997 CD-ROM version of Encyclopaedia Judaica.

The second of the two books is *Real Jews*: Secular vs. Ultra-Orthodox and the Struggle for Jewish Identity in Israel by Prof. Noah J. Efron of Bar Ilan University. As the subtitle implies, this book is a socio-political study of the impact of the chareidim on the cultural and political landscape in Israel. Here, likewise, the author scrutinizes the chareidi mode of conduct and our stand on social issues from a totally political perspective while placing little to no emphasis on the underlying ideology that makes us tick. The premise of Efron's book is to address a far different question. In his Preface he writes:[2]

> Why do the ultra-Orthodox seem like an undifferentiated horde to so many of the rest of us here in Israel? And why – beset by bombs, hunger, and hopelessness – do so many of us see as our primary enemy, as the *real* cause of all our problems, the great mass of men in black?

In other words, he is addressing the question that I posed in the introduction of this book: why are the chareidim hated and shunned?

So, it appears that other, more accredited individuals have preceded me in probing the mysteries of the chareidim. What does my book provide that the others do not?

Well, obviously it does not reach the same conclusions, but, in addition to that, the two main answers to this question are:

- Of the books that critique the distinction between chareidim and non-chareidim, mine is the only "pro-chareidi" book in English.

---

[1] Heilman, *Defenders of the Faith*, Shocken Books, New York 1992, Prologue p. xii.

[2] Efron, *Real Jews*, Basic Books, New York 2003, Preface p. xvi.

- My book is about the relationship between chareidim and other Orthodox Jews and not between chareidim and secular.

But what is equally important: Mine is the only book in English that presents a concise, clear-cut definition of a chareidi.

And, if I say so myself, I do quite a job of it. Thus far, I have devoted not less than four complete chapters to defining, explaining, and illustrating exactly what is a chareidi – on top of being "concise." Why did I [think that I] have to do that?

The answer is that I have accepted upon myself the thankless burden of performing a feat that, heretofore, has never been attempted – I have set upon to disprove the Theory of Evolution. No, I don't mean the Darwin Theory of Evolution. That can be left to the capable pens and lectures of such luminaries as Rabbi Eliyahu Dessler and Rabbi Avigdor Miller, ZT"L. I mean the Theory of Chareidi Evolution.

What's that?

I will explain. First, let me restate (and rephrase) my definition:

Chareidiism is the ideology of Leviticus 26:3 in accordance to the commentary of Rashi and Torat Kohanim. A chareidi is one who upholds that ideology.

Plain and simple.

Yet, I don't seem to have much company. Of all the four authors of the books in my "bibliography," only one of them, Rabbi Moshe Grylak, bothers to make a point of defining exactly what a chareidi is. On page 15 of his book *The Charedim: Who are We Really?* He states:

> Any Jew who is affiliated with the Jewish people, who believes in G-d and his Torah and that it was publicly handed down at Mount Sinai; a Jew who pledges full allegiance, with no reservations, to the Halacha as determined by the Shulchan Aruch and a consensus of its commentators and who is not politically Zionistic (i.e., Herzelian or nationalistic) – is to be regarded as an adherent to the chareidi stream of the Jewish people.

That works for me (although I have no need for the proviso about the politically Zionistic).

This leaves the other three authors, two of whom are noted college professors, as delinquent in this minor detail.

I will excuse Rabbi Noigershall because, if one scrutinizes his book, it becomes apparent that his advocacy is not so much centered on the antagonism toward "chareidim" in particular, but rather the antagonism toward Orthodox, mitzvah observant Jewry in general. True, the chareidim are the strongest champions of many of the issues that he addresses but, with the ostentatious exception of the draft issues, the issues are actually basic issues of religious versus secular that affect all Orthodox

Jews. As such, his use of the term chareidi is merely a synonym for "staunchly religious Jews" and a precise definition is not required.

I cannot be so forgiving toward the academicians. One would expect of these scholarly college professors who call themselves historian and philosopher (Efron) or sociologist, anthropologist, and ethnographer (Heilman) and who have undertaken the task of explaining to the world the plan and purpose of chareidim, to provide a concise definition. Yet, the anticipated concise definition is conspicuously absent; and the question in my mind is: what does this say to us?

No, they do not fully neglect the issue; that would be rather impossible. As they must, Heilman and Efron each devote an opening chapter, 29 and 41 pages respectively, to presenting the requisite background information about the chareidim to enable the reader to understand who they are. Heilman titles his chapter *Who are the Haredim?*; and while Efron titles his chapter *History*, his opening line is, "*Who* are Israel's ultra-Orthodox and where did they come from?" Nonetheless, there are serious shortcomings with their lengthy narratives, not the least of which is that, after the 29 or 41 pages, we are still not clear as to who qualifies as a chareidi and who does not.

Heilman does indeed *describe* chareidim. On page 12 he writes:

> Later, as the distinctions among the observant became clearer, evolving modern Hebrew began to use *dati* as a generic term for the "religious," though in common usage it became associated with those observant Jews who by and large had accommodated to modern lifestyles. "Haredim" became reserved for those religious people who had not made such accommodations and compromises.

And he goes on to delineate some of the various factions, notably comparing Hasidim and Mitnagdim and discussing Agudath Israel. Yet, he does not *define* them. We still don't know what it is that makes a chareidi chareidi. As his chapter title suggests, he dwells on the *who,* but barely touches the *what*.

In Heilman's defense, one can argue that a precise definition is only vital when discussing the chareidim in relation to others who are not chareidim. Heilman's work is not for this purpose and, as such, it may be sufficient to be apprised of *who* he is studying even if we don't know *what it is* that makes them that way.

This line of defense might hold up if this would be all that Heilman wrote; but it is not. Heilman actually got a second chance – that of authoring the entry on **Haredim** that appears in current editions of the CD ROM version of Encyclopaedia Judaica. Since it is an encyclopedia, it is more vitally essential to provide a clear "*what*" definition and, since it is the venerable Encyclopaedia Judaica, it has got to be accurate.

Indeed, this time Heilman does a slightly better job. He does attempt to state a concise definition, and it may have been valid if he hadn't spoiled it himself by throwing in too much salt. In the section under the subtitle *Definition* he writes that the term "haredim" *currently* refers to:

> ...those most extreme of Orthodox Jews who, **although they have changed over time** (emphasis mine – YH), claim to have made no compromises wit[h] contemporary secular culture or essential changes in the way they practice their Judaism from what the tradition and Halacha have sanctified throughout the ages.

Boy, am I confused! "...although they have changed over time..."? You mean, what they are now is not what they used to be? Then, what were they before and in what way have they changed? And what do we expect them to be tomorrow?

I have a feeling that Heilman doesn't really know, and in a few more pages, I will explain why that is. Heilman continues by discussing the identifying characteristics of chareidim – how they dress differently, speak differently, and act differently than other religious Jews. It appears as if he is forced to diagnose the "condition" based on the symptoms. This would imply that there is no available diagnostic laboratory test to positively identify the "ailment."

Let's turn to Efron. I previously mentioned that Efron provides a chapter entitled *History* in which he presents the anthropological background of his subjects (us chareidim). The chapter is aptly titled because he presents a historical backdrop and nothing more. When we compare with Heilman who titled his chapter *Who are the Haredim?*, we may acknowledge that Heilman indeed follows through on his title by pointing out who he includes in his study. His approach is as if to say "I can't define them for you but I will show you how to identify them." Efron doesn't even do that. He opens his chapter with the words, "Who are Israel's ultra-Orthodox and where did they come from?" and then promptly proceeds to answer the second half of the question (where we came from) while totally ignoring the first half (who we are). Presumably, he contends that the answer to the second half ipso facto answers the first half, but such is not the case. If one does not have an ideology-based *"what"* definition of a chareidi, as do Rabbi Grylak and myself, then one does not have a clue as to *who* they are nor *where* they came from. It escapes me how one can hope to make a reader understand the kulter-kampf between chareidim and non-chareidim if one cannot first explain:

- What is a chareidi?

- Why does he do what he does and not do what he doesn't?

- Why, in spite of our "backward," primitive, isolationist demeanor, is the population of chareidim growing? – Yes, of course we have lots of kids,[3] but, what keeps the vast majority of them within the fold? Why do we gain more adherents from the outside than we lose from the inside? What does it offer to its members besides restrictions, restrictions, and more restrictions?

- What is our agenda? – To be sure, Efron devotes a great deal of textual real estate to discussing the secular *perception* that chareidim are trying to take over the country. In fact, he titles one chapter (72 pages!) *Rabbis and Ayatollahs: **The Protocols of the Elders of Bnei Brak***. But the looming question – "for what ultimate purpose?" – remains unanswered (it is not even addressed).

In contrast to my stated vindications of the other authors, Prof. Efron cannot be excused for overlooking this essential issue. This is because in the course of his work, Efron is compelled to play the numbers game. Hence, innocently tucked away on page 90, in the course of his discussion on educational funding, Efron casually declares one of the most pivotal statements of that section of his thesis as an undisputed established fact, "Haredim represent *approximately 7 percent* of the population..." (emphasis mine – YH). This chapter is not the place to deal with the integrity of this figure,[4] yet it escapes me as to how we can assess the quantity of chareidim if we are not apprised as to what constitutes a chareidi to begin with?[5]

---

[3] Included in this question is: why are chareidim so eager to have such big families while the mainstream population is not?

[4] Suffice it to say that the Israeli government has not conducted an official census since 1995 and the next one is scheduled for 2008. The best current indicator that we have is the electorate. In the two previous elections (2003 and 2006) the combined constituency of the two chareidi parties, UTJ and SHAS, were 16 and 18 seats respectively. Even the lower figure reflects representation of over 13 percent of the population. Bear in mind that the chareidim [exclusively] include some factions that maintain that it is Halachically forbidden to vote! Additionally, Efron himself notes on the following page that the chareidi population is child-heavy which means that a greater proportion of the chareidi population is below voting age. Also note that Efron writes on page 145 that "the purchasing power of the Hareidi community ... is somewhere along the line of 15-20 percent of the population." Not bad purchasing power for a mere 7 percent, the poorest to boot! After I wrote all this, I reached page 242 where the percentage magically changed to "one in ten Israelis." That's a 43% increase over the 7 percent on page 90.

[5] This same problem haunts us to the very conclusion of his book. On page 273, 2 pages before the finish line, he writes, "...according to Boston University

So let us return to our initial question: exactly who are those that, in Efron's eyes, are included in the chareidi society?

With Efron I am just as confused. Although Efron never presents a definition, he certainly implies one. He spends the bulk of his History chapter depicting his chareidim as the religious Jews who, since the 1800s, opposed the credo of the Enlightenment and subsequently of Zionism. He presents them as a "movement" that was launched in that era by Rabbi Moshe Sofer (Chatam Sofer) whom he portrays as "the first ultra-Orthodox Jew."[6] Lovely. This "definition" holds true all the way to the last page of that chapter. From that point onward, no part of the book deals with clashes with Zionism or Zionists per se nor even with "enlightened" Jews, but rather, as his subtitle indicates, with the secular.[7] He does not contend that the masses are afraid that the chareidim will intrude on their Zionist aspirations, only that they will intrude on their secular lifestyle.

One aspect that makes this so confusing is that let us consider that there are three entities: (1) the totally (24/7/365) secular, (2) the totally (24/7/365) religious, which, I suppose, is what we generally agree constitutes the "ultra-Orthodox" or chareidi, and (3) there are the hybrids – those who observe Shabbat and kashrut and attend prayers but when it is not Shabbat or prayer time, they are usually at work or recreation in a largely non-religious atmosphere. While it is clear that Group 1 and Group 2 are the two primary competing subjects of his book, where does this third delegation stand according to Efron? They are certainly not chareidi, but are they secular?

The natural assumption would be they are neutral bystanders and do not personify either of the parties that are discussed in his book. But even this is far from clear, certainly to my understanding and, I daresay, even to Efron's. When one does not have a clear, one line, definition to define a chareidi then the vague descriptions that are offered in such writings become mired in inaccuracies and inconsistencies. Let's look at what

---

economist Eli Berman, for almost 25 years, rates of childbirth among the ultra-Orthodox have been 2½ to 3½ times as great as secular birthrates. Yet… the populations of ultra-Orthodox relative to secular have grown far less than childbirth rates would suggest. To parse this data accurately would require complicated analysis and the collection of new data…" Don't you think it might also require a clear definition as to what counts as ultra-Orthodox? It's been 273 pages and we still haven't got one.

[6] Efron, *Real Jews* page 22.

[7] It is vital to note the distinction between an "enlightened" Jew and a secular Jew. An enlightened Jew, what we call a qualified *apikores*, is one who is familiar with the Scriptures and basic tenets of Judaism and of Halacha, yet he believes that these can be reconciled with non-Jewish society albeit with much compromise. A secular Jew, what we call an *am haaretz* or *tinok shenishba*, is

Efron writes in his Introduction:[8]

> Soon after the war, I flew El Al to the United States. I was squeezing back from the bathroom through a crowd of ultra-Orthodox Jews noisily[9] praying in front of the emergency exit, when a flight attendant caught my eye and, smiling slyly, whispered in Hebrew, "You open the door, I'll push." I smiled back and found my seat.

Ultra-Orthodox Jews? By what measure? Efron doesn't tell us. My assumption is that the flight attendant was ready to push *all of them* out regardless of whether they ordered Glatt Kosher or even if they or their sons had served in the army and insist upon reciting the prayer for the welfare of the State of Israel in their synagogues. Oh, I am certain many, if not most, were indeed ultra-Orthodox, but is ultra-Orthodoxy the collective raison d'etre of this "crowd?" It appears that according to Efron, and probably most of his readership, any Jew who prays in a *minyan* on a plane is ultra-Orthodox,[10] at least while he is praying.[11]

Then, perhaps, Efron should define a chareidi as "a Jew who prays with a minyan on a plane." Yet, Efron presents ultra-Orthodoxy as a movement launched by Chatam Sofer in the 1800s. Does he mean to imply that were it not for Chatam Sofer, there would be no Jews forming prayer groups on El Al planes today?

I am still confused.

I couldn't help but wonder why Efron is so fixated on this undefined 1800s Chatam Sofer characterization, but I might have let it pass as his personal conjecture if not for one vexing concurrence. Although Heilman,

---

one who knows nothing of substance about Judaism and who shuts out religion from his active life. Admittedly, both for Efron's purposes and for mine there is no practical difference. Both entities unite seamlessly as the "brethren, haters, and shunners." This distinction is only important to understand the struggle of the Chatam Sofer.

[8] Efron, *Real Jews* page 4.

[9] This adjective is very telling. As it lends nothing to the story, it only serves to cast aspersions on the activity and, thus, to compromise Efron's claim to objectivity. I have both observed and participated in these "crowds" and I can attest to the fact that the participants typically make every effort not to raise their voices, that they can be barely heard above the din of the jet engines even at ground zero and that virtually no uninvolved passengers are even aware that the prayers are going on – unless they need the bathroom.

[10] More than anything else, this story serves to illustrate that, in many cases, an event that is presented as a focused intolerance toward chareidim is in actuality a universal intolerance toward religious observance in general.

[11] In all fairness to Efron, Efron indeed acknowledges this diversity in the Preface of his book where he writes that in relation to the secular "there is no monolithic 'us' or 'them.'"

in his personal convictions (he calls himself "modern Orthodox") and in the format and premise of his writing, is very different than Efron, and although he presents a deeper and more intimate perspective of the chareidim, he concurs with Efron on this point – that the existence of the chareidim dates back merely 200 years!

Like Efron, Heilman contends that:

> To trace the social and psychological origins of haredi angst and traditionalism, one must go back at least 200 years to Europe, where most Jews then lived. As an organized and identifiable movement, Orthodoxy, from which the haredim emerged, originated there and then in opposition to the rapid change and religious reform that was beginning to sweep Jewish life. This began with three intertwined forces that shook the world in the eighteenth century...[12]

Professor Heilman has taught us a few "facts": (1) Orthodoxy is a movement, (2) the haredim "emerged" from the "Orthodox," and (3) all this "began... in the eighteenth century."

And do you know what makes this commonly held premise so utterly amazing? It is that both Efron and Heilman write their collusive theories immediately after they themselves write that the chareidim themselves maintain otherwise!

You see, we chareidim don't actually think of ourselves as chareidim. We think of ourselves as just plain standard Jews. The real Jews. In fact, I wrote that there are plenty of Jews who meet my definition of chareidi who would never think of themselves as chareidi and might even disdain such a label. This segment doesn't want to be termed *chareidi* – only Jewish. That's fine with me. It is primarily non-chareidim who promoted the use of the term *chareidim* or alternatively, *ultra-Orthodox*. Both Heilman and Efron agree with this. Heilman writes: [13]

> Yet while other Jews increasingly use the designation, ironically haredim generally do not use it to refer to themselves. Rather, in their vernacular Yiddish, they commonly call themselves *Yidn*, Jews, or more specifically *erlicher Yidn*, virtuous Jews. This insider name implies their conviction that, contrary to what others may suggest, they are *not* a separate sect called "haredim" nor a subgroup in a new homeland for Hebrews but very simply the true Jews.

Efron echoes this idea.[14] In the opening paragraph of his chapter on the History [of chareidim] he writes:[15]

---

[12] Heilman, *Defenders of the Faith*, Shocken Books, New York 1992, p. 14

[13] Ibid. p. 12

[14] I have a hunch that Efron read Heilman's book.

[15] Efron, *Real Jews* p. 16

This is how they view themselves. The term they most commonly use to refer to themselves is *Yidn*, Yiddish for "Jews." The name reflects a profound truth about Haredi self-image. In their view, they are not a *sort* of Jew, they are simply Jews: real Jews, true Jews, good Jews, gold-standard Jews, platonic Jews, the ideal from which all other Jews deviate... The Jews who stood at the foot of Mount Sinai to receive the Torah were like them. For as long as there have been Jews, there have been Haredim. All the rest... are recent corruptions of the true practice of Judaism, which Haredim alone carry on.

Thereupon, they each proceed to inform their readers that they know better and that the chareidim are a modern age society whose origins can be traced to cultural upheavals that occurred within the past two hundred years.

And before that... there were no chareidim! Just some pre-historic cavemen. Oh, sure, there were Jews. But they weren't chareidim. Couldn't have been. They were different Jews who wore tunics and turbans. Chareidim wear black frocks and shtreimels. They can't be the same ones. The pre-historic Jews weren't acclimated to industrialization and urbanization so they became extinct. From their surviving remnants arose a new species – the modern, enlightened, secular Jew and a mutant sub-species that can be called "chareidim."

Yes, chareidim are mutants because if they weren't here yesterday and they are here now they must have evolved! And how does something evolve if not from sudden mutation? That's how evolution works. That's how everything works because everything evolved. The whole world evolved. Every intelligent person knows that the whole world came about through evolution. That's what the great scientists say; that is what they teach in all the great universities; that is what has been proven beyond the shadow of a doubt. Only under-educated, unenlightened, primitive, backward people could question the truth of evolution.

People like us.

We chareidim do not believe in evolution. We believe in Creation. We believe that G-d created the world in six days. We also believe that G-d created the chareidim in six days – from the first day of Sivan until the sixth day of Sivan in the year 2448. For six days G-d sanctified his nation, and on the seventh He gave us his Torah.[16] On that day it is written, "***Vayecherad*** *kol ha'am asher ba'machaneh* (and the entire nation who were within the camp ***trembled***). [17]

---

[16] The sages of the Talmud debate whether the Torah was given on the sixth or seventh day. See Rashi on Exodus 19:15 s.v. *Heyu.*

[17] Exodus 19:16. The root of the word *Vayecherad* is the same as that of the word "chareidi."

We didn't evolve. We were always here – since "Creation." Whether with cloaks and khaffiyahs, tunics and turbans, frocks, knickers, and shtreimels, dark suits and black fedoras, we are the ones who upheld Leviticus 26:3 (not to exclude the rest of the package) in 2448 and we are the ones who uphold it today. We've been doing business for over 3300 years throughout the globe without altering our original corporate charter nor our basic *modus operandi*.

The academicians cannot accept this. It is difficult for the evolutionists to believe that G-d created the world. Yet, even among those who believe in G-d, many find it hard to believe that G-d created the Jews; and many who believe that G-d created the Jews find it hard to believe that G-d created the chareidim.

We chareidim think that evolution is absurd. Recorded history – which amazingly goes back no further than five to six thousand years – has yet to document any instance of any extant creature becoming more complex than it ever was. No one has yet caught a jellyfish even thinking about growing a backbone. But evolutionists have a lot at stake. So much so that they are compelled to advocate the absurd.

As I wrote in the introduction to this book, the controversy between the belief in spontaneous evolution versus Creation is merely a manifestation of the controversy over belief in G-d. The "evolution" of the theories of evolution is fueled by the need for the autonomous man to find an alternative to the existence of G-d. This is because, to such a person, the implications of the existence of G-d, i.e., that he (the human) is a subservient and accountable being, is too menacing for him to handle. By clinging to the belief of a "plausible" alternative, the evolutionist can declare that he is not beholden to a G-d, to any master plan or to any spiritual morals. It doesn't matter if the plausible alternative is patently absurd – such as the popular "Monster Soup Mutation" theory – as long as it remains even remotely plausible.

In our case, there is something similar at stake. The mere concept that the chareidi might be the paradigm Jew and that all who are racially Jewish descended from chareidim – as the academicians unanimously acknowledge as being the unequivocal stance of its adherents – is, indeed, quite menacing to the non-chareidi. Menacing is an understatement. It is downright hostile as it presents an invasive challenge to the very legitimacy of his rejection of its tenets. Unlike the less knowledgeable secular masses, these scholars cannot ignore the challenge. They know too much.

Behold, the theory of evolution comes to the rescue. Evolution espouses the idea that everything that is in existence today is a mutated descendant of something that used to be structurally different. Nothing can be viewed as "original" – even (especially?) chareidim. Hence, since chareidiism evolved from a different form of Judaism, it cannot claim to be the original brand of Mosaic Judaism that was ordained and styled by G-d Himself at Mount Sinai. In other words, chareidim cannot call themselves the exclusive authentic, genuine-article Jew. This creates room for non-chareidi, non-Orthodox, and even *Halachically* non-Jewish people to claim that they just as much (or even more closely) personify the "original" Jew – if there is one. That is how an intelligent evolutionist Jew such as Tommy Lapid[18] can say to Noah Efron, "*They* say that they are the real Jews. *I* am the real Jew! If Moses were around today, or Maimonides, they would recognize *me* as the true Jew, not the ultra-Orthodox."[19] Whoahh!! Is he talking about the Moses of whom Rashi twice writes that his office was the Beit Midrash (House of Study)?[20] Does he mean the Maimonides who writes that every single Jewish male must study Torah day and night until the day of his death[21] and who writes that any Jew who fully commits himself to the service of G-d is exempt from national service?[22] And don't you think that Bar Ilan professor (and Harvard and M.I.T. Fellow) Noah Efron would find this claim to be a bit absurd?

Apparently not. Efron is a fellow evolutionist. Efron does not study Chumash with Rashi and he is more familiar with Heraclites than Maimonides. Efron rejoins:

> The surprising thing is not that he thinks that; he has good arguments and – as one must say about such hypotheticals – he could be right. What's surprising is that it matters so much to a very secular member of

---

[18] It is entirely possible that by the time this book reaches market Mr. Tommy Lapid will be a political non-entity to the extent that younger readers may wonder who he is (was?). Mr. Yosef (a.k.a. Tommy) Lapid is a Holocaust survivor who co-founded a political party whose sole platform was to combat chareidi influences and institutions in Eretz Israel. In the 2003 elections, his party, named Shinui, won an amazing 15 seats in the Knesset with no agenda other than the aforementioned. His victorious motto and his only stipulation for joining Ariel Sharon's coalition was, "Anybody but SHAS!" In 2005, he pulled his party out of the coalition when Sharon struck a deal with UTJ (the Ashkenazi chareidi party). In January 2006, his party was showing so badly in the polls that it was questionable if Shinui would win any Knesset seats at all in the upcoming March elections. Thereupon, Mr. Lapid was compelled to retire from the Knesset. At the time of Efron's research, Lapid was the undisputed champion of the anti-chareidi secular masses in Eretz Israel.

[19] Efron, *Real Jews* page 14

[20] Rashi Numbers 9:6 and Numbers 27:2 based on Sifri and Talmud Bavli Bava Bathra 119b

[21] Maimonides, Yad HaChazaka, Mada, Hilchot Talmud Torah 1:8,9

[22] Maimonides, Yad HaChazaka, Zeraim, Hilchot Shmitta V'Yovel 13:12,13

a very secular parliament just what Moses and Maimonides might think of him.[23]

Did you get that? Tommy Lapid could be right! According to Efron *what* Tommy Lapid thinks is not absurd. Of course it's not. Moses and Maimonides were up to date and tuned in with their times, not like the chareidim who are centuries out of date. What is absurd, says Efron, is only *why* Tommy Lapid feels the need to think that way. After all, neither Moses nor Maimonides was Israeli.

But there is something even more important at stake. And that is that, through this theory of evolution, non-chareidim can relieve themselves of the onerous and formidable "fable" that their very own ancestors were dyed-in-the-wool chareidim. "Heaven forbid, my forefathers couldn't have been chareidim. Chareidim didn't evolve until the eighteenth century!"[24] As long as chareidiism is an era, a temporary passing fad that "will fill the planet with sound and splendor, then fade to dream stuff and pass away," something that was not here yesterday and won't be here tomorrow, then Heilman and Efron, et al, can maintain the luxury of claiming to be familiar with chareidim and yet harbor no qualms about why they themselves are not chareidi. However, if they were to acknowledge that chareidiism, i.e., Leviticus 26:3, is G-d the Father's prescription for success and immortality and that it was the credo of their very own ancestors, then they might have some explaining to do.

So now we can understand why the academic community cannot define chareidim with any ideology based definitions. They are afraid to. They are afraid of discovering the true age of the chareidim. The minute one presents a concise, ideology based definition of chareidi, it becomes apparent that this ideology has been around for quite some time, that it is the ideology of his ancestors, and that it is still just as vibrant as ever. If the ideology is 3300 years old, then, so are the chareidim. We have been here longer than any "other kind" of Jew and we don't seem to have any plans to "fade to dream stuff and pass away" anytime soon.

So, to review, the theory of evolution saves the day. Evolution allows the academicians to view chareidiism as a recently introduced *mode of conduct* without a proven ideological premise. This way, the *behavior* can be scrutinized and not the ideology. Furthermore, the behavior, which is perceived to be totally man-made, is conceivably subject to challenge and modification. Accordingly, Efron, for most of his 275 pages, talks of

---

[23] Efron, *Real Jews* ibid.

[24] Unfortunately for many, if not most, they do not need to go back even as far as the eighteenth century to acknowledge full chareidi ancestry.

nothing but chareidi behavior and nary a word on chareidi ideology.[25]

But ignoring the ideological underpinning can have nothing but fatal repercussions. It is the proverbial ostrich that deals with danger by sticking its head in the sand. Thus Efron fails to note the fallacy of Shinui's battle cry as he critiques it in his Preface:

> Still, the greatest part of Shinui's success must be attributed to the power of their simple message: It's us or the ultra-Orthodox, and we will defeat them before they defeat us.[26]

Sure, that's their message. But what is their plan? More specifically, what exactly are they trying to defeat? To the enlightened evolutionists – and there are hundreds of thousands of them, hence, their "success" – we are a new age sect of fundamentalists who are socially uncooperative. That's what Lapid and his minions think we are and that is what Efron thinks we are. In fact, Lapid thinks that they have been around longer than us, because Moses and Maimonides would identify with them. They are more with the times, more "PC" – more educated and scientific. In short, more realistic and down-to-earth, so they will surely outlast us. But, according to Rabbi Grylak and me, we are not a modern fundamentalist cult. We are adherents to an ideology. A venerable and quite successful ideology. We don't adhere to it merely because our elders preach it to us. We adhere to it because it makes sense to us, because it makes good on its claims, because it works.

There is only one way to fight an ideology. You must have a better ideology. One that looks and sounds better; one that works better. Shinui has no ideology, no ammunition; yet, thousands believe that they will win the war.[27] It is because they think that we evolved from an extinct species, and, as such, we are ourselves susceptible to extinction. It does not serve their interests to believe that we were created in our pristine form 3300 years ago, and, through our adherence to Leviticus 26:3, that we have perpetuated ourselves in identical form ever since. Who was it that said that the first rule of battle is: Know thy enemy?

The absurdity of this evolutionary exposition is truly startling. Efron so much as says so himself. Let's take a fuller look at what he writes. We will start on page 17:

---

[25] Efron does make some casual references to the chareidi ideal of "toratam omanutam" (his spelling) on pages 18, 62, and 97. None of these references include any sort of analysis as to what this ideal is based on.

[26] Efron, *Real Jews* Preface page xv

[27] As I wrote above in footnote 18, the Shinui party imploded in January 2006 (after these words were drafted). Make no mistake about it, nobody "defeated" them – there was nothing of substance to defeat. Of their own accord they "faded to dream stuff and passed away."

By the middle of the sixteenth century, there were 10,000 Jews in the Holy Land by some estimates, and more were arriving from Europe each month. Most of these Jews set up in Jerusalem or Safed, which ever since has remained, along with Bnei Brak, the hometowns of most ultra-Orthodox in Israel. It is with these pioneers in mind that Haredim maintain that it was they who led the Jewish return to the Holy Land, not the secular Zionists.

Comment: This makes sense because, by all accounts, there were no secular Zionists in the sixteenth century. But wait! Efron can wiggle out of this:

This point is debatable. Modern historians insist that those pious Jews who settled in Palestine almost half a millennium ago were hardly direct forbears of today's ultra-Orthodox. Like Heraclites, the Greek philosopher who observed that one never steps into the same river twice, these scholars hold as an axiom that the pious Jews of 500 years past are not, cannot be, the same as those of today. But today's ultra-Orthodox point to many similarities. Like us, they point out, the Jews...settled into an austere life dominated by prayer, study, and work...these Jews considered study the best of all possible pursuits...

All that is why today's ultra-Orthodox – who have no truck with Heraclites in the best of circumstances – see themselves as the natural heirs of the Jews of Palestine of five centuries ago.

Comment: So the gloves are off. While we chareidim maintain that we are the updated model of the same mechanism that has existed for centuries, the modern historians insist otherwise. Though he neglects to explain where the "old" Jews have disappeared to, at least he has secured an ally – Heraclites. Presumably, Heraclites' point is that a river is essentially the water that it comprises. Since, in any given spot at any given moment, the original water is flowing out and other water is replacing it, the actual water, i.e., "river" that one steps into now is not the same river that he stepped into a moment ago. Accordingly, when one generation of "pious" Jews "moves on" and is replaced by another, the new generation is not the same brand of people as the previous.

I think that Efron is swimming against the current with his reference to Heraclites. Logic dictates that Heraclites would concede the following: (A) Both bodies of water are equally deserving of the term "river." (B) This new river, even if different, is occupying the exact same space and carrying out the exact same function as was the previous "river." (C) The molecular composition of the substance in the current "river," H_2O, is identical to the molecular composition of the substance in the previous "river." The new river did not evolve out of the old one, it merely took its place.

Ergo, if one's perception of anthropology is evolutionary such that a human being used to be a jellyfish, thus the DNA, molecular makeup, and the functionality of the ancestor does not match that of the descendant, then it is possible to argue that the ideas and behaviors of a previous generation does not match the ensuing generation. But, even to Heraclites, a new river is the same H_2O as the old river doing the same thing in the same place. The molecular composition of the "pious Jews of 500 years past" was $Xd_{20}Lv_{26}D_6$ (Exodus 20, Leviticus 26, and Deuteronomy 6 – the three most fundamental passages that are dealt with in this book) and, lo and behold, the chareidim of today are composed of the exact same $Xd_{20}Lv_{26}D_6$ and they do the identical activities in the identical synagogues and yeshivot! If you can call both bodies of water "rivers" then you can surely call both generations of pious Jews "chareidim."[28]

Now, Efron tells us when the chareidim really turned up. First, he devotes 2½ pages to relating the advent of the Enlightenment. Now on page 21:

> A backlash was inevitable… For those of a traditional leaning, it seemed that, *for the first time in their history* (emphasis mine – YH), Judaism was being devastated by Jews themselves. Something had to be done, as one leader of the counterchange insisted, "to restore the glories of the past."
>
> That leader was Moses Sofer…He raised an old Talmudic dictum – "innovation is forbidden by the Torah" – to high and inviolable principle. …Sofer determined that if Judaism were to survive with any integrity, it had to survive intact, in its totality…

Comment: The italicized phrase "for the first time in their history" is the deepest flaw in Efron's theory. I will elaborate shortly. Read on:

> Moses Sofer was, in short, the first ultra-Orthodox Jew, just as Moses Mendelssohn had been the first "Enlightenment Jew." This is an important turning point because it illustrates that only when "modern" Jews came into being, ultra-Orthodox Jews came into being too.

Comment: If one agrees with his first statement – that Chatam Sofer was the first ultra-Orthodox Jew, then the second one, about Moses Mendelssohn, is plausible. I think both statements are nonsense. The only agreement I have is that the first chareidi was indeed named Moses and

---

[28] Efron does not appear to be totally oblivious to this argument. He seems to allude to it when he presents the chareidi side of the debate, albeit with much less conviction. Subsequently and without any further explanation, he rejects this assertion out-of-hand. This can only be because Efron is himself a "modern historian." So much for objectivity.

that he was also a *sofer* (scribe).

> The conjunction seems odd at first. In ways most evident to the eye, pious Jews had simply remained pious Jews… they dressed as their great-grandparents had, spoke the same languages…observed the same rites, and so forth. But something important had changed in their attitudes…They now viewed themselves as different: purebred Jews, not like all those other mutts.

Comment: What Efron seems to be saying is: suppose you have 100 assorted brown lizards in the desert, 90 of which happen to be chameleons. You then transport the whole lot to a grassy meadow and 90 of them (the chameleons) turn green. The ten that have remained brown have undergone a drastic change for they have now discovered that they are not chameleons. Apparently, Efron assumes that, until now, they hadn't an inkling that they are not chameleons.

What Efron is suggesting is akin to what another renowned secular-but-religiously-knowledgeable Jewish thinker, Prof. Woody Allen, suggests in his celebrated philosophical treatise *Without Feathers* when he describes his mythological Great Roe: "The Great Roe is a mythological beast with the head of a lion and the body of a lion, though not the same lion." Likewise, Efron's chareidi has yesterday's mannerisms of the pious Jew and today's mannerisms of the pious Jew, yet they are not the same pious Jews. Note that Efron himself writes earlier that the immigrant Jews of the middle sixteenth century that settled in Jerusalem and Safed were of European extraction with more "arriving from Europe each month." How much could the sixteenth century European Jews possibly differ from the eighteenth century European Jews (and which month initiated the difference)? Efron and Allen appear to be quite similar. If there is any difference, it is that Efron is serious.

> Zeno would have admired the paradox. Sofer introduced to Judaism an innovation perhaps as radical as any the religion had absorbed during its long history: the idea that innovation itself was forbidden and had always been forbidden. The irony grows. Sofer's innovation gave rise to a new sort of Jew, one who accepts as an axiom that the very notion of a new sort of Jew is nonsense…

Efron is saying that, being that the world and people and the Jews are driven by the forces of evolution, the Jews were always changing, and that was Okay. All of a sudden, some pious Jew decides on his own that we weren't supposed to be doing any of this alleged changing for all these centuries and if the Jews keep on changing, they won't stay the same, so he put a sudden stop to all this changing business so that they can stay the same and – Voila! – something different! Introducing the new unchangeable same-as-yesterday chareidi. "New" and "same-as-yesterday" are quite a paradox.

I think that if Zeno read this he would say, "Efron, maybe you should consult with the dean about taking a Sabbatical. Chareidiism is an ideology. All ideologies are inherently unchangeable because the minute you change one, you have made a different ideology. If the ideology isn't new, the chareidim aren't new, either."

In fact, Chatam Sofer was an old chareidi. A chareidi by *my* definition – he knew Chumash with Rashi. Specifically, he knew the Rashi in Leviticus 26:15 that I quoted that says that the first level of the *seven below* draws in the second and third until rock bottom. Chatam Sofer was not introducing anything new. He was merely echoing an age-old truth[29] to his followers because there was a danger that they may lose sight of it. And that is that you can't change something, even a little bit, and expect it to retain the same properties. A pious Jew has always been $Xd_{20}Lv_{26}D_6$ and it is this molecular composition that has given it its resilience and durability. The Lv_{26} part of the compound contains the Manufacturer's warranty. (Incidentally, this part of the compound is the "secret" element that I extolled in the Preface of this book.) You tamper with that, even if you are sure that you have a superior product, you have voided the warranty. Moses Mendelssohn didn't hear the message and so he never learned the secret. He thought that $Xd_{20}D_6$ was enough to be a Jew. If you alloy it with some other elements such as S (Science), Lt (Literature), and Nz (German) you'll have even a better Jew. He never forgot his Chumash but he forgot his Rashi. When his new alloy decomposed, there was no warranty.

But to all you science-minded readers, how do I *scientifically* disprove Efron's theory of spontaneous mutation?

It's relatively simple. Suppose someone claims that he can prove that a thoroughbred horse evolved out of a turtle 50 million years ago. If I can prove with the same standards of proof that thoroughbred horses were *already* in existence 60 million years ago, then his theory sustains a broken leg and has to be shot.

Now, I already wrote that, with my definition, we learn that a chareidi is composed of $Xd_{20}Lv_{26}D_6$ – something that Efron and Heilman don't seem to acknowledge – and if you actually study the Talmud, Maimonides, and pretty much any work of Jewish scholarship written before the advent of the printing press, it is evident that the pious Jews of those times were likewise composed of $Xd_{20}Lv_{26}D_6$.

But I have more to say. As I noted just a few pages back, Efron at-

---

[29] Rashi had written it 800 years earlier and he didn't make it up, either.

tempts to alleviate the absurdity of his evolutionary theory by claiming that this new mutation was, as are all non-Creation entities, a product of cause-and-effect. Their evolution at that particular time was a reaction to an unprecedented circumstance that had *never happened before*. He wrote, "it seemed that, *for the first time in their history*, Judaism was being devastated by Jews themselves." This implies that were it not the first time in their history that "Judaism was being devastated by Jews themselves," even Efron would expect the chareidim to show up a bit earlier. Now, the book jacket tells us that Noah J. Efron teaches history at Bar Ilan University. I must comment that if, in his view, the Enlightenment was "the first time in our history that it seemed that Judaism was being devastated by Jews themselves," *Jewish* history is not his specialty.

Now, here's the real history of the chareidim:

The first chareidi was a fellow named Moses Amramson. In the Hebrew year 2448 (c. 1312 B.C.E.), he ascended Mount Sinai and took dictation from the Boss on a Handbook on how to be a pious Jew. Included was Leviticus 26 which outlines the terms of the deal that I discussed at length in Chapter 1. Henceforth, the chareidim were officially open for business. Before he even had a chance to distribute the copies, some of the new unconfirmed members, who weren't related to the founders of the organization, broke the rules and reconstituted the contraband idolatry – the Golden Calf – that they had pledged to leave at the door. Unfortunately, a few of the confirmed members dabbled with the contraband and thus challenged the integrity of the entire newborn chareidi movement. This original Moses knew that, for now and always, the rules have to stay the same (it was part of the secret) and he declared the first chareidi mantra: *Mi L'Hashem Eilai!* (Whoever is for G-d shall side with me!) Immediately, his entire tribe as well as the vast majority of the confirmed members pledged allegiance to $Xd_{20}Lv_{26}D_6$, the "secret" molecular makeup of the chareidim, and Moses managed to get another copy of the Handbook. The matter was dropped but not forgotten.

The fledgling chareidi society hobbled on for another ten months when the first actual "devastation by Jews themselves" erupted. Moses Amramson had a disciple and relative named Korach Kehati who signed on to Shinui. Korach Kehati felt that the chareidi leadership was wielding far too much power which stopped short of his desk. Kehati went so far as to claim that what Moses taught wasn't genuine and that he wrote up most of the Handbook himself. To that end, he gathered up 250 well-educated MPs[30] and dressed them up from head to toe in blue woolen robes. This group became known as Adat Korach or Korach Kehati's

---

[30] Members of Parliament, i.e., Sanhedrin

Klan. They held a clandestine meeting in the Tabernacle courtyard where they donned the blue robes and burned incense. The fire got out of control and the entire KKK went up in smoke. Korach promptly dropped out of sight but, on the way out, he had a sudden change of heart and he himself declared what was to be – then and always – the official chareidi mantra: *Moshe Emmet V'Torato Emmet* (Moses is genuine and his Torah is genuine).

To this day, this mantra serves as the prime battle cry of the chareidim and it has, whether spoken or unspoken, led us to triumph over every adversary that has challenged the chareidim throughout the generations. And there have been many.

Things calmed down a bit after the Korach incident and for the remainder of his tenure, despite a few isolated incidents of deviancy from the rules, Moses Amramson's ideology and leadership were never again challenged. The chareidim were here to stay.

Just prior to his death, Moses Amramson passed the mantle of leadership and the "secret" to his most devoted disciple, Joshua Fishman.[31] Joshua was such a close reflection of his great master that his 28-year stint as leader of the chareidim went, likewise, unchallenged.[32] Yet, Moses himself had predicted that it wouldn't last and that new ideas would repeatedly penetrate the protective "clouds of glory" and stir up controversy from within. The challengers arose and, each time, the chareidim produced a capable leader who answered the challenge and rallied the faithful with the spirit of *Moshe Emmet V'Torato Emmet*. None of whom was "the first" and none employed any original tactics. The game plan was always the same – just do what it says in the Handbook, the same Handbook that Moses gave us in 2448, and, don't forget the secret.

Joshua passed the secret on to the Elders of the nation, and not a moment too soon. In the days of the Judges, another early "Enlightenment" started to take shape as some communities thought that Judaism could be enhanced by mixing in some of the niceties of foreign cultures. Thus, they introduced the philosophies of the idol Baal into the nation. It is hard for us to understand what were the alluring attributes of this wor-

---

[31] Joshua bin Nun. "Bin Nun" is Aramaic for "son of a fish." The verse in Chronicles I 7:27 confirms that Nun was Joshua's father's actual name. Despite this, I recall hearing an additional commentary that the term "son of a fish" is meant to indicate that he is a descendent of the tribal patriarch Ephraim who is characterized as a fish (Genesis 48:16). At present, I cannot locate this commentary.

[32] As Pirkei Avot (1:1) tells us, this original Joshua Fishman was the divinely chosen successor to assume the role of director of operations for Moses' comprehensive education system – Torah U'Mesora (*Moshe kibel **Torah** m'Sinai u'mesaro l"Yehoshua*).

ship, but judging from the way that masses of unlearned spirit-searching Jews flock to the Far East and study the teachings of Zen, Confucius, and Buddha to this day, such behavior can scarcely be deemed peculiar. There is much room to say that the followers of Baal did not stop observing Shabbat, donning *tefillin*, or eating Kosher, but merely wanted to expand their horizons and fit in with the surrounding cultures. Even then.

Presently, a "leader of the counterchange" by the name of Gideon ben Yoash came up to bat. Like the Chatam Sofer, this fellow made a career of opposing the followers of Baal to the extent that he was nick-named "Baal-Beater." He actually scored some smashing victories and didn't do too badly on the battlefield against Midian, either. He managed to contain the adherence to Baal until his demise but he couldn't eradicate it. He did not declare a mantra but you can bet that he was pushing *Moshe Emmet V'Torato Emmet*. The message: Judaism doesn't need any artificial additives.

Like the modern "Enlightenment," the subversive appeal of Baal plagued the Jews for hundreds of years. Finally, in the era of the first Temple, the situation got so out of hand that the *Maskilim* (followers of Baal) claimed 450 prophets – all of them false – and the chareidim were down to just one – fully genuine – who was still doing business; known to all as Elijah Tishbee.[33] He single-handedly contested (literally) the paradox of being a Jew and a Baalist (the secularists of that era). The big issue of the time was the economy as it hadn't rained for a while and the GNP was next to nil. The leader of the Baalist party was King Achab himself and, as the secular are so fond of doing, they blamed the chareidim. Elijah was able to unequivocally demonstrate that it was not the chareidim that were holding up the rain clouds. The onlookers were so impressed that they declared a new mantra: "G-d is the A-lmighty!" which is a more concise and more sophisticated variation of *Moshe Emmet V'Torato Emett*. The 450 prophets had to resign their seats and the economy immediately improved. The Baalists never won another election.

New and different "Enlightenments" kept popping up, but to us chareidim, it was becoming an all too familiar pattern. In the Second Temple era it was a recurring theme. First, Alexander the Great opened up the country to Greek culture and philosophy and when they made a hard sell to the Jews, lots of them were buying. These Jews called themselves Hellenists and they urged their fellow Jews to "see the light" – there's more to life than toil in Torah. Once again the chareidi leadership held firm. This time it was a fellow named Mattis Hasmonai, the Kohen Gadol

---

[33] Legend has it that his real name was Pinchas Elazari and he was Gideon's main sponsor. See Rashi's commentary to Judges 6:8.

from Upper Modiin (Kiryat Sefer). Hailing from the tribe of Levi, he adopted Moses' original mantra of *Mi L'Hashem Eilai*. Regardless, his true message was *Moshe Emmet V'Torato Emmet*: "Don't buy anything new – it's not made to last." His sons assembled a small army and vanquished the Hellenists. To the untrained eye it appears that the victory was due to raw courage, cunning and brilliant strategy. But the Maccabees knew better. They knew that they won this round only because they remembered the secret. They taught us that darkness can overwhelm us only when we forget the secret. And so, in the depths of winter when the days are shortest and the nights are darkest we light a single candle[34] to remind us of the secret and to dispel the darkness.

The duration of the Second Temple period saw a non-stop parade of new ideologies pass through like traveling snake-oil salesmen. First were the students of Zadok and Baituse who inaugurated the Sadducees. In their wake came the Samaritans and the Essenes and, eventually, the early Christians (*Minnim*). All of these "enlightened" sects were reincarnations of Korach, of "Judaism being devastated by Jews themselves," Jews who maintained that we can eliminate Lv_{26} from the formula and still remain "Jews" – Jews who forgot the secret. And in each reincarnation there was another Moses [the] Sofer. They were such leaders as Shimon ben Shetach, Nochum Ish Gam Zu, Rabbi Yochanan ben Zakai and Rabbi Akiva. During this era, the chareidim went under one of their numerous synonymous monikers – the *Perushim* (Pharisees).[35] Yet they were the same chareidim composed of the same secret molecular formula – $Xd_{20}Lv_{26}D_6$. They inherited the secret from Shimon the Righteous who got it from the last of the Prophets who got it from the Judges who got it from Joshua who got it from the original Moses [the] Sofer.[36]

During the post-Temple Talmudic era there were no new major "Enlightenment" style challenges but Jewish society was split into the dual-personality entity that has characterized us to this very day. There

---

[34] Though our prevailing custom is to light an additional candle each night, the essential commandment is one candle per household.

[35] This designation is the one that the followers of the Gaon of Vilna, who established the first European-chareidi communities in Eretz Israel, initially took for themselves. Technically, it is even now the official term for "today's" chareidim. The term "chareidi" is a more recent variation that was adopted by non-chareidim. Note that the hardcopy version of Encyclopaedia Judaica that was originally published in 1972 does not include an entry entitled Haredim or even Ultra-Orthodox. The expression was hardly in use. It is only the CD-ROM version that was released in 1997 that saw fit to add such an entry. For more on this subject, see Chapter 9.

[36] Pirkei Avot 1:1

were clearly two streams: the *Chaveirim* – the learned, fully mitzvah observant, equivalent to today's "Orthodox," and there were the *Amei Haaratz* – the unlearned, traditional or Masorati style Jew. Yet from this time onward for many centuries the subservience to the nations of the world was heavy and threatening. The pagan cultures of Rome gave way to Christianity, the "religion of love," and somewhere around the third century C.E. they shut the lights on "Enlightenment" by officially incorporating into their doctrines that the Jews are unrepentant Christ-killers and are doomed to eternal damnation. Anti-Semitism was now officially sanctioned as a justified societal norm. In the middle of the seventh century, the Jews were likewise ostracized for rejecting Muhammad. The Jews were widely dispersed into small enclaves throughout the Eastern Hemisphere and they had to do their utmost just to retain their Jewish identity and to band together to ward off the physical threats to their existence. For a while, new assimilationist ideologies were largely absent because, in this setting, it was no longer possible to pretend that we can eliminate the Lv_{26} and still remain Jews.

All of this changed around the year 1450 C.E., although it was a bit too early to notice. A man named Johannes Gutenberg perfected[37] the movable type printing press and the world woke up from its slumber. For the first time, the written word could be mass-produced and widely distributed.[38] Knowledge and literacy began to proliferate throughout Europe. Mathematicians, scientists, astrologers and navigators could publish and disseminate their ideas and discoveries and, consequently, pool their knowledge so that others could study their works and improve on them. The understanding of the physical, cosmic, chemical and biological sciences grew by leaps and bounds over the course of the next three centuries until a new religion arose: *Atheism* – the worship of science and of Man's technological know-how; the idea that Man now knows enough to control his own destiny and that only Man can better Man. And, with this, came liberalism, democracy, and tolerance.

Until now, the non-Jewish masses were characterized as boorish, illiterate, uncouth and superstitious. Thus, it was actually the non-Jewish world that was gaining in literacy and knowledge. The Jews were traditionally among the most literate people in the world and they were always tuned into the arts and sciences. It's not so much that the Jews

---

[37] There is a bit of controversy as to whether he actually invented it and there is no doubt that more primitive methods of block printing predated him. Yet he is credited with fashioning the mechanism that enabled mass-produced printing.

[38] Ironically, one of the first things that was mass-produced and distributed was the aforementioned Handbook including Leviticus 26. Unfortunately, his edition did not include Rashi.

"wanted in" – they had "been there" first. You might say that the non-Jews were catching up to the Jews. The enlightened non-Jews pretended that they were willing to forge an alliance with the Jews (though they still wanted first billing). Of course, none of this was truly new; it was a more sterile, godless Hellenism repackaged in a veil of humanism and tolerance. Unlike Greek Hellenism, the sales pitch was: you can buy this product without selling out on what you have. This new product is godless so it is compatible with all religions (talk about a paradox!). It looked new, and the educated, intellectual, "enlightened" Jews of Western Europe were buying.

But the Jews of Eastern Europe were not. At least, not all of them. These were the chareidim of Europe. The Jews who hadn't forgotten the secret. The Jews who were composed of $Xd_{20}Lv_{26}D_6$ until now and who remained that way.[39] They were the Jews of Poland, Galicia, Lithuania, Hungary, Romania, and Russia. The enlightenment engulfed the Jews of Germany, France, Italy, and Austria and it was moving into Hungary. It just so happened that the most revered and influential Torah scholar who was located at the most Western extreme of the Hungarian region was indeed Rabbi Moses Sofer. He was an unparalleled scholar and an unyielding (to quote Prof. Heilman) "Defender of the Faith." He was the appropriate person in the appropriate place at the appropriate time.

Yet, he did not produce the chareidim. The chareidim produced him. He did not develop $Xd_{20}Lv_{26}D_6$; he developed from it. In one sense he was our leader, teacher, and master, but in a truer sense he was our representative. He was the one that the chareidim put forth to vocally oppose the Maskilim. But there were others. Many others. And if it would not have been him, it would have been someone else.

Undoubtedly, the Chatam Sofer and the Gaon of Vilna, as well as the Baal Shem Tov and others, played a key role in helping the chareidim of 200 years ago preserve their adherence to Leviticus 26. And, granted, the Gaon of Vilna indeed encouraged his followers to bolster the Jewish *yishuv* (settlement) in Eretz Israel. Nevertheless, when we recognize that the chareidi enterprise is a 3,000-plus year continuum, it becomes clear that these great personages alone do not account for why there are chareidim in Israel today. The European Ashkenazim cannot claim to be the only chareidim or the first chareidim – even if they are the only ones who wear *shtreimels*, frocks, and knickers. Any Jew that is composed of $Xd_{20}Lv_{26}D_6$ is chareidi regardless of his national origin; and such Jews

---

[39] It cannot be denied that the Jews of Eastern Europe did a better job of retaining their chareidi status simply because the aforementioned tolerance that devastated Western European Jewry was slow in coming. Indeed, outside of the big cities, it barely got there at all.

have always existed in Israel and throughout the Sephardi communities in North Africa, Turkey, Asia Minor, and Yemen. Indeed, the Ashkenazim are not necessarily the original chareidim of Eretz Israel, yet it is undeniable that the influx of Ashkenazim in the 1800s infused a European Ashkenazi flavor into the adherents of Leviticus 26 and they became the dominant force in the Torah community. Accordingly, the Ashkenazi chareidim personify the common perception of what is generally considered "chareidi" today.

So now we have a different perspective on history. It is quite unlike the history that is taught in Bar Ilan University and Queens College. The history that is taught there is evolutionary history: The world is constantly changing and the inhabitants of the world are temporary guests. The world came into being with no designs for Man – Man simply evolved; Man came into being with no designs for the Jews – the Jews simply evolved; the Jews came into the world with no designs for the chareidim – the chareidim simply evolved; and the chareidim have no designs for the future because their motto is *HaChadash assur min haTorah* – What is new is forbidden from the Torah. They are part of the past and they will stay there, and the evolving future will move on without them.

But I never attended a college or university. I am not sophisticated enough to acknowledge evolution. I only believe in Creation. Creation means that things don't change. They stay the way they have always been from the time that they were created. Men have always been men and apes have always been apes, turtles turtles, and thoroughbred horses horses. As long as the world has existed there has been Man.[40] Man is a constant in Creation. And as long as there has been Man, there has been knowledge of G-d. Torah is a constant. Within mankind, the Jews are a constant and within the Jews the chareidim are a constant. We are in the past and we are in the present and it is we, and only we, that one can be assured shall be here in the future.

Why?

Because *Moshe Emmet V'Torato Emmet.*

---

[40] This statement is predicated on the fact that the Jewish calendar begins from the "formation" of Adam the First Man. There is quite a bit of debate among Torah scholars as to how much "real time" the world was in existence before the debut of Man. I am not taking sides in this debate. Whether the actual time was 5 days or millions or billions of years, our contention is that it was all a concerted preparation for the advent of Man. Man is the culmination of Creation and, therefore, the entire span of Creation was one prolonged Creation of Man.

Author's note: The upcoming chapter is a lengthy and intricate Talmudic discourse. It is intended to illustrate how chareidim think differently (or more profoundly) with regard to some of the primary tenets of Judaism. It is targeted toward the more learned and studious reader and it is not subtle. In short, it is a sermon. If you are not up to taking in a full length sermon but would still like to take in the message of this chapter, then you may prefer to skip to the last few pages – I would recommend Part IV on page 168.

Chapter Six

Getting to the Heart of the Matter

The chareidi view of the commandments

Part I – The Heart beats…the Odds

"I'm a good Jew at heart. G-d understands me."

How many times have we heard this sentiment, emanating predominantly from a non-observant or marginally observant Jew? The observant Jew will typically respond with, "Try telling the tax authorities that you have been paying your taxes at heart. I'm sure they will understand." or "I suppose your heart will go to paradise but we can't be sure about the rest of you."

Regardless, it cannot be said that this sentiment is totally without basis, for even (especially) chareidim are wont to quote the well known Talmudic phrase, "The Holy One requests the heart."[1] It must be that the chareidim understand this phrase differently than the average consumer.

What lies at the heart of the chareidi mindset?

We stated our definition of chareidi as one who adheres to the directive of the verse in Leviticus 26:3 to observe the commandments with toil in Torah. Thus far, we have elaborated on the import of the "toil in Torah" aspect. We suggested that this aspect is what distinguishes the chareidi from the NCOJ. It would seem that in the "commandments"

---

[1] Talmud Bavli Sanhedrin 106b

department, the chareidi and NCOJ stand on equal footing. But even this can only be true if both entities conceptualize the significance of commandments in the same way; and I, for one, am not convinced that such is the case. I am not clear as to how NCOJs conceptualize the significance of commandments nor does it seem as if there is total collusion among their ranks.

The chareidim have a bit of an edge. We can learn these concepts from the words of the Talmudic sages; however, their words are succinct. Their implications must be excavated from beneath the surface – and this requires a bit of toil.

The last words of the Mishna in tractate Makkoth[2] characterize the chareidi perception of commandments:

> Rabbi Chananya ben Akashya says: The Holy One wanted to confer merit on Israel, accordingly, He increased for them [the quantities of] Torah and commandments as it is written, "G-d desires, for the sake of deeming him (i.e., the individual Jew) as righteous, [that he is] to enlarge the Torah and to strengthen it."[3]

This statement implies that G-d did not "have to" give us such an extended list of commandments nor such a vast and complex Torah, but that He did it in order to enable every Jew to readily attain righteousness. How are we to understand this? Can commandments be superfluous? Isn't every commandment essential? Doesn't each one embrace a unique and vital purpose?

The Talmud gives us a clue[4]:

> Rabbi Smalai expounded: 613 commandments were dictated to Moses – 365 negative commandments corresponding to the days of a solar year and 248 positive commandments corresponding to the number of organs in a human being. Said Rav Hamenuna: What is the [indicative] verse? "Torah was commanded to us by Moses as a legacy…"[5] *Torah* has a numerical value of 611[6]; *Anochi* (I am the L-rd your G-d) and *Lo Yihiyeh* (There shall not be any other gods before Me) were heard directly from the mouth of the Almighty.

> [King] David came and reduced the amount to eleven as it states, "A song to David. G-d, who will reside in Your tent, who will dwell in Your

---

2 Talmud Bavli Makkoth 23b

3 Isaiah 42:21

4 Talmud Bavli Makkoth 23b-24a

5 Deuteronomy 33:4

6 Tav = 400, Vav = 6, Resh = 200, Heh = 5. 400 + 6 + 200 + 5 = 611.

holy mountain? One who walks with simplicity, one who performs righteousness…"[7] Isaiah came and reduced the amount to six as is written, "One who goes with righteousness, one who speaks with straightforwardness…"[8] Michah came and reduced the amount to three as is written… Isaiah returned and reduced the amount to two as is written… Habakuk came and reduced the number to one as is written, "And a righteous man with his loyalty shall he live."[9]

Hey, hold on there! How many commandments are there? Aren't there supposed to be lots of them – for our own benefit?

Another question: What is the significance that Moses relayed to us 611 commandments and that we received two commandments directly from G-d? Didn't all of the commandments emanate from G-d? Many of us are familiar with the Talmudic legend[10] that as G-d uttered the first commandment the entire nation fell dead. G-d dispersed a divine dew and revived them. He then uttered the second commandment and, once again, the entire nation fell dead and were again revived. Thereupon, they insisted on hearing the commandments only via relay through Moses. It seems that the direct commandments were limited to two only for this "technical" reason. If the Jews would have had more stamina, perhaps they would have heard three or thirty or all of them. Is this truly so, or is there some special significance that they heard these two, not more and not less?

Lastly, it is a splendid bit of symbolism that the number of negative commandments corresponds to the days of the solar year and that the number of positive commandments corresponds to the number of organs in the human body, but are we to understand this as merely a mnemonic symbol or is something deeper than this being implied?

The Maharsha[11] confronts all of these issues and presents a detailed explanation of this obscure Talmudic passage. He begins by quoting some earlier commentaries, one of which maintains that the later Prophets (David, Isaiah, etc.) were not actually reducing the quantity of commandments but were merely categorizing them into groups to enable people to progressively reach greater levels.[12] The Maharsha rejects this idea by

---

[7] Psalms 15:1-5

[8] Isaiah 33:15

[9] Habakuk 2:4

[10] Talmud Bavli Shabbat 88b

[11] Rabbi Shmuel Eliezer Eideles one of the most popular late-era commentaries on the Babylonian Talmud. His commentary is included in most editions.

[12] It is not clear what this means. I surmise that it may be that each category represents a more advanced level to pace a person's spiritual growth (similar to

noting that at one point the Talmud derives that one need not cover all eleven line items (in the case of King David's list) to qualify for the trophy, but, actually, any one of them will suffice. This approach does not concur with the idea of a sequential progression.

The Maharsha goes on to offer his own explanation. He begins by quoting the commentary of Maimonides to the aforementioned Mishna comprising the statement of Rabbi Chananya ben Akashya. Maimonides states:

> And it is among the principles of our faith in the Torah that if a person should fulfill *any one commandment* of the Creator's 613 commandments as it should be fulfilled, and he does not combine with it any intent of an earthly nature whatsoever, but rather that it is done for its own sake out of love [for G-d]... he is deserving of life in the World to Come. This is because, as there are numerous commandments, it is not possible (i.e., likely) that a person, over the duration of his life, will not perform at least one commandment fully and as directed.

To summarize, Maimonides is telling us that we need only perform one solitary commandment with complete devotion and our fortune is made.

Based on Maimonides, Maharsha interprets the statement of Rabbi Chananya ben Akashya to mean that there are two vantage points – that of Man in the physical world and that of G-d in the spiritual world. From G-d's spiritual "vantage point" physical embodiments have no significance in and of themselves. They are only instruments that enable the physical man to enact a spiritual impulse. This means to say that the physical form of the daily *tefillin* and *tzitzit*, the *matzoh* of Passover, the *shofar* of Rosh Hashana, the *sukka* of Sukkot, etc., are, in actuality, nothing but instruments through which Man can display his allegiance to G-d and forge a connection. This is all that G-d requests from Man.

In other words, in G-d's eyes, there is only one commandment – **Emunah** (*Loyalty to G-d*).[13] This automatically splits into two commandments, the positive and the negative, similar to a Venn diagram – *A* and *A-complement*. *A* is **Anochi Hashem** (I am the L-rd your G-d...). This is the positive – to be loyal to G-d, to acknowledge G-d as One, to fulfill *Anochi Hashem*. *A-complement* is **Lo Yihiyeh** (There shall be no other

_____

the 12 step plan that I alluded to earlier). This is difficult to comprehend because it is hard to see how any one category is more advanced than another.

[13] I am calling this one commandment Emunah as that is what the Maharsha indicates and it concurs with the terminology in Habakuk (And a righteous man, with his Emunah shall live). I believe that this supreme commandment is what the *Chovot HaLevavot* and others refer to as *Yichud Hashem*, acknowledging the Oneness of G-d.

gods before Me). This is the negative – not to be disloyal to G-d, to disavow any other power, to observe *Lo Yihiyeh*.

All that Man has to do to merit life in the World to Come is to fulfill this *one* commandment of Loyalty or *Yichud Hashem*, which, in effect, means to fulfill *Anochi* and to observe *Lo Yihiyeh*. This is what the Psalmist[14] refers to as *Sur MeRah* (turn away from evil) i.e., observe *Lo Yihiyeh* and *VaAseh Tov* (do good) i.e., fulfill *Anochi*. Hence, the Psalmist writes[15]: "Who is the man who desires life (World to Come) who has a longing for days to see [pure] good? ...Turn away from evil and do good, seek peace and pursue it." Fulfilling *Anochi* and observing *Lo Yihiyeh* is the complete ticket. Maimonides implies that this goal is achieved by a single pristine fulfillment or observance. What a deal!

It pays to waste no time to achieve this one commandment of Loyalty. Paradise awaits! But, just a second – slow down. How exactly does one carry out this commandment in "real-time?" We physical beings cannot connect to the spiritual CPU without a graphical user interface.[16] So G-d has developed one for us with a full set of applications and utilities. 611 to be exact. There are 247 positive commandments, all of which are applications for accessing *Anochi*. Likewise there are 364 negative commandments, all of which are "bugs" that will trigger *Lo Yihiyeh* (and crash the system). According to Maimonides, any single time we access *Anochi* or consciously avoid a "bug" (observe *Lo Yihiyeh*) we "score a hit." Rabbi Chananya ben Akashya is telling us that G-d, in His unbridled benevolence, gave us a host of methods of achieving this single commandment of Loyalty to G-d to facilitate each of us to make the grade at least once in his life and to earn a share of Eternity.

The point is that, although each commandment is indeed different and has a distinct physical imprint, at the "receiving station" they all accomplish a like result – lighting up a display of Loyalty to G-d. All of the commandments of the Torah are a light switch for this one light. Therefore, performing one commandment properly has the same result as if one has performed numerous commandments or even the entire Torah. It is similar to the quaint carnival game where one has to hit a disk with a sledgehammer whereupon a puck flies up a shaft. If it flies high enough it rings a bell and the contestant wins a prize. It shouldn't matter if he uses a sledgehammer, a baseball bat, a paddle, a shoe, or whatever. If he hits it hard enough the bell rings and sounds exactly the same. One cannot discern what striking implement was used by the sound of the bell. Even if

---

[14] Psalms 34:15

[15] Ibid 34:13, 15

[16] No, the Maharsha does not use this terminology.

he uses two or more items to do the job, the bell sounds the same as if he used one. So, whether with one stick or 100 sticks, if he hits it right and rings the bell he gets his prize, and if not, not.

Of course, he is well advised not to quit after one success, but this is not merely because the goal is to win more prizes, but because a Jew must be loyal to G-d (and display said loyalty) *all of the time*.

The Maharsha goes on to explain the significance of the symbols. Man was given a body to enable him to "do" – to perform positive actions – and, consequently, to fulfill *Anochi*. Therefore the quantity of commandments (bell ringers or light switches) was set to correspond with the quantity of parts of the body. The most vital human organ is the heart and every other organ is subordinate to it. Therefore, says Maharsha, the heart represents the parent commandment of *Anochi* that we heard directly from G-d and all the other organs represent the physical manifestations of *Anochi*, i.e., the 247 positive commandments that we heard from Moses.

On the flipside (literally), the negative commandments are represented by the number of days in the solar year. This is because the observance of *Lo Yihiyeh* and negative commandments is fulfilled when we have the opportunity and temptation to transgress them. G-d empowered our evil inclination, also called the Satan,[17] to present us with ample opportunity to transgress. This is actually for our benefit as in this way we can "ring the bell" of Loyalty to G-d by, technically, doing nothing. The Hebrew term "HaSatan" (*the* Satan) has a numerical value of 364.[18] This is because the Satan is empowered to test our loyalty 364 days a year. Only one day is his power restrained, the Day of Atonement. On the Day of Atonement almost all physical activities are proscribed and we focus on refraining from all of the negative commandments on the list. This is the purest manifestation of the *Lo Yihiyeh* side of the Loyalty commandment. By restraining ourselves on the Day of Atonement we make a clear declaration (ring the bell) of *Lo Yihiyeh* and in this way we likewise merit a share in the World to Come. Since G-d's *Lo Yihiyeh* is equivalent to all of Moses' 364 negative commandments, when we observe *Lo Yihiyeh* on the Day of Atonement it is considered as if we observed all 364 earthly prohibitions (which, in effect, we have) and thus we are atoned for the failed opportunities that transpired throughout the year.

With this in mind, the Maharsha offers an explanation to a puzzling passage in tractate Eruvin[19]. The Talmud relates that for 2½ years the

---

[17] Talmud Bavli Bava Bathra 16a

[18] *Heh* = 5, *S'in* = 300, *Tet* = 9, *Nun* = 50. 5 + 300 + 9 + 50 = 364.

[19] Talmud Bavli Eruvin 13b

students of Shammai and the students of Hillel debated the issue of whether it is more "convenient" for Man to have been created or more convenient to not have been created. The Talmud resolves that they "counted" and concluded that it would be more convenient for Man to not have been created and now that he is created, he should scrutinize his actions.

The questions abound: What is the crux of the argument? What is meant by the adjective "more" and what is meant by the term "convenient?" What was counted and how does that resolve the issue?[20] And, most vexing, if the merciful G-d created Man and said "and behold it is very good"[21] then is it not obvious that being created is to our advantage?

Says Maharsha that in line with our discussion we can explain it as follows. From G-d's vantage point there is only one two-sided commandment – Loyalty to G-d – which can be achieved via either of two approaches: (1) action, by fulfilling *Anochi*, or (2) inaction, by observing *Lo Yihiyeh*. Clearly, if Man was not created[22], he would be incapable of the *Anochi* approach though he would excel at observing *Lo Yihiyeh*. The observing of *Lo Yihiyeh* would be quite convenient. Conversely, if he is created, he now has the opportunity to fulfill *Anochi* but is likewise susceptible to transgress on prohibitions and negate *Lo Yihiyeh*. Only the *Anochi* approach would be convenient. Each situation has a gain and a risk. The debate centers around which of the two positions is the "more convenient" approach of achieving Loyalty.

To resolve the dilemma, the group took a rather mathematical approach – they simply counted and compared the quantity of positive commandments versus the quantity of negative commandments to determine what are the true "odds." The resulting tabulation was, as we know, 365 negative commandments versus 248 positive ones. This means that for every two opportunities that we have to earn paradise we have close to three opportunities to botch it up. Not such favorable odds. Based on this calculation, the group concluded that it would be more convenient for Man to have not been created because, in that condition, it would be a cinch to observe the numerous negative commandments although he is

---

[20] The classical interpretation is that they simply took a vote and concluded as they did based on the opinion of the majority. The notion that a deep philosophical issue is resolved based on how many members of either party showed up to the plenum on that day is a bit difficult to digest, especially if the vote fell squarely along party lines.

[21] Genesis 1:31

[22] I must postulate that the intention here is not to say that Man would not exist at all, but rather, that he would exist without any physical form. This would somewhat alleviate the obvious question as to how is it possible for Man to be virtuous in his observance of *Lo Yihiyeh* if he does not exist?

thereby hindered from performing any positive ones. The fact that he is created into a physical form is not a convenience as the odds are not in his favor. Therefore, now that he is created, his only recourse is to overcome the odds by "scrutinizing his actions," i.e., by capitalizing on his ability to perform actions and focusing those actions on those that fulfill *Anochi*.

With this, the Maharsha goes on to interpret the verse, "I am asleep, yet my heart is awake." (***Ani yeshaina v'libi ehr.***)[23]

Ani yeshaina – I am asleep. We would be at an advantage were we to be asleep – i.e., not physically created – because, in that way we would be in full compliance of the 365 negative commandments. Maharsha notes that the numerical value of *yeshaina* (asleep) is 365.[24]

V'Libi ehr – yet my heart is awake. Maharsha quotes a Midrash on this verse:

> Says Rabbi Chiya bar Abba: From where do we know that the Holy One is the heart of Israel? As the verse states, "The rock of my heart and my portion is G-d."[25]

In G-d's realm there is but one commandment, the positive side of which, *Anochi Hashem*, is represented by the heart of the human body which is the root of vitality for all of the other organs. As Man was indeed created, he must activate his heart, i.e., scrutinize his actions to fulfill *Anochi*.

We now have a clearer understanding – the chareidi understanding – of the Talmudic edict, "The Holy One requests the heart." The heart represents the sole positive commandment from G-d's vantage point and likewise translates into all of the positive commandments in our physical world. To be a "good Jew at heart" one must focus his actions toward fulfilling *Anochi* and "beating the odds." And he must undertake those actions for, if not, it would be more convenient if he were not created.

Finally, the Maharsha offers his explanation to the ensuing lines of the Talmud which states that King David reduced the number to eleven, Isaiah reduced it to six, Micah to three, Isaiah again to two, and, ultimately, Habakuk reduced it to one. He says that we now understand that every physical commandment is merely a method of fulfilling *Anochi* and that any individual one is equally capable of achieving this goal and conferring the doer with a share in the World to Come. Nevertheless, not all the commandments are equally accessible as some only apply to cer-

---

[23] Song of Songs 5:2

[24] *Yud* = 10, *Shin* = 300, *Nun* = 50, *Heh* = 5. 10 + 300 + 50 + 5 = 365

[25] Psalms 73:26

tain classes (e.g., Kohen or Levi), to particular callings (e.g., farmers, landowners, moneylenders, employers), to the different genders, and at specified times (e.g., day or night, festivals, Shmitta and Jubilee, etc.) As such, King David endeavored to isolate those commandments that are accessible to all people at all times and to package them into categories to facilitate the individual to find at least one convenient commandment by which to merit Eternity. He compiled eleven categories. Subsequently, Isaiah merged them into six categories that are more rudimentary and that every human being is expected to uphold. Micah was able to further glean the list into three fundamentals: doing justice, loving kindness, and behaving modestly before G-d. Isaiah further presents that of these three, the two that involve inter-human relations are the primary ones. Finally, comes Habakuk and brings us right back to where we started; that all of the commandments are actually exercises in one grand undertaking – faith and loyalty to G-d – and that this endeavor is in affect for all Jews at all times.

Part II – Pulling at the Heartstrings

We now understand what is the true essence of a Torah commandment in the heart of a chareidi. In G-d's realm, all of the commandments are one (Loyalty or *Yichud Hashem* via *Anochi/Lo Yihiyeh*), so we can accurately construe that G-d's oneness fuses all of the commandments together. In our earthly realm, each commandment takes on a distinct characteristic and is relegated to its specific time, place, and constituency. Yet, our sages tell us of certain commandments that their intrinsic value is, of itself, equivalent to all of the other individual commandments. On this note, three commandments[26] are singled out for special recognition: Keeping the Sabbath, the *tzitzit*, and our old friend, reciting the *Shema*.

Why are these three so special?

Based on our discussion, the answer is self-explanatory (but I will explain it, anyhow): they all explicitly symbolize *Anochi* and *Lo Yihiyeh*.

Let us examine the *Shema*. In Chapter 3, we observed that the recital of *Shema* is a realization of toil in Torah study and that it can single-handedly entitle the recitor to the accompanying benefits. At that point, I

---

[26] To be fair, throughout the Talmud and Midrash, we find seven commandments that are ascribed with this attribute: the three that I discuss here plus charity, circumcision, settling the Land of Israel, and, in a negative connotation, the sin of idolatry. The three that I discuss are, nevertheless, outstanding as for each of them we find sources that relate them to the other two, not to mention the ensuing discourse here. Obviously, I do not mean to preclude Torah study, which, as has been already discussed at length, is on a plane of its own.

was somewhat at a loss trying to explain *why* the reciting of the *Shema* is such a potent feat. But now, once we have determined that the entire body of commandments is the advancement of the concepts of *Anochi* and *Lo Yihiyeh*, we notice that this declaration encapsulates this ideal, and does so repeatedly.

Hence, the opening line:

Shema Yisrael – Hear O Israel

Hashem E-loheinu – The L-rd is our G-d ➔	**Anochi Hashem E-lohecha** – I am the L-rd your G-d
Hashem Echad – G-d is One ➔	**Lo Yiheyeh elohim acheirim** – There shall not be any other gods before me

Here we have it, all 613 commandments in one breath. We have just now recited the complete body of Law as it exists in G-d's realm.[27]

In the first paragraph of *Shema*, we dwell a bit on this ethereal concept that we must love G-d with all our heart, soul, and strength and we must study the Torah and teach it to our children. Although this paragraph introduces to us the commandments of *tefillin* and *mezuzah* as a way of affirming our commitment, it really makes no mention of any general requirement for performing physical commandments. This is because, in this paragraph, we are discussing the commandment at the "receiving end." There is but one two-part commandment and it is not physical. Indeed, in many prayer books, it is annotated that when reciting the first paragraph of *Shema* one should bear in mind that he is fulfilling the commandment of *Yichud Hashem* as well as *Kabbalat Ohl Malchut Shamayim* (acceptance of the yoke of the Kingdom of Heaven).

The second paragraph brings us down to our neck of the woods. Here G-d speaks to us in our physical language and tells us what we must do "over here" to fulfill the one commandment "over there." There are three parts to this diktat: (a) the requirement to fulfill positive commandments – to love G-d and to serve Him (*Anochi*) – and the reward for compliance, (b) the admonition against transgressing negative commandments – the focus is on worshipping foreign powers (*Lo Yihiyeh*) – and the punishment for said transgression, and (c) a repetition of the requirement to study the Torah, to teach it to your children and to post these instructions on one's person (*tefillin*) and on the doorposts (*mezuzah*). For this paragraph, the user-friendly prayer books instruct us to bear in mind *Kabbalat Ohl Mitzvot* (acceptance of the yoke of obligation to fulfill the commandments).

Finally, we recite the passage of the commandment of *tzitzit*. The

---

[27] See Maharsha tractate Menachot 43b s.v. *U'Reitem*

Talmud in tractate Berachot[28] inquires as to why this paragraph qualifies as the closing paragraph of the declaration of *Shema* (perhaps it is bothered that it does not deal with the generalities of love of G-d and of studying and teaching Torah.) The Talmud responds that it features five matters that one must internalize on a daily basis – (1) the commandment of *tzitzit*, (2) recalling the exodus from Egypt, (3) acceptance of the yoke of performing commandments, (4) the prohibition to entertain thoughts of heresy and idolatry, and (5) not to entertain thoughts of sinfulness. Despite this five-point list, Maimonides[29] cites only two of these features – numbers 2 and 3 (in reverse order) – as the primary reasons for including this passage in the Shema. Specifically, in order to explain why the sages appended this passage to the other two passages, Maimonides remarks that this paragraph "also entails the command to recollect all of the commandments" (Feature #3). In his following item, he validates why we recite this third paragraph even at night, when the obligation to wear *tzitzit* does not apply, by explaining that it mentions the exodus from Egypt (Feature #2) and, that by reciting this passage with the *Shema* on a daily and nightly basis, we fulfill our obligation to "recollect the day of your exodus from the Land of Egypt all of the days of your lives".[30]

Of these two qualifications that are cited by Maimonides, Keseph Mishna[31] seems to favor the second qualification as the more comprehensive one as he asks why Maimonides even bothers to cite the first qualification. He answers that the second qualification serves to explain only the significance of reciting this passage but it does not explain in what way this passage is linked to the other two. The first explanation illustrates how this passage is related.

I thought it a bit curious that according to Maimonides, and more so in light of the comments of Keseph Mishna, the first of the five features that the Talmud mentions as to why this passage is included – the basic commandment of *tzitzit* – being completely ignored, does not seem to figure significantly (or at all) into the equation. Additionally, the gist of Keseph Mishna's comment (why does Maimonides cite the first qualification?) seems to suggest that Maimonides' first qualification by itself would be insufficient cause to include this passage. Perhaps it is because, although this passage "also entails the command to recollect all of the

---

[28] Talmud Bavli Berachot 12b

[29] Maimonides, Yad HaChazaka, Ahava, Hilchot Kriat Shema 1:2,3

[30] Deuteronomy 16:3. The sages (T.B. Berachot 12b) derive from the terminology that this recollection must be undertaken each day and each night.

[31] Commentary to Maimonides by Rabbi Joseph Karo author of Shulchan Aruch. Maimonides, Yad HaChazaka, ad loc.

commandments," it would still be only a "distant relative" to the first two passages as there are other passages that underscore this concept that are much closer in proximity and linguistic style[32] to the other two – in other words, there are "closer" relatives.[33]

Our current trend of thought, however, casts a new light upon this matter and helps us to realize that this passage may be more closely related than it appears and that the concept of the *tzitzit* is vitally significant.

The Torah commands that the *tzitzit* should include a string of *t'chelet* (light blue wool). Thereupon, one should gaze upon the *tzitzit* and thereby "recollect all of the commandments of G-d".[34]

How does the *tzitzit* inspire one to recollect all of the commandments of G-d?

Herein lays a dispute between Rashi and Nachmanides.[35] Rashi posits that the numerical value of the word *tzitzit* is 600.[36] The traditional number of strings (after they are doubled) is eight and the traditional number of knots is five. $600 + 8 + 5 = 613$ or the total number of commandments.

Nachmanides is not comfortable with this explanation as (a) the Torah's spelling of the word *tzitzit* omits the second *Yud* thus reducing our numerical count by ten and (b) the number of strings and knots, although they are traditional, are not mandatory. Nachmanides contends that the impetus for recollection is the string of blue wool as the word *t'chelet* is a consonantal of the word *tachlit* which means "all encompassing purpose." Furthermore, he quotes the Talmud in tractate Menachot[37] that states that the reason for the color blue is that "*t'chelet* resembles the sea, the sea resembles the sky, and the sky resembles the Throne of Glory."

The words of these scholars are sufficient to us and "all those who

---

[32] Deuteronomy is Moses' narrative and reflects a unique style. The passage of *tzitzit* is in Numbers (15:37-41).

[33] One prominent example would be Deuteronomy 7:12.

[34] Numbers 15:39

[35] Rabbi Moses ben Nachman also known as RaMBaN. He lived approximately 150 years after Rashi and is without question one of the most venerated commentators of his era. In his introduction, he states that one of the objectives of his commentary is to challenge Rashi's opinions. His commentary is much more elaborate than is Rashi's.

[36] *Tzadi* = 90, *Yud* = 10, *Tzadi* = 90, *Yud* = 10, *Tav* = 400. $90 + 10 + 90 + 10 + 400 = 600$.

[37] Talmud Bavli Menachot 43b

add, detract".[38] Yet, if I may be so bold, I wish to suggest two additional ideas, in line with our discussion; one is a complement to Rashi's opinion and the other is a complement to Nachmanides.

Idea #1 – We have just previously stated that the entire body of commandments from G-d's realm is condensed into the two commandments that were heard directly from G-d: *Anochi* and *Lo Yihiyeh*. We further stated that *Anochi* and *Lo Yihiyeh* are themselves condensed into the two phrases of the opening line of *Shema*: **Hashem E-loheinu** (*Anochi*) and **Hashem Echad** (*Lo Yihiyeh*). There is room to suggest that these two edicts can be further condensed into the two words, *Hashem Echad*[39]: **Hashem** = *Anochi Hashem* and **Echad** = *Lo Yihiyeh lecha elohim acheirim*. Aside from the tradition of five knots and eight strings, there is also a tradition to the number of windings between each knot. The accepted Ashkenazi[40] custom is the following order: Top knot › 7 windings › Second knot › 8 windings › Third knot › 11 windings › Fourth knot › 13 windings › Fifth knot. The most popular explanation for this sequence of numbers is that the first three groups, $7 + 8 + 11$, add up to 26 which is the numerical equivalent to the four letter name of G-d[41] (the one that appears in *Shema* which we mask by colloquially saying "Hashem"). The last group, 13, is the numerical equivalent of the word "*Echad*".[42] Hence, the 39 windings say to us "*Hashem Echad*" which, according to my thesis, is a condensed version of *Anochi* and *Lo Yihiyeh*. As such, this represents "all of the commandments of G-d."

Idea #2 – Rabbi Chaim of Volozhin[43] made the following observation: The Talmud in tractate Menachot (the passage that Nachmanides refers to) sets out to explain why, of all colors, *t'chelet* (light blue) is chosen for the special string. The Talmud does not bother to first ask why it is that any special colored string is mandated to complement the white strings in the first place. The implication is that, to the sages of the Talmud, the impetus for having one colored string in the company of

---

[38] Talmud Bavli 29a

[39] It doesn't end there. There is yet room to condense these two concepts into the first two and last two letters of the four letter name, and further, into the Yud and the Heh of the first two letters themselves. Read on.

[40] The Sephardim have a different tradition so this idea wouldn't apply to them. I thought it sort of fanciful that this idea works in consonance with Rashi's numerical explanation as Rashi was Ashkenazi. Nachmanides, who opts for the more colorful explanation, was Sephardi.

[41] *Yud* = 10, *Heh* = 5, *Vav* = 6, *Heh* = 5. $10 + 5 + 6 + 5 = 26$

[42] *Aleph* = 1, *Chet* = 8, *Dalet* = 4. $1 + 8 + 4 = 13$

[43] Ruach Chaim on Avot 3:1. Rabbi Chaim of Volohzin was one of the foremost

uncolored strings is patently obvious, the only question is: why this particular color? He asks, what, then, is the impetus that was so obvious to the sages of the Talmud?

He goes on to explain that the purpose of the *tzitzit* is to cause us to recollect all of the commandments of G-d. We know that there are two forms of commandments – positive and negative. Positive commandments entail some form of action. With this action we create, build, or remedy some spiritual entity that must be created, built, or rectified. A positive commandment is often referred to as an *assiah* (action or deed), but, additionally, is characterized as the manifestation of a *zechira* (commemoration). Negative commandments entail restraint. With this restraint we obstruct a potentially dangerous force – which would come about if we commit the prohibited act – that would damage or destroy a "healthy" spiritual entity. In other words, we fulfill negative commandments by protecting or guarding what is spiritually intact against destruction. A negative commandment is referred to as a *shemira* (safeguard).

White represents what is spiritually pure, clean, and intact. It says to us that we must stand on guard and protect the white from becoming sullied or colored. Color (any color) represents the converse of white. It is something that contains some degree of darkness, something that is spiritually "tainted," something that is not completely pure or intact, something that requires *tikkun* (rectification). Color says to us that we must do something positive to dispel the darkness and to bring it closer to white. In this way, the white strings represent all of the negative commandments that are characterized as a *shemira* from defilement. The colored strings represent all of the positive commandments that demand some form of *zechira* (and *assiah*) to enact a spiritual *tikkun*.

Now we understand why it is so fundamentally essential that one string must be colored and the remainder should be white. It is by gazing on this contrast of color against the white that we can simultaneously recollect all of the commandments of G-d – i.e., the negative commandments represented by the white strings and the positive commandments represented by the colored string. This was well understood by the sages of the Talmud. Their only question was why, of all colors, was *t'chelet* the color of choice to represent the positive commandments? To this they answer that *t'chelet* resembles the sea, the sea resembles the sky, and the sky resembles the Throne of Glory.

With this explanation we can look at the words of the passage of

---

students of the Gaon of Vilna. This portion was adapted from an address delivered by Rabbi E. Svei at a sheva berachot celebration in Philadelphia, Pennsylvania in June, 1977.

tzitzit with added clarity. The Scripture states[44]:

> *"...and you shall place on the fringe at the edge a string of t'chelet.*
> *And it will be for you for a fringe and you will view it and you*
> *will recollect all of the commandments of G-d and you will per-*
> *form them and you shall not explore after your hearts and after*
> *your eyes, as you are prone to following after them. In order that*
> *you should recollect and perform all of my commandments and*
> *be holy for your G-d. I am the L-rd your G-d that I have extri-*
> *cated you from the Land of Egypt; I am the L-rd your G-d."*

And you shall place on – along with – ***the fringe*** –the white strings
that comprise the fringe – ***a string of t'chelet*** – a string of a contrasting
color which is to be *t'chelet*. ***And it will be for you for a fringe*** – the
white and the *t'chelet* combined – ***and you will view it*** – the contrast of
blue on white – ***and you will recollect all of the commandments of G-d***
– both the positive and the negative commandments – ***and you will per-***
form them – the color will inspire you to carry out the *zechira* and the
assiah and to perform the positive commandments – ***and you shall not***
explore after your hearts and after your eyes, as you are prone to fol-
lowing after them – the white will enjoin you to observe the *shemira* and
not to transgress on the negative commandments. The passage repeats:
In order that you should recollect (tizkaru) and perform (va'assitem)
all of my commandments – *zechira/assiah*, the positive commandments
– ***and be holy for your G-d*** – *shemira*, the negative commandments. ***I am***
the L-rd your G-d that I have extricated you from the Land of Egypt –
Anochi Hashem E-lohecha asher hotzeiticha…; ***I am the L-rd your G-d***
– *Lo Yihiyeh lecha elohim acheirim.*[45]

As I indicated, the first of these two ideas, the one that deals with
numerical symbolism, is akin to Rashi's explanation which is, likewise,
premised on numerical letter values. The second idea which focuses on
the contrast of the blue colored string is akin to Nachmanides who, likewise, emphasizes this feature. But, aside from that, within the scope of
our discussion, there is another quite noteworthy distinction between these
two ideas. The first one describes how the *tzitzit* remind us of all of ***G-d's***
commandments, i.e., G-d's "two" spiritual commandments of *Anochi* and
Lo Yihiyeh as represented by the phrase "*Hashem Echad.*" The second

---

[44] Numbers 15:38-41

[45] This negative connotation can be inferred from the "unneeded" repetition of
the positive phrase as we find in the exegesis of the Passover Haggadah of the
end of the verse in Exodus 12:12: *Ani Hashem – Ani Hu V'Lo Acheir* (I am
G-d – I am He and none other).

idea describes how the *tzitzit* remind us of all of G-d's **commandments**, i.e., the physical positive and negative commandments that exist in *our* realm.

We can now turn our attention to the third "special" commandment – the keeping of Shabbat. Two concepts that we "discovered" in connection to the *tzitzit* come back to visit us when we examine the essence of Shabbat. The first is that the positive commandments, the *Anochi*, are characterized as a *zechira* and that the negative commandments, the *Lo Yihiyeh*, are characterized as a *shemira*.[46] The second concept is the significance of the number 39 as the numerical value of the phrase "*Hashem Echad*" which we posited as a reference to *Anochi* and *Lo Yihiyeh* fused together.

In the first version of the Ten Commandments, the fourth item reads, "Remember (*Zachor*) the day of Sabbath to sanctify it." In the second version of the Ten Commandments, it reads, "Guard (*Shamor*) the day of Sabbath to sanctify it." The sages explain that when G-d uttered this commandment to Moses (which only occurred once), He sounded both words in a single utterance "what a human mouth cannot pronounce and what a human ear cannot discern."[47] If Man cannot perceive such an utterance, what is achieved thereby?

Here, once again, G-d is "laying down the law" on His terms (more accurately – *using* His terms). We are taught that Sabbath observance is an *Oht*, a sign of acknowledgment, that G-d created the world and is the Master over all of creation, that all that we accomplish during our working days is by His will, and, consequently, our achievements will not be one iota more productive by working "overtime" nor will they be any less productive if we conform to His work schedule and take a day off. In short, it is a declaration of faith and loyalty, an embodiment of the *single* commandment of **Emunah** (faith or loyalty) that underwrites the entire fleet of 613 subroutines á là the Prophet Habakuk. Of course, to us multidimensional beings, there must be a positive aspect and a negative aspect; but to G-d, they are one and the same. Therefore, G-d instructs us to observe the Shabbat in His non-dimensional superhuman terminology – to do the *zachor*, the *Anochi*, and to observe the *shamor*, the *Lo Yihiyeh*, with a single utterance (which, most likely, did not occupy any unit of time). Of course, this is way too abstract for us, so, we must break it down into discernible physical components.

The sages tell us that Shabbat is a microcosm of the World to Come.[48]

---

[46] See Rashi's commentary on Deuteronomy 33:9 s.v. *Ki Shamru*

[47] Talmud Bavli Shavuot 20b

[48] Talmud Bavli Berachot 57b

It is an ethereal time wherein we are visitors in G-d's domain. As such, we truly only observe two commandments – *Zachor* and *Shamor*, a variation of *Anochi* and *Lo Yihiyeh*. The regular part of the week is *olam hazeh*, this world, where we have 611 other commandments to observe.[49] We perform our obligations during the weekdays by utilizing 39 types of activities. In other words, during the week, we sanctify the 39 types of activities by executing them to carry out the commandments and to pursue our livelihoods. On Shabbat we sanctify the same 39 types of activities by refraining from their execution. In this way, throughout all seven days of the week we can make 39 declarations of G-d's supremacy; with our (weekday) actions and our (Shabbat) inactions we scream out, "*Hashem Echad.*"[50]

Part III – Home is Where the Heart(h) Is

By now, you have probably noticed a pattern or, shall we say, a recurring theme. Let us review the list of characters:

Emunah – Yichud Hashem	
Anochi Hashem	*Lo Yihiyeh*
Positive commandments	*Negative commandments*
Aseh Tov	*Sur MeRah*
Hashem E-loheinu	*Hashem Echad*
Hashem	*Echad*
T'chelet	*White*
Zachor	*Shamor*
Weekday	*Shabbat*

Can we add to this list? (Please, no!)

Well, call me cruel (it may be one of the nicer things I hear when this book comes out), but I am not dismissing the audience just yet. It's time to get a bit personal.

As we recall the statement of Rabbi Chananya ben Akashya – that G-d wished to confer merit upon the Jewish people and, accordingly, He loaded us up with all kinds of virtue-heavy commandments and an inex-

---

[49] We can actually observe Shabbat during the week when we actively prepare and when we delegate special things for Shabbat.

[50] Though I do not pretend to speak for the composer, I believe that this concept may be amply represented in the words of the acclaimed *Lecha Dodi* poem that all Jewish congregations recite on Friday evenings written by the Kabbalist Rabbi Shlomo HaLevi Alkabetz of Safed. The opening stanza states: *Shamor V'Zachor B'dibur Echad* (*Shamor* and *Zachor* in a single utterance) / *Hishmiyanu E-l HaMeyuchad* (Was sounded to us by the Unique G-d) / *Hashem Echad U'Shmo Echad* (G-d is One and His name is One) / *L'Shem U'L'Tiferet*

haustible program of Torah study and, as such, we are never lacking for scoring opportunities – we may not help but notice that this system seems to bypass a significant portion of the population (possibly the majority): those of the female persuasion.

Evidently, women have a very meager connection to the positive commandments. Indeed, there are but three positive commandments that are designated specifically for women and two forms of obligatory offerings (aside from personal sin offerings) and they are required to partake in matzoh and *marror* (bitter herbs) on Passover, *kiddush* on Friday nights, *havdalah*, Grace after meals and *mezuzah*.[51] They are also obligated in the Rabbinical commandments of *megillah*, Chanuka lights, four cups of wine on Passover, and blessings of enjoyment. After these, the pickings are slim.[52] Clearly, Rabbi Chananya ben Akashya's uplifting homily does not endow the women with the full range of benefits. Could it be, as some feminists assert, that G-d is interested in a discriminatory system of virtue in an effort to bar women from paradise?

I believe that most of us would consider such a notion patently ridiculous. Moreover, this assertion can hold true only if one believes that men and women are two distinct competing species of human-kind who manage to cohabitate when the conditions for such happen to be favorable. Furthermore, such an opinion relies on the assumption that G-d "Himself" can be characterized as male in a biological sense.[53] Ironically, these (mis)conceptions are propagated mostly by those who consider themselves as liberal and egalitarian.[54] The "chauvinistic" charei-

---

V'L'Tehilla (For renown, for majesty and for praise).

[51] The issue of prayer is a bit complicated.

[52] Women are exempt from all time oriented commandments besides *matzoh* and *marror* and the Rabbinic ones I mentioned. They are likewise totally exempt from the ever present obligation of Torah study, the essential obligation of marriage and reproduction, and from the pilgrimage on the festivals except for the special *Hakhel* that follows the sabbatical year. Though a woman may be a *mohel* and a *shochet*, it is certainly not the norm. Virtually all the laws of testimony and judicial proceedings, establishing the months, warfare, commerce, trade and agriculture, and the Temple service are outside of their jurisdiction. The communal requirements of building the Temple and appointing a king are undoubtedly carried out by the men. Of course, if they do engage in trade and commerce and agriculture, they are obligated to all the tithes, charity, and apportioning, paying workers on time, sending away a mother bird, and they are obligated in the levirate marriage. All of these, however, are actually negative commandments that are transformed to a positive (*lahv hanitak l'aseh*).

[53] No, I haven't overlooked Rashi's commentary on Numbers 20:1. Also of interest is Rashi's commentary on Numbers 5:12 although Rashi himself negates the biological connotation in his commentary on Exodus 15:3.

[54] This brings back fond memories of the bumper sticker slogan that was

dim believe otherwise.

To review the question, we are asking that if the purpose of such an extensive list of commandments is to give us maximal opportunity to merit virtue, why are women denied a large share of this opportunity?[55] (Note – we are not asking, as the Talmud in Berachot[56] asks, how do women merit paradise if they have so few obligations, but rather, why is it that they were not given as much opportunity as were the men?)

Numerous Rabbinical scholars explain that men were created to civilize this world by engaging in industry, production, commerce, mastering the sciences, and, when necessary, warfare. To this end it was necessary to imbue man with fierce and passionate drives to motivate him to reach his full potential. These drives generally fall into three categories of lust: lust for wealth (*kihnah* – envy), lust for bodily pleasure (*taavah* – craving), and lust for glory and fame (*kavod* – honor). Although these drives cause man to succeed, they are simultaneously tremendous obstacles for self-discipline and for forging a path to G-d. To compensate for this shortcoming, G-d gave us [men] a full spectrum of "channels" to Him in the hope that every man will find at least one that can suit him. Conversely, women were not meant to be the instigators of all the above achievements and therefore there was no need to instill in women these lustful drives at the same scale as men. As such, their conduit to G-d is not fraught with obstacles to the same degree; hence, they have no need for such a full range of commandments.

While this explanation seems to adequately explain why it is not necessary that women should be as burdened as the men, it still falls somewhat short of explaining why they are held back from performing many of the commandments. Of course, based on the response of the Talmud in Berachot that I (parenthetically) alluded to earlier – that women merit paradise by means of supporting, encouraging and enabling their menfolk[57] to study and perform commandments – it follows that women are actually not excluded from any commandments, but rather, can be active participants in a supporting role. Still this avenue entails being fully dependent on the achievements of the men (who, to be fair, do not

---

disseminated by the feminist movement at the height of its renaissance three decades ago: "When god made man, she was only kidding."

[55] Indeed, the Talmud in tractate Kiddushin 34a excludes mezuzah from the commandments that do not pertain to women using the argument, "This commandment is followed by the urging of the Torah 'In order to increase your days' – i.e., extend your life. [Can we claim that only] men require life and women do not require life?"

[56] Talmud Bavli Berachot 17a

[57] Even women who are not married can support their sons, parents, siblings, and/

always get the job done); and so we ask, why is it that women do not have independent access to these channels?

Perhaps, the rudiments of the Maharsha and the trend of our discussion can satisfy this question, as well.

Many readers may be familiar with the following discourse as it is a very popular generic sermon that is frequently presented at *sheva berachot* celebrations:

The Talmud in tractate Sota states[58]: **Man (*Ish*) and Woman (*Isha*) – if they are worthy, G-d is with them; if they are unworthy, a fire consumes them.** Rashi explains that the Hebrew spelling of the word *ish* (Man) is *Aleph-Yud-Shin*. The Hebrew spelling of the word *isha* (Woman) is *Aleph-Shin-Heh*. They are essentially the same root, except that the man has a *Yud* and the woman has a *Heh*. The Hebrew letters *Yud* and *Heh* comprise an abbreviated version of G-d's name. When Man and Woman are worthy, i.e., they conduct their relationship according to the Will of G-d, they sustain G-d's presence between them and the letters *Yud* and *Heh* of G-d's name that He contributes to their essence is preserved and, in turn, preserves them. If they are unworthy, He withdraws His presence and thereby withdraws the *Yud* that is His contribution to Man and the *Heh* that is His contribution to Woman. In both cases, the resulting essence are the Hebrew letters *Aleph* and *Shin* which spell out the Hebrew word *esh* (fire) to indicate that their relationship will transform into a fire of rage and consume them.

Typically, the homily ends here and the speaker goes on to hurriedly wrap up his speech and convey his blessings to the newlywed couple before the non-dairy frozen dessert completely melts into oblivion. But, for us chareidim, it may be a tad bit too soon to relax and enjoy the dessert. The discourse continues.[59]

Why exactly is it that, of the two divine letters, the man is bequeathed the *Yud* and the woman is bequeathed the *Heh*?

For this we must study a passage in Talmud tractate Menachot[60]:

Rabbi Judah the Prince asked of Rabbi Ami: What is the meaning of the verse, *Have trust in G-d for all Eternity for with Ya-H* (the abbreviated name of G-d that consists of a Yud and a Heh) *G-d has formed*

---

or the community in general. Nobody needs to be left out.

[58] Talmud Bavli Sota 17a

[59] This portion is a continuation of the address that was delivered by Rabbi E. Svei as noted above (note 43). This also appears in Sefer Kehillat Yitzchok by Rabbi Isaac Neeman of Janowa (Vilna, 1900) attributed to Rabbi Elyakim Getzel of Zambrow.

[60] Talmud Bavli Menachot 29b

worlds [61]...? This concurs with the exegesis of Rabbi Yehuda bar Rav Iloyi who expounded, "These are the two worlds that the Holy One created – *olam hazeh* (this world) and *olam haba* (the afterlife or the World to Come) – one of which was created with the letter *Heh* and the other was created with the letter *Yud*; but I still cannot determine if the World to Come was created with a *Yud* and the present world was created with a *Heh* or vice-versa. When we find the verse, ***These are the products of the heavens and the earth*** (i.e., this world) ***in the course of their creation (b'hibaraam)*** [62]... and we expound "Do not read the word as *b'hibaraam* (in the course of their creation), but rather *b'Heh baraam* (with the letter *Heh* they were created)." [63] I now understand that it is the present world that was created with the *Heh* and, consequently, the World to Come is created with the *Yud*. And why was the present world created with a *Heh*? Because this world resembles a three-sided structure (i.e., a structure with a roof but with less than four walls that is not fully enclosed) that whoever wishes to exit may do so...and why is the World to Come created with a *Yud*? To symbolize that the righteous who inhabit it are few in number (as the letter *Yud* is the smallest of all Hebrew letters)...

Thus far, we understand that the letter *Yud* is symbolic of the World to Come and that the letter *Heh* is symbolic of the present world. Now, let us note a passage in tractate Bava Metzia [64]:

And Rav said: All those who follow the counsel of their wives will eventually fall into *Gehinnom* (Hell) as is written...Said Rav Pappa to Abaye: Is there not a popular adage, "If your wife is petite, [it is advisable to] bend over to whisper to her [to seek her opinion]?" This is not contradictory! This statement [of Rav] is regarding [outside] worldly matters, this statement [of Rav Pappa] is regarding household matters. Another version: This statement [of Rav] is regarding heavenly (spiritual or religious, i.e., other-worldly) matters, this statement [of Rav Pappa] is regarding present-world matters.

If we consider the second version of the Talmud's solution, we can perceive a deeper reason [65] why G-d created mankind in two genders,

---

[61] Isaiah 26:4

[62] Genesis 2:4

[63] This is derived from noting the tradition that the letter *Heh* in this word is purposely inscribed a different size (smaller) than the normal size of the letters being penned. This distinction signifies that we view the letter *Heh* as separate from the rest of the word, as if it is a distinct word. Hence the word *b'hibaraam* is broken into two words – *b'Heh baraam*.

[64] Talmud Bavli Bava Metzia 59a

[65] Obviously, I mean in addition to more superficial biological reasons. We may fool ourselves to think that the biological phenomena are the main factor

male and female. *Man*[66] must simultaneously manage his status in two worlds – *olam hazeh* and *olam haba*. His job in *olam hazeh* is to maintain and enhance [quality of] life for himself and others. He does not need to actively acquire life or a life-sustaining world as they are both already present. Rather, his job is to preserve this world and the life it supports. In short, his mission in regard to *this* world is a passive one of *shemira* (guarding or preserving) as is signified by the white of the *tzitzit*. In this world, *Lo Yihiyeh* dominates – do not do what is destructive to your existence.

Additionally, he has a second mission – to make use of this *olam hazeh* and his allotment of life to create and build an afterlife, an *olam haba*. This World to Come must be created and life therein must be earned. This is the *zechira* and *assiya* that is signified by the *t'chelet* in the *tzitzit* that indicates that there is something active that must be done. This is dominated by *Anochi – I am G-d who extricated you from the Land of Egypt to be your G-d*. Come close to Me and prolong (immortalize) your existence.

The Talmud states that initially the first *Man* was a man and woman fused together.[67] One reason for this is that the Torah tells us that *Man* was created in G-d's image. This can be understood in a physical sense that just as G-d is One and is neither distinctly male nor female but a (The) complete indivisible all-encompassing being, the original *Man* was also a single complete physical being. However, *Man* cannot be G-d and *Man* cannot be One, *Man* is merely "one." He who is One (G-d) can think all thoughts, utter all words, hear all sounds, and be all places as One. He who is "one" (*Man*) can think one thought, utter one word, hear one sound, and be in only one place at any one time. Likewise, he can only focus his efforts on one goal at any given time. Yet, he has two missions or, as is our trend, one complementary two-fold mission.

This two-fold mission is a bit much for "one" *Man* to handle. G-d understands this and proclaims, "It is not good for *Man* to be by himself,

---

because we notice that all vertebrae and even many plants are male and female and none of this *olam haba* talk applies to them. With this discussion we may have to alter our thinking that it is only once mankind had to be created male and female for spiritual reasons that G-d implemented this system throughout the entire animal and plant kingdom for biological consistency (and to throw off the non-believers).

[66] I italicized the term *Man* here to denote that the term in this context is gender neutral. I mean man and woman alike. All the associated male pronouns (he, his, etc.) are similarly gender neutral.

[67] Talmud Bavli Berachot 61a

I shall make for him a *complement*[68] who will be opposite him." Evidently, a two-fused-into-one being can only exist in G-d's realm where *Anochi* and *Lo Yihiyeh* are One and *Zachor* and *Shamor* are One (and, I suppose, white and *t'chelet* are One) but not in this world where everything is merely "one." Consequently, as with everything else we discussed, G-d has to break down the intact entity into two sub-units and so He does. He makes "one" *Man* into two people: male and female – *ish* and *isha*.

Although they both have the same attributes of humans – intelligence, power of speech, free will, emotions, and consciously guided activities – they are designated for two distinct, yet complementary, purposes. To the woman, the *isha*, He contributes the *Heh*, the *Lo Yihiyeh*. This is to signify that her primary function is to manage the *shamor*, the preservation of the integrity of this world. To the man, the *ish*, He contributes the *Yud*, the *Anochi*. This is to signify that his primary purpose is to enact the *zachor* and *assiya*, to create and acquire a share of the Eternal world. True, they are both cautioned to observe all the negative commandments. Nevertheless, his job is to distance himself from material involvement as if every day is the Day of Atonement[69] whereupon all the negative commandments are a "done deal" and to focus on Torah study and the active performance of positive commandments. The woman has no such stipulation to engulf herself in "holiness." She is entitled to and, as I am saying, expected to, spend the bulk of her time facing the challenges of the material world. Indeed, just as the woman is distanced, i.e., "out of proximity," from the positive commandments, the man is *meant* to be distanced (out of proximity) from the negative commandments.

Thus we note that the complementary relationship between man and woman cannot be simply stated that he is the scholar (and/or breadwinner) and that she is the homemaker (and/or breadwinner), whereupon they combine their talents and mix and match their responsibilities to form a viable team, but rather that they are, each one, specifically groomed to specialize in a different phase of our two-phased objective. Hence, the Talmud states that if they are worthy they will complement each other

---

[68] This translation of the term *ezer* may be slightly more articulate than what we are used to (typically: helpmate) though I maintain that it is no less accurate.

[69] This means to conform with the ideal status prescribed by Rabbi Shimon ben Yochai who spent 13 years in a cave with no clothes, no gadgets, no women, and the barest minimum of food. In such a setting, negative commandments are a moot point as there is barely any opportunity to sin. Most of us, must settle for the Rabbi Yishmael ideal and we must work, cohabitate with others, etc. Still, even Rabbi Yishmael will agree that a man's involvement with the material world should be kept to the minimum that he requires.

(*ezer*)[70]; but if they are unworthy, they will instead become opponents. Just as an army has ground forces and air forces and sea forces that do not oppose each other, but rather, complement each other, and that is what enables the army to succeed, so too, a man/woman union has *olam hazeh* forces and *olam haba* forces that are meant to complement each other and not oppose each other. It is only in this way that they can succeed as an integrated whole. It is obvious that the ground forces have no need for planes and the air forces have no need for tanks. Woman, in her role as the complement (*ezer*) of Man, has no need for *tzitzit*, *tefillin*, quorums and public Torah reading, *sukka* and *lulav*, etc., as they in no way assist her to accomplish her part of the joint mission. If a woman feels that she is incomplete without assuming an active role in these activities, it is most likely because she is not successfully involved in a complementary relationship[71] with her male counterpart.[72]

In such a situation, where Man does not live up to the obligations that are signified by the *Yud* and/or Woman does not preserve the integrity of the *Heh*, G-d withdraws His deposit, the *Yud* and *Heh*, and goes Home. The couple has failed at their joint mission of creating and earning a World to Come. The alternative world is a world of fire.

Part IV – A Heart Filled with Anxiety

The previous section has a bit of a harsh conclusion. Trust me, evangelism and fire-and-brimstone preaching are not my game. Its purpose was merely to take the principles that are set down by the Maharsha's elaboration of the passage in tractate Makkoth and to apply them to the intergender relationship to offer a perspective as to the chareidi view of what makes such a relationship fulfilling and successful. It is in no way meant to imply that individuals who have not been totally successful (or even those who have been totally unsuccessful) in forging and/or maintaining a healthy union with a cross-gender counterpart are doomed to Hell and damnation. It is merely meant to imply that such a union, when undertaken in the manner prescribed by the Torah, is an integral "surefire" (get it?) method of enabling both parties to achieve their maximum potential and to confirm reservations for the better place.

Thus far, we have studied the passage in tractate Makkoth with the commentary of the Maharsha to understand that the foundation of all of the commandments is a single commandment, *Emunah*, comprised of

---

[70] Rule of thumb: The more he compliments her, the more she complements him.

[71] See note 57 above.

[72] I want to be very clear that I am by no means suggesting a greater degree of blameworthiness for either gender. I am speaking bluntly where such is the case regardless of what are the circumstances that brought it about.

two complementary components, *Anochi* and *Lo Yihiyeh*. Thereupon we noted that this theme is reflected in certain specific commandments and, likewise, in the structure of human society.

Let us review the newly expanded list of *Anochi/Lo Yihiyeh* impersonators:

Emunah – Yichud Hashem	
Anochi Hashem	Lo Yihiyeh
Positive commandments	Negative commandments
Aseh Tov	Sur MeRah
Hashem E-loheinu	Hashem Echad
Hashem	Echad
T'chelet	White
Zachor	Shamor
Weekday	Shabbat
Man (ish)	Woman (isha)
Yud	Heh
(Acquiring) Olam Haba	(Preserving) Olam HaZeh

What is the chareidi supposed to make of this?

Want my opinion? (Don't answer!) I think the lesson is that it applies to everything. I mean *absolutely* everything!

In the eyes – and heart – of a chareidi, every single activity or conscious inactivity can be characterized as a fulfillment of *Anochi* or a transgression of *Lo Yihiyeh*. This is not restricted to what is listed among the 248 positive commandments and the 365 negative commandments, it applies to anything that a Jew does or refrains from doing. If the activity serves to display loyalty to G-d and to bring the individual closer to fulfilling his ultimate purpose, he is fulfilling *Anochi*. As we saw in Part I, *any* complete unmitigated fulfillment of *Anochi* is an "Admit One" ticket to G-d's world. If the activity is not one of loyalty, it is ipso facto one of disloyalty that serves to distance the individual from G-d, thus, a transgression of *Lo Yihiyeh*. It is an invitation to be shunned by G-d and left to the forces of chance.

Thus G-d the Father says to us: *Im b'chukotai teileichu* – If you are to walk within my statutes,[73] if you fulfill *Anochi*, **then**…And I will walk in your midst, and I will be for you for [a] G-d.[74]

This is one of G-d's utterances for us all to hear. But He is not finished, He has a second utterance: *"V'Im b'chukotai timasu* – And if in

---

[73] Leviticus 26:3

[74] Ibid. 26:12

my statutes you will display loathing; and if your souls will repulse my judgments; to desist from performing *all of my commandments* for you to nullify my covenant."[75]

What commandment did we learn is G-d's version of *all of my commandments*?

That's right, it's *Lo Yihiyeh*. Only, to be a bit scarier, according to the Maharsha, any individual commandment, or even action, can be a transgression of *Lo Yihiyeh*. Hence, to G-d, that single transgression or undesirable activity can be deemed as not performing *all of my commandments*. **Then what**? "...I will likewise walk with you in happenstance and I will also smite you sevenfold in accordance to your sins."[76]

Well, what do you know? We have come full circle to the credo of the chareidim, One Above and Seven Below.

The sincere chareidi takes all this very much to heart. Everything he does is either a fulfillment of *Anochi* or a transgression of *Lo Yihiyeh*. This means that when a Jew eats, he is either fulfilling *Anochi* or transgressing *Lo Yihiyeh*. The distinction is based, not only on what he eats, but on where, when, how, and why he is eating it. Any of these prepositions can account for the distinction between fulfilling *Anochi* or transgressing *Lo Yihiyeh*; but he is doing one or the other, never is he doing neither. The same applies to what comes out of the mouth. It is not only what he says but where, when, how, and why he says it. Both work and play must be either a fulfillment of *Anochi* or a transgression of *Lo Yihiyeh*. There is no middle ground. Here again the factors are what he is doing together with where, when, how, and why. Every time he sleeps, every time he cohabitates, again, either *Anochi* or *Lo Yihiyeh* – one or the other. And, yet again, every time a coin or bill comes out of his pocket, or goes into it.

This idea is liable to make someone a wee bit anxious, don't you think?

That is why chareidim are chareidi.

Are we done yet? Just about. I have one final correlation.[77]

This entire discourse follows the analysis of the Maharsha who, in turn, bases his thesis on Maimonides' commentary on the Mishna in Makkoth.[78] The reality is that not many chareidim are well acquainted with this specific commentary of the Maharsha nor even with this spe-

---

[75] Ibid. 26:15

[76] Ibid. 26:24

[77] Parts of this discourse are adapted from a lecture delivered by Rabbi Asher Weiss in Har Nof, Jerusalem, December, 2004.

[78] Mishna Makkoth 3:16

cific commentary of Maimonides on the Mishna. I must concede that suppose the reader of these lines were to randomly approach a common chareidi and say to him, "I just read somewhere that everything you do is either a fulfillment of *Anochi Hashem* or a transgression of *Lo Yihiyeh!*" the response could range from total disagreement and perhaps even a challenge of the statement to an agreeable "Yes, I have seen this concept in the *Mussar* (Jewish Ethics) books"; and, even then, the likelihood of his quoting these specific commentaries as his source are a certain long shot.

Yet, every chareidi is taught from his youth that his actions throughout his life must engender one trait: *V'Nikdashti b'toch B'nei Yisroel* (And I will be sanctified among the Children of Israel).[79] This is the great commandment of *kiddush Hashem*. In general, it means that every Jew is a representative of the Creator of the universe and his commitment to embodying this role must be so resolute that he must guard the honor of G-d's great Name with his very life. This commandment also comes with a complementary counterpart: *V'Lo tichalilu et shem kadshi* (You shall not desecrate My Holy Name).[80] This is commonly referred to as *chillul Hashem*. Any action that might besmirch the honor of G-d's name must be avoided at all costs, even under total duress. No price is too high.

In the initial description, this obligation is only enforced in specific extreme circumstances. One need only forfeit his life to refrain from transgressing the three cardinal sins of murder, idolatry (the literal *Lo Yihiyeh*), and immorality. At a second level, we are taught that during a time of heretical decrees one must forfeit his life to refrain from transgressing any law or even an established custom such as to alter the Jewish mode of dress. All of the particulars of these obligations are enumerated by Maimonides in Hilchot Yesodei Torah.[81] After composing nine articles of law that describe the *what, where, when,* and *how* of the Jew's obligation to offer the ultimate sacrifice (as well as when it is forbidden), Maimonides adds a catch-all article:[82]

> Any person who willfully and without duress transgresses on *any one* of all the commandments that are stated in the Torah with a haughty disposition to provoke [G-d], this is a desecration of His Name (*mechalel et Hashem*)... And, similarly, anyone who abstains from a transgression or who performs a [single] commandment not for any [personal] reason at all, not for fear, or for awe, or for the quest for [personal] honor, but

---

[79] Leviticus 22:32

[80] Ibid.

[81] Maimonides Mada Hilchot Yesodei Torah 5:1-9.

[82] Ibid. 5:10

rather, only for the honor of the Creator, Blessed is He, … this is one who is sanctifying the Name [of G-d].

This assertion of Maimonides seems to parallel the assertion he made in the commentary on Mishna in tractate Makkoth. Any *one* *commandment*, when executed impeccably, is a complete manifestation of *Yichud Hashem* and carries the status of a *kiddush Hashem* and ensures the individual of his share of paradise. It is as if he performed all of the commandments of the Torah. Conversely, any single transgression is a strain of *Lo Yihiyeh*. When it occurs due to carelessness or craving, it is viewed as a lost opportunity that can be rectified. However, if it is performed wantonly and without duress, with the knowledge of its severity, it is a full-fledged commission of *Lo Yihiyeh* and a desecration of G-d's Name, a *chillul Hashem*. It is as if the individual has transgressed the entire Torah. A conscious *chillul Hashem* cannot be fully atoned for in this world.

So now, once again, let us review the final cut of the parallel concepts to *Anochi* and *Lo Yihiyeh*:

Emunah – Yichud Hashem	
Anochi Hashem	Lo Yihiyeh
Positive commandments	Negative commandments
Aseh Tov	Sur MeRah
Hashem E-loheinu	Hashem Echad
Hashem	Echad
T'chelet	White
Zachor	Shamor
Weekday	Shabbat
Man (ish)	Woman (isha)
Yud	Heh
(Acquiring) Olam Haba	(Preserving) Olam HaZeh
Im B'Chukotai Teleichu	V'Im B'Chukotai Timasu[83]
V' Nikdashti (Kiddush Hashem)	V'Lo TiChalilu (Chillul Hashem)

We now have a possible answer to a question that was posed way back in the beginning of this book (Introduction).

Hear the word of G-d, those who are anxious (chareidim) toward his word…

We asked: What is the word of G-d?

In true Jewish style, let us answer the question with a question: How

---

[83] It follows that we can add to the list Bracha (the Blessing) and Kelala (the Curse) as well as Mt. Gerizim and Mt. Eval. But it is unnecessary as it would not add anything to our current discussion.

often has G-d ever spoken to all of us?
　Just once.
　And what did He say?
　He said *Anochi* and *Lo Yihiyeh*.[84]

---

[84] See Talmud Bavli Sanhedrin 99a.

Chapter Seven

An Educated Consumer
(or: Chareidiism 101)

Chareidi ideology in eight easy lessons

"I don't understand why the chareidim…"
"Doesn't it say…?"
"How come it's kosher enough for him, but not kosher enough for you?"
"Now, all of a sudden, we are not allowed to…"
"Where is it written that…?"

Secular Jews and NCOJs seem to have a hard time understanding chareidim. Indeed, it is for this reason that I am writing this book. All too often, when a particular issue is in the limelight and the chareidim promote their (predictably unpopular) position, non-chareidim recoil in shock as if this position is a newly concocted bombshell coming out of left field.

The amazing thing is that the perspectives and ideals of the chareidim have been virtually unchanged for the past 2300 years.[1] There is probably no socio-political or theological structure currently in existence that can claim such consistency and longevity.[2] What's more, there is no other culture that can claim a higher rate of literacy throughout its history, that has produced such a volume of books on its theology, philosophy and codes of law over the course of generations and which continue to be printed in massive quantities, and that has such a high percentage of

---

[1] I chose this figure because chareidi Judaism is a clear manifestation of the teachings of the Talmud. As such, I am designating the onset of the Talmudic era, which began with the masters of the Mishna as an appropriate point of reference. This era began shortly after the construction of the second Temple after the expiration of the Men of the Great Assembly. Of course, this was merely a continuum of Torah Judaism that truly began at the Exodus 1,000 years prior.

[2] Christianity (only 2,000 years old) has undergone numerous changes and reforms since its inception and its original doctrines would likely not be recog-

adherents that continue to study these works and writings that are so archaic.

These works are quite profuse and exceedingly accessible. They adorn the shelves of most Orthodox synagogues, study halls and yeshivot. They are available in all mainstream Hebrew book stores and the most fundamental works find themselves in the homes and private libraries of most common Orthodox Jews who have any degree of identification with Torah Judaism, scholars and laymen alike. Almost all of the essential texts can boast modern translations into the mother tongues of the non-Jewish world with English at the head of the pack. It's all there for the asking.

A cursory examination of these venerable works would certainly shed much light upon the philosophies of Orthodox Judaism in general and on the *weltanschauung* of the chareidim in particular (which, in my view, are one and the same). It would address all of the exclamations at the head of this chapter.

Alas, many are those who work all day and watch TV all night and read John Grisham or Harry Potter books all Shabbat (or study for their college exams). They simply can't seem to allocate any quality time for cursory examination. And thus, it remains that not only secular Jews but even many NCOJs have a hard time understanding chareidim. In fact, my observations tell me that many religious people know scarcely little about their religion and, I daresay, that this lack of knowledge is the leading cause of discord between theirs and the Torah camps.

This is not to say that all chareidim (and know-it-alls like me) are accomplished scholars and know all that there is to know. The scope of knowledge is virtually limitless as the verse says, "Its measure is longer than the earth and is wider than the sea."[3] The difference is that the chareidi recognizes that Judaism comprises a vast body of knowledge. He knows that there is so much more to know. It is also clear to the average chareidi that no matter how much he knows about any given subject, there are others who know more. In short, he knows more than the rank and file yet is conscious of how little he knows.

The brethren, haters and shunners are those who not only do not know what the chareidim know, but more tragically, are not conscious of

---

nizable today. Islam (merely 1400 years old) comprises numerous factions, each claiming that their doctrines are the "original" ones and no one really knows. I don't know much about the Far-Eastern cultures but it seems evident that most Asians (with the possible exception of the Indian Hindus) that emigrate outside of their indigenous environment do not uphold traditional practices.

[3] Job 11:9

what, or how much, they don't know. Many have a solid religious family upbringing and a commendable elementary school and often high school religious education. They fool themselves into believing that this is sufficient for a lifetime. As I wrote in the introductory chapter, this is one of the hazards of *consumerism*.

What you don't know, can hurt.

Years ago, I read an issue of the *Jewish Observer* wherein Rabbi Moshe Sherer wrote an open letter to a non-Jewish fellow who underwent a Reform "conversion" to Judaism. This gentleman had written into some non-Orthodox publication to voice a grievance. He opens by describing his devotion and sincerity throughout the six month conversion process, and states that he is fully committed to his "Jewish" identity, and that he, as well as the Reform community that he joined, considers himself to be a full fledged member of the Jewish nation. He goes on to complain bitterly that he is quite taken aback that *"Now* I am told that the Orthodox Jews refuse to acknowledge my Jewishness and that I and my children are considered to be gentiles."[4] The inflection of the letter was that *after* being cajoled and instructed as to how to become a Jew, **now** he suddenly finds out that to the more *Jewishy* Jews, everything that he has done is "not good enough" and to them (i.e., us) he is back at square one. In other words, it looks to him as if the contract was revised after he signed on the dotted line – a classic case of changing the rules in the middle of the game. In the tone of the letter, he was ascribing to the Orthodox the blame for his predicament.

Rabbi Sherer responded to this letter in his publication. He opened by expressing his sympathy to this fellow for the unfortunate heartache that he is enduring. But he then goes on to explain how the Orthodox definition of Jewishness is the standard that has existed throughout the ages. There is nothing new about it. It is the more modern "streams" of Judaism who have revised the rules. If he would have investigated the Orthodox position at an earlier stage, he would not be stricken by a sudden revelation. To some degree, he is at fault for not investigating mainstream (read: Orthodox) Judaism. To a greater degree, his Reform mentors are at fault for not "enlightening" him as to the acceptability of his status within mainstream Judaism. The Orthodox cannot be faulted for not providing information that was never requested. *The information was always available.*

It is one thing for a non-Jew to be unversed in the precepts of Ortho-

---

[4] I have contacted the Jewish Observer in an effort to locate this item. To date, I haven't succeeded. This story and quotation are completely from memory. I apologize for any inaccuracies.

dox Judaism. It is surely understandable and typically excusable. Yet, it remains that if he is contemplating becoming Jewish, it behooves him to, at the very least, pick up the basics. If you wish to play the game, you better learn the rules. If there are new versions to the game, and those are the rules that you learn, you will not be able to contend with people who continue to play the game by the original rules. If it's a different set of rules, it's a different game. This unfortunate fellow was unaware that Orthodox Judaism and Reform Judaism are two different games.

Unfortunately, it is not only the non-Jews who don't know the rules to the game. Sadly, the majority of the Jewish people don't seem to know the rules. These are the secular Jews. Many of them do not know the rules because they were never taught the rules. They are not aware that there is much to be gained by "playing the game" (every player wins something!) or that there even is a "game." Others are quite aware that there is a "game" to play with a distinctive set of rules. Their issue is that they are not interested in playing the "game." As I wrote in the introductory chapter, this book is not focusing on the secular Jews.

This book focuses on Orthodox Jews. All Orthodox Jews are aware that we are here to "play the game." I would actually *define* the Orthodox as those Jews who are committed to "playing the game." I would postulate that, in some ways, the difference between the Orthodox and the affiliated non-Orthodox (traditional or *Masorati*) Jew is similar to the difference between an amateur and a professional. An amateur plays for "fun" and he plays when he "feels like it" – if he doesn't feel like it, he doesn't play. A professional plays to win, as if his livelihood depends on it, for, if he is indeed a professional, this is truly the case.

I would likewise venture that every Orthodox Jew (chareidi or not) considers himself a professional. So, how would I differentiate between the chareidi and the NCOJ?

My answer would be, as I just wrote, Orthodox Jews are those Jews who are *committed* to "playing the game." The chareidim are those Orthodox Jews who are committed to *winning it*.[5]

What do I mean?

Recall in Chapter 1, that I laid down my definitions for a chareidi versus an NCOJ. An NCOJ merely observes the commandments, i.e., he plays the game, as is indicated in the first level of the *seven below*. A chareidi observes the commandments with *toil in Torah*. Why? As I clearly illustrated in that chapter, it's because that is how we win all the wonderful prizes (timely rains, prosperity, international dominance, military su-

---

[5] Winning does not mean to defeat an opponent. Judaism is not a competitive sport. Everybody can win.

periority, children, etc.) that are listed in the passage in Leviticus 26. Evidently, *toil in Torah* is the difference between merely playing the game and winning it.

This phenomenon needs no explanation. As any participant in any contest knows, the second[6] requirement to succeed is to know the rules. Ideally, all of them, but certainly, the key ones. The more of the rules that one knows, the more likely he is to excel. To be a "grandmaster," one must "master" the rules. Not only the rules. He must know the essential strategies. A grandmaster almost always wins. But grandmasters aren't born. They start at square one and they learn to master the game. And that can only be done with persistent toil.

I am not even attempting to conceal the fact that a main objective of this book is to win over the hearts and minds of my Jewish brethren who, for lack of understanding what a chareidi really is, might tend to be hateful or shunful of their chareidi coreligionists. My goal is to help this segment to relate to us and, ideally, to identify with us. In short, I am trying to sell the product.

To whom?

Why, to consumers, of course.

And, to this end, I feel it is worthwhile to adopt the motto of a well known, very successful, Jewish businessman, Mr. Sy Sims. In the course of doing business, Mr. Sims never tired of saying: ***An Educated Consumer is our Best Customer***.

What does he mean?

Generally, when people shop, their primary concern is the price. People would like to acquire the desired goods for the lowest possible expenditure. If one merchant sells a suit for $100 and a second merchant sells a suit for $150, it seems rather elementary that one would prefer to buy at the first merchant. They are both suits, so why pay more?

However, there may be a reason to pay more. The wares of the second merchant may be worth more – if they are of superior quality. Thus, the consumer has a secondary concern – value. Everybody knows that $100 is less than $150, but not everybody knows that hand tailored worsted wool is more valuable than mass produced double-knit polyester. Only a consumer who is educated in the materials and craftsmanship of a product can recognize value.

Mr. Sims is trying to relate the message that his merchandise is a superior value. Thus, even if it may be priced higher than other competing merchandise, a customer who recognizes value will determine that it is worthwhile to buy his merchandise. It follows that the educated con-

---

[6] Wouldn't you like to know the first one? See page 183.

sumers, i.e., those who have done their homework and have learned to recognize value, are the ones who will patronize his establishment. Ergo, an educated consumer is his best customer.[7]

It is my aim to illustrate that to be chareidi is a superior value. A simple consumer will not understand this unless he does his homework and thus becomes an educated consumer. So, it's time for a crash course in chareidiism. Let us call it: *Chareidiism 101.*[8] The idea is to present a curriculum that comprises the most fundamental and concise texts that enable one to become familiar with the specifications and features of the "product."

Let's be clear on this. This is *not* a curriculum *for* chareidim. They know what to study; nobody needs me for that. Nor is it a curriculum on how to behave like a chareidi. For that, you need only grab the nearest Kitzur Shulchan Aruch, open it up, and do exactly as it says. I can guarantee that any Jew who studies Kitzur Shulchan Aruch and endeavors to follow it to the letter is assured of a share in the World to Come.[9] This is a curriculum *about* chareidim; about how to think like a chareidi and how to see the world through the eyes of a chareidi. It is for one who wants to understand what "makes us tick." (Actually, that's what this book is, but this book is actually a cheap substitute for the real McCoy stuff that I will discuss here. One can read this book in a week, but this "crash course," if truly followed, would probably take a number of years.)

So what is on the curriculum of my crash course in chareidiism?

My course would comprise three prerequisites and three core texts.

The three prerequisites would be:

- *Maimonides 13 Principles of Faith* and the *Six Constant Commandments*

- *Chumash with Rashi*

- *Ethics of our Fathers* (*Pirkei Avot*)

---

[7] There may be another explanation that is a bit cynical: Nowadays fewer and fewer people include dress clothes in their wardrobe. Of late, dress clothes are the exclusive domain of businessmen, lawyers, bankers, and politicians (and then, Jews). In other words, only people with higher educations are interested in his line of clothes. Thus, an educated consumer is his best (you might say – only) customer.

[8] I thought it more dignified than "Chareidiism for Dummies."

[9] This guarantee is underwritten by Tanna D'Bei Eliyahu in T.B. Niddah 73a and it is not even void where prohibited.

The three core texts would be:

- *Messilat Yesharim* (Path of the Just) by Rabbi Moshe Chaim Luzzato

- *Chovot HaLevavot* (Duties of the Heart) by Rabbi Bachya Ibn Pekuda

- *Menorat HaMaor* by Rabbi Yitzchak Abohav

Let's discuss it.

Lesson 1 – Maimonides' 13 Principles of Faith – What's in it for all of us?

All of us Orthodox Jews are, well, Orthodox Jews. But, as I wrote in the Introduction, some Orthodox Jews who do not consider themselves chareidi view the chareidim as "other" Orthodox Jews. To the extent that chareidim may be "different," what makes them that way?

The place to start examining what may be different about chareidim is at the point at which all Orthodox Jews are the same. What collectively defines all Orthodox Jews is that we share a common belief – a belief in Orthodox Judaism. We cannot be a cohesive group unless all of us primarily believe the same basic principles. I have no doubt that if we were to put any number of Orthodox Jews into cubicles and ask each one to compose a list of ten or more primary Orthodox beliefs based on their upbringing and their studies of Tanach (Scripture) and Talmud (no philosophical works at this stage, that would be cheating), no two individuals would compile an identical list. Traditionally, Orthodox Jews have a difficult time agreeing with each other about anything. Can anybody compose a comprehensive list of beliefs that will be universally accepted?

Thankfully, about 830 years ago, a great, yet controversial Jewish thinker arose who took upon himself this awesome task. Though it took some time, his saintliness prevailed and so, by a common consensus, we have universally adopted Maimonides' 13 Principles of Faith as our credo.

It is worthwhile to be familiar with these principles. They are:

1. G-d is the Creator of all that exists.

2. G-d is a being of absolute uniqueness. He has always existed and will exist forever.

3. G-d has no body or conceivable form.

4. G-d precedes all and succeeds all.

5. G-d is the sole object of any and all prayers.

6.   All of the teachings of the Prophets are true.

7.   Moses was the supreme Prophet and his prophecy excelled over all who preceded or succeeded him.

8.   The entire Torah that we have was dictated to Moses.

9.   This Torah will never be altered or replaced.

10.   G-d is aware of all of our thoughts and deeds.

11.   G-d rewards those who perform his commandments and punishes those who transgress them.

12.   The imminent coming of the Messiah.

13.   The eventual revival of the dead.

Despite the centrality of the 13 Principles, it is a sad reflection on our society that so few Orthodox Jews, even chareidim, are capable of reciting the entire list. Some of the more consumerist NCOJs may have never actually examined the list and, as such, they are not truly conscious about some of the items that are included. This can cause them to lose sight of some of the principles. But the chareidi, even if he cannot readily recite the whole list, must be always conscious of every single one.

To emphasize this, here's what I would do. First, I would ask the students to review the list and mentally record their impressions. Thereupon, I would ask them to put the list away and to leave it untouched until the last day of the course. At that time, I would instruct the students to look at them again and to determine if these principles convey the same meaning to them as when they looked them over on the first day. If they are unchanged, the student failed the course. If they are enhanced, the student passed. There is no need for any exams.

Lesson 2 – Messilat Yesharim: Chapter 1 – The Object of the Game

In Lesson 2, I would interrupt our study of the remaining prerequisites and, instead, I would introduce *Messilat Yesharim*.

Why so soon?

I began the course by emphasizing that all Orthodox Jews, chareidi or not, collectively maintain a set of beliefs. This is *what* every Orthodox Jew is expected to adhere to. After this *what*, the remainder of the course is to explain *why*.[10] Why must we uphold this set of beliefs? What are

---

[10] There will be no *how* in this course. That is left to Intermediate Chareidiism

they based on and what do they do for us? What are we trying to achieve?

In other words: *WHAT IS THE OBJECT OF THE GAME*?

Recall that earlier I wrote that knowing the rules is the *second* requirement to succeeding at a contest. But open the rule book to any game and you will notice that it does not immediately describe the rules. There is usually a preamble: *The object of the game is…* Such as: *The object of the game is to be the first player to move all his pieces to the home region. **The first player to accomplish this wins!***

The first thing that the chareidi needs to know is "the object of the game," because the chareidi is playing the game to win. The goal of Rabbi Luzzato (henceforth, Ramchal) in writing Messilat Yesharim is to help us win the game. And so, in Chapter 1, he clearly and succinctly depicts the "object of the game":

> The foundation of piety[11] and the root of an unblemished service [of our Creator] is that it be clarified and verified by each person as to what is his (the individual's) obligation in His world, and to what he must apply his sights and his orientations in all that he toils his entire life. And what our sages have taught us is that a person was created for no other ultimate purpose than to derive enjoyment from G-d and to take pleasure in the aura of His Presence which is the true enjoyment and the greatest pleasure of all the pleasures that can exist. And the location of this pleasure is actually in the World to Come… However, the road through which to arrive at this destination is the present world…

So there you have it. The chareidi believes that we are here in this world to reach a goal. All of our "sights and orientations" must be pointed toward that goal (or else we will never reach it). As such, the chareidi has a premise to guide his every action and his every thought and opinion – "does this activity or perspective serve to bring me closer to my goal or to distance me from it?"

The chareidi, almost by instinct, knows whether a given thought or action is conducive toward reaching his true goal. Still, even (read: especially) the most successful players and performers couldn't get to the top without a coach. Ramchal doesn't let us down, but rather, as an expert coach, he goes on to establish a step-by-step program for reaching our goal. We will elaborate on this in a later lesson. Understanding just this much is sufficient for Lesson 2.

———————

(102) which, as stated above, is almost totally Kitzur Shulchan Aruch.

[11] His use of the term chassidut to mean "piety" is not referring exclusively to the particular groups of Orthodox Jews who today call themselves Chassidim but

Lesson 3 – Chumash and Rashi – Getting Beneath the Surface

Until about 250 BCE the written Torah – the "Bible" – was a closed book. It was the exclusive domain of us Jews. That's because it was written in the Holy Tongue (what we'll call Hebrew) and there were no translations into any other language. If you didn't happen to speak Hebrew,[12] you were out of the loop. Along came the Greek emperor Ptolemy Philadelphus and, with a heart full of brotherly love, he commissioned the first translation into a foreign language (though it was still Greek to most people). From that time onward our Torah became "public domain." Now you can find a copy in any hotel room. Our Rabbis considered this breach to be a great catastrophe and, indeed, it is one of the reasons for the fast of the Tenth of Tevet. In 1956, a bigger disaster occurred. A significant segment was relegated to the motion picture industry courtesy of Cecil B. DeMille and Charlton Heston. Definitely worth fasting again.

As a result, today in the Western world, Jew and non-Jew alike are equally versed in the stories of Creation and Adam and Eve, Noah's Ark and the Great Flood, Joseph and his coat of many colors, the Egyptian servitude, the Exodus, the ten plagues and the splitting of the Sea of Reeds, receiving the Law, the Golden Calf, the spies, etc. along with some choice idioms such as "Love thy neighbor as thyself" and "Man does not live by bread alone." It follows that a familiarity with the text of the Torah is not indicative of even being Jewish, let alone of being Orthodox, and certainly of being chareidi.

But the chareidi knows that the Torah is not just a storybook. It is actually a very profound treatise which contains all you need to know about who we are, where we come from, why we are here, where we are headed, and how to get there. That's quite a neat package; only, that it comes gift wrapped in a storybook wrapping. This wrapping is on so tight that it won't come off, and so, the only way to reach the true goodies in the package is to look through the wrapping. This is very difficult for (at least) two reasons. One is that it requires no small amount of skill, practice, piety, and a bit of x-ray vision – what we call *ruach hakodesh* (a spirit of holiness) – and nobody can attain any of these things without guidance from the masters. The second reason is that there are layers upon layers of this "wrapping."

To truly master the art of penetrating the many layers of wrapping

---

to the larger group of Torah observant Jews that subscribe to his "program." In this context, it is a synonym for what is today called chareidi as I emphasize in Chapter 9.

[12] Note that from the period of the Babylonian conquest, even Jews did not speak

requires the successful completion of Advanced Chareidiism (Chareidiism 103, likewise beyond the scope of this book). I myself am still struggling with this course. However, as in most endeavors, the key is to "break the ice." Once one has learned how to unwrap the outermost layer, his ability to penetrate additional layers is greatly enhanced.

Accordingly, throughout the generations, we have been blessed with scholarly luminaries that have undertaken the task of enabling us to penetrate at least some of these many layers of wrapping. The most prominent and universally recognized of which is Rashi. I have already sung the praises of Rashi in Chapter 1 and there is no need to repeat them. The plus point of Rashi is that, in such a succinct manner, he provides us with the most rudimentary, yet comprehensive glimpse as to what lies beneath the outer wrapping and launches us on our quest to penetrate further. Undoubtedly, Rashi is not alone among the great masters and when I invoke Rashi it is certainly not to the exclusion of any of his colleagues. There is so much further to go, but this is a crash course, remember?

There is no question that, according to my definition, Rashi, as well as all of his colleagues, was a full fledged chareidi. It follows that when one studies Chumash with Rashi, he sees the Chumash as a chareidi sees it. When one reads the Chumash without Rashi, he sees it as Cecil B. DeMille sees it.

Lesson 4 – Pirkei Avot – The Unbroken Chain of Tradition

In Chapter 9, I discuss the evolution of the term *chareidi* and note that at various eras throughout our history, other synonymous terms were employed in reference to this ageless social group. One of the synonyms employed by the Talmud is the term *chassid*[13]. As such, the Talmud in tractate Bava Kamma (30a) states:

> Rav Yehuda said: This individual who wishes to be a *chassid* should strive to uphold matters relating to [restraint from] property damage. Rava said [he should strive to uphold] matters relating to Pirkei Avot and some say matters relating to [prayer and] blessings.[14]

Hebrew in their daily lives, only Aramaic.

[13] Literally: one who exemplifies kindness. The term chassid is most commonly used to describe one who conducts himself with *midat chassidut* meaning one who goes beyond the letter of the law. However, Rashi in tractate Menachot (40b s.v. *Chassidim*) defines them as "those who are speedy to do mitzvot," which is remarkably similar to his definition of *haChareidim* in Isaiah 66:5.

[14] It is well worth seeing Maharsha's commentary on this passage.

I hereby lay claim to Rava's stamp of approval that Pirkei Avot is one of the most essential elements of chareidi ideology.[15] I think most of my peers would put it even stronger: Pirkei Avot *is* chareidi ideology. To the letter. I would go so far as to say that it is the chareidi's corporate charter. As a supplementary definition for *chareidi* to the one that I pose in Chapters 1 and 2, I would also say that a chareidi is one who subscribes to all that is written in Pirkei Avot. Actually, Pirkei Avot is nothing more than an elaboration of the principle of Leviticus 26:3. But that is saying a lot.

You may think that I am designating Lesson 4 for extolling the virtues of Pirkei Avot because it is a limitless treasure trove of chareidi morals, ethics, and ideals that, for the most part, seem to begin with the second Mishna wherein we hear the words of Shimeon the Just who said: "Upon three things the world stands – Upon [the study of] Torah, upon the Service [of G-d], and upon the distribution of kindness."[16]

This is not entirely true. For, if this was so, I may as well begin the course at Pirkei Avot and end the course at Pirkei Avot. It is, after all, the charter of the chareidim so what more do we need?

Aside from all of the morals, ethics, and ideals of the chareidim, it tells us something else. There is a distinct message in Pirkei Avot which warrants its position as Lesson 4 on my curriculum. Without internalizing this message, all of the other teachings of Pirkei Avot would be of a greatly reduced potency and as such, the value of this message is equivalent to the sum total of these teachings. Yet, many Non-Charadei Orthodox Jews who have studied Pirkei Avot seem to overlook this crucial message (which is either *why* or *because* they are not chareidi). And it is all contained in the very first Mishna.

The very first Mishna in Pirkei Avot states as follows:

> Moses received the Torah at Sinai and he handed it down to Joshua, and Joshua [handed it down] to the Elders, and the Elders to the Prophets, and the Prophets handed it down to the Men of the Great Assembly.

What is the significance of this introduction?

Rabbi Ovadia of Bartenura[17], the renowned commentator of the Mishna, explains as follows:

---

[15] This does not imply that we may overlook the issues of controlling damages or relating to G-d. These issues are for the more advanced courses. Pirkei Avot must be a part of the introductory course.

[16] Pirkei Avot 1:2

[17] Rabbi Ovadia of Bartenura was born in Italy, circa 1440, and immigrated to Jerusalem where he died in 1516. He is revered as the primary commentator to the Mishna on the same scale as Rashi is revered as the primary commentator on Chumash.

I contend that due to this that this tractate (Avot) is not dedicated to the expounding of [the details of] any specific commandment from the commandments of the Torah, as is the case with all the other tractates of the Mishna, but rather it is completely [composed of] ethics and morals, and the wise men of the nations of the world have likewise composed treatises, which they conjured by themselves, in the ways of ethics, how one man should relate to his comrade; *therefore*, the Tanna (Second Temple scholar) began this tractate with the statement "Moses received the Torah at Sinai…" to say to you that [of] the morals and ethics that are contained herein, the sages of the Mishna did not conjure them by themselves, but rather, even these were told [by G-d to Moses] at Sinai.

What is he telling us?

He is saying that one can study and appreciate the myriad pearls of wisdom that are found in Pirkei Avot, yet, he may view these teachings merely as logical suggestions that may emanate from the mind of any wise man such as Benjamin Franklin – who, incidentally, quotes some sayings of Pirkei Avot in his Poor Richard's Almanac, without crediting the source. As such, this individual considers himself free to approve or reject the morals according to his personal code of ethics. The purpose of this introductory Mishna is to alert us that this "chareidi charter" was dictated to Moses at Sinai *by the Holy One Himself* and that this G-d-given legacy has been handed down intact until the sages of the Second Temple era saw the need to eternalize it in writing.

In the previous lessons we learned that the chareidi (1) maintains a set of beliefs, (2) works toward reaching an ultimate goal, and (3) understands the Torah at a more profound level than the superficial text. In this lesson we learn that the chareidi (4) holds on to a value system which, any Orthodox Jew must acknowledge, was ordained by G-d at Mount Sinai and that this system has been in effect *non-stop* ever since the Jewish people attained nationhood in the year 2448.

That's 3300 years and counting!

Lesson 5 – Menorat HaMaor – The Code of Jewish Ethics

Although I shall never cease heralding Pirkei Avot as the most comprehensive anthology of chareidi morals and ethics, it remains as only one component of the larger picture. In fact, the entirety of Pirkei Avot only deals with one subject – social relationships. Of this there are a few categories:

- One man's relationship to his fellow man (Examples: Judge each man to the sector of merit; Do not judge your peer until you have reached his situation.)

- Man's relationship to himself (Examples: If I am not [responsible] for myself, who shall be [responsible] for me?; Who is rich? He who is satisfied with his share.)

- Man's relationship to G-d and G-d's relationship to man (Examples: Do not be like a servant who serves the Master for the sake of reward...; Conform your will to be as His will so that He will conform His will to be as yours.)

- A student's relationship to his master and a master's relationship to his student (Examples: Make for yourself a master; Let the honor of your student be as beloved to you as your own honor... and the fear of your master should be as your fear of Heaven.)

- A judge's relationship to the litigants (Examples: Be deliberate in judgment; When the litigants come before you, you must view them as equally wicked...)

- A Jew's relationship to the Torah (Examples: You are not required to complete the task, yet, you are not free to desist from it; Such is the manner of Torah. You shall eat [only] bread with salt, you shall drink water by measure...)

There remain numerous subjects, both practical and philosophical, that it doesn't touch upon. These subjects are widely distributed throughout the vast expanse of the Talmud. Some examples:

Although Pirkei Avot states some profound comments about the World to Come, there is no mention about the Messiah or Revival of the Dead. This is covered at length in tractates Sanhedrin and Sota. We find the subject of death and mourning in Moed Katan; marriage, divorce, and man-woman relationships scattered in all tractates of Nashim and in Niddah; Heavenly judgment in tractate Rosh Hashana and repentance in tractate Yuma; prayer in tractate Brachot; honoring one's parents in tractate Kiddushin; our love of Eretz Israel in tractate Ketubot; evil gossip and baseless hatred in tractates Gitten, Bava Bathra, and Erechin; the commandments of *tefillin*, *tzitzit*, and *mezuzah* in (believe it or not) tractate Menachot; circumcision in tractate Shabbat, etc.

You really need to know your way around.

Now, we know that the Orthodox Jew's day to day activities are governed by the Halacha. The Halacha is our law. Sure enough, all of the Halachic rulings of the Talmud were eventually compiled into codified digests – notably Maimonides' Yad HaChazaka, the Tur Shulchan Aruch and all of its "derivatives" – and so we have the law at our fingertips. But this course does not concern Halacha. Accordingly, I am not referring to the Halachic aspects of all these subjects but rather the philosophical ideas and concepts that shape our perceptions; the profound sayings of the sages that go beyond Pirkei Avot. These philosophies were handed down through the unbroken chain of tradition along with the teachings of Pirkei Avot. And just as the Mishna states about Pirkei Avot, these scattered philosophies are every bit as divine and every bit as relevant as is the Halacha. So if the law must be compiled into a codified body, is it any less important that the philosophies of Jewish living that were dictated to Moses at Mount Sinai be codified as well?

Rabbi Yitzchak Abohav thought so, and so, he compiled for us the *Menorat HaMaor*.

Menorat HaMaor is our Shulchan Aruch for Talmudic (i.e., chareidi) ideology. In some ways, it is very similar to Maimonides' Yad HaChazaka. Just as Maimonides gleaned from the entire Talmud all of the Halachic rulings on every subject and compiled them into a compendium of Talmudic law, Rabbi Yitzchak Abohav gleaned from the entire Talmud all of the Aggadic literature on every subject into a compendium of Jewish thought. In fact, he is so thorough at integrating all of the pertinent teachings into a given subject that there were occasions predating sophisticated CD-ROM Torah libraries that, when I needed to locate a particular passage, I would open Menorat HaMaor to the appropriate subject and expect to see it referenced. I was rarely disappointed.

Also, just as Maimonides organized the material into 14 books,[18] each one categorizing a field of law, and then divided each book into sections for the specific related subjects, and then subdivided each subject into chapters, so too, Menorat HaMaor mimics this style by organizing the material into seven "Lamps,"[19] then each Lamp into precepts, each precept into sections and each section into chapters.

Here the similarity ends. Whereas Maimonides presents the Halachic rulings in concise "bite-size" pieces, Menorat HaMaor fuses the Aggadic literature into lengthy prosaic lessons interspersed with his personal insight. In this format, his style is very much like that of the Ro"sh.[20] To some extent, I myself am imitating this style in some of the exegeses that I propose in Chapter 3.

---

[18] Maimonides entitled this work Yad HaChazaka (the Mighty Arm) to allude to this number of fields of Halacha as the numerical value of the word Yad is 14 corresponding to the 14 books.

[19] Here, also, the title of the book is intimated as the Menorah was a seven branch candelabra. The primary Lamps are: (1) Avoiding what is unnecessary, (2) Restraint on improper speech, (3) Performing the commandments, (4) Torah study, (5) Repentance, (6) Peace and love for fellow man, and (7) Humility.

[20] Rabbi Asher ben Yechiel. From the later Rishonim (Medieval scholars), he

Lesson 6 – Chovot HaLevavot – The Truth About G-d

Thus far in our course, we learned how a chareidi looks at himself, at the Torah, and at his religion. There is One more Component that needs to be examined in detail. That is how the chareidi perceives G-d.

Of course, our perception of G-d is summed up in the first four items of the 13 Principles of Faith. The third of which is that we believe that G-d has no physical body nor any humanly conceivable form whatsoever. And certainly G-d tells us through the Prophet Isaiah, "For My [manner of] thinking is not your [manner of] thinking, and your ways are like Mine, says G-d."[21] Yet, we learn in Lesson 2 that our ultimate goal is to derive enjoyment from G-d and, as we will discuss in Lesson 7, this is contingent on striving to emulate Him as well as to serve Him. Consequently, we cannot be fully exempt from maintaining some humanistic perception of G-d so that we can try to understand how to serve and emulate Him.

This is a most daunting task and it may be well nigh impossible if not for the assistance of *Chovot HaLevavot* (Duties of the Heart).

I cannot offer a better overview of Chovot HaLevavot than that which the author, Rabbi Bachya Ibn Pekuda, himself presents in his introduction. He opens by positing that there are three categories of sciences: (1) Physical sciences such as chemistry, physics and medicine (2) Abstract sciences such as mathematics, astrology, and music and (3) Philosophical and theological sciences. He continues that the wisdom of our Torah represents this third category and that it is vital to study this wisdom to understand our essential obligations. He continues that there are two categories of obligations: (1) the obligations of the limbs, i.e., the commandments, and (2) the obligations of the heart. He notes that there are ample works that define the first category of obligations but he does not find comprehensive works that adequately define the second category, the duties of the heart. His first impulse was that perhaps they are not so truly important but he says that after much introspection he concluded that such is not the case. Thereupon, he set out to compose a work that properly defines the duties of the heart.

At the end of his introduction, he explains that he would depict the duties of the heart as a structure with ten chambers, each one leads into the next.

---

fostered in the era of the Poskim by compiling a Talmudic compendium of Halacha. His work was of a more prosaic style and was not codified. His son Rabbi Jacob ben Asher codified his work into the format that later became the Shulchan Aruch.

[21] Isaiah 55:8

As each chamber has its own portal, he refers to them as ten gateways:

Gateway of:	In it he describes:
Oneness	How to understand the meaning that G-d is one.
Discerning	How to discern G-d's presence in every aspect of Creation.
Service of G-d	That we are indebted to G-d for our existence and we must display that gratitude by serving Him willingly.
Trust in G-d	How we must internalize that anything that happens to us is directed by G-d.
Specifying our actions	How we must sanctify all of our actions as a manifestation of His will.
Subjugation	That we must banish our personal motives from our actions.
Repentance	How to repent from our wrongdoings.
Personal account	How to maintain a "clean slate."
Abstinence	Our obligation to avoid indulgence in things that lead us away from service of G-d.
Love of G-d	The attachment to G-d that we are trying to achieve through all of the above.

Undoubtedly, these obligations are not easy to fulfill and few, if any, are those who truly succeed. At least the chareidi can be aware of what obligations he has. The typical NCOJ hasn't a clue.

Lesson 7 – Messilat Yesharim – The twelve step program

I introduced *Messilat Yesharim* in Lesson 2 because, more important than knowing the object of the game, what I really needed to emphasize was that *there even is* an object of the game. That itself is a novel idea to many consumers. I then interjected the next four lessons – Chumash with Rashi, Pirkei Avot, Menorat HaMaor and Chovot HaLevavot – as collectively they help us understand why it is worthwhile to play the game. In other words, they provide a fuller understanding as to what the esoteric term "derive enjoyment from G-d" means so that we can conceptualize this "object of the game" in tangible terms. Now, it is time to take a broader look at Messilat Yesharim because, not only does he elaborate on "the object of the game" but he completes the training manual by telling us "how to play."

Let us pick up where we left off. Ramchal begins his masterpiece by presenting a general overview of our purpose in existence, "to derive enjoyment from G-d." He explains this to mean that although we are born into this physical world, our true goal is eternal pleasure in the ensuing spiritual world. In order to be comfortable in that world, our job in this one is to make ourselves more spiritual. To this end, he adopts the program of spiritual progression that the Talmud quotes from Rabbi Pinchas ben Yair and that I already referenced in Chapter 3:

> From this Rabbi Pinchas ben Yair states: (1) Torah brings one toward (2) vigilance; vigilance brings one toward (3) alacrity; alacrity brings one toward (4) innocence; innocence brings one toward (5) abstinence; abstinence brings one toward (6) purity; purity brings one toward (7) piety; piety brings one toward (8) humility; humility brings one toward (9) fear of sin; fear of sin brings one toward (10) holiness; holiness brings one toward (11) the Divine spirit; the Divine spirit brings one toward (12) revival of the dead.

So now we have a clearer concept of the object of the game. It is to become a most spiritual being that, at its most sublime level, is characterized as the power to revive the dead, which Ramchal describes as a virtual partnership with G-d. As this is reminiscent of immortality, I termed this goal as trying to reach the peak of Mount Neverest. And it is every bit as formidable. Legend has it that the Gaon of Vilna set out to implement the agenda of Messilat Yesharim and he claimed that he could not progress further than Level 5 (Abstinence).

We notice that Rabbi Pinchas ben Yair's road map comprises 12 station stops and, indeed, the remainder of Messilat Yesharim is a detailed elucidation on how to attain each successive level of this arduous climb. This is what I call the 12-Step program of "Chareidi Synonymous." The very first step of this program is the *toil in Torah* that I put forward in Chapter 1 as the foundation of chareidi ideology as indicated by Rashi in Leviticus 26:3. But even this is only the first step! It is a mere launch-pad for our liftoff toward the stratosphere. There is so much further to go, but without this *toil in Torah* we will never even reach Level 2.

And so, finally, after these seven lessons, we understand what motivates the chareidi. The chareidi understands that his purpose in life is to try to reach the peak of Mount Neverest and everything he does – every action, every thought, every opinion – is aimed at coming closer to this magnificent goal. He cooperates with the "rest of society" only in situations where the rest of society shares in this goal. When this is not the case (as is the norm) he travels alone.

Lesson 8 – The 13 Principles of Faith and Six Constant Commandments – Knowing is Believing

As I indicated in Lesson 1, this final lesson is more of an epilogue of the total course than a lesson unto itself. The purpose of this course has been to explain how a chareidi thinks and what motivates his behavior. Here, as the concluding segment we will look at how the chareidi puts it into practice.

In Lesson 1, I listed the 13 Principles of Faith and I indicated that we would revisit these principles at the end of the course.

There is a well known anecdote that a certain Chassidic Rebbe was explaining to one of his disciples what distinguishes between the disciple and the Rebbe. He said, "You (the disciple) believe that G-d exists. I *know* that G-d exists."

When it comes to the NCOJ and the chareidi, the opposite is true – the NCOJ may know the 13 Principles of Faith, the chareidi *believes* the 13 Principles of Faith.

How so?

In Chapter 1, I explain the true difference between the NCOJ and the chareidi. The chareidi is the *one above*, the subject of Leviticus 26:3. The NCOJ is the initial level of the *seven below*, the subject of Leviticus 26:14. These two societies live next door to each other on opposite sides of an imaginary fence. Superficially, the distinction between these two camps is not readily discernible and these two entities dwell side by side both performing commandments. But Rashi tells us that this sameness is an illusion for all are not pointed in the same direction. The chareidi is striving to get to the top of Mount Neverest. This starts with *toil in Torah* and is propelled by internalizing the 13 Principles of Faith. Conversely, says Rashi, the NCOJ at Level 1 of the *seven below* is susceptible to falling level by level as far as Level 7. Even though the highest level of the *seven below* performs commandments and is therefore relatively virtuous, it is the first level in a gradual descent that culminates in *Kofer B'Ikar*, denouncing all that is G-d, the total nullification of the 13 Principles.

Lacking *toil in Torah*, the integrity of the 13 Principles is all that remains; it is all that prevents the NCOJ from further decline. Yet it stands in great peril. The chareidi requires his *toil in Torah*, not only because it is the first step toward his ascent to the top of Mount Neverest, but because it preserves his faith. It keeps him from joining the *seven below*.

His worst enemy is *Kofer B'Ikar*, lack of faith. He must always be conscious of the 13 Principles of Faith so that he knows what he must protect through his *toil in Torah*. And so, his belief system cannot be passive; it is not enough to know the 13 Principles. He must be proactive; he must *believe* the 13 Principles.

To facilitate this, the Sefer HaChinuch tells us that, of all the 613 commandments, there are six commandments that are constant and incessant; obligations that we must fulfill at each moment of our lives:

1. To acknowledge G-d as the supreme and all-powerful Creator of all that exists.

2. To disavow the existence of any other power or deity.

3. To designate G-d as the sovereign of Creation.

4. To harbor love for G-d.

5. To harbor fear of G-d.

6. To [actively] desist from following one's base desires.

Now we know the answer to all of the inquiries at the opening of this chapter:

"I don't understand why the chareidim…"

"Doesn't it say…?"

"How come it's kosher enough for him, but not kosher enough for you?"

"Now, all of a sudden, we are not allowed to…"

"Where is it written that…?"

The answer is that the chareidi has a mission to fulfill and he is very focused on this mission. Therefore, everything that he can do is measured. It is measured by the distance between him and the top of Mt. Neverest. If the activity reduces this distance it is acceptable. If it increases the distance it is unacceptable. What's more, he cannot afford to be idle from pursuing his mission. And so, the chareidi is always busy. Even when he is stuck on the subway, even when he is sick in the hospital or imprisoned and he cannot toil in Torah or perform commandments, even when he cannot actively proceed on his ascent to Mount Neverest, he is busy. He is busy observing the six constant commandments, he is busy protecting his faith, he is busy maintaining his status as the *one above* for the One Above.

Chapter Eight

Cops and Rabbis
(or: Dear Kindly Rabbi Krupnik)

Accepting authority and submissiveness

Excerpted from the original screenplay of a famous Broadway musical:

Riff:	Why, if it ain't Lieutenant Schrank.
Jets:	Top o' the day, Lieutenant Schrank.
Riff:	And Officer Krupke.
Jets:	Top o' the day, Officer Krupke.
Lt. Schrank:	I'll give you the top o' the head.
Officer Krupke:	Hey, you, get down.
1st Jet:	But we're havin' such fun.
2nd Jet:	We enjoy the playground.
Riff:	See, it keeps us deprived children off of the foul city streets.

And a bit later:

Lt. Schrank:	You're gonna start makin' nice with the Puerto Ricans from now on... 'Cause if you don't... and I catch any of you doin' any more brawlin' in my territory... I'm gonna personally beat the ... out of every one of you...

Anybody know who Lt. Schrank and Officer Krupke are? That's right, they are policemen. Anybody know who Riff and the Jets are? That's right, the Jets are a gang of street punks and Riff is their leader.

Riff and his gang are very polite to Lt. Schrank and Officer Krupke. But they are not very cooperative with them. They do not seem to respect these hard-working civil servants very much. You see, Lt. Schrank and

Officer Krupke give them advice that they do not ask for; advice like "Hey, you, get down" and "you're gonna start makin' nice with the Puerto Ricans from now on." The street punks don't feel like getting down (especially when such role models as Lt. Schrank and Officer Krupke tell them to) and they certainly don't feel like making nice to the Puerto Ricans. They don't like anybody telling them what to do. Nobody does. And since they are always crossing paths with policemen whose job it is to tell them what to do, they harbor a chronic dislike for policemen.

I was once reflecting upon this part of the production and I had a nagging thought that something about this act seems eerily familiar. I have heard this story before. Perhaps this particular scene is not so original. After perusing a much, much older book, I came across it – the original chareidi version of this performance. I like to call it South Side Story[1] and here are the main characters:

Gang Leader – Riff van Korach

1st Jet – Dathan ben Eliav
2nd Jet – Abiram ben Eliav

First Police Officer – Lieutenant Moses Schrank
Second Police Officer – Sergeant Aaron Krupke

In the early part of the story our Riff van Korach and his gang have a few tiffs with the "police." Lieutenant Moses instructs him to put a set of fringes with a single blue woolen string on the corners of his cloak. Riff gets his whole gang to wear blue woolen cloaks with no fringes at all. Further, Lt. Moses instructs him to place a parchment with two passages from the Torah on his doorpost. Riff has his gang put complete Torah scrolls in the rooms instead. For some reason, Riff and his gang do not feel like being very cooperative. Ironically, it is not because the task is difficult that they do not comply. If anything, their approach is the more costly and difficult one. The issue is simply that they do not want any "policemen" telling them what to do.

This concept is more clearly illustrated by Riff's two favorite henchmen, Dathan and Abiram. Just like Officer Krupke says to the Broadway Dathan and Abiram "Hey, you, get down," Lt. Moses tells the original Dathan and Abiram "Hey, you, get up here!" And they are just as eager to comply – "We will not come up! If you must preside over the people, must you preside over us, as well?"[2] Incidentally, this is not the first

---

[1] This refers to the South side of the Tabernacle where this story took place.

[2] Numbers 16:12,13

altercation between Dathan and Abiram and Lt. Moses. They had crossed paths years earlier when Officer Moses was just a rookie walking the beat. What respectful greetings did they have for him then? "Who appointed you an officer and a judge over us?"[3] Guess Officer Moses wasn't wearing his badge.

A bit further along into these productions we see just how deeply this sentiment of chronic dislike can penetrate one's soul.

Let's get back to the Broadway version.

Riff is upset that there is another gang of punks who inhabit his territory (the aforementioned Puerto Ricans). He does not savor competition so he sets out to challenge the rival gang and its leader into a decisive "rumble" which I suppose means a duel with multiple duelists on each side. To formally arrange this rumble he holds a "war council" with the rival gang leader at the local soda fountain. Things start to get a bit rowdy and Officer Krupke shows up again:

1st Jet:	Top o' the evening, Officer Krupke.
Officer Krupke (to Riff):	You!
Riff:	Me, sir?
Krupke:	Yeah, you. Didn't you hear me?
Riff:	Yes, sir. I got twenty-twenty hearin'.
Krupke:	Then why didn't you answer me?
2nd Jet:	His mother told him not to answer cops.
Krupke:	Wise apple, you want me to run you in?
2nd Jet:	Indeed not, sir.
Krupke:	I oughta run all you punks in. What are you standin' around here for?
Riff:	You see, sir, we're afraid to go home. Such a bad environment.

Eventually, Officer Krupke gets called away before managing to disperse the gang and, being a musical, the gang erupts into a cheery song all about Officer Krupke which bears the unmistakable message: Get offa my case!

---

[3] Exodus 2:14

The story is quite similar in the chareidi version. The minute that Riff van Korach is out of earshot from Lt. Moses and his partner, Sgt. Aaron, he erupts into his own song which relates the following fable:[4]

There was a poor widow who lived in my neighborhood with two daughters. Her sole possession was one small field which was her lone source of sustenance. She was about to plow her field when in walks Lt. Moses and warns her, "Take heed not to plow with an ox and an ass together." When she was ready to plant, again comes Lt. Moses and warns her, "You may not sow your field hybrid crops." Eventually, it came time to reap and Lt. Moses again admonishes, "You must forgo *leket* (gleanings), *shikcha* (forgotten bales), and *peah* (one edge of the crops)." When she was ready to store the produce the friendly Lieutenant informs her, "You are obligated to relinquish the priestly portion (*teruma*), and separate the first and second tithes." The widow suffered all this in silence and obeyed the authorities but when she evaluated this she determined, "It is not worthwhile for me to maintain this field and to undergo this burden." She thereupon sold the field and bought two lambs in order to profit from their wool as well as from their offspring. When the lambs first give birth, comes Sgt. Aaron and demands, "Give me the first born, for so it is commanded..." Later, when she was about to shear the sheep, Sgt. Aaron demands, "You are obligated to me the first shearings, as G-d has commanded..." Says the widow, "See how far I have fallen into a trap and cannot get out!? Let me slaughter the sheep!" As she slaughters the sheep, Sgt. Aaron returns and says, "I am entitled to the forearm, the jawbones, and the abdomen." Says the widow, "Even when I slaughter the sheep I am not free of him. I will consecrate the slaughtered sheep and now we will see his response!" After she consecrates the sheep, Sgt. Aaron approaches and says, "Now, I am entitled to it all because the Holy One has said, 'All *cherem* (consecrated properties) in Israel will be for you.'" And so he takes it all from the helpless widow and she and her two daughters are left with nothing and die of starvation.

Quite a tale, isn't it? I must comment that, since it is not entirely implausible,[5] it makes an impression. And it does not exactly portray Lt. Moses and his Law Book, nor the general chareidi lifestyle, for that mat-

---

[4] Yalkut Shimoni 750

[5] Some points are a bit implausible. Like most cases of those who slander Jews and chareidim by misrepresenting the facts, the picture is tainted by leaving out some minor details. For one thing, the obligation for the "first shearings" does not take effect with less than five sheep whereupon each fleece must weigh at least 12 *sela* for a total minimum of 60 sela. At that point the requirement is to give 1/60 or one sela out of 60 (less than 2%). Secondly, the second tithe remains the property of, and is to be consumed by, the owner. Thirdly, as much as this poor woman was obligated to surrender *leket, shikcha,* and *peah,* if she is

ter, in a positive light. Now, we may think that such a Hyde Park soap box speech wouldn't draw too sizable a crowd but the indications are that our Riff van Korach drummed up quite a following. And do you know why?

It's because he was able to appeal to the most basic and fundamental of human emotional needs. It's the one that I talked about in the introduction to this book. It's called independence, autonomy, and self determination. It is the longing of the human being to be the master of his own destiny – to be in control. And that means that we have a natural aversion to letting other people dictate our lives. Nobody wants to be policed. Nobody. Me, neither – you can put yours truly at the top of the list.

Still, even though nobody wants to be policed, that doesn't mean that we shouldn't be. Let's make one more comparison between the Broadway production and the chareidi version. In the Broadway version we left off at the scene where Riff and his cronies pour out their souls to the now off-stage Officer Krupke to explain why he "has them all wrong." Riff does not see the benefit of taking up the Officer's kind offer to "run him in." He also doesn't think that it is worthwhile to follow his advice about "makin' nice with the Puerto Ricans." This turns out be a serious error in judgment. By the end of the rumble, Riff makes a hasty – and permanent – departure from the entire production with a knife in his gut. No question, had he made nice with the Puerto Ricans or even had himself "run in," he would now be in much better shape (better to be "run in" than "run through").

In the original chareidi version there was also a rumble. Lt. Moses had strongly advised Riff van Korach, his henchmen, and his fellow Levites to be content with their status and not to decide for themselves how much fame and fortune they are entitled to. No good will come of it. When Korach and his band stubbornly insisted that Lt. Moses and Sgt. Aaron do not dictate the terms, it culminated in a rumble. The entire landscape began to rumble. By the time the dust settled, Korach and his gang of hooligans were stationed at the subterranean level. I suppose that some stages have a trap door – they exited stage center. In any case, here again, there is no doubt that if Korach had been more mindful of Lt. Moses' advice he would have lived to see a lot of *nachas* (delight) from his great-great grandchildren.[6]

---

truly poor she is eligible to receive *leket, shikcha,* and *peah*. Thus, in a real case scenario, the "system" does more to ensure her survival than to starve her to death. Of course, the whole story presupposes that G-d ignores her and does not reward her loyalty with material blessing. This denial of G-d's providence is the hallmark of the *seven below*.

[6] Korach was a direct paternal ancestor of the Prophet Samuel. See Rashi Numbers 16:7 and I Chronicles 6:7-13

At this stage (pardon the expression), I would like to point out one crucial distinction between these two performances. In the Broadway version the gang leader was a young hot-headed juvenile delinquent from a broken home who most likely never finished high school. In the chareidi version, the profile of the antagonist is much different. Our Korach is from the wealthiest of Jews, from the most distinguished of families, well connected, (happily?) married, and well educated. I find it puzzling that someone from such an illustrious background does not exhibit a bit more prudence. I am not alone. All of the classical Midrashim ask the identical question, "Korach who was clever, what made him consider this foolishness?"[7] They answer that his spiritual vision led him astray. He was able to foresee some very distinguished dignitaries among his descendents and thus calculated that he is obviously being short changed from his own allotment of dignity.

At least one commentator expounds that this is only half the picture.[8] This only explains why Korach thought that he could challenge the authorities and succeed. But the underlying motivation was nothing but jealousy. Initially, Riff van Korach didn't reject the concept of tribal princes and High Priests. There was nothing irrational about it. That is, as long as he could be one or the other. But as soon as he saw some other folks get the job, and he knew that he would have to answer to them, his perceptions changed. All of a sudden it doesn't make sense. What was logical up until Election Day becomes anathema the day after the [unfavorable] returns are in.

It would be one thing if he was merely uncooperative but it did not end there. From not studying and not complying (*seven below* Levels 1 and 2) he:

- Loathed others who were complying (Level 3)

- He despised the "authorities" and rebelled against them (Level 4)

- He caused others to rebel (Level 5)

- He denied that the commandments were given by G-d (Level 6)

And when somebody is this close to Level 7, I suppose he's as good as there. And all this because he felt that he shouldn't need to play second fiddle to his younger cousin and, accordingly, not to his older cousins either.

But how did it happen? He was so clever!? And he was learned, too. He did study. He had some toil in Torah under his belt. He should never

---

[7] Quoted in Rashi Numbers 16:7 s.v. *Rav Lachem*

[8] Rabbeinu Bachya Numbers 16:1

have set foot into the Camp Kelala. What went wrong?

The answer must be that the purpose of toil in Torah is to reap all of the benefits of the Bracha camp which culminates in "…And I shall put my sanctuary in your midst… And I shall walk in your midst and be your G-d…" As such, the true purpose of toil in Torah is to get close to G-d – to try to reach the peak of Mt. Neverest. This is what we chareidim call *Torah L'Shma* (studying Torah for its true purpose). Korach toiled in Torah but not in order to get closer to G-d. It was in order to clinch that coveted spot as tribal prince. Once he didn't get it, the toil in Torah was suddenly valueless and all that Moses had taught him, just as suddenly, became illogical.

In the course of my stated goal of championing the Torah lifestyle, which I have only for cultural reasons termed the "chareidi" lifestyle, I cannot evade the obligation of trying to solve the grand riddle. And that is: now that I have staked my claim that this "chareidi" ideology is the paradigm Orthodox ideology that is mandated in Leviticus 26 (and Psalms 1), has been successfully practiced for thousands of years, and brings on the most satisfying and successful living, why are NCOJs not chareidim? In other words, why do so many Orthodox Jews – Jews who have gone to Orthodox day schools and yeshivot and who are at least as clever and intelligent as I am, those who go to synagogue every Shabbat like I do and sit through[9] the same Torah reading and hear the same pronouncements from G-d about "going in My statutes" and "choosing life," Jews like my friend Morton (see Introduction) – why do these Jews not see things the way the chareidim see them?

Certainly, I have not been totally neglecting this issue. In Chapter 1, I wrote that the NCOJ knows the Chumash while the chareidi knows Chumash with Rashi. Only one who knows Chumash with Rashi knows that "choosing life" and "going in My statutes" involves toil in Torah. Since the NCOJ is by definition one who is not tuned in to Rashi's frequency, his receiver misses the signal. Yet, this begs the question as to why the NCOJ does not bother to take a closer look at the fine print.

In some cases the answer is that they are just plain too busy. All normal human beings want one thing in life – success and prosperity (I consider these to be one thing). This is what Thomas Jefferson calls "life, liberty, and the pursuit of happiness." Now, according to Leviticus 26:3 (per Rashi), only toil in Torah guarantees success and prosperity. Without it, the chances of success are just that – subject to chance. In other words, without toil in Torah, one is left with unproven and unguaranteed methods of achieving success. G-d calls it *happenstance*. It is a much

---

[9] You might notice that I didn't use the phrase "listen to."

more arduous method of achieving success (and it doesn't always work). What emerges is that someone who is not involved in toil in Torah is so busy seeking success and prosperity the hard way that he doesn't have time to stop and think that perhaps there is a more efficient method.

In Chapter 7, I offered another approach to this question. I wrote that the chareidi plays the game to win while the NCOJ plays the game for sport. If one is not playing the game to win, then there is no urgency to master all of the rules.

But the question keeps coming back to haunt us. If one is playing the game anyway, why not play it to win? There can be only two answers:

- They do not truly value the prize OR-

- They are not prepared to be bound by *all of* the rules (or both).

The first of these answers has similarly been previously addressed in these pages. Both in the Introduction to this book and again in Chapter 7, I discussed the importance of understanding the nature and the value of the "product" (remember Sy Sims?). This is the most basic issue of consumerism, so basic that it doesn't need to be included in my list of Consumer Hazards for it is the root of them all. Indeed, this is the essence of the first level of the *seven below* – *Lo lamad* – to not study and, consequently, to not know "what it's all about." The only remedy for this problem is consumer education which is the theme of Chapter 7 and indeed of the entire Book One. As such, to this point we have been discussing NCOJs who are *Lo lamads* – consumers.

But, not every NCOJ is a *Lo lamad*. I have known many people who do not advocate chareidi ideals who know quite a bit. Aside from personal acquaintances, these include quite a few Orthodox journalists who have penned the op-ed columns that inspired me to write this book. Some of whom are very intelligent, some of whom are very clever, some of whom are very learned.

Just like Korach.

Korach could have gotten very far in life. Indeed, he had gotten very far. But Lt. Moses told him one thing he wasn't ready to hear – "*Rav Lachem!*" You have gone far enough! You are not permitted to go further. You are restricted from your ambitions.[10] One early twentieth-century commentary[11] suggests another hidden meaning: *Rav Lachem* – you have a *Rav*, a Rabbi, a master. Although you are an exalted tribe, you are still

---

[10] This explanation is based on Nachmanides Numbers 16:5.

[11] Rabbi Zalman Sorotzkin, Oznayim L'Torah, Numbers 16:7. I have not found any Talmudic, Midrashic, or earlier commentaries that suggest this idea in relation to this verse. Nevertheless, this commentary mimics a comparable Talmudic exegesis in tractate Sota 13b with regard to G-d's admonition of Moses in Deuteronomy 3:26 where the verse uses the exact same phrase – *rav lach*.

subordinate to the Kohen (who, incidentally, is also from your tribe). You are not of the highest rank, he outranks you. Korach had a problem with this. He had a problem accepting orders from anyone except G-d Himself. He was ready to be G-d's lieutenant, except that G-d already had one and He didn't need another one. Korach was very clever. He knew it all. He didn't need any intermediaries between him and G-d. He can decide for himself how to carry out the commandments.

He didn't want to be policed.

Orthodox Judaism is very intrusive. Like the police it tells us what to do. Like Lt. Schrank and Sergeant Krupke, it gives us advice that we don't ask for. Not only does it tell us what we can and cannot do – all societies do that – not only does it tell us what we can and cannot eat – there are some cultures that do that, too – it also tells us what we can and cannot say, what we can and cannot see, what we can and cannot read, what we can and cannot hear, and what we can and cannot think. It tells us who we can and cannot marry and after we are married it tells us when we can and cannot touch the one we married. Even what it lets us eat, it tells us when we can eat it and when we can't. It tells us how to do it, too. How to work, how to play, how to study, how to pray, how to make love, how to make war and how to put on our shoes. Nobody knows this as much as the chareidim.

I have already written in the Introduction to this book why secular Jews are non-observant. To be observant, one must believe in at least these articles of the 13 principles of faith:

1.   There is a G-d who created us and everything that we can perceive. (Principle 1)

2.   G-d gave us rules – His Torah. (Principles 8 and 9)

3.   G-d is aware of everything that we do (and say and think) – in other words, He knows if we follow the rules. (Principle 10)

4.   G-d will reward us for compliance and punish us for transgression of the aforementioned rules. (Principle 11)

I wrote that some secular Jews simply don't believe in G-d. They never get to first base. Why don't they believe in G-d? They may say that it is because they don't see Him. Of course, we will say something else. We will say that it is because they don't look for Him. And why don't they look for Him? It is because this group is very intelligent. And they know that if they look for him they may actually find Him. And if they find Him, they will not be able to intellectually reject articles 2, 3, and 4. And they will have to follow rules that they are not prepared to follow. If they find G-d, G-d will control their lives. They don't want any G-d controlling their lives so they must make sure that there isn't One.

This group is easy to comprehend. The other secular Jews are a bit more puzzling. They claim to believe in G-d yet still reject article 2. And if not article 2, then articles 3 or 4. How they manage to do this is beyond me. They must be even smarter than the first group. But it shows me one thing – that even if one believes in G-d, he can still find some pretext to avoid subjecting himself to following rules that he is not prepared to follow.

Whenever I have carried out a conversation with an irreligious Jew or have read an op-ed piece written by one on the topic of religion, no matter what masterful rhetoric is put forth, I always perceive him conveying the same subliminal message: religion invades my life and tells me what to do – and I refuse to be policed!

"I refuse to be policed!" This is the mantra of the irreligious.

But now, we come to Jews who are not truly irreligious – yet not what we call Orthodox. These are the Conservative, Traditional, or *Masorati* Jews. These are Jews who, not only believe in G-d, but they, in theory at least, also believe in articles 2, 3, and 4. So they are amenable to following some basic rules so that G-d, who knows what they do, shouldn't get angry and punish them too much. But not all the rules. Not the ones that intrude into their lives like not watching television on Shabbat or not eating at non-kosher restaurants. They are only up to following the rules that they feel like following and, in general, these do not include rules that would make them alter their personal agendas. They will fit some rules into their agendas but will not fit their agendas into anybody's rules. No matter Whose. This is because they don't try to think like G-d; they expect G-d to think like them. So, if they don't see the logic in these rules, or they think that they are not up to date, then certainly G-d would think so, too, and would not expect them to obey such inconvenient rules. I suppose that this will explain why Masorati Jews are not Orthodox.[12]

With this, we have learned something frightening, and that is: we may actually believe in the primary articles of faith and still resist the demand for control over our lives that comes along with them. This is a

---

[12] A more precise explanation is that to be Orthodox, one must believe in all 13 principles of faith. Though these Jews may accept the four that I mentioned they seem to reject some others, most notably the two that bind us to the Talmud and the Oral law and, by extension, Shulchan Aruch. These are Maimonides' principles 6 and 7 which proclaim that all the words of the Prophets are true and that Moses was the father of all Prophets. It is only through Moses and the Prophets and subsequently the sages and Rabbis (the heirs to the Prophets), that we have established the tenets of Orthodoxy.

fundamental struggle in human emotion and it is relentless. Ultimately, it shadows us into the Orthodox camps.

It is the members of the Orthodox camps that begin to take G-d's presence seriously. Orthodoxy understands that G-d is not merely subjecting us to a few rules to inconvenience us and to test our loyalty to Him; G-d actually expects us to "walk in His statutes." Every step. G-d wants us to live a complete lifestyle that is strictly regimented and is starkly at odds with the rest of human society. It is not something that we prefer to do. G-d dictates our lives. But we are all human. We long for self-determination. Not all of us are prepared to take dictation. In fact, we have to be trained to take dictation.

I was born Orthodox and I was raised Orthodox and I have spent my entire life in the company of my fellow Orthodox Jews. I can only parrot the words of Rabbi Avigdor Miller that, collectively, we Orthodox Jews are the most exalted people on earth, a kingdom of priests and a holy people. Yet we are struggling. We are struggling with our yearning for self-determination and our reluctance to relinquish control to a Higher authority. We have always struggled. Lt. Moses told our very Orthodox forefathers, "You have been rebellious with (against) Hashem, from the day that I have come to know you."[13] No, things haven't changed much. I have observed this struggle within our community and I myself am engaged in it no less. I consider this the defining point of Orthodoxy.

Although there are no clear demarcation lines, and most of us fall into the gray areas, at least I can see the extremes. Those that are most successful in the skill of taking dictation can be called chareidim. For, according to the Prophet Isaiah, those who pine for the word of G-d are what he calls *chareidi*. And those who toil in Torah are pining for the word of G-d because that's where it's at. Those who are least successful at taking dictation and who, despite observing the commandments, are not seeking out the word of G-d are the non-chareidi and even anti-chareidi Orthodox Jews. And when I have discussions with or read op-ed pieces by those at this extreme, I hear the same subliminal message. "I know what the Torah says, you don't have to tell me (even though I only spent four years in yeshiva and couldn't wait to get out). I don't need to be policed!"

In my opinion, this, more than anything else, explains why intelligent and learned NCOJs are not chareidi.

Of course, if we would receive all the orders and details straight from G-d, it might be a bit less discomforting. But that doesn't happen any

---

[13] Deuteronomy 9:24

[14] Deuteronomy 10:12

more. G-d let us hear him say *Anochi* and *Lo Yihiye* and then He turned it over to His legal team to hash out the details. And this legal team also comprises the police force. It began with Lt. Moses and Sgt. Aaron. Ultimately, Lt. Moses promoted Cpl. Joshua who empowered the Elders who empowered the Prophets who empowered – the Rabbis. And so it has been for the past 2,000 years. The Rabbis tell us what G-d wants – despite the fact that we may not all see the logic to it. It is on their shoulders to give us advice that we don't ask for. It is their job to break the news to us about what else G-d forbids us to eat (and drink if you live in New York), what new activity is prohibited on Shabbat, how much longer we have to wait for our wives to regain their purity, how many people we can invite to our weddings, which cell phones to use and what restrictions to impose before we think of connecting to the internet. It is a thankless job, but someone's got to do it. They are the police – and nobody, but nobody, is happy to see the police.

Well, almost nobody. There is always a small minority who can come to terms with the police. These are the ones we call the *law-abiding citizens*. You see, a policeman is a civil servant, as is a Rabbi and a Kohen. He is just a representative of the law. He doesn't make it up, he just lets you know when you are violating it. If one doesn't respect a policeman, it is actually an indication that he doesn't respect the law itself. But to make it look like he is not actually disregarding the law, the delinquent doesn't *acknowledge* the law. His demeanor says that there really is no such law, the policeman is making it up himself. The policeman is not more authorized than I am to make up laws, so I certainly don't have to obey this over-imaginative policeman.

Korach's problem wasn't Moses. His problem was with Whoever passed him up for his younger cousin at the board meeting that elected the tribal officers. Korach knew that the final decision rests with G-d, the Chairman of the Board, but you can't exactly badmouth the Chairman and expect to stay on in the organization. So he had to blame the president of the company, Moses, and convince all his fellow employees that the president is making up the company policies behind the back of the Chairman and that nobody can complain about it because the only way to the Chairman's office is by way of the president's. He was so convincing that he convinced himself that the president was making up the policies. The Chairman would never overlook such a distinguished employee with an impeccable record. But in truth, it is just these kinds of controversial decisions that the president doesn't make himself. He will only do it with the full backing of the Chairman.

Korach was very clever and very logical. He did not see the logic in Moses' actions. Thus he claimed that Lt. Moses' orders were so illogical that he must be making them up. But his logic had one fatal flaw. It is not easy to tell people that you can't drink the tap water, that you can't take that medication on Shabbat, that you will have to reserve twin beds for most of your long awaited pre-planned vacation, that you shouldn't invite the entire office to your daughter's wedding. These are precisely the rules that nobody is interested in making up.

"And now, Israel, what does Hashem, your G-d request from you? Only for you to fear Hashem, your G-d, to walk in all His ways..."[14] G-d wants one thing from us – to fear Him, to be loyal to Him, to follow His directions, to turn over the reins to Him – to relinquish control. It is not easy. No human being wants to do that. And so the sages ask, "Is the fear of G-d such a trivial endeavor? Yes, to Moses (who spoke these words) it is indeed a trivial endeavor."[15] Moses got all of the details directly from G-d. It didn't take much to convince him that these rules are genuine. But we only heard the rules from Moses. Like Korach, it is easy to convince ourselves that they are not logical and that they are not genuine.

Nobody wants to be policed. Not even chareidim. We all want to be on equal terms with G-d. Adam and Eve wanted that. That was the sales pitch of the serpent: "Just one bite out of this fruit and you can be a competitor with G-d; you can decide *for yourselves* right from wrong; you can create your own worlds; you can go into business for yourselves." He neglected to tell them the full price, but G-d had already told them. G-d said, "If you eat that fruit, you will have to get down from the top of Mount Neverest and deal with death and decay. This is My domain, and, although I am happy to share it with you, in My domain there can be only One boss. If you want to control your own life you must descend into the world of Man; and the world of Man is the world of happenstance." For us Homo sapiens, the opportunity to be our own god is too tempting a deal to turn down, and so they bought it. They paid the price then and we pay the price now. We are forever struggling with this serpent.

G-d wants us to remedy this problem so that we can get back to the top of Mount Neverest where we belong. So after 2,000 years of chaos,[16] He revealed Himself to us and told us the word of G-d. He told us *Anochi* and *Lo Yihiye*. Here is what to do and what not. He told us *Im bechukotai telechu* and *V'Im bechukotai timasu*. Here is where to walk and where not. "I have created the *yetzer hara* (evil inclination), but I have created the Torah as an antidote."[17] But following the Torah means relinquishing

---

[15] Talmud Bavli Berachot 33b

[16] Talmud Bavli Sanhedrin 97a (also see Rabbi Aharon Feldman, *The Juggler and the King,* Feldheim Publishers, Chapters 14.1-14.3)

[17] Talmud Bavli Kiddushin 30b and Bava Bathra 16a

our claim to autonomy and self-determination. It means obeying the police. One can only stand to be policed if he understands who the policeman really is. The policeman is the one who tells us up front exactly what the Judge is going to tell us later. To be chareidi means to heed the word of G-d, the Judge. And He appointed Rashi and a host of other policemen to tell us how to do that. And even if they give us advice that we don't ask for, and even if the advice may not seem so logical, they are really only relaying to us the expert advice of the ultimate Judge.

So, when Lt. Schrank and Officer Krupke tell Riff and his gang that they should "get down" and that they should "start makin' nice with the Puerto Ricans" they are not just bossing them around. They are giving them the recipe for a longer and more productive life. I'm sure Riff would love to be here to confirm that. Same thing for when Lt. Moses tells Korach "your position is high enough" and to his buddies "Hey, you, come up here." He wasn't making anything up. I am sure that Korach would love to be here to tell us all how genuine Lt. Moses is but, presently, he is still stuck in the sauna. And when the writings and the rulings of the Rabbis over the generations and of the living Rabbis of our generation give us advice that we don't ask for and that may not meet our own sense of logic, they are actually just telling us what we need to know to get back to the top of Mount Neverest where we will be able to live forever. And for those of us who want to get there, that is advice worth listening to.

Chapter Nine

What's in a Name?

The true meaning of the term "chareidi"

I have discussed this book with countless people and I can say one thing for sure – nobody appears to have a hard time understanding what I am trying to do. This is no surprise as the chareidim and their role in society are timely subjects in today's day and age. Everybody knows, or thinks they know who the chareidim are. They are all over the Jewish and Israeli news.

The word *chareidi* – or *hareidi* or *haredi* or whatever – is scattered (read: splattered) throughout every Jewish periodical; it reverberates over the airwaves, on the planes and buses, through the chambers of the Knesset and the Israeli Supreme Court, through the halls of the schools and universities, in the cafes and bars of Tel Aviv, Herziliya, and Haifa, in the barns of the Kibbutzim, in the army barracks and police stations. Undoubtedly, in today's lexicon of Jewry, whether religious or secular, whether in Israel or in the Diaspora, the word *chareidi* is a household term.

It wasn't always this way. In fact, the term *chareidi* in its present day usage and connotation is surprisingly new.

How new?

Well, as I wrote in a footnote (35) in Chapter 5, the venerable everything-you-could-ever-possibly-want-to-know-about-Judaism-and-more Encyclopaedia Judaica, in its hardcopy version originally published in 1972, does not include an entry entitled *Haredim* or even *Ultra-Orthodox*. Apparently, as of that point in time, neither expression was much in use. It is only the CD-ROM version that was released in 1997 that saw fit to add such an entry. Evidently, somewhere in the span of this 25-year interval the term *chareidi* has staked its claim.

Where did it come from and how did it get here?

The term *chareidi* is actually just one of a host of synonymous terms that appear within Jewish literature to connote some variation of devoutness. In Chapter 4, I mentioned that the "prescription" of Leviticus 26:3 – performing commandments with toil in Torah as a means to success – is echoed by King David in the opening chapter of Psalms:

> Fortunate is the man who has not walked in the counsel of the wicked,
> and in the path of sinners he has not stood and in a session of scoffers he
> has not sat; but rather *has made the Torah of G-d his desire* and in His
> Torah he will articulate daily and nightly. And he shall be as a tree [firmly]
> planted along the tributaries of water, that yields its fruit in its season
> and its leaves shall not wither, and *all that he shall do will succeed...*
> Not so the wicked...[1]

At the conclusion of this opening chapter, King David identifies his
heroes: For G-d knows the way of the *tzaddikim* (righteous ones)...[2]

In the eyes of King David, the Jews that follow this prescription –
i.e., the members of the *one above* camp of Leviticus 26 which are the
Jews that I wish to call *chareidim* – are to be referred to as *tzaddikim*.[3]
This term and three others comprise the set of synonymous terms that are
included in the poetic liturgy that we recite on the Sabbath and Festivals:

Through the mouth of the straightforward – *yesharim* – He is praised.

And through the words of the righteous – *tzaddikim* – He is blessed.

And through the tongue of the altruists – *chassidim* – He is exalted.

And through the innards of the holy – *kedoshim* – He is sanctified.

These four terms, among others,[4] can be found repeatedly throughout the Scriptures, particularly in Psalms. Indeed, relative to these others,
the term *chareidim* is dismally scarce. Essentially, it was the Prophet
Isaiah, a direct descendent of King David, who introduced to us the term
chareidim in this context.[5,6]

New synonymous terminology surfaced in the Talmudic era. The

---

[1] Psalms 1:1-4

[2] Ibid. 1:4

[3] See Rashi's commentary on Isaiah 66:5 s.v. *Chareidim*

[4] Some terms that come to mind are *anavim* (humble ones) and *yerayim* (G-d
fearing).

[5] Isaiah 66:5. There is only one other place in all of Scripture where the term
chareidim is used in this context: Ezra 10:3.

[6] Nevertheless, it is curious to note that the initials of the four terms that are listed
in the Sabbath liturgy are highlighted in many prayer books as they spell out the
name of our forefather Isaac (Y – *yesharim*; Tz – *tzaddikim*; Ch – *chassidim*; K
– *kedoshim*; Y[i]-tz-ch[a]-k = *Yitzchak*). It is interesting that in Genesis (27:30),
the verse juxtaposes the term chareidi with the name Yitzchak – "*Vayecherad
Yitzchak charada* (and Isaac trembled a trembling)" as if to associate the term
chareidi to the other four prominent terms.

Mishna mentions two terms: *Perushim* (Pharisees; literally – those who segregate themselves [from heretical influences]) and *chaver* (literally – friend or member) to connote those who remain steadfast to traditional Halachic observance. In addition, we find the term *talmid chacham* (literally – wise student) to connote a Torah scholar or one who is learned. All of these terms are repeated in the gemara with the addition of the term *tzurba d'rabbanan* – a young (literally – sharp or witty) Torah student.

So now we are faced with five or more scriptural terms and approximately four additional Talmudic terms and, as I noted above, the term *chareidi* is probably the scarcest of all. Not only does it only appear twice in the Scriptures but aside from one passage in the Talmud that quotes and expounds upon the verse in Isaiah 66,[7] it is not stated at all in the entire Talmud! Yet today, for better or for worse, it is the terminology of choice. How did this come about?

Firstly, I must concede that the modern usage of the term and the mistaken concept of chareidim as a nouveau religious socio-political movement did indeed develop in the wake of the Enlightenment. In a book in Hebrew about the life and times of Rabbi Meir Simcha HaCohen of Dvinsk, it states:[8]

> In opposition to the terrible danger of Enlightenment and Zionism that hovered over the nation, the Sages of Israel commenced to coordinate in order to protect the autonomy of the observers of Torah. In various central locations, chareidi organizations sprouted:
>
> ■ In Hungary – *Irgun haKehillot haChareidiot* (Organization of Chareidi Communities) – established 1869.
>
> ■ In Galicia – *Kehal Machzikei haDat* (Congregation of Upholders of the Faith) – established 1878.
>
> ■ In Germany – *Hitachdut HaChareidim* (Union of Chareidim) – established 1887.
>
> ■ In Poland and Russia – *Knesset Yisrael* (Assembly of Israel) – established 1906.
>
> ■ In Galicia and Bukvina[9] – *Histadrut Chareidim* (Order of Chareidim) – established 1912.
>
> My argument in Chapter 5 is that this concept of a new movement is

---

[7] Talmud Bavli Bava Metziah 33b

[8] The Ohr Somayach, Bergman, Asher, Hebrew self-published Bnei Brak 5761 pp. 108-9

[9] No, I don't know why it lists Galicia again and I also never heard of Bukvina.

fundamentally erroneous because, in reality, there was no *new* movement but rather a rejuvenation of the socio-political organizational framework of the original 3,000 year old "movement." This socio-political framework had existed before, notably during the second Temple era but, as I wrote there, it fell into disuse in the post-Talmudic era due to universal persecution and had to be reconstituted in the 18th century when a new wind of tolerance swept the world. Those *one-aboveniks* of the second Temple era called themselves *Perushim*,[10] yet they characterized today's chareidim in every aspect – they were motivated by the Rabbinic interpretations of Mosaic law, they were a [minority] political presence, they were hated and shunned by many of their brethren, and...they persevered!

Note that three out of the five above mentioned organizations used the term *chareidi* to characterize their essence. I cannot be certain as why they chose that particular appellation but it is reasonable to assume that it was modeled from the passage in the Talmud in tractate Bava Metziah 33b which expounds on the verse in Isaiah 66. Nevertheless, it is just as worthwhile to note that two of the organizations did not use this term. This indicates that the term was somewhat popular but not necessarily the "global" standard. As the book states, these five organizations were founded to give a voice to the traditional Halachically observant camp of European Jewry to counteract the pressures and political influences of the assimilated "elite." They were meant to represent all of "Orthodox" Jewry and not to create distinctions *within* the Orthodox camp. Thus, the term *chareidim,* when used, was merely an official title but the adherents were referred to simply as the *mitzvah observant* or *shomer-Shabbos* Jews – both within the camp and without. Yes, of course, there were *Chassidim* and *Mitnagdim*, but, for the most part, there were no *chareidim*. Some of these organizations eventually merged into what is the present day Agudath Israel, which likewise did not adopt the term.[11] In America, until very recently, everyone is pegged – Satmarers are called Satmarers, Bobovers are called Bobovers, Lubavitchers are called Lubavitchers, and the *mitnagdim* are called Agudah-niks. Until the past decade, nobody was called *chareidi*.

---

[10] As I annotated in footnote 35 in Chapter 5, even today the term Perushim is the official term for the descendants of the original Ashkenazi chareidim who arrived in the eighteenth and nineteenth centuries. It is more that non-chareidim began to call them chareidim, and that is what stuck.

[11] The Machzikei haDat of the Galician Chassidim remained independent. The Rebbi of Belz, ZT"L survived the Holocaust and made his way to Eretz Israel where he reestablished the Machazikei haDat organization which remains vibrant to this day.

Now, let's set the Wayback Machine for 1918. After the British conquest of Palestine, Dr. Chaim Weizman prevailed upon the British mandatory government to establish an official Chief Rabbinate for the Jewish communities in Palestine. The purpose of this Chief Rabbinate was more to showcase the Jewish establishment in preparation for eventual statehood than for the purpose of helping the Jewish residents observe Halacha. The *Perushim* of Jerusalem, led by Rabbi Joseph Chaim Sonnenfeld, ZT"L, could not abide by the standards of this Rabbinate and immediately established an independent Rabbinate that initially called itself *Vaad HaIr L'Makhelot haAshkenazim – HaEida haChareidit* (Municipal Committee for the Ashkenazic Communities – the Chareidi Congregation). Even then, it was known simply as the Vaad HaIr; the term "*haChareidit*" merely lagged on as the caboose. At that point in time, the Vaad HaIr was associated to some extent with Agudath Israel. After 1948, they split away from Agudath Israel as a result of differences of opinion on how to relate to the new irreligious state. Because of this split, coupled with the fact that the old city of Jerusalem was lost to us and an undefined Palestine became a smaller and more-defined State of Israel, they dropped the *Vaad HaIr* and changed their name to the *Beth Din Tzedek* (Court of Justice) *L'Makhelot haAshkenazim – HaEida haChareidit.* Henceforth, to the present they are known as the *Bedatz* (more accurately: *BeDa"Tz* – acronym for *Beth Din Tzedek*). In relation to the Zionist establishment, this faction was relatively weak and self-contained though they made a lot of noise due to their affiliation with Neturei Karta. Thus, although they represented the long standing *Yerushalmim* – i.e., the *Perushim* – they did not represent the entire gamut of the *one above* camp such as the Agudah-based "yeshivish" Jews, the newly developing chassidic communities, the *mitnagdim* in Bnei Brak, nor the Sephardim. The appellation of *chareidi* was theirs and theirs alone. And they didn't use it too much, either.

So, after all this, how did the term *chareidi* come to encompass the entire *one above* contingent and evolve from an exclusive members-only realm into the vernacular of the outside world?

The answer is that there are two realms of influence where the Eida haChareidit assumed the dominant role on behalf of the *one-aboveniks* that propelled them into the public arena.

The first is their active and aggressive opposition to the secularists and the institutions of the irreligious State of Israel vis-à-vis the more passive defiance that has characterized the other factions. Although all of the *one above* factions identify uniformly with the core issues – Shabbat observance and street closures, uninhibited Torah study and the infrastructure to support it, modesty in public, and respect for the dead – it was the

Eida haChareidit that had the temerity to issue public proclamations decrying the breaches, to call for demonstrations,[12] and to actively challenge the edicts of the government. To be sure, this is far from absolute; all of the factions comprise some members who are more zealous and, conversely, many who are not interested in confrontational endeavors. I intend to discuss this subject at length in a later chapter. What is certain is that, whether in the forefront or not, the Eida haChareidit dominated the headlines.[13]

This is one primary factor that has ensured the entity known as *chareidim* an indelible spot on the Jewish sociological map and it answers the second half of my lead question – how the term chareidi penetrated to the outside world. The as-of-yet unanswered question is: what caused this appellation to spread and to become the umbrella term for the entire *one above* community, something that only evolved over the past three decades?

In line with this first realm of influence, the most convincing theory would probably be that, ever since the founding of the state, the two most concentrated hamlets of the *one-aboveniks* has been the Meah Shearim-Beis Yisrael-Geula section of Jerusalem and the town of Bnei Brak. These two communities fought long and hard to win the insular characteristics that all stringently observant pious Jews value – absolutely no motor traffic on Shabbat enforced by barricades in the streets, no public breaches of modesty, no non-kosher shops, etc. Initially, these were the only two such urban communities in all of Eretz Israel. Jerusalem carried the pre-eminence of being Jerusalem and its insular ghetto was indeed dominated by the Eida haChareidit. As such, this enclave became known to all as the *chareidi* area of Jerusalem. Consequently, all who reside there, regardless of their personal affiliations, are identified as chareidi.[14] It is only over the course of the past few decades that the stringently observant came to infiltrate and establish other urban areas which followed the same model as the parent enclave – Jerusalem neighborhoods such as Bayit Vegan, Tzanz-Unsdorf-Mattersdorf, Sanhedria Murchevet, and, more recently, Har Nof, Kiryat Belz and Ramat Shlomo; the chareidi neighborhoods of Ashdod and Netanya; and new towns such as Beitar

---

[12] Although there is no denying that the demonstrations typically escalate into violent confrontations, it must be stressed that the Eida itself never condoned nor incited any kind of violence.

[13] I am not overlooking the Neturei Karta. For our purposes it would be too confusing to make a distinction between the Eida and the Neturei Karta although they are not truly one and the same.

[14] This is called: guilt by association.

Illit, Kiryat Sefer, Ramat Beit Shemesh and El-Ad. As all of these communities essentially emulate the Meah Shearim-Beis Yisrael-Geula model despite the fact that their leadership is not specifically governed by the Eida haChareidit, they are all termed *chareidi* communities and, consequently, the inhabitants are all *chareidim*.

I have a second, much more subjective theory based on the second realm of influence of the Eida haChareidit: *the quickest way to a man's heart is through his stomach.*

To a large degree, all the various factions of what are today known as chareidim were capable of maintaining their standards among themselves and did not need to rely upon the other factions for much, except for one thing: everybody needs to eat – and the food has got to be kosher.

As the Eida haChareidit took the most uncompromising stance on Halachic as well as political issues they did not wish to rely upon the Kashrut standards of any Jewish faction. As the concept of organized Kashrut certification agencies was coming into vogue they could not ignore the call-to-arms to establish their own Kashrut agency that adheres to the strictest standards of Halacha. They needed to be able to certify every primary type of food because they wanted their community to eat Bedatz Eida haChareidit certification and nothing but. Any local Rabbinate could certify that a given product is *Kosher* but a product that the Bedatz certifies is *Kosher L'Mehadrin* ("Appropriate for the Meticulous" – i.e., the most meticulous level of Kashrut). I am not certain if they are actually the first mehadrin agency but they are certainly the foremost – the Rolls Royce of Kashrut agencies. Other mehadrin agencies – Agudath Israel, Machzikei haDat of Belz, Chug Chatam Sofer, and, more recently, Shearit Yisrael, among others – have rivaled them. Moreover, most of today's chareidim are not overly selective and rely on a broad range of mehadrin agencies. Yet, there is no question that the most universally accepted certification is Eida haChareidit.[15] Common indicators include the fact that most wedding halls in Israel (certainly in Jerusalem) that serve the general chareidi public strive to carry the Eida haChareidit supervision and that if one requests "Glatt Kosher" meals on El Al airlines for flights out of Tel Aviv, he gets meals certified by the Eida haChareidit.

As a result, the mainstream stringently observant[16] community has

---

[15] Virtually all of the mehadrin agencies incorporate Eida haChareidit foundation foods into their products. Conversely, the Eida haChareidit does not rely on any other agency even for foundation foods, they insist on checking out the source food themselves.

[16] As I wrote in a footnote in the pilot chapter, I disdain the term ultra-Orthodox.

long been united in this that they respect and appreciate the Bedatz Eida haChareidit certification. Prior to the proliferation of so many mehadrin agencies, the stringently observant might say, "I only eat *Bedatz*" or, alternatively, "I only eat the *chareidi hashgacha*." Thus, when it came to the fare on the Shabbos table or to their upcoming *simcha*, all of the "frummies" were proud to identify with the Eida haChareidit.

Now, despite my insistence throughout this book that the true definition of a chareidi is solely an ideological status and that external symbols and habits are superficial and inaccurate, I certainly cannot argue that these superficial indicators are the popular basis for identifying who is a chareidi. No doubt, the most commonly applied indicator for determining who is a chareidi is the individual's appearance, how he or she dresses and grooms. In short, a chareidi is somebody who looks like a chareidi, and I suppose that this is probably true more often than not. Still, externalities are just that – externalities; superficial and quite often misleading. A more accurate, though still imperfect, indicator would be one who visibly upholds chareidi disciplines, one of the most basic of which is what he will and will not eat. And, as a rule of thumb, chareidim are adamant on mehadrin certification. Thus, in the eyes of the non-chareidim, the Israeli *one above* community was distinguished in that they would cohesively rely on, eat, and serve "chareidi" kashrut. This cohesive conduct stuck to them so that over the years, the term chareidi became more of a unifying icon. Thirty years ago, before we were all called *chareidim* one might say, "The *mehadrin* Jews insist on chareidi kashrut." Today, however, things have changed and the same observer would more likely say, "The *chareidi* Jews insist on mehadrin kashrut."

Although this second theory may not be as authoritative as the previous one, I do feel that, at the very least, it does make a significant contribution to the phenomenon. What is more important is that it suggests that, whether I like it or not, most people base their criteria for identifying chareidim on their appearance and ritual behavior rather than on what they think and believe. And that brings me to the main gist of this chapter and, indeed, to this entire section of this book.

Everything that I have written in this chapter on this point is the material for an introductory chapter, not an epilog. After all, in my real introductory chapter I posed the question "Who are the chareidim...?" Yet, I consciously neglected to address the topic of "Where did the term *chareidi* originate?" until now because it truly is not that important. What is important is not so much the question "how did we come to be called chareidim over the past few decades?" as is the question "what has the term chareidi come to mean over the past few decades?" In other words, I am not so concerned as to where the term came from; my concern is:

where is it going?

Before we go on, I think it is worthwhile to review the fundamental ideas that I have been promoting throughout this volume:

- A chareidi is one who buys into G-d the Father's contractual deal (heretofore: policy) as stated in Leviticus 26:3 in accordance to Rashi's commentary adapted from Torat Kohanim which stipulates that our side of the deal involves performing the commandments with "toil in Torah."

- Toil in Torah does not mean that every Jew must drop everything and dedicate his life to nothing but Torah study. Toil in Torah means that every Jew should continue doing what he does best with the aspiration of creating a society that functions along the guidelines of the laws of the Torah as well as do whatever he can to increase the knowledge of the laws and philosophies of the Torah among all the members of this society and, subsequently, among all of mankind. This latter aspect ideally entails some level of personal study and, at the very least, full scale support – moral and financial – of those who can study more intensely.

- Man's ultimate purpose is to come as close to G-d as he can. This is accomplished by emulating His traits.

- The very minimum *implementation* requirement to be chareidi – in conjunction with the ideological adherence to chareidi principles[17] – is to observe the commandments at their most basic level, not to wantonly violate any negative commandments and to recite *Kriat Shema* twice a day[18] (and mean it).

- Every Jew is invited to the party – Black tie (and suit and hat and velvet kipa) optional.

The ideology that I am trying to promote throughout this entire project is the ideology of Torah, pure and simple, the way it would be presented by Rashi himself were we to be sitting at his feet 900 years ago.[19] I do not seek to add to it nor to subtract from it. In a nutshell, it is what we

---

[17] These would be the concepts that were covered in Chapters 6 and 7 – Maimonides Thirteen Principles of Faith, Pirkei Avot, Messilat Yesharim and Chovot HaLevavot.

[18] See Kitzur Shulchan Aruch 45:23

[19] Moreover, I am not promoting any particular subjective understanding of the verse or of Rashi's position. If the reader sincerely maintains an interpretation of the Torat Kohanim that differs with mine, then I urge him to follow his own viewpoint.

Ashkenazim call *Yiddishkeit*. Ideally, it would follow that the best term for the followers of this discipline would be, well – Yidden!

Oh, how I wish this was so. Alas, it seems that, although all Jews – all Yidden – are encouraged to buy into G-d's policy, there are many uneducated consumers who cannot recognize value; and they are not signing up. And so, King David looks upon those who do sign up and he calls them *tzaddikim* and he calls them "fortunate." And Isaiah calls them *chareidim* and he says that "we will see in their rejoicing." And I am attempting to write a book that is a guide for the consumer; a book that tries to explain why it is worthwhile to sign up for the policy, why it is worthwhile to be a chareidi. But who am I? I am not King David and I am not the Prophet Isaiah. I am just an unemployed chareidi who took on a new line of work, a policy agent (you can't beat the commission), and I am looking for buyers. I have a nice smile, an effective pitch, and a proven product – so, why am I having a hard time?

I once read a booklet that was put out by Proctor and Gamble that explains the entire process of bringing a new product to market. It told the true story of the history of one of their most successful innovations – the disposable diaper. It led the reader through every step of development from the initial idea,[20] researching marketability, researching and choosing raw materials, product design, developing the prototype, product testing, test marketing and, the final and most crucial step – naming and packaging the product. This last step is a whole science in itself and numerous names were suggested and considered by the best heads in the business. They eventually marketed it under the name Pampers and we all know that it was, and remains, a great success. The message of the booklet is that every individual step must succeed in order for the product to succeed. If it fails in the earlier stages, it usually means the product was never viable. But if it fails in the last step, it means that poor packaging and publicity scuttled an otherwise very useful and seaworthy vessel.

I fear that the term *chareidi* has, of late, evolved into a troublesome and highly charged expression. So much so that many who easily fit my definition, indeed, who would most likely fit anyone's definition, are uncomfortable with the appellation. One of my mentors, a very prominent Rabbi from one of the "blackest" neighborhoods in Jerusalem, said to me through his long beard and *bekesha*, "I would say that I don't consider myself a chareidi."

Why did he say that? Obviously, he wasn't defining chareidi using

---

[20] Believe it or not, the story goes – from the booklet – that it all began when one chief executive of P & G was babysitting for his grandchild. As he struggled with the cloth diaper he told himself that there must be an easier way. He broached the subject at the next board meeting and the rest is history.

my definition. He certainly has no trouble with Rashi's commentary on Leviticus 26. He must have been drawing on the "other" definition.

What is the "other" definition of a chareidi?

Noah Efron presents a 275-page study to address the question of why the chareidim are hated and shunned by the secular masses in Eretz Israel. Toward the end of the 275 pages he can present no better answer than to posit that Israeli secular Jewry, much like the general non-Jewish Western societies, in order to ascribe moral credence to its hedonistic culture, needs to designate a distinct not-as-hedonistic population as a sinister "other," a black sheep, the scum that we dare not view as viable counterparts and certainly dare not associate with, emulate, or contribute toward their existence. To some degree the Palestinian Arabs can play that role, but during the more peaceful interludes, when there is no other agenda but to confront the domestic disorder within our own domain, the secular masses have to conjure a closer, more domestic "other." The chareidim are the natural – and virtually unopposed – candidates for this vital role. As such, writes Efron:

> It is my opinion – or guess, I suppose – that hating Haredim, despite its recent setback, is a growth industry because Haredi-hating is a defining element of Israeli identity and is perhaps on the way to becoming *the* defining element of Israeli identity. Palestinian suicide bombers pose a more bloody threat to the safety of Israelis than the ultra-Orthodox ever would, but ultimately it is still the ultra-Orthodox who provides the most useful foil for Israelis seeking to understand ourselves. In the end, the Haredi is the better "other."[21]

This appears to be a universal human need. The nations of the world need a black sheep and, for this coveted honor, we Jews have been designated the Chosen People. Yet, it doesn't end there. The enlightened assimilated elite, the *maskilim*, likewise need a black sheep (after all, they are assimilated), so they turn their attention to the *datiim*, the Orthodox. This is the point to say *dayenu* – enough. We *datiim* are not assimilated to the non-Jews and we do not need to emulate this trend. But Orthodoxy itself is plagued with consumerism and, as I enumerated in the hazards of consumerism, notably hazards #2 and #3 and specifically hazard #6: *A consumerist Jew is in danger of regarding himself to exist on a plane that is separate from other religious Jews…*, an Orthodox Jew so afflicted will likewise make judgments using Western standards. That being the case, an Orthodox Jew who has fallen victim to hazard #6 of the consumerism syndrome will also need to designate a black sheep, a "different" Orthodox Jew who does not share his Western values – a sinister "other"

---

[21] Efron, Real Jews, Basic Books, New York 2003, p. 264

– for himself. And who fits this bill more than the Leviticus 26:3 chareidi?

And so, to many Westernized consumerist mitzvah observant Jews, the term chareidi has come to mean the "other." I believe that this connotation is what my Rabbinic mentor had in mind when he made his comment.

In order for a given population to qualify for the distinguished role of a distinct, sinister "other," they must fulfill two stipulations:

- They must be distinct

  AND –

- They must be sinister.

Consequently, an Orthodox Jew who feels compelled to view the chareidi as the "other," must incorporate into his core definition of chareidi whatever distinguishing and adverse characteristics happen to be available. This tends to be a bit tricky because, on the surface of things, we are all hewn out of the same stone and we pledge allegiance to the same belief system but, with a bit of creativity, it can be done. The result will be some of the more opinionated and, might I say, inflammatory definitions among those suggested in the beginning of Chapter 1:

- Ancient backward out of date Jews (Distinct and somewhat sinister; socially out of touch).

- Jews with beards that aren't trimmed, funny black hats, long coats and long dresses, thick stockings, and wigs. (Distinct; non-conforming).

- Jews that don't work (Sinister and somewhat distinct).

- Jews that don't pay taxes even if they do work (Sinister).

- Jews that go around collecting money (Sinister).

- Jews that don't go to the Israeli army (distinct and aloof), who throw stones on Shabbat and burn Israeli flags (Sinister).

- Jews that won't eat in your house (Distinct; anti-social).

But, as I mentioned in Chapter 1, these definitions are intrinsically flawed because the minute one incorporates specific adverse traits – such as stone throwers, draft dodgers, flag burners, *chiloni* haters and parasites – into his core definition of chareidi, it follows that one who does not indulge in these stimulating pastimes cannot be chareidi. He must be something else. But what? There must be another, less controversial term for my kind of chareidim, but what is it? Oh, there are plenty of potential candidates – *yesharim, tzaddikim, chassidim,*[22] *kedoshim, yerayim, anavim* – but nobody implements them. Why not? Are there no such people?

Alas, in the eyes of these consumers there are none. *Every* chareidi throws stones at cars, burns Israeli flags and evades the army. If they didn't actually do it, it's because they never had the chance. It absolutely must be so because that is what a chareidi is. None of them work or pay any taxes. All of those ultra-Orthodox fellows in the Diamond Exchange complex only sit and play pinochle all day long. Oh, all right. There are a select few who work but those aren't real chareidim. They can't be because a chareidi is by definition someone who doesn't work. So this fellow must be a – a – let's see now, I don't use the term *yashar* and I wouldn't call him a *tzaddik* so I guess he's a – a not-so-bad Jew who likes to dress like a chareidi. That must be it. A not-so-bad Jew in chareidi drag. But I'll bet he won't send his kids to the army so he must be a real chareidi but, then again, he's working so I suppose there must be some chareidim who do work. I wonder how he avoids paying taxes because no chareidim pay taxes…

As I wrote in the Introduction, if this syndrome was restricted to secular non-observant Jews we would write it off as a consequence of *shiabud malchuyot*, the yoke of exile, and there would be no need for a book such as this one. After all, Torah-observant Jews ought not shape their *hashkafot* based on the opinions of the non-observant. But it was articles such as this one that prompted me to take on this project:

> What could have brought another Jew and an Israeli, growing up in his own country, to deface a Jewish house of worship and to wish its occupants dead?
>
> I thought about it. Perhaps it was someone who had seen ultra-Orthodox Jews throwing stones at cars traveling on nearby Bar Ilan road one Sabbath. Perhaps it was someone who'd watched bearded, black-suited Jews on TV ignoring the siren for Israel's fallen during Memorial Day, or who had read endless newspaper articles about how the ultra-Orthodox were receiving army exemptions, subsidized rentals, preferred mortgages, and educational stipends despite the fact that they burn the flag of the country in which they live and spit in the faces of those whose pockets they empty with such cynical arrogance, for that is the picture our television and newspapers paint, based unfortunately on the awful reality.
>
> I, of course, and my family…are not guilty of any of those crimes. We

---

[22] Here I obviously mean the Talmudic connotation and not today's social connotation. See Rashi in T.B. tractate Menachot 40b s.v. *Chassidim.*

serve in the army with pride. We support the State with our taxes and pay our bank mortgages, and our children's unsubsidized college tuition. We deplore the disgusting manipulations of corrupt, self-serving "religious" politicians who callously use our G-d and His holy Torah to siphon off funds desperately needed for the unemployed, the handicapped, social and educational programs, handing them over to those perpetuating a parasitical lifestyle that is as far from Torah values as it is possible to imagine.

But how could the "stupid kid" who wrote those hateful words know that? After all, we don't raise our voices in protest when religious extremists achieve yet another victory against the State and its well being. We don't say out loud what many of us believe, that the greatest tragedy for the Jewish people in the land of Israel is the fact that there is an intermingling of synagogue and state. We don't say loud enough: "One nation, one draft" and those who won't serve, and won't work, and won't pay taxes, can leave and try their luck siphoning off funds from the welfare offices in Williamsburg. We don't object that the National Religious Party is out there with all the rest, its hand outstretched to get its share, its political agenda geared to its own narrow constituency's interests, and the Torah, and G-d, and justice and the public good be damned.[23]

Who wrote this article? Evidently, it is someone who attends an Orthodox synagogue, is a champion (and expert) of "Torah values" as well as of "justice and the public good," and is careful to write "G-d" with a dash. Actually, this writer is a renown and prolific author and journalist who resides in a quite religious suburb of Jerusalem, no stranger to the "ultra-Orthodox."

There is much to comment upon this article and, indeed, the upcoming part of this book (Book Two) is slated to deal with it in detail, but, for the moment I wish to focus on her statement that, "I, of course, and my family...are not guilty of any of those crimes." From the article to this point we have learned:

- The ultra-Orthodox (chareidim) ignore the siren for Israel's fallen during Memorial Day.

- They collectively receive army exemptions, subsidized rentals, preferred mortgages, and educational stipends – apparently, it is only them and for no particular reason.

- All of the above beneficiaries burn the flag of the country in which they live and spit in the faces of those whose pockets they empty

---

[23] For the full text and creditation of this article, please see Appendix B at the end of this book (page 307).

with such cynical arrogance.

- The picture that our television and newspapers paint is based on the "awful reality."

- Everything listed above constitutes a crime (probably not including the picture painted by the television and newspapers because it is based on the awful reality).

- The writer and her social circle are not guilty of any of those crimes (perhaps they are guilty of different ones but not these.)

In other words, this mitzvah observant writer, who does not consider herself chareidi, is in one class of Torah values – presumably because they observe the siren and serve in the army with pride – while all these "criminals" are in another class which happens to be "as far from Torah values as it is possible to imagine." There are no such criminals in her class. No siree, there can't be! Once they transgress these crimes they are automatically assigned to the "other" class. It is the criminality that *defines* the classes. And so, the chareidi, or, in this case, the "ultra-Orthodox," is defined as the "other" – or, perhaps, worse.

I am reminded of the following story: The Coca-Cola company wanted to market their product in some third-world Asian country. They produced labels that read "Coca-Cola" in that country's script and they inquired how to say "Enjoy" in the local language. They stocked the product in the markets and strategically displayed signs in the native tongue that read "Enjoy Coca-Cola!" After all this, scarcely anyone would try their product. After a bit of investigation they were able to detect the problem. They discovered that in the local language Coca-Cola means "snake on a stick."[24]

Now, here I am, spearheading a selling campaign using all the popular slogans: "Try being chareidi – it's the real thing!" "Chareidiism gives life – have a chareidi and a smile!" "*Yesh chareidim, yesh chaim!*" yet, sales are down. What is the problem?

Perhaps I am not speaking the local language.

Men are from Mars and speak with the Martian dialect; women are from Venus and speak with the Venusian dialect. I must be from planet Isaiah-66 (one of the moons of planet Meah Shearim-Bnei Brak where all of us aliens come from – I actually arrived on the MIR space station) and I speak in the *Isaiahish* dialect. In Isaiahish, *chareidi* means a *one-abovenik* which means one who sees *Anochi* or *Lo Yihiyeh* in every deed (Exodus 20); one who lives by *Im b'chukotai telechu* (Leviticus 26); and

---

[24] I have no idea if there is a grain of truth to this story. In fact, I am quite skeptical.

one who declares these two ideas twice daily when he says *Hashem E-lokenu Hashem Echad* (Deuteronomy 6); hence, the secret chemical formula, $Xd_{20}Lv_{26}D_6$. Now, all of us chareidim actually speak Isaiahish so we know that the product is actually a brand of refreshment. As the providers, we know what the product consists of. But to the consumers who do not speak in the Isaiahish dialect, when they see the billboards and advertisements promoting the product, it says to them "snake on a stick" and they decline to even read the brochure.

Case in point:

From the time that I initially undertook this project I have been pondering about how I will get this published. It was clear from the outset that, although the *hashkafic* perspective of this book would undoubtedly conform with the values of the mainstream chareidi publishers such as Targum Press and Feldheim Publishers, this book is intended to stray beyond the placid confines of Torah *hashkafa* and confront the stormy realm of today's socio-political standoffs. It is intended to be both contentious and pretentious (if not audacious). Although I have the strongest connections with some of these printing houses,[25] it was no surprise to hear them say that this book is too touchy (and cynical) for their mandates. I actually expected this and so I set out, as I knew I would, to seek a publisher that produces Torah works that has a bit more flexibility.[26]

One of the most promising candidates was a relatively new East Coast-based Jewish publishing house that I will call Rishon Publishers. I anticipated that Rishon would be interested in this work, for one reason, because it looked like a perfect fit for their corporate mission which, according to their website, was:

> ...to publish quality, popular Orthodox Jewish scholarship that is both sophisticated and accessible to a general readership. If you have a book or an idea that you think fits our mission, please contact us.

Further, they state:

> We publish books of Jewish scholarship, both traditional and academic, on any issue of contemporary or scholarly relevance. Some examples are contemporary Halacha, Biblical studies, philosophy/Jewish thought, history of Jewish customs and biographies.

> We do not consider technical academic works for publication because

---

[25] The chief editor of Targum is a neighbor as well as a relative of mine and the chief editor of Feldheim is a former *chavruta* (study partner) of mine from Natwich.

[26] I did not "discover" Mazo Publishers until well after this incident. Chaim Mazo is one of the best kept secrets in the Orthodox publishing industry.

they are too specialized for the general public. We are, however, interested in academic works that can be understood and embraced by non-specialized readers.

We only accept books that are written in English. However, English works with occasional foreign phrases in the text or footnotes are acceptable.

We only accept submissions that adhere to Orthodox Jewish beliefs, albeit interpreted in as inclusive a manner as possible.

I knew my book fit the descriptions that they listed and didn't expect that aspect to be an issue. In terms of this being a "sophisticated work of Jewish scholarship" on an "issue of contemporary or scholarly relevance" that "adheres to Orthodox Jewish beliefs" it was certainly right down the pipe, particularly for one who accepts "inclusive interpretations." For a second reason, they seemed to have scored some early success by handling an exceedingly controversial work so it was evident that they don't shy away from material that may be somewhat contentious. It seemed to me that, to the contrary, they would be intrigued by a work that had the potential to stir up a bit of commotion.

I readily put together my package including a cover letter and the half-finished manuscript and emailed it to the publisher, one Rabbi Alan Tuderman, to the United States 6,000 miles away. A mere 37 minutes later I received a reply from 6,000 miles away that began as follows:

Dear Yechezkel,

Thank you for submitting your manuscript. While it seems like a book I would want to read, it does not fit in with Rishon's mandate. It looks more like a Targum or Feldheim book.

Boy, was I thrown. I am certain that, beyond the cover letter, he could not have properly read any substantial share of the book over the 37 minutes. The issue could not be the sophisticated scholarship or even the contentious or aggressive thrust of the book. The issue was nothing more than the perceived affiliations of the particular faction of Orthodox Jews that were designated as the protagonists (I suppose the word "Chareidi" in the sub-title tipped him off). Evidently, "Orthodox beliefs albeit interpreted in as inclusive a manner as possible" might include any possible hashkafa *except* chareidi. I promptly emailed him back as follows:[27]

---

[27] Edited for brevity and clarity. I wish to express my appreciation to Rabbi Tuderman (not his real name) for granting me permission to disclose this correspondence.

Dear Rabbi Tuderman,

Thank you very much for your quick reply. I wonder if it wasn't a bit too quick.

I, as a typical conceited wannabe author, think that it is more than a book that you would want to read, it's a book that you would want to sell. Of course, I can't argue with the boss but I am a bit curious as to what precisely is Rishon's mandate. Based on the brief paragraphs that are on your website I see every reason for it to fit in. Apparently, you are avoiding books that smell from Targum / Feldheim. Just to understand, I would like to know the distinction that you want to maintain between your books and Targum / Feldheim.

As for my book, as far as the hashkafa part goes, it would likely fit with Targum / Feldheim books. However, this book is meant to veer off of hashkafa and get involved in confrontational social issues. Although I did send a copy to M… at Targum, I truly speculate that Targum will say that it is too confrontational as well as cynical and they need to keep [away from controversy].

Anyway, let me know if I am supposed to consider this a full-scale rejection (and I will accept it as such) or just a first impression blues. In case of the latter, I do urge you to give it a serious once-over (I don't think you are being fair to yourself if you don't).

Remember – Don't judge a book by its cover letter!

Here, again, the reply was immediate, brief and startling:

[No greeting]

In short, selling the Chareidi world to non-Chareidim is an admirable goal but not one for Rishon. If anything, *we would be doing the exact opposite.* (Emphasis mine – YH)

"If anything we would be doing the exact opposite." I suppose this means that Rishon's mandate in providing sophisticated works in Orthodox Jewish scholarship is better served by selling the non-chareidi world to chareidim than by selling the chareidi world to non-chareidim. Did he realize what he was saying in our language? As I noted, it was obvious that he hadn't read (or, at least, comprehended) any substantial portion of my book. If he had, he would have learned to speak Isaiahish and he would realize that he is telling me, "Selling *im b'chukotai telechu* to adherents of *im b'chukotai timasu* – i.e., *one above* to the *seven-belowniks* – is an admirable goal but not one for Rishon. If anything, we would sell *im b'chukotai timasu* to the followers of *im b'chukotai telechu – seven below* to the *one-aboveniks*." So much for inclusive interpretations of Orthodox beliefs!

Of course, he didn't mean exactly that, but close to it. He doesn't speak Isaiahish and so, in his language, *chareidi* means "snake on a stick." He already knows what a chareidi is so the idea of considering a conflicting opinion is a bit disquieting as if to say, "I better not read too much of this book lest I discover something that will change my perception." It's not just a "snake on a stick," it's a dead "snake on a stick."

Many people cannot or do not want to understand this book because they have preconceived ideas of what a chareidi is. The biggest challenge that I face in writing this book is the hurdle of getting the reader to release his grip on his preconceived notions and to define *chareidi* using the definition that the chareidim use. It is a daunting task. Even my Rabbinic mentor was discouraging. He said, "If you want to sell Yiddishkeit, then go and sell Yiddishkeit. Leave the chareidim out of it. Get the word out of the book."

After the experience with Rishon that I related above, I could well see his point and I thought long and hard about it. But, if you are reading this, it is clear that I couldn't go through with it. This is because, on the lips of both the protagonists and the antagonists, the community that adheres to Leviticus 26:3 is the one that is today called *chareidi*.

It must be abundantly clear by now that this half of the book is meant to be a portrayal of who the chareidim truly are. The upcoming half of the book is meant to deal with who everybody else thinks we are. And these two entities are certainly not the same. We are not a society that does *a*, *b*, and *c* and that does not do *x*, *y*, and *z*. This characterization confuses people who observe, sometimes inaccurately, chareidim not doing *a*, *b*, and *c* or actively doing *x*, *y*, and *z*. We are a community of people who are devoted to upholding and maintaining a long-standing system of values and beliefs. To rephrase that into English, it is not accurate to say that chareidim are Jews who don't work, don't pay taxes, evade the army, dress in outlandish garb, throw stones, burn flags, hate secular Jews, etc. All of these characterizations are distortions. What is indeed accurate are statements such as:

- [Chorus:] The chareidim are those who promote observance of commandments with toil in Torah…

  … a portion of whom dedicate their lives to Torah study and are not employed in a gainful enterprise.[28]

---

[28] This is actually the case in many fields of employment in the secular world, particularly what is categorized as a "civil servant" including police and law

- [Chorus:] The chareidim are those who promote observance of commandments with toil in Torah...
  ... most of whom opt to avoid military service.

- [Chorus...] ... many of whom prefer to dress in traditional garb.

- [Chorus...] ... a few of whom zealously defend these values and are predisposed to forceful tactics.

- [Chorus...] ... some of whom distance themselves from those who are not [as] observant.

None of these "adverse" characteristics are constants and, as such, they do not warrant being included in the core definition of the term chareidi. But as long as Jews, Orthodox or not, require a distinct, sinister "other," a "snake on a stick," this misconception will persist. This is why I disagree with my Rabbinic mentor. It wouldn't matter if we were called *yesharim, tzaddikim, chassidim, kedoshim, yerayim, anavim, Perushim* or *chareidim*. To us, the *one-aboveniks*, all of these lofty terms are one and the same. To the *seven-belowniks* any given term presently in vogue that refers to the "other" kind of Orthodox Jew means "snake on a stick."

It is not my desire or intention to make distinctions or categories within observant Judaism. We are all the children of G-d the Father. He says so Himself, "Sons are you to *Hashem* your G-d; you are not to make leagues..."[29] This can be understood not as two distinct statements but as one relational statement – *because* we are all equally the sons of G-d the Father, we, *therefore*, have no business dividing ourselves into separate "leagues." But G-d does designate two camps. He says *Im b'chukotai telechu* which He calls "*et haChaim v'et haTov*"[30] (the source of life and all that is good) and he says *V'Im b'chukotai timasu* which He calls "*et haMavet v'et haRah*"[31] (the source of death and all that is evil) and he tells us, all of us, where to stand – "*u'bechartem b'Chaim!*"[32] (And you shall choose life!) He does not make distinctions between His children,

---

enforcement personnel, firefighters, paramedics and emergency service personnel, politicians, lawmakers and judges. All of these people generate no revenues and are supported totally by their communities – the taxpayer's dollar. To us, the full time scholars are another (more exalted) class of "civil servant." By engaging in the purest form of toil in Torah and, thus, enticing G-d to make good on His side of the deal, they provide a most essential community service and we are happy to support them.

[29] Deuteronomy 14:1. This verse is being interpreted in accordance to the exegesis of the Talmud in tractate Yevamot 14a.

[30] Deuteronomy 30:15

[31] Ibid.

[32] Deuteronomy 30:19

but by our choosing to stand in different places, we segregate ourselves.

With this in mind, I am thinking that perhaps I should acquiesce to the opinion of my Rabbinic mentor. Chareidi means "snake on a stick" to too many people. And, therefore, for anyone who feels the need to incorporate these adverse characterizations into their core definition of chareidi, I am not suggesting to them to embrace chareidiism. Certainly not their concept of charediism. I am merely suggesting that they embrace Leviticus 26:3 as Rashi teaches it. You might say to embrace *Yiddishkeit* – albeit Rashi's *Yiddishkeit*. This is what G-d mandates. This is what King David praises. Don't aspire to be chareidi, just to be a Leviticus 26:3 Jew or, better yet, a $Xd_{20}Lv_{26}D_6$ Jew. Be a *one above* Jew or a Davidic Jew or call it whatever you like. Perhaps, even reread this book and replace every instance of the term *chareidi* with the alternative term of your choice. But, one note of caution: If you try this exercise or commit to being this kind of Jew, you will readily discover that there is no substantial difference between yourself and those that *you* currently call *chareidi*.

Chareidio-active Fallout

A chareidi perspective on rebellious youth and fallout

Author's note: Technically, this chapter does not belong in this volume. The chareidi position on social issues is the subject matter for Book Two and this particular chapter – which discusses the phenomena of chareidim who stray from the path – is slated to be one of the final chapters of the entire project. Nevertheless, due to the timeliness and the relevance of this topic, and in light of a plethora of recent publications that address this issue and that have received much attention, I felt drawn to jump ahead and prioritize this chapter, albeit out of sequence. This chapter not only analyzes the issue in line with the principles of One Above and Seven Below, but it also provides valuable insights on how to overcome some of the hurdles. It is in the sincere hope that readers may truly benefit from this chapter that I have resolved to include it in this edition of the book.

Note that this chapter is not intended to substitute for professional or Rabbinic advice in the event of real-life situations.

I have a very close friend who I will call Sruly.[1] Sruly is one of the sharpest, most quick-witted snappy-one-liner artists that I have ever known (a mentor of sorts), a Tzanzer *einikle*[2] (from two lines), and a confirmed chareidi. He once remarked to me matter-of-factly, "I know that I will never go *off the derech*. I wouldn't be able to stand back and watch while my kids become *baalei teshuva* (penitents)!"

I am pleased to report that it's been at least twenty years now and, true to his word, Sruly has not gone *off the derech*. In fact, I cannot off-handedly think of anybody from my yeshiva friends and acquaintances that have gone *off the derech*. And with this, I am prepared to make one of the boldest claims among all that I have made throughout this book:

As a rule, chareidim do not go *off the derech*!

---

[1] Of course that's not his real name. His real name is Yisroel. Just Sruly is what I have been calling him for over 30 years.

[2] A direct descendent of Rabbi Chaim Halberstam of Tzanz, the progenitor of the Tzanz, Klausenberg, Sighet-Satmar, and Bobov Chassidic dynasties.

Hold everything! Stop the presses!

Am I naïve? Am I blind? Are there not tens and hundreds (if not thousands) of chareidi *noshrim³* and *shababniks⁴* frequenting the seedier haunts of Jerusalem and New York? Are there not ever-increasing help organizations created specifically to attend to these wandering souls? Has not the general Orthodox press – and ever more so, the chareidi press – devoted countless articles and issues in its periodicals of recent years to address this plague?

The answers to these questions in reverse order are: Yes, it has. Yes, there are. Yes, there are. No. And no.

Here is what I mean to say:

From the chareidi perspective, going *off the derech* (heretofore OTD) may not be what we think it is. It may differ somewhat from the general perception. So first, let us examine the general perception.

What do we know about why young Jews go OTD? Let's first see what the experts have to say. There is no need for me to disclose that I am not the first writer that is addressing this issue (nor that I am not an expert). I am sure that many readers are aware that the Agudath Israel of America monthly periodical, *The Jewish Observer*, ran a number of issues devoted exclusively to this topic over the course of the past few years. In addition, a book was very recently published entitled, "Off the Derech: How to respond to the challenge" by Mrs. Faranak Margolese.⁵ This work is an in-depth study of the problem of why observant Jews forsake observance. This book has served as a wake up call throughout the greater Orthodox community and is heralded for its thoroughness and candor.

The author's basic premise is that there are three components to a healthy and positive attitude toward observance:

- The feeling component

- The belief component

- The implementation component

The *feeling component* means that if someone is going to embrace a highly demanding discipline such as Orthodox Judaism, they must feel positive, comfortable, and secure about the religion and those who practice it. If they acquire negative feelings due to being coerced, shamed, or

---

³ Israeli term for "dropout" which is its literal meaning.

⁴ Israeli term for street bum.

⁵ Margolese, Faranak, *Off the Derech*, Devora Publishing Company Jerusalem, 2005

humiliated in the name of religion or by observing insincere, miscreant, or hypocritical behavior from other Jews, especially those who are potential role models, they are likely to get "turned off" and rebel. This can be rephrased as the emotional aspect.

The *belief component* means that they must believe in the authenticity and pragmatism of Judaism. It has to make sense. After all, if it is not the "true religion," why practice it? This is the intellectual aspect.

The *implementation component* refers to how readily one can maintain the rigors of Orthodox religious observance in the face of physical challenges. These challenges come in the form of adverse forces within the community or environment usually coupled with weakness of character or health, social, marital or financial difficulties. This can be rephrased as the logistical or practical aspect.

According to Mrs. Margolese, all of these components interact to influence a person's commitment toward observance. In an ideal situation, all three components are in a positive mode – a person feels good about his religion, believes in it, and is up to weathering all the challenges – and, consequently, he remains fully observant. Unfortunately, in many situations one or more of these components do not score passing grades. In an extreme case, where none of the three components generate satisfaction, it is relatively inevitable that the subject will forgo observance. Most situations are more complex. One may feel good about Judaism yet question its beliefs or, conversely, he may maintain a strong intellectual appreciation yet be disillusioned by all the insincerity that he encounters. One can be facing neither of these issues yet find it difficult to maintain observance in Moosejaw, Saskatchewan, on the Berkley campus, while stationed aboard the USS Nimitz, or if he cannot hold down a job or sustain a marriage.

The author notes that these components are not of equal import, nor do they relate equally at various stages of life. She maintains that the emotional aspect is most influential, followed by the intellectual aspect and, least significantly, by the logistical aspect. The emotional aspect is the first player to show up as it stakes its claim from early childhood onward. The intellectual aspect does not normally kick in until adolescence and the logistical aspect typically asserts itself from early adulthood. These factors help explain why some people who experience similar events react differently. As we know, some people are more predisposed to emotional influences – the SFs of the Myers-Briggs scales – while others may be predisposed to intellectual influences – the NTs.[6] It

---

[6] This may be a bit incoherent to readers who are not familiar with the ideas of Carl Jung and personality typology. In a nutshell, SFs are people who tend to

is a reasonable assumption that these inborn personality traits will impact the way an individual values Orthodox Judaism's ideology and/or conventions. Likewise, these factors shed light upon why one person rebels at a relatively young age and others who seem to have a rock solid foundation take a left turn further down the road.

In terms of "how to respond to the challenge," her conclusions are relatively self-evident. We, as parents and educators, must do our utmost to bolster positive impulses in all of the three areas and to maintain and promote a religious environment that meets the emotional, intellectual and logistical needs of our charges.

Firstly, I must comment that this is overall a superb work, long overdue, and I highly recommend it. All that she wrote is "to the point" and can be applied to the general Orthodox Jewish population across the board, chareidim and non-chareidim alike. Having said that, I must comment that despite the thoroughness of her work with regard to the general Orthodox population, if we wish to narrow our perspective and focus primarily on the chareidi faction (which narrow-minded people like me certainly wish to do), something is lacking. This is because, although Mrs. Margolese's book aptly describes why Jews from "observant" backgrounds forsake observance, it comes up just a touch short when it comes to discussing why Jews go "off the derech." You see, before we can determine the aspects of going off the derech we have to define one crucial detail:

The derech to where?

Where does the derech takes us? How are we supposed to get there? How do we know if we are on the right course – or off of it?

Mrs. Margolese's book doesn't spell this out. It only talks about abandoning observance. And, what exactly is "observance?"

One thing that greatly impresses me about the author's manner is that she is meticulous about defining her terms. Notwithstanding, she concedes that there is one term that is exceedingly troublesome. Lamentably, it is the term that appears most frequently in her work – *observance*. In her introduction she writes: "Even defining observance, the first and seemingly most simple step, was complex."[7]

---

acquire information through Sensory processes (S) and make judgments based on a subjective Feeling (F) technique, i.e., employing likes and dislikes and humanistic considerations. These tend to be the more "feely" types. NTs are people who gather information through abstract iNtuitive processes (N) and make judgments based on a more objective Thinking (T) or logic-based technique and they are the more "brainy" types. Of course, there are also STs and NFs and all this is just a fraction of the whole picture.

[7] Margolese, Faranak, *Off the Derech,* Introduction pg. 15

I wholeheartedly agree that this is a complex step, and I will explain why I agree (though somehow I have a nagging suspicion that this is not what the author meant). According to the principles that have been posited in this book, there are two realms of "observance":

- The observance of Leviticus 26:3 – If you are to walk within my statutes (*Im bechukotai telechu*)

- The observance of Leviticus 26:14,15 – And if you do not hearken to Me... (*V'Im lo tishmau li...V'Im bechukotai timasu*)

We previously pointed out that according to Rashi, the first realm of observance – observance that is integrated with toil in Torah – is the currency to buy all of the ensuing benefits and is our admission ticket to Camp Bracha. I would like to call this realm *Torah observance*. This is the credo of the chareidim.

The second realm, mechanical mitzvah observance that is not supplemented with toil in Torah, is inherently substandard and, left to itself, it will eventually deteriorate into non-observance and culminate into heresy.[8] In relation to *Torah observance*, a comparable term for this realm might be *mitzvah observance* or *compliance* but, all through this book, I have employed a more concise term. I have called it *consumerism*.

The author indeed goes on to say that she settled on the most rudimentary – and universal – definition available, "For clarity's sake, I use a classic definition of 'observance' – the *halachic* observance of Shabbat and *kashrut*."[9] In short, her book and all of the statistics that she associates to it, is addressing the lowest common denominator of Orthodox Jewry. It is addressing the consumers.

This being the case, we can now postulate as to why she makes no attempt to define an even more fundamental term: what is the *derech* as in "*off the derech*?" I think that we can safely assume that there is no true need for her to define "the derech" because it is patently obvious that, to the consumer, the definition of "the derech" and the definition of "obser-

---

[8] This does not happen overnight. Often it is a slow process that involves several generations. Many Jews who are at the top level of the *seven below* manage to maintain a lifelong holding pattern. This will not last indefinitely. Inevitably, their offspring will either discover "Torah observance" or decline further.

[9] By this, I assume she means rudimentary kashrut. I have noted in other places within this book that the Kitzur Shulchan Aruch (45:23) presents a slightly more expanded description of minimal observance – (1) Not publicly transgressing any basic commandments (which is generally characterized by observing Shabbat and kashrut as Mrs. Margolese writes) plus (2) reciting the Shema twice daily (though, obviously, this stipulation is restricted to the male population).

vance" are one and the same. Being observant, which currently means merely "the *halachic* observance of Shabbat and *kashrut,*" is "the derech."

And, indeed, so it is in the mind of the NCOJ! Let us recall that the NCOJ is defined as the population that is at the uppermost level of the *seven below* – those that observe mitzvot but who stay uninvolved in toil in Torah. To the NCOJ, the "*halachic* observance of Shabbat and *kashrut*" as well as any other ritual commandment is the end-all and be-all of Orthodox Judaism. That is as far as "the derech" goes.

Now, I already conceded that I am not an expert on this subject, but if my assumption is correct, I think I have a much simpler explanation of why "mitzvah observant" (consumerist) Jews go off the derech. I didn't get this idea from a 400-page book, I got it from a one line bumper sticker. The bumper sticker read[10]:

If you don't know where you are going, any road will get you there!

If mechanical observance of commandments (*mitzvah observance* or *compliance*) with no involvement in toil in Torah is, in itself, the finish line, then it is quite obvious that although to many Jews these commandments will offer a sense of religious identity and fulfillment, there will be many others who will ask, "What for?" Performing commandments merely for the sake of religious identity is not much of a derech. Many Jews from Orthodox homes may not feel such a pressing need for religious identity. They would rather eat what they want and do what they want on Shabbat and settle for a bit less religious identity. Keeping Shabbat and kosher and coming to shul and wearing *tefillin* cannot be an end goal. And as long as I don't know what the end-goal is, perhaps any road will get me there.

So now we can see a clear cut reason why consumerist mitzvah observant Jews leave observance: They do not see religious observance as a means to an end! To these Jews, either there is no ultimate goal or they do not identify with the ultimate goal. If one does not believe that there is a pot of gold at the end of the rainbow, he will not invest his energies in following rainbows.

This is what I stated way back in the Introduction of this book as Consumer Hazard #5: *A lack of knowledgeable conviction to inspire subsequent generations to remain within the fold.*

For this population, to simply maintain the status quo of religiosity is an uphill battle. As Mrs. Margolese is defining observance as the bare minimum, she is discussing Jews whose starting point is the uppermost level of the *seven below*. It follows that her book is predominantly[11] dis-

---

[10] It was the one just below *Don't follow me, I'm lost too!*

[11] In her section on statistics at the back of her book, she presents figures relating

cussing why people descend from Level 1 of the *seven below* to Level 2 and lower. When we look at it from this perspective the answer to her thematic question (on the cover of the book) "Why observant Jews leave Judaism" is self explanatory. We are talking about consumerist Jews – Jews whose starting point is Level 1 of the *seven below*, Jews who are already in the *"V'Im bechukotai timasu"* camp and, consequently, are *already* off the derech by Rashi's (and Torat Kohanim's) definition. This being the case, it is no surprise that one falls from Level 1 downward. Rashi tells us that it is the natural cause-and-effect.[12] It is what we should *expect* to happen!

This is because there is absolutely no safety apparatus intervening between Level 1, mechanical compliance, and Level 2, non-compliance.[13] Likewise from Level 2 to Level 3 to Level 4 ad infinitum (Level 7). So, in addition to the problem of undermining the essential purpose of being observant, we have "natural causes" for people to fall from compliance to non-compliance, similar to the reason why many people who walk at the edge of an unsafeguarded cliff fall off – gravity! When a force that pulls one down gets hold of somebody and there is no safety harness to prevent being pulled down, down he goes. It is all but inevitable. Mrs. Margolese's entire work is an analysis of what are the "gravitational forces" that pull consumers from Level 1 downward. In this capacity, her identification of the three primary components – the emotional, intellectual, and logistical aspects – are very relevant.

All of the above rides on the premise that *the derech* and *observance* (or is it *compliance?*) are one and the same. I have a bit of trouble with this premise, at least, when we are discussing chareidim. As Sen. Joseph Lieberman once said, "We see [this issue] through a very different set of eyes."[14]

To the chareidi, merely being compliant or mitzvah observant is not true observance. It doesn't meet the standards of Rashi and Torat Kohanim. There is a more sublime level of observance – Torah observance. And until one accepts upon himself *Torah* observance, he has not yet even

---

to the religious upbringing of the 466 valid applicants who responded to her on-line survey. The two categories that can be termed as chareidi would be "Black Hat/Yeshivish" and "Chassidic." Each of these groups comprised 12% of respondents. This says that 76% of the respondents are from non-chareidi backgrounds.

[12] Rashi on Leviticus 26:15 s.v. *L'Hafrechem*

[13] Rashi's commentary on Leviticus 26:14 s.v. *V'Lo Taasu* – "Once one does not study [Torah] he will neglect to perform [mitzvot]."

[14] Acceptance speech for running mate for the Gore / Lieberman Presidential campaign August 16, 2000. I voted for Bush. I am not from Florida.

begun to embark upon "the derech." He remains a consumer.

So now, what does a chareidi mean when we talk about the derech?

Let's start from the finish line and move our way back to the starting gate.

In Chapter 7, I wrote at length that chareidi ideology dictates that we are here in this world for some ultimate purpose. I called this "the object of the game." Ramchal explains that this purpose is to become as much like G-d and, consequently, as close to G-d as we can come. Since the optimal status is the ability to revive the dead, I termed this goal as reaching the peak of Mount Neverest. For achieving this, Ramchal calls upon the 12 step development course set out by Rabbi Pinchas ben Yair, meaning, that there are twelve virtuous character traits that one must master to advance to the finish line. The very first of these traits – the starting gate – is *Torah*. I understand "Torah" to mean the Torah oriented wisdom and perception that can only come about through toil in Torah study. Without achieving this initial trait it is impossible to advance further and certainly impossible to reach the finish line. This is why only with the dimension of toil in Torah can one aspire for the Bracha of the *one above* (or, One Above). Mere mechanical observance of the commandments, compliance, without toil in Torah cannot get the job done.

As such, when a chareidi talks about "the derech" it means the road to the top of Mount Neverest. So at least we know where we are supposed to be going. We also know that to get there, we must start at square one. It cannot be bypassed. As Rabbi Pinchas ben Yair tells us, the starting point is the acquisition of Torah. This is what is meant by *Torah observance*. Coincidentally, Leviticus 26:3 tells us that just reaching this starting point is the secret to success *in this world* (the other 11 steps are for maximum success in the next one). This is what I called the *one above* camp or the camp of Bracha. To us, going OTD means moving away from toil in Torah (Torah observance), or moving out of Camp Bracha.

Now we understand why very few true chareidim go OTD. Who, in their right mind, would want to leave the confines of Camp Bracha and wander into Camp Kelala?

But, alas, can I deny what we can all readily observe – so many young people from chareidi backgrounds who are aimlessly drifting? After all, what about the 24% of OTD respondents to Mrs. Margolese's on-line Web survey who indeed hail from chareidi backgrounds?[15]

---

[15] Here, I am referring to the figure quoted above in footnote 11. I don't know whether to be encouraged or discouraged by this figure. On one hand, the statistic that non-chareidi OTDs outnumber the chareidi OTDs by more than 3 to 1 seems to indicate that the problem is less than one third prevalent in chareidi circles.

Undoubtedly, we chareidim certainly do face a problem, but it is not the identical problem. Remember that I contend that there are two realms of observance. Each of these realms maintains its own set of characteristics.

The Mishna in Pirkei Avot discusses four types of scholars.[16] At the two extremes we have the most successful scholar who is described as one that is "quick to hear (comprehend) and resilient to lose (i.e., forget what he learned)," and the least successful scholar who is described as one that is "resilient (slow) to comprehend and quick to lose." Between these extremes we have the more consistent types: the one that is "quick to comprehend and quick to lose" and the one that is "resilient to comprehend and resilient to lose." Of these two types, the former is considered "one whose loss overcomes his gain" since, at the end of the day, despite having initially taken in an abundance of material, he has forgotten most of it and has wound up unlearned. His efforts bear little fruit. Conversely, the latter of the two is considered "one whose gain overcomes his loss" since, despite only being able to absorb a much smaller volume of material, he doesn't forget any of it and his efforts pay off.

When we look at these two realms of observance we see something very similar. Each realm has its own set of characteristics. The non-chareidi mitzvah observant realm is easy to come by. When a person is born into a family that observes mitzvot and is himself trained to perform mitzvot, we consider him to be *Frum From Birth* (FFB). The implication is that one *can be born* a mitzvah observant Jew. On the flip side, we have repeatedly claimed that if this mitzvah observance is not charged with toil in Torah, it is susceptible to rapid deterioration. As I wrote above, this is due both to a natural "gravitational" pull away from observance and, in a more practical sense, to not seeing an ultimate goal and purpose for religious observance. Thus compliant mitzvah observance is "quick to obtain and quick to lose."

The chareidi, Torah observant, realm is a bit different. To understand where we are going with this, we must review a point that was discussed back in Chapter 3 – *Everything You Always Wanted to Ask*. In that chapter, I observed that within chareidi society, as with virtually any value system or "ism," there are varying degrees of adherence. Roughly, I broke

---

On the other hand, perhaps only 1 out of 4 "Orthodox" Jews is chareidi to start with, in which case, the problem spreads evenly across the board. This is one reason why statistics such as these are so unreliable. Of course, the most distressing thing is that there were 466 OTD respondents from our brethren regardless of how they started out.

[16] Pirkei Avot 5:15

it down to three primary levels which I nicknamed *hot, lukewarm* and *cold*. Allow me to add to this another insight about value systems which I maintain to be fully applicable to chareidiism: people aren't born with these ideals, they are all acquired.

These insights converge to tell us that no matter how staunchly chareidi the native environment, it does not make someone truly chareidi. As chareidi is an ideology, no one really qualifies until he is capable of internalizing it. Doubtless, a chareidi upbringing gives one quite a head start, and can make the path a smooth one to follow, but it won't get him there. You might say that within the chareidi community, every individual starts out as a 2nd degree chareidi who I referred to as the "I am a chareidi because I was born a chareidi" chareidi. From this beginning one can move up to 1st degree, move down, fall out, or remain where he is. Thus, although it is in vogue to call one *Frum From Birth*, it makes no sense to call one *Chareidi From Birth*. The full commitment to a chareidi lifestyle must be nurtured. The message of Leviticus 26 is that as much as the Torah and all its benefits are a rightful heritage for all the Jewish people, G-d the Father is not *giving* it to us. He is *offering* it to us to purchase, to acquire. It comes at a price, it comes with toil. It does not come for free.

So what is actually happening when we a see a member of the chareidi camp going OTD?

The answer is that, in most cases, we are not looking at a 1st degree chareidi who has targeted a goal and has toiled and achieved but rather somebody who, despite his upbringing, never bought into the deal and, consequently, he never received the goods. In the chareidi world the problem is not that somebody went OTD, the problem is that he never started out.

So, now we understand that when we are dealing with two different realms of observance, the problems of non-observance that apply to each are two different problems. In the NCOJ world, the challenge is not in getting people to get on the derech. That is relatively easy, "quick to obtain" – *frum* Jews are born that way. The challenge lies in the "quick to lose" aspect – avoiding the gravitational pull to give it up. That is what Mrs. Margolese's book is about. For the chareidi, the opposite is true. Once we have paid the price and acquired our ideology, we do not readily forsake it. We have an ultimate goal to strive for. We are "resilient to lose." Our issue is acquiring it in the first place because, as nobody is actually born with it, it is "resilient to obtain." This is what my book is about.

So it is not too surprising that my friend Sruly and all of my yeshiva friends remain loyal to the cause. They have toiled and they have arrived and they have "obtained." They see the pot of gold at the end of the rainbow and, so, they are not "quick to lose." As a consequence, my bold assertion that *true* chareidim do not go off the derech may not be so remarkable after all.

Let us summarize in one line what we have learned to this point: In the chareidi world, the problem of our youth going OTD is not really about going OTD – *Off the Derech* – but rather it is about never getting *On the Derech* despite their chareidi upbringing.

By now you may be thinking: "So, who cares whether we call it '*off* the derech' or '*not on* the derech'? The fact remains that there is a substantial portion of people brought up in the chareidi community who have fallen out. What difference does it make what you call it, it's the same problem?"

I care. And I care for the following reasons:

- Knowing the true nature of the problem gives us a clearer focus on how to deal with it. This is a manifestation of the classic concept of treating the disease rather than treating the symptoms.

- Knowing the true nature of the problem allows us to combat the malicious accusations that the "system" is not genuine and does not deliver on its promises.

Though the first point is the more significant one, I prefer to address this latter point first. I will subsequently return to the first point.

As long as the problem, as it affects us, is looked upon as the identical problem that is in the general non-chareidi world, people use it as ammunition to equate chareidi society to non-chareidi society. Many people take advantage of this perceived failing in order to vilify the integrity of the system. They remark, "See how many of their offspring are out on the streets? There must be something terribly wrong with the system. Why should I even consider being chareidi?" In short, if people do not remain chareidi, it means that the product must be faulty.

When we understand what is really going on, we can recognize that the challenge lies in the marketing, not in the product. I mentioned earlier that G-d never really gave us the Torah, but rather, He offered it to us for purchase. Being that I consider the Torah to be the most sophisticated wireless communication device, I would like to draw an analogy to a more popular, albeit less sophisticated, wireless device – the cellular telephone.

Suppose somebody approaches you and offers you the most advanced, state-of-the-art, quad-band, you-name-it-it-does-it cell phone absolutely free. Isn't that a great gift? Except that it's not really a gift. That is because, in order to benefit from it there are two requirements of you, the recipient:

- You must make sure that the device's power source is always charged.

- You must subscribe to a service provider to obtain connectivity. This typically entails a monthly service charge plus variable charges for air time and other features (plus VAT where applicable).

If even one of these two requirements isn't met, the device is not going to function and the gift that the benefactor so generously endowed becomes nothing more than a fancy status symbol and a very pricey paperweight. Sure, it's a wonderful machine that can give you access to the entire world but, to accomplish that, you must make a commitment and pay a price. Your "absolutely free gift" winds up costing you a bundle. Hopefully, the benefits are worthwhile.

G-d the Father (the Singular One) is a very shrewd "Businessman." When He gave us His Torah and the gift of Judaism, it looked like a free gift. But He was actually doing what all the "other" wireless communications companies have been doing for decades: give away the "device" for next to nothing and hook the customer on the extended service contract, without which the device is nothing more than a useless status symbol. And so, He tells us (need I say where?) that in order for the "device" to work, we must sign a long term service contract with the Service Provider – of which there is but One.

The observance that observant Jews (FFBs) are born with is like being given the main body of the cell phone. To be *mitzvah observant* means to merely keep the phone charged – it will turn on and off and maintain its memory and perform calls to emergency numbers but, in general, it does not communicate. To be *Torah observant* means to purchase the service contract and to enjoy full functionality. In all cases, when we see someone forsaking observance it means he is discarding his "cell phone." For the consumerist NCOJ, the mitzvah observant Jew who never was interested in, or possibly even aware of buying the service contract, such a move makes sense and does not surprise us. The phone does not communicate and how many games of Snake can one play, so why keep it? In his circles, no one was urging him to buy the service contract. For the NCOJ, holding on to the charged cell phone was the total picture and we perceive our failure when he throws it out.

For the one born into the chareidi community, the picture is slightly different. The 2nd degree chareidi was born into an environment where the primary focus in life is not just to brandish this fancy "cell phone" but to buy and uphold a long-term service contract, as well. To us, going OTD is not characterized by discarding the phone but rather by abstaining from buying the service contract. Thus, we ought not lament our failure when we see someone discarding his disabled "cell phone." After all, it's disabled. It isn't communicating. We really must lament our failure at a much earlier stage when he abstains from taking the requisite steps to enable this priceless device to begin with. Unfortunately, it is not easy to discern when this occurs because it is a passive non-deed. When we see that the individual is still holding his "cell phone" – i.e., he keeps up his appearance and goes through the motions – we may not readily notice that he never had his device enabled. This is especially true if he takes care to keep it charged as when he compliantly continues to keep Shabbat and *kashrut* and wear his *tefillin* albeit in a mechanical context. In most cases, even in our circles, we do not concede that one is OTD until he takes the dramatic visible step of discarding his "cell phone" but all that means is that we missed the actual break-off point.

In truth, the 2nd degree chareidi is not much different from his non-chareidi brother. As I wrote in Chapter 3, he is as much a consumer as is the non-chareidi and he is subject to most of the associated hazards. Consumerism is the avowed enemy and it can only be vanquished with toil in Torah which he has not yet undertaken. The difference lies in that the NCOJ is brought up to view Orthodox observance as a repository of religious identity. The rituals that must be observed – Shabbat and kashrut, etc. – must be upheld only in order to sustain this religious identity. When he forsakes it, it is because he does not fancy a need for such religious identity. The chareidi is brought up to view observance as a life-enrichment program, a wellspring of *Bracha*. When he rejects chareidi-style Torah observance, it says to us something more profound than that he merely has no need for Jewish identity. It says to us that he just doesn't see the Bracha and his life isn't being enriched or, at least, he doesn't think it is.

Now that our analogy is fully developed, allow me to substantiate my claim that the problem does not lie in the product but rather in the marketing.

All of the cell phone companies are doing booming business. They have no problem marketing their product. That is because people feel a dependency on constant, dependable, far-reaching communication. In this physical world, people readily acknowledge that these fancy devices can successfully provide the sought after communication and that it requires an investment on their part, so they line up in droves, dig into their pockets and sign on the dotted line. They know it works because they see it working and so they buy.

In the spiritual world of authentic Judaism it is much more difficult for people to perceive that the exact same phenomenon is in place. We must obtain the spiritual "device," sign the spiritual contract, pay the spiritual, if not physical, price and only then is the communication guaranteed to work. It is much more difficult to market this concept than a physical cell phone for several reasons:

- The physical cell phone provides immediate measurable gratification which justifies the commitment and cost. We can physically see that the physical cell phone physically works when physically enabled. Conversely, G-d's wireless communication device, although it promises ultimate satisfaction, does not necessarily deliver on-the-spot gratification.

- Because we can physically perceive that the physical cell phone works, nobody dares to claim that it doesn't work. Such a claim would never be taken seriously. Conversely, for the spiritual "device," for every one individual (like me) who wishes to claim that the "device" delivers world-wide connectivity *once we sign up*, there are hundreds if not thousands more that refute this claim. They indeed constitute an overwhelming majority and they are taken quite seriously.

- The physical cell phone deal is individualized. This means that I can be assured that, as long as I pay my subscription and charge my phone, my cell phone will work even if yours does not. With G-d's deal, even though no individual will be short-changed, the full benefits package is subject to group participation, a factor over which the individual has limited control.

- Even though mankind has survived several millennia without the benefits of a physical cell phone, people are convinced that they cannot function without one. G-d's Torah, His wireless device, has been responsible for keeping us in business for over 3300 years and yet people aren't convinced that they need it!

- There are no special deals on the spiritual device. A few pages back, I commented that the service is not for free. That was an understatement. The price is exorbitant. I wrote a complete chapter earlier in this book (Chapter 8, *Cops and Rabbis*) to emphasize just how steep is the price – it's about as steep as Mount Neverest itself. As I said in that chapter, the terms of this service contract totally intrude upon our lives and dictate to us (just about) which eye to open first in the morning and which to close last at bedtime and everything in between. It means that we can't do whatever we want to and that we must do things we would prefer not to. Yet, the price is the price – there are no breaks. You might say the price is prohibitive. Not only do I contend that it is the main reason why the irreligious do not buy religion and why the marginally religious do not buy chareidiism, but the main point I was trying to illustrate with my exposition on Korach was that as a result of the exorbitant, inflexible, intransigent price, people who are not prepared to pay it will say anything to undermine the product – that it doesn't really work, it is fake and not genuine, it wasn't really manufactured where it claims to have been, and that there are other competing models that work just as well (if not better).

The upshot is that it is a formidable task to market this concept. The life-enrichment program and the wellspring of Bracha are not so easy to perceive as, in reality, they look quite different from the way people envision them to look. Countless people who never tried it are knocking it and that is why so many of our own never acquire it. Yet those that do are ready to "swear by it." People who are truly chareidi, 1st degree chareidi, tend to stay chareidi. In fact, as I wrote in the opening of this chapter, the retention rate within chareidi circles is remarkably strong. I cannot off-hand think of anybody that invested in genuine toil in Torah who felt that he could find a better product somewhere else.

We can now return to the first of the two reasons for our modified perspective of the problem of fallout that I enumerated earlier (page 241) – *Knowing the nature of the problem gives us a clearer focus on how to handle it.*

I commented earlier that when one who was born into a chareidi environment forsakes observance, it indicates that he does not perceive the Bracha of the benefits package. This is despite the fact that, technically, he is supposed to be experiencing it. As long as this is the case, we need to introspect on why this is so and what we can do about it.

The process of transforming our young uncommitted chareidi youth into full-fledged committed chareidi adults is what we call *chinuch* (colloquially: education). This term tends to mislead us because if we scrutinize its literal meaning we find it to mean "training" as in training a new recruit, or, to stick with our analogy, training a new cell-phone customer how to use his device. The misleading aspect about this term is that it presupposes that the trainee is *already* recruited or that the customer has *already* bought the service. Our discussion bears out that this is not always so and for the *mechanech* (literally: trainer; in practical terms: parent and/or educator) to act on this assumption can be both erroneous and hazardous.

In other words, every parent and teacher must be aware that, despite the literal meaning of the term, *chinuch* is not limited to training a confirmed customer. In many, if not most cases, the task just as much involves promoting the product – or soliciting the customer – to begin with.

I firmly believe that one of the main causes of losing our "customers" is that we do not acknowledge that they are just that – customers. And there is no way we can train them how to use the product if they do not first buy it. We take for granted that they are sold on the product because *we* are sold on the product. And when the customer is skeptical, we see him as a disgruntled buyer rather than as an inquisitive shopper. We are blind to their hesitations and apprehensions and they sense that we are not sensitive to their concerns. And so, since they have not committed themselves to the purchase, even though we think they have, they walk out of the store. We have lost a customer.

Accordingly, to get somebody onto the derech means to interest him in the product. We cannot overlook this step. This comes *before* we show him how to use it. This is typically known as *salesmanship* and, although I mentioned twice so far that I am not an expert on why Jews go *off the derech*, I did spend about twenty years in the diamond business so I can claim to know something about salesmanship. As some of the most fundamental rules of salesmanship are also the most fundamental rules of chinuch, they must be applied accordingly.[17] Let us examine the most relevant of these rules and see how we can apply them within the framework of chareidi society:

Rule #1 – The firmer the firm, the firmer the sales

A good salesman for a weak company is like a good jockey on a slow horse. Don't expect him to win too many races. In order for the salesman to succeed, the company that he represents must be rock solid. People tend to avoid doing business with a shaky company even if the product is infallible.

This brings us to the topic of *shalom bayit* – tranquility in the home. There is no argument that chinuch starts at home. Every educator and youth professional acknowledges that a weak home – poor *shalom bayit* – is the weightiest card in the game. Mrs. Margolese devotes a complete chapter to this issue and it is certainly on target. The main point is that every human being naturally seeks out a comfortable, stable, and pain-free environment. Ideally, no place fits this bill better than the home. Yet, not all homes are ideal and so, when conditions at home are more explosive than those on the streets, the streets will more than compete with the home for "home field advantage."

Nothing casts our children off the derech faster and surer than breaches in *shalom bayit*. All of the bracha of the Bracha camp goes unnoticed by

---

[17] Mrs. Margolese corroborates this concept in a quotation on page 67 of her book. Here, I am merely elaborating on the idea.

a young person when it all remains outside his front *mezuzah* and none of it penetrates within. The Talmud in tractate Gittin says that "when a man divorces his original wife, even the altar of the sanctuary sheds tears."[18] Do you know why the altar sheds tears? I'll tell you. It is because all the time that the couple was at odds, there was an endless supply of *korbanot* (sacrifices). Now that they have finally divorced, the altar is worried that the constant flow of korbanot may finally come to an end.

What is the chareidi take on all this?

Two things. First, there is a secret to maintaining healthy *shalom bayit* which only the chareidim know. Not all of us, unfortunately, but at least the most dedicated chareidim. And from whom do we learn this? Well, from the wisest of all men, of course (and the one with the most wives – although he didn't exactly bat 1.000, either). King Solomon tells us "When G-d is pleased by the ways of a man, even his (the man's) enemies make peace with him."[19] The Midrash expounds:[20] Rabbi Yochanan says, "his enemies" refers to his wife as is written "...the enemies of a man are the members of his household."[21] Thus, we are told that one who goes in the ways that please G-d or, in other words, one who "walks within My statutes..." – yes, we are back to Leviticus 26:3 – is placing an order for an overnight express door-to-door delivery of *shalom bayit*.

The second thing is not explicitly mentioned by King Solomon with an accompanying Midrash so I suppose it may be even a bigger secret. I will credit this concept to Rabbi Avigdor Miller, ZT"L. And the big secret is this:

The time to work on *shalom bayit* is *before* you get married![22]

Remember, that according to chareidi ideology, being Jewish entails a clear objective. In this book, I have figuratively called it striving to reach the peak of Mount Neverest. What the objective really is, is to perfect one's character and gain wisdom and to then work on improving society and the world at large (and when you're done with that, you can...). Every individual needs to have a plan as to how he intends to approach this objective. As I wrote in Chapter 2, the Talmud in tractate Berachot[23] offers two valid plans – one sponsored by Rabbi Yishmael and one spon-

---

[18] Talmud Bavli Gittin 90b

[19] Proverbs 16:7

[20] Yalkut Shimoni 954

[21] Michah 7:6

[22] I know. For many readers it's too late!

[23] Talmud Bavli Berachot 35b

sored by Rabbi Shimon ben Yochai (perhaps there are others, but these are the only two that I am familiar with). And, as the cell phone companies say, you have to pick the plan that's just right for you.

Getting married also entails a clear objective and it will only succeed if the objective for getting married is an extension of the objective to reach your ultimate goal. Otherwise, the objectives will conflict and one will be sacrificed for the other. Thus, when one searches for a marriage partner, it pays to see to it that he or she shares your ultimate objective and is suited to your specific plan.

Those chareidim that implement these two secrets invariably fare much better than the rest of the population in this regard. Yet, there are no guarantees. Even the most dedicated chareidim are vulnerable. The opening chapters of Job tell us that the more devout we are, the more we are tested. The higher up we go, the harder the climb. At times, when we have the strength to move up, the other members of our team can't keep up with us. It is oft times easier to share the objective at a lower level than at a higher one. Furthermore, when we are faced with circumstances that are out of the ordinary we sometimes become different people than those who we ordinarily are. These issues can loosen even the tightest ships in our fleet and be the cause of more *korbanot*.

To deal with this, there is one more chareidi secret presented by one of my all-time favorite chareidim, King David. This comes from the Talmud in tractate Berachot:[24]

King David writes, "For this shall a *chassid* (i.e., chareidi – see Chapter 9) pray to you at his time of finding, only that a flood of many waters shall not reach him."[25] Rabbi Chanina says, "time of finding" refers to [finding] a wife as is written, "He who has found a wife has found [that which is] good."[26]

This tells us that no matter how chareidi we are, if we do not pray for G-d's help, we are liable to be washed away in the tsunami. And if you are not yet married, there is no better time than the present to start praying.

So now we know the chareidi take – One must be on the derech to maintain *shalom bayit* and one must maintain *shalom bayit* to stay on the derech.

Rule #2 – Understand what a customer is

---

[24] Talmud Bavli Berachot 8a

[25] Psalms 32:6

[26] Proverbs 18:22

A customer is somebody that you have an obligation to service. He has no obligations to you.

Some businessmen imagine that they "own" their customers. And with that mindset they feel that they are empowered to dictate the terms. Although there are many people who allow themselves to be stage-managed by people they are giving money to, most customers are not patsies and when they sense that they are not seen to be on par with the salesman, they take their business elsewhere.

Most parents think that they "own" their children. This assertion is indeed well grounded by virtue of that:

- We physically "create" them and bring them into existence

- We raise and nurture them for years and years at great expense

- They resemble us in appearance and mannerisms

- The Torah saddles them with various obligations of respect and fear and prohibitions against striking and cursing their parents

- At the earlier stages, they don't really have the option of taking their business elsewhere

These truths lull us into the false impression that the child is duty-bound to go in the path that we set for him.

A learned chareidi knows better. Once, while visiting my in-laws, I encountered a young neighbor of theirs – quite chareidi – who had some children in tow. As I was mildly acquainted with this fellow from previous visits, we struck up a conversation. At some point I asked the rhetorical question, "So, are these your kids?" He immediately gave me the proper answer, "No, these are G-d's kids. I just take care of them."

Here is one fellow who has the right idea. Our children are not truly ours. The Talmud tells us: "There are three partners in [the formation of] a person – the Holy One, his father, and his mother..."[27] This implies that while they are our bodily "issue" that we have physically produced and, as such, can be considered to be subordinate to us, their soul and spirit comes from a completely external source which is totally unique and independent and does not rank beneath ours.

This means that we parents are not the highest authority figure in the rearing of our children. There is a third, silent, senior Partner who grants us supreme authority yet who retains ultimate veto power. In the final analysis, we are merely caretakers for His charges. Try as we may to steer our children where we want them to go, He may have other plans

---

[27] Talmud Bavli Nidah 31a

for them. Just as in the previous topic, *shalom bayit*, we understand that parents can only succeed when they are in harmony with each other, both parents together must work in harmony with the senior Partner. In the event of a "difference of opinion" among the partners, we will only be successful with our children if we set our sights to get the child to where He wants him to be as opposed to where we want him to be.

This teaches us that even parenthood has boundaries, and we are not authorized to overstep our bounds. The Talmud dictates: "*For always*, a man should *never* instill excessive dominance (*eimah yeteirah*) within his household..."[28] All of the self-help books in existence discuss the issues of overbearing control and emotional abuse. There is no question that *eimah yeteirah* stands shoulder to shoulder with poor *shalom bayit* (which often coincide) to destroy young people's self esteem and sense of security and, consequently, their faith in the merits of the "product." I need not elaborate on this topic.

Sadly, the empowerment that the Halacha allocates to parents and teachers can enhance the incidence of *eimah yeteirah* even within chareidi circles. After all, at least one of the two examples offered by the Talmud involved a chareidi.

It is vitally important to be able to distinguish between legitimate parental authority and *eimah yeteirah*. As a postscript, it helps to look at *Kibud av v'em* as a bonus for doing our duty and not as remuneration. Think of it as a privilege and not as our due. If nothing else, this outlook serves to relieve the frustration that develops when the anticipated honor is not forthcoming.

Rule #3 – Know your product

Consumers do not make good salesmen. Enough said.

Rule #4 – The salesman must believe in his product

Imagine walking into a Cellcom (or Cingular) franchise and sitting with the sales clerk for 20 minutes as she shows you all of the latest models and details the various unbeatable service plans. In the middle of all this, her own cell phone rings and she reaches for a Pelephone (T-Mobile?)! No better way to disillusion your customer.

Now, everybody is aware of the dangers of hypocrisy. It is bemoaned in almost every article and book as one of the primary contributors to fallout. It probably ranks at the top of the list immediately behind abuse and rejection. Actually, it is itself a by-product of abuse and rejection.

---

[28] Talmud Bavli Gittin 6b

What I wish to point out is that there are two dimensions to hypocrisy: hypocritical behavior and hypocritical belief. These can also be rephrased as (respectively) *active* hypocrisy and *passive* hypocrisy. Doubtless, the classic scenario of when the father motor-mouths his way through the Torah reading while admonishing his kid to pay attention will do it every time. When a child sees that his parent or teacher does not practice what he preaches, he loses faith in the whole "system." This is what I mean by hypocritical behavior or active hypocrisy and there has been so much written about this that there is nothing for me to add.

The lesser known dimension is when a parent or teacher shows little enthusiasm for his Jewishness even though he observes the command-ments meticulously *and* toils in Torah. A prominent American Torah leader[29] is known to have remarked that the reason that so many children of Orthodox families abandoned religion in the 1900s, both in Europe and America, is because they observed their fastidiously devout parents sighing and saying, "*Oy, s'iz shvehr tzuzein ah yid* (Whoa, it is difficult to be Jewish)!" even though it was truer then than ever. Our sages tell us, "In accordance to the level of hardship will be our reward."[30] This means to say that tradition maintains that our ultimate reward will more than compensate for the unwelcome discomfort. Yet, there is something in a sigh that creates the impression that the individual is not fully confident in a proportionate reward.[31] Though this may be excusable in the face of real hardships,[32] when we display this lack of enthusiasm under more subtle conditions we may be engaging in a passive form of hypocrisy which does not go unnoticed by one who is on the lookout for it.

I mentioned earlier that the payoff for upholding G-d's contract is not always immediate and clearly recognizable. At the same time that we are trying to sell the product to our charges, we ourselves often encounter difficulties that test our own confidence in it. Sometimes our challenge is similar to a salesman who must sell off a load of inventory right after the manufacturer publicly announces a massive recall. We can never let our-selves lose faith in our product if we want to stay in business.

---

[29] I am not certain as to exactly which Torah leader this was. My recollections are that it originated from Rabbi Aaron Kotler, ZT"L. Other versions attribute this remark to Rabbi Moshe Feinstein, ZT"L.

[30] Pirkei Avot 5:23

[31] I certainly do not mean to say that the impression is accurate, only that one who chooses to look at it from this negative perspective has what to base it on.

[32] Obviously, it is not my or anyone's place to be judgmental of how people react to hardships, particularly those that we, thankfully, have never suffered. The Talmud in tractate Berachot 5b tells of certain great sages who could not accept suffering even though they were fully aware of the associated reward.

Rule #5 – Have an effective pitch – accentuate the positive eliminate the negative

This rule is self-explanatory. The popular adage about life is "No pain, no gain." When it comes to the trials and tribulations of chareidi-style religious observance, these words are truer than true.

The well known Mishna in Pirkei Avot tells us:[33]

> Such is the manner of acquiring Torah: meager bread with salt you shall eat, water by measure you shall drink, and upon the ground you shall sleep, and a life of discomfort you shall live, and in the [study of] Torah you shall toil. If you [are prepared to] do so, you are fortunate and well off. Fortunate in this world, and well off in the World to Come. [34]

Nobody wants pain and everybody wants gain, but, in our world, we cannot have the gain without some measure of pain. If we focus on the gain, the overall picture will be gainful. If we focus on the pain, the overall picture will be painful.

Rule #6 – Get to know the customer

Any salesman worth his salt makes it his business to get to know as much as he can about his customer and to establish rapport. The more he knows about "where the customer is coming from" the more he knows about where the customer wants to get to and the more effectually he can enable the customer to get there. And, since success breeds success, the customer remains loyal and comes back for more.

Somehow, when it comes to raising children, this concept can get lost. I can think of several reasons for this, but these are the main ones:

- We think we already know where the customer is coming from

- We are not prepared to view our children as customers

The latter of these two reasons is technically the topic of rule #2 above so there is no need to reiterate it. Let us focus on the first of these reasons.

Every human being has distinct inborn character traits and a personal set of physical and emotional needs. These factors, coupled with environmental conditions, are what make each person unique. In the world of child-rearing we sometimes assume that these inborn traits can be readily

---

[33] Pirkei Avot 6:4

[34] Many commentaries (e.g., Rashi) understand this Mishna not to mean that these hardships are absolutely imperative but that in many situations they will be part of the deal and a lasting commitment is only possible when the scholar is prepared to accept them if need be.

modified to the traits that we want them to have (and that we may ourselves possess). We feel that the child is fully capable of conforming to our values. This rule is here to teach us that such an assumption may be a tragic mistake.

Experienced salesmen know better. They are aware that diversity lies in the customer, versatility lies in the product. This means that the typical customer is not about to change himself to conform to the product; rather, the salesman must tailor the product to fit the customer.

The simplest analogy is a shoe store. Suppose a customer walks into a shoe store and asks for a size 10½ shoe and the store just happens to be out of size 10½. Can we even consider asking the customer to accept a size 10? Would we consider the customer stubborn and inflexible because he refuses to modify his shoe size to match what is available? As much as the customer would like to do it, it is beyond his capabilities. At the very best, we may possibly consider taking a narrow cut size 11 and insert an insole and, thereby, service the customer by *modifying the product to fit him*.

When it comes to Torah education, even in our circles, parents and educators tend to get mixed up. Sometimes they view the Torah – or, the "system" – as if it is the customer and the child as if he is the product. Either the child has to conform to the system's demands as a "one-size-fits-all" or we have to tailor the child to fit. For example, if we set the Torah's "specifications" for two sessions a day, four hours each, with another two hour session at night and the child is fit for one long and one short session with time for himself in between, we commonly attempt to modify the child's capabilities as opposed to adjusting the specifications. Usually, it's like asking a customer to change his shoe size.

With this introduction, let us discuss a sequence of applications of King Solomon's sage counsel, *"Chanoch l'naar al pi darko* (train the youth according to his manner)."[35]

In our society, we generally create peg-boards with uniformly round holes. Yet, we seem to be coming across an uncomfortable percentage of square pegs that don't readily fit into all the nice round holes. Hence, the question becomes: do we square the holes or do we insist on rounding the pegs and subsequently reject the pegs that cannot be rounded? We believe that Torah ideals have sufficient versatility to enable every individual to adapt them to his set of needs. There must be round holes for the round pegs and square holes for the square pegs.

There are a number of doctrines of emotional and psychological phenomenon that reflect the diversity of human behavior. These doctrines

---

[35] Proverbs 22:6

help us understand where our children are coming from and what traits can and cannot be modified. Sadly, some chareidim tend to invalidate them as religiously unfounded and based on atheistic and immoral premises. While this may be true concerning the outlandish theories of Sigmund Freud, some of the more contemporary doctrines are too relevant to be dismissed. These include some of the ideas of Carl Jung and personality typology[36] or enneagrams,[37] Maslow's hierarchy of needs, or Glasser's five basic needs, not to mention Rabbi Dr. Abraham J. Twerski's theories on self-esteem. Many of these ideas have parallels in the words of our sages and are quite valid. It pays to be familiar with them.

Rule #7 – Find out what the *customer* wants. Identify with the *customer's* objectives and service the *customer's* needs.

This topic, basically an expansion of the previous one, is the second installment in our "*Chanoch l'naar al pi darko*" sequence.

We have all seen those tacky mottos: "The customer is always right", "Every customer is our only customer", "We put the 'U' into Value", "Please Disturb", "Unconditional satisfaction starts with 'U'", "We are specialists because our customers are special", etc., etc., etc.

Many businesses prominently display these mottos in bold lettered signs. Do you know why they do that?

If you answered that it is to make the customer feel worthy and appreciated, you are only half right. The other half of the reason is to *remind the salesman* that it is his job to make the customer feel worthy and appreciated even though his true motto is, "I am in business to make money and that is the only reason I put up with nuisances such as you."

Customers do indeed need to feel worthy and appreciated. They also need to feel that they are being heard and that the salesman is as much concerned about the customer's goals as he is about his own. The skilled salesman knows that this is part of his job and a key to his success. The minute he puts his interests ahead of the customer's is the minute that the bold lettered sign changes to "Going out of business." In short, the customer's success is his success.

This opens up to us a second – somewhat more chareidi-specific – application of the verse *Chanoch l'naar al pi darko* – with an emphasis

---

[36] I have alluded to Myers-Briggs Typology Indicators (MBTI) in other places in this book (Chapter 2) as well as earlier in this chapter.

[37] For a more thorough exposition on enneagrams from an Orthodox Jewish viewpoint check out the book Awareness: *The Key to Acceptance, Respect, Forgiveness and Growth* by Dr. Miriam Adahan, Feldheim Publishers.

on the term *"darko"* – *his* derech.

Who's derech?

I expect that most people who study this verse conclude that it means the trainee's derech. Yet, it appears that this occurs only when they study it. When it is put into practice, we sometimes notice a bit of confusion. By the methods employed, it is evident that there are those who understand *"darko"* – *his* derech – to imply the *trainer's* derech.

In the chareidi world there is a tendency for parents and teachers to take a personal stake in the development of their charges to the extent that they feel personally affronted if the child or student does not fully reflect their personal standards. They do not measure success by the achievements of their disciples but rather by their own achievements. There is a general tendency in all streams for parents to want their children to be successful in the areas in which they themselves fell short; and, in our circles, where many of us have reached spiritual levels beyond that of our youth, it is common for us to expect our current spiritual level to be the child's starting point. Hence, we subject our children to restrictions that we ourselves were not restricted from in our youth. Of course, we are merely inculcating true Torah values into our youth; nevertheless, we must not forget that what was "resilient to obtain" for us may be just as "resilient to obtain" for our offspring despite (or, perhaps, due to) the spiritually enhanced atmosphere of their upbringing.

To this end, for the purpose of gathering material for this portion of this book, I took note of and picked up a copy of a recent release entitled *Unchosen*: The Hidden Lives of Hasidic Rebels by Hella Winston.[38] Firstly, I must comment that this book is for mature audiences only and should only be read by individuals who have an active involvement in *chinuch* and fallout issues. In her book, Ms. Winston profiles the life experiences of several young adults who rebelled against the conventions of their native Chassidic communities. Books like this (and thank G-d there are not too many of them) serve as a stark revelation of the inherent pitfalls that arise in an inflexible, impersonal, one-size-fits-all environment.

While reading this book, I paid special attention to those specific factors that contributed to each individual's rebellious course. What, in my view, stood out most with respect to the two main subjects – Yossi, the young man from the Satmar community and Malkie, the young woman from the Chabad community – was that both of them were brought up to be stringently observant by parents who themselves were not brought up that way. The parents voluntarily developed a self-imposed zeal for their

---

[38] Beacon Press, Boston USA 2005

Chassidic societies that suited themselves and, seemingly, they took for granted that they could readily instill this zeal into the psyches of their children. Though this may not necessarily be the critical element in Malkie's case, in the case of Yossi, the young man from Satmar, we are shown that his father's most pressing concern over the waywardness of his son was the backlash to his own prestige and standing within the community. His rants and overtures were focused exclusively on the shame that Yossi was bringing upon his family. Clearly, the father was not prepared to compromise any of his hard earned standards and modify the requirements – within the acceptable limits, of course – to help his son find a way to remain comfortable within the camp.

Now, as the book itself demonstrates in the cases of the other subjects, this phenomenon is certainly not restricted to families that are newcomers to the intense chareidi or Chassidic lifestyles; it occurs even in long established chareidi families.[39] Nevertheless, people who have "upgraded" to the chareidi genre often harbor personal insecurities that make them more vulnerable to these challenges and less prepared to deal with them.[40]

Regardless of where it occurs, if the salesman cannot focus on what the customer needs, he will soon be focusing on his need for customers.

Rule #8 – Do not oversell the customer

Let's expand the previous two topics even more.

Aggressiveness is the trait of a wise salesman; over-aggressiveness is the trait a foolish salesman.

When a customer walks into the store and explains to the salesman what he is shopping for, the salesman commonly asks him how much money he is planning to spend. If he is skilled he will be sure to show the customer precisely what is available in the specified price range, point out its strengths and limitations and gauge the customer's responses to sense if he can "talk him up."

Sometimes an overambitious salesman will immediately try to get the customer to spring for the big ticket item. If he would like to see this customer again, this is not such a good idea.

---

[39] At least one other subject, a young woman, underwent some horrific abuse.

[40] This is actually a natural side effect of such a dramatic lifestyle change and it has been plaguing us ever since we chareidim came into existence. According to my sources, we chareidim were sworn in on 6 (or 7) of Sivan 2448 and barely 40 days later (16 Tamuz) we lost our composure and turned our attention to a golden calf. The Midrash (Tanchuma Ki Tisa 19) comments that the instigators of this debacle were the newcomers to the Jewish people.

Today's cell phones can do amazing things with features such as MP3, 4, and 5, SMS, MMS, LMS, XLMS, internet, email, Bluetooth, home theater, radar detection, PDA, world time, scientific calculator, 16 million quadraphonic ringtones and every game Nintendo has ever produced. But lots of people only need them to make calls (some only to take calls). So here's a sales tip: If the customer wants the basic model for $9.99/month then sell him the basic model for $9.99/month. Hopefully, you will see him again when he is ready for the $89.99 cable and satellite system and you will get your big commission then. If you insist on burdening the customer with an overloaded system that he is not ready for, he may think that as much as he doesn't need the useless digital camera feature, he doesn't really need the whole tootin' thing. It's cheaper to use a pay phone. The device is a hassle and is working against him and not for him.

For us chareidim, even though our game is to sell the concept of toil in Torah we must be careful not to try to sell a first time buyer more toil in Torah than he is ready for. And this takes us to yet a third application of *Chanoch l'naar al pi darko*. This application is merely an enhanced version of the one previously discussed but it carries the distinction of being *exclusively* specific to the chareidi world. In fact, I consider this application to be the root of one of the most serious problems within the chareidi world, and one that is instrumental in keeping chareidi youth-crisis personnel working overtime (and the previous applications keep them busy enough). In my opinion, this is the main area of weakness in chareidi chinuch that doesn't readily apply to the NCOJ circles (who have more than their hands full).

Like the previous application, this variation has a similar emphasis on the term "*darko*" – *his derech* – as there is yet a third mystery candidate for the identity of the shadowy pronoun "his" in "*his* derech." This is due to the fact that many sincere and well intentioned chareidi parents and educators, in their zeal for advancing mitzvah observance with toil in Torah misread the "*his* derech" to read "*His* derech" with a capital "H."

In Chapter 2, I introduced the two schools of thought presented by Rabbi Yishmael and Rabbi Shimon ben Yochai. To summarize, Rabbi Shimon ben Yochai asserts that a Jew should forsake all earthly endeavors and fully immerse himself in Torah study and he should depend on external entities to provide for his basic needs. Rabbi Yishmael maintains that one may not rely on external sources for sustenance and, consequently, must supplement his Torah study with the requisite amount of gainful occupation. The Amoraic sage, Abaye, qualified these two views by stating that "Many have attempted to do as Rabbi Yishmael and have succeeded, [and many have attempted to do] as Rabbi Shimon ben Yochai and have not succeeded." Our assessment was that Rabbi Shimon ben Yochai indeed personifies the ultimate ideal that is the true "Will of G-d." Still, there is no question that this ideal calls for an intense commitment, strict discipline, denial of material comforts, and a self-imposed social insularity that most human beings are not geared to handle. In practice, most people are only capable of implementing the more "down to earth" style of Rabbi Yishmael.

Many in chareidi circles hold that the proper way of rearing our youth is to aggressively promote the ultimate ideal of Rabbi Shimon ben Yochai as a universal standard because, after all, both sides agree that that is the consummate Will of G-d. It is as if they read the verse, "Train the youth according to *His* (G-d's) derech." Although there is no question that our desired objective is to produce as many Rabbi Shimon ben Yochai's as we can, it does not pay to set a lone standard and to undermine Rabbi Yishmael's position along the way. Abaye warns us that it's not always going to work. It's like trying to sell a motorcycle to a twelve year old kid who wants a bicycle. If he's not ready for it, or qualified to use it, and doesn't have the money for the registration, gas, and insurance, not only is this motorcycle going to sit around unused (or, worse, it may be mis-used), but, for lack of a bicycle, he's not going to get anywhere at all. In fact, he very well may resort to thumbing rides and wind up in places he wouldn't otherwise be going to.

I think that Abaye's message is that if we try too hard to make Rabbi Shimon ben Yochais out of potential Rabbi Yishmaels we will not wind up with more Rabbi Shimons, only with less Rabbi Yishmaels. We can always try to sell them the motorcycles after they have outgrown the bicycles, but we don't want to lose any customers.

So now we understand the two main "derechs" upon which to lead our young 2nd degree chareidi – that of Rabbi Shimon and that of Rabbi Yishmael. After all this, reality tells us that even the more genial Rabbi Yishmaelist route is a hearty challenge. This is because we have within our ranks the 3rd degree chareidi as well – the QOF chareidi[41] who is not prepared to actively engage in toil in Torah but still feels comfortable within the camp (for now). For this specimen, we have to recognize that the basic realm of mitzvah observance or compliance – i.e., the elemen-tary derech that is espoused in Mrs. Margolese's book – also constitutes a derech. If this is the extent of the derech that this child is prepared to undertake, it may not pay to try to push even the Rabbi Yishmael ap-proach.

---

[41] If you have forgotten, the QOF was introduced in Chapter 3 as the most ideologi-cally superficial chareidi. QOF stands for Quaker Oats/Fagin and is defined in Chapter 3.

Rule #9 – Some customers are *buyers*, others are *shoppers*

Sometimes a customer walks into the store knowing exactly what he wants. He understands the product, he knows the value, he has the right amount of money, he is ready to buy and he does. Don't we wish all customers were like that?

Such a customer is called a *buyer* and is the commercial equivalent of the motivated and inspired, natural born, 1st degree chareidi. Unfortunately, for us salesmen (and parents and teachers) there are not enough of these kind of customers to go around (life would be kind of dull if there were). Most customers are *shoppers*. They need to be sold on the product. They need to evaluate the pros and cons and check out other items in other stores before they are ready to commit themselves and part with their currency.

Now, the product that we are selling is a commitment to Torah observance. Okay, so how does one come to get "hooked" onto Torah observance? Well, why don't we look at the Torah itself and see what it says? Surprisingly, the Torah presents not just one, but two methods of achieving a commitment to Torah observance; and they are both right next to each other in the same weekly portion.

The Torah in the portion of Jethro relates the episode of the Revelation and receiving the Torah. The primary recipients were the more than 600,000 certified adults from the proper descendants of Jacob (plus wives, children, adolescents, elders, and Levites). Rashi[42] quotes the Midrash that all of these Jews were of one mind behind Moses and, as such, we can consider them all to be bona fide 1st degree chareidim. The Torah relates a bit later that even before Moses "laid down the Law" they all proclaimed that "All that G-d has spoken we will do and we will study – *Naaseh V'Nishma*."[43] The Talmud relates that the Jews were rewarded with spiritual "crowns" for their valiant demeanor of trusting in G-d and signing the contract without demanding to read the fine print.[44] Let us call this sublime "blind faith" approach the *Naaseh V'Nishma* method.

What is not so readily noticed is that earlier in that portion we are introduced to another approach. The Torah tells us that Jethro "heard" all that G-d did for Moses and for His nation, Israel. Whereupon, Jethro arrives to cast his lot with the fortunes of the Jewish people as the first

---

[42] Rashi, Exodus 19:2 s.v. *VaYichan*

[43] Exodus 24:7

[44] Talmud Bavli, Shabbat 88a

righteous convert.

When Jethro recounts his observations to his son-in-law, Moses, he remarks, "I now know (*Attah yadati*) that G-d is greater than all other powers…"[45] Rashi (ad loc.) comments: "**From all other powers** – This teaches that Jethro was familiar with every form of idol worship; that he did not overlook a single deity from sampling its manner of worship."

Jethro could not accept G-d on blind faith. He had to do some comparison shopping. Only after he checked out all the competing brands and was satisfied that the G-d of Israel is the All-Powerful deity bar none could he consecrate his life to His service. Let us call this scrupulous investigative approach the *Attah Yadati* method. Jethro valued this method, so much so that the Midrash states that, upon giving his daughter to Moses as a wife, Jethro stipulated with him that the first-born son would be designated for idolatry.[46] Many understand this to mean that Jethro insisted that at least one son should arrive at the truth of G-d via the same means as he did.

It emerges that the Torah details two methods of accepting the Torah – *Naaseh V'Nishma* for the buyers and *Attah Yadati* for the shoppers. Needless to say, the *Naaseh V'Nishma* approach is the safer and more direct route but it does not afford the peace of mind of the riskier *Attah Yadati* approach. And in this generation, we certainly need peace of mind.

So now we have yet a fourth application of the topic of *Chanoch l'naar al pi darko*. Besides the question of whether our customer is more attuned to Rabbi Shimon ben Yochai's *derech* or to Rabbi Yishmael's *derech* (or neither) we must also evaluate whether he is a *buyer* or a *shopper*. We must recognize that not all of our offspring are automatically buyers. No matter how effective a sales pitch we have, some customers will insist on shopping around. Despite the inherent dangers, it may still be necessary to give the child a bit of slack and to allow him to check out the competing merchandise. As long as he is not ready to buy, we actually have no choice.

Rule #10 – Be patient. Just because the customer is not interested today does not mean that he won't be interested tomorrow.

Do you have time to take a one question survey? Okay, here's the question:

At what age does an Orthodox Jew become an adult?

---

[45] Exodus 18:11

[46] Mechilta, Jethro, Tractate Amalek, Section 1

Now, I haven't actually conducted this survey so I will have to specu-late the results. My guess is that about 2 out of 3 respondents would answer "at the time of bar or bat-mitzvah." It is our tradition that every Orthodox Jew is considered an adult at the onset of adolescence. At this age, 13 for a male and 12 for a female, the subject is obligated in all of the relevant commandments and is liable for damages and for full judicial punishment for any transgression. This includes the death penalty where applicable. Likewise, at this age, a male is eligible to be counted in a *minyan* (prayer quorum), a *mezuman* (Grace after meals quorum), and to recite blessings and Torah readings on behalf of others. A 13-year-old boy is eligible to be a witness for the sanctification of the new moon and thus establish the dates of the festivals of which the entire Jewish nation is obliged to uphold. He is likewise eligible to be a witness for capital cases and to determine the marital status of a woman. He can be a king and if he is from the order of priests (Kohen) he can perform the duties of the High Priest on the Day of Atonement.

That is quite a load of responsibility.

Nevertheless, I am certain that some learned respondents will point out that only from the age of twenty on up is one eligible to be included in the national census, to receive a portion of the Land of Israel, and to enlist in the army. Moreover, it is only from the age of twenty that his fixed value for vows reaches the full value of fifty shekels.[47]

I have conducted a great deal of research to explain this discrepancy and, frankly, I am stumped. If one is mature enough to kill or be killed in a court of law, must perform every single commandment, and can be a king and High Priest, why doesn't he count in the census? Why can't he go out and fight and receive a portion of the land? Why is his fixed value for vows less than the full value? The only conclusion that I could arrive at, based on the Mishna in Pirkei Avot,[48] is that from the age of 13 and on, a Jewish male is physically and emotionally capable of taking on the trials and tribulations of performing the commandments. Still, he is ex-pected to remain within the docile confines of the insular community until the age of 20. Until this time he is a student and a follower – i.e., a

---

[47] There is also a tradition that until the age of 20, one is not liable for punish-ments meted out by the Heavenly court. Though this has a basis in an Aggadic passage in the Talmud (tractate Shabbat 89b) and is supported by Rashi in his commentary on Genesis 23:1 (s.v. *Vayihiyu*) and Numbers 16:27 (s.v. *U'Nesheihem*), there is no firm Halachic basis for this. As such, there is much debate among Torah scholars as to what are the "terms and conditions" of this "exemption." See Question 69 of Kaba D'Kashiyata from the responsa of Chelkat Yoav. See also Pardes Yosef on Genesis 23:1.

[48] Pirkei Avot 5:21. See commentary of Rabbi Ovadia of Bartenura.

consumer. Only after seven years of shouldering and absorbing the Torah's ideals is he ready and eligible to face the "outside world." At 20, he is expected to marry and rear young Jews. He must now be a parent, a teacher, and a leader; no longer a consumer but a provider.

What is clear is that these seven years of adolescence reflect a developmental phase, a prolonged dress rehearsal. The epoxy of Torah values is mixed at the age of 13 but it does not fully harden until the age of 20. In the meantime, conditions are constantly testing the tensile strength of the compound. Even though from the age of 13 one is obligated to behave religiously like an adult, until he has all of the responsibilities of adulthood, even the physical worldly ones, he is not considered a full-fledged adult. This creates a seven year "twilight zone" in which the adolescent is not compelled to play the game "for keeps." Effectively, he can afford to remain a consumer and, as long as he does, as I wrote so many pages ago, there may be no essential difference between the chareidi and the young NCOJ.

This topic brings us back to the main theme that I have been presenting throughout this chapter, that when a 17, 18, or even 19-year-old (or even older) adolescent seems to make a sharp left turn, it does not necessarily mean that he is going off the derech but that, perhaps, he has not yet embarked. It happens so often that when people appear to be going off the derech what we are really seeing is that it is taking them a bit longer to get onto the derech. He has not yet arrived at the critical stage when the store is about to close and he must make up his mind about his purchase. He is still shopping! In most cases he is stalling off making the purchase because it demands such a heavy price. He is still hunting around in hopes of finding a better deal. We need not despair or panic. If we play our cards right, and bide our time, we can show the customer that he will not find a better deal anywhere he looks. We just need to do our best to keep him close to the store, and, if he wants to shop around, we need to let him know that we will be here waiting when he is ready. Most people, by the time they enter their twenties, are aware that the longer they avoid committing themselves to a firm set of values, the more they will fall behind. At some point everyone realizes that the store is about to close. Let's take a tip from Sy Sims and hope that, in time, the customer will become educated enough to recognize a good value. Like the future children that Sruly was "afraid of," so many of them eventually come back.

Rule #11 – Never antagonize the customer. Always leave the door open for reconciliation

My father gave me this advice when I was working in his business.

Though it may seem elementary, we must bear in mind one thing: For what kind of customer do we need to be so cautioned? Without a doubt, it is for a customer who is *asking* to be antagonized, such as one who holds onto the consignment merchandise too long or who is delinquent in paying his bills. Despite the heartache he causes, it is still not worth antagonizing him. Perhaps the elderly proprietor, the old codger, will retire or pass away and his more conscientious son will take over. Whereupon, the customer's business may turn over a new leaf, but the new proprietor, who doesn't owe you anything and who remembers how you antagonized his boorish papa, will look for other suppliers. Or, perhaps, this worthless, wayward customer may malign you to other more worthy potential customers. In cases like these, you stand to lose more than just a customer.

This topic invokes a variation of the *eimah yeteirah* issue that was discussed way back in rule #2. At that point, the emphasis was on the effects of overstepping authority, excessive control and domination, and emotional abuse toward even well behaved and well adjusted children. This current rule adds to it the issues of intolerance and rejection toward children who are not toeing the line. In this case, we may feel more in place to come down hard on the budding "deviant and rebellious son." This rule indicates that such a short term approach does not come without a long term effect. Seeds that are planted in the hearts of young people often sprout many years later. If they are flower seeds we may see beautiful late bloomers, but if they are weeds, then a full-grown weed is precisely what we get.

Rule #12 – Understand that you will not win every potential customer

All of the previous rules are tips on how to relate to our customers to enable them to "buy with confidence" and, consequently, on how to increase sales. This final rule is merely a message to the salesman that no matter how skilled we are, it is not totally up to us. Ultimately, the customer has the final word. Inevitably, there will be instances when the customer walks out of the store never to return, leaving the hapless salesman to wonder, "What have I done wrong?"

In a recent conversation, my mother said to me, "There are three things which you cannot force a kid to do. You cannot force him to eat, you cannot force him to sleep, and you cannot force him to learn." Now, in my mind I said, "Come on, everybody knows that!" and, indeed, to us professional parents all this may seem rather elementary. But some of us may be surprised at how many people think otherwise, at least initially, and subsequently learn rules like this the hard way. Still, most people seem to get it sooner or later.

Where my mother may not have been accurate is in the correct number of "things." There are more than three of them (How about getting a kid to sit still?). Just, some of these "things" may be a bit harder for some people to learn. In my estimation, one very relevant example stands out: You cannot force a child – or anybody – to believe.

Now, when the objective reader looks at this rule in print, it seems to be even more elementary than the three basics. But many parents find this even more difficult to accept. They assume that if this child was born to us, he automatically shares our values. They simply cannot believe that a child of theirs does not believe. And they try to make him believe. Since we are discussing a child who has shuttered his eyes and his heart from accepting our values, it is all but a foregone conclusion that, at least for now, nothing is going to change. This would be a good time to remember rules #10 and #11, which advise us not to burn our bridges behind us. Accordingly, a wise parent may bite his tongue and take a deep breath and hope for a better tomorrow.

Alas, not all parents have the strength to do this. Not only do they refuse to believe that their offspring does not believe, but they likewise refuse to believe that they cannot bring their offspring to believe and, as a result, they lose their wits. And they panic. And they despair. And they take it out on themselves, on each other, on other family members and other educators, and they resort to tactics which violate all the previous rules, and, because they refuse to relinquish control, they lose control.

This is a disaster.

Not even the best salesman can boast a perfect success rate. After mastering all the "good management" rules, there will always be customers who are just not interested. The same goes for our "customers." As long as we avoid the dangers of mismanagement – poor *shalom bayit*, *eimah yeteirah*, hypocrisy and ignorance, and recognize the numerous applications of *Chanoch l'naar*, the rest is up to the customer. A good portion of those who go off the derech are those who were never interested. They do not identify with the goals of Jewish nation nor with that of the individual Jew. We can illuminate the "derech," we can write books such as this, but we cannot make people look and we cannot make people think.

This rule declares that a salesman has no grounds – and no right – to get discouraged. Nobody bats 1.000. Like everything else about chareidi life, the affliction of fallout is not anything new. It is part of the package and always has been. Remember that I have asserted that chareidiness by my definition goes all the way back to Adam the First Man. Well, so does fallout. Ever since Creation it has transpired in the best chareidi families. Adam, Noah, Abraham, Isaac, King David and King Hezekiah, all of whom maintained an open line of communication to G-d the Father Himself, all saw at least one of their offspring go way off the derech. And we are not better salesmen than they were.

Moreover, as my friend Sruly pointed out, the situation is never hopeless. A Jew can leave generations of observance behind, but he cannot erase them. They are there and waiting to beckon to his descendents no matter how estranged they may be. "The Torah is bundled and is lying [unguarded] in a [public] corner – anyone who wants to study it may come and study it."[49] Fortunately, many of these "apostate" Jews are doomed to experience Sruly's most horrific fear – to stand back and watch helplessly as their children become *baalei teshuva*.[50]

Conclusion

"Remember what Amalek did to you on the derech as you came out of Egypt. That he chanced upon you (*karcha*) on the derech and he cut down the weaklings who were trailing behind you…"[51]

The world outside of the Camp Bracha, the camp of the *one-aboveniks*, is the world of *keri*,[52] chance and happenstance. It is the world of Amalek that culminates in *kofer b'ikar* – denial of G-d's presence. It is the fate of the *seven below*.

Why were we susceptible to Amalek's attack in Refidim? The Midrash explains that it was because our hands weakened their hold (*rafu yedeihem*) on the Torah.[53] When the finest members of our nation weaken their grip, the weaker ones that "trail behind" fall prey to the ravages of Amalek – and get lost in the world of chance and happenstance.

As I just wrote, the problem of fallout has always been with us. We must face it and deal with it but no matter whose book you read, we cannot eradicate it. It pays to internalize the famed advice of Rabbi Nachman of Bratslav: "The entire world is [like] a very narrow bridge and the main principle is not to become frightened at all." Don't panic and don't lose your grip.

When we look at the issue of fallout within the chareidi world in

---

[49] Talmud Bavli Kiddushin 66a

[50] The chareidi world relishes the chareidi curse – the most menacing thing we can say to our anti-chareidi "enemies": May you live to see every one of your children return to a life of Torah!

[51] Deuteronomy 25:17,18

[52] Leviticus 26:23,24

[53] Midrash Tanchuma, Exodus, Beshalach 25

comparison to how it is presented in the more general Orthodox world by writers such as Mrs. Margolese, my feelings are that in the chareidi world, the picture is not as bleak. The chareidi world is the more firmly rooted one at the same time as it is the more demanding and exacting world. As such, our strengths are more acute but so are our challenges. Even though the chareidi version of the product – Torah observance – is in plentiful supply in the chareidi side of town, it still remains a hard sell because it is so much costlier than the non-chareidi version – compliant mitzvah observance. In spite of this, we can boast a higher rate of customer satisfaction and loyalty. Lamentably, in those circles where there is less of a commitment to toil in Torah, there will continue to be heavy casualties for, as Rashi maintains, it is inevitable.

In the final analysis, regardless of our position, we truly are all in one boat. The way we must respond to the challenge is in most areas identical. As Mrs. Margolese writes, we must make our realm of observance to be emotionally, intellectually, and logistically palatable. For those of us who are committed to Torah observance, although we will never bat 1.000, we have the means of managing the situation. As is the case for any commercial enterprise, our worst enemy is mismanagement. If we can avoid mismanagement, we have won half the battle (the bigger half). And, as is likewise the case for any commercial enterprise, it is necessary to have a comprehensive business plan. Bear in mind that just as I wrote that the time to work on *shalom bayit* is before we get married, the time to work on fallout is *before* we meet trouble. Before we even begin to deal with whether or not the youth is on or off the derech we must first establish a clear derech. And this can only happen with our own toil in Torah.

We all obtain pearls of wisdom from our elders. Back when I was a young trainee in my father's office, I observed him admonishing a veteran employee, "Never examine a diamond near an open window." I immediately piped up, "Dad, what did it cost you to learn that lesson?" He responded, "About $1,200." I always look back at that exchange and appreciate the fact that something that cost him $1,200 to learn, I merited to learn for free. Henceforth, I use this anecdote as the basis for one of my personal mottos:

Some folks learn things the easy way, other folks learn them the hard way, and yet other folks don't manage to learn them at all.

The keys to success are within our reach – if, like Sruly forebode, we don't force ourselves to learn these lessons the hard way.

Appendix A

Transmission Failure

Author's note: In the earlier stages of this project, I wrote an autobiography chapter that I expected to instate as an intrinsic part of this book. My objective for writing this chapter is described in detail in the Author's Foreword at the beginning of this book.

As it transpires that the full version of this chapter runs in the neighborhood of 70 pages, I had to make a cost/benefit analysis. I felt that the chapter in its entirety was too long and cumbersome, too personal, too revealing, too distracting, and ultimately, counterproductive.

After mulling over a number of options (detailed in the Author's Foreword), the most practical solution seemed to be to create this anthology of excerpts. These excerpts were culled out of the original finished chapter intact and, for the most part, have not been re-edited. As a result, certain passages that allude to concepts or incidents that were related in the omitted portions may be a bit unclear. I apologize for any inconvenience that this may cause.

*It goes without saying that everything that is presented is factual, although some incidents will obviously reflect a subjective point of view. With very few exceptions, all of the people that are mentioned are real people with fictitious names (the rest are fake people with real names). In order to further protect "the innocent", I felt it prudent to conceal the identity of my hometown. As such, I refer to my hometown as **Natwich**, which is an acronym for **N**orth **A**merican **T**own **W**ith an **I**ntegrated **C**ommunity of **H**ebrews. The neighborhood of my early childhood (until the age of 11) is being called **Rainbow Beach** and the name of the new neighborhood (from age 11 until we made aliya) is being called **Hammerstone Hills**. Names of other places such as **Syracuse Park**, **Oak Crest** and **Maccabee Hebrew Day School**, are also fictitious.*

I am always interested in feedback from my readership on

this and any part of the book. If any readers are genuinely inter-ested in the unabridged 70 plus page version of this narrative, they may request it from me by email. If I do establish a web site for this book (under consideration) and sense a substantial level of interest, I may make it available through the web site.

As is every author, I am grateful to anybody who takes the time to read my material. I hope you find these excerpts enjoy-able and inspirational.

Excerpt 1 – The opening pages of the chapter. My father's ordeals during the Holocaust

I am writing a book about chareidim. I think that I can do that be-cause I profess to be one. At least that is my opinion.

How do I come to be chareidi? Was I born one? Is anybody? Is one automatically chareidi because their mother is chareidi?

Whether or not I was born chareidi is a moot point. There are many Jews who are chareidi like myself who always felt chareidi despite the fact that they were not born into a chareidi environment. Likewise, there are many religious (*mitzvah* observant) Jews who were not born into a religious environment. Nevertheless, they always felt religious and there-upon gravitated toward *mitzvah* observance. We can call these fine people observant Jews "waiting to happen." Many of today's chareidim did not originate as such but were "chareidim waiting to happen."

The important thing is that, although always strictly observant, I was not brought up to be chareidi. The looming question is, "Why not?"

The fact is that both my parents have long and strong roots in the Chassidic "ultra-Orthodox" genre. Nevertheless, it seems that such roots, when replanted, do not stand a strong chance of reproducing a specimen like the original as long as the environmental conditions are not ideal. Such was the status of middle 1900s America. The horticulturists of our nation have since done a fine job of developing the proper environmental conditions to enable the American species of chareidi to thrive and even to adapt to other terrains. This is a testimony to the resilience of the chareidi plant (a bit like a thornbush that is aflame yet doesn't burn). Yet, in parts of America, there were times when only the strongest and most purebred specimens were capable of producing fruit.

My father was born in the late 1920s to a Chassidic family near Munkacz in what is now Ukraine. He studied at a local cheder and under-went a traditional Chassidic upbringing. Life was normal until he was fourteen years old.

Even though World War II began in 1939, life in Munkacz remained relatively placid until the deportations of 1944. But 1944 eventually came. On the last day of Passover the Jews of Munkacz were instructed to vacate their homes and to assemble at a local brick factory. It was actually a couple of weeks until the deportations were carried out. When my father's group came, the Germans checked the number of Jews against their list and announced that there was one missing. My father noticed that his mother wasn't there. He told the officer that his mother was missing but he thought he knew where to find her. With this, he ran back toward his home and then to the synagogue that was two doors away. He entered the synagogue to find it vacant except for his mother who was standing in front of the open ark entranced in prayer. He tugged at her clothes and said, "They are waiting for us. We have to go now." She turned to him and said, "It's all right. We can go. I am sure that the Holy One B"H has heard my prayer."

They reached Auschwitz exactly one week before the holiday of Shavuot. Though no one truly knew what was in store, the rumors had filtered through and the trepidation was tangible. My grandmother held my father back from alighting from the train. She noticed that everyone was told to abandon their luggage at the rail side. With a motherly instinct she opened their suitcase and took out some extra shirts and slacks and a sweater and proceeded to "overdress" my father. A Jewish camp inmate, whose job it was to clear the train, climbed on and harshly ordered them to alight. My grandmother stalled until she finished the overdressing but they were promptly forced off the train.

The man reached over and grabbed my father in the course of yanking him off the train, but then he stopped. He looked at my father and asked, "How old are you?"

"Fourteen," was the reply.

"No, you are not fourteen. You are eighteen."

My father was not comfortable being bullied by this stranger. "Excuse me, but I am not eighteen, I am fourteen."

The man looked in his eyes and said firmly, "Yingele (young man), here you listen to what you are told, and I say that you are eighteen." And with that, he hurled him off of the train.

My father did not appreciate that exchange and he never saw that stranger again.

The men were separated from the women and each group had to pass through the initial selection. My father caught up with his father and they stood in line for the selection. When my grandfather's turn came he was asked his name (same as mine), his age (late 40s) and if he could work (affirmative). He was sent to the right.

Then came my father's turn. He was asked his name and then his age. By now he was beginning to think that maybe that belligerent stranger knew something he didn't. He drew himself up tall and said, "I am eighteen." (Don't forget the extra layers of clothes).

"Kenst du arbeitin? (Can you work)?"

"Javald. Ich ken arbeitin."

He was sent to the right.

Simultaneously, his mother and two sisters were subjected to the women's selection. My grandmother was selected for immediate entry to the World of Truth. My two aunts were allowed to remain in this one. They were subsequently transferred elsewhere and eventually to Bergen-Belsen where they were liberated. They married immediately after the war, immigrated to New York, raised small families (observant), and lived (relatively) happily ever after.

Meanwhile, my father and his father were transferred to Mauthausen. One day, after a few weeks in Mauthausen, his barracks was ordered to line up outside. The inmates lined up in six rows. The Nazis divided the six rows into two groups of three rows each and both groups were transferred to smaller satellite camps. My father and his father were in different groups. After the war, my father found out where the second group went. He also found out that there were almost no survivors from that group.

My father was sent to Melk, a work camp in Austria that was actually part of a Luftwaffe base. Because the camp was full of Luftwaffe personnel, there was a much smaller concentration of SS guards at that camp (not that it makes much difference to us but the Luftwaffe didn't care much for the SS, either). Nazis are Nazis but still the Luftwaffe Nazis were a tad less vicious than the SS, simply because they had more pressing concerns than doing in the Jews, especially from late 1944 and on.

As in many of the camps, the religious Jews banded together and managed to exist on a somewhat higher plane of morale than the non-religious. My father tells of one man called Koppel the Calendar who managed to memorize the Hebrew calendar before being deported. He was the only one who knew when *Rosh Chodesh* and the Jewish holidays fell out. Another man managed to build a *sukka* by putting wood and branches on top of an abandoned boxcar. He invited my father and others (one at a time) to sneak in with their rations to say the blessing "to dwell in the *sukka*." Most of the religious (Hungarian) Jews actually survived the nine or so months in Melk.

As the Allied Forces closed in, the SS liquidated the satellite camps (and most of the inmates) and they herded the survivors and marched west. The survivors from that region were concentrated at a camp named

Ebensee. I have seen photos and have read accounts about Ebensee. It can only be described as the land of the living dead (this, in addition to the piles of dead that did not happen to be living). By the time my father arrived, in the last weeks of the war, it was total chaos. Very few guards, no work, no food, no room to sleep, nothing but starvation, sickness, and death.

But – it was spring. The guns could be heard and the planes could be seen. For the living there was the dream of imminent liberation. And for the religious, there was G-d. On May 5, 1945, a flag was hung from the watchtower to signify that it was over. The next day, my father, 15 years old, stood holding the hand of Rabbi Yehoshua Grunwald, the Rebbi of Chust, as they watched the American tanks roll in.

Shortly before the liberation, one prisoner came across a *shel yad* from a pair of *tefillin*. The *shel yad* was conveyed to the most prominent religious spiritual leader that was present, the Rebbi of Chust. He concealed this treasured find until the day of liberation a short time later. On the day of liberation the Allied Forces brought in a mobile field kitchen and prepared a meal of meat and rice. Two lines quickly formed – a long line at the kitchen waiting for a ration of the hearty food and a much shorter line in front of the Rebbi of Chust waiting to say the blessing and don the *shel yad*. My father stood on the short line. It seems that the food was too rich for the undernourished systems of most of the inmates. My father relates that many people who partook of the offerings of the long line began to die. Many others who partook of the offerings of the short line began to live.

Excerpt 2 – A bit of background about my mother's parents

My mother is American born, the eldest of five siblings. Her father was born and raised in the Hungarian town of Kleinvardein in 1902. I recently discovered that the Rebbi of Klausenberg was born in 1905 and lived in Kleinvardein from 1912 until right after World War I (1919). Though neither of them is still with us, it is safe to assume that they knew each other as youngsters.

My grandfather's great grandfather was the Rabbi of Irshau (Hungary) and was a contemporary, acquaintance, and correspondent of the Chatam Sofer. This ancestor's daughter (I guess that means a great-great-great aunt) became the second wife of one of the Chatam Sofer's most accomplished disciples, the Maharam Shick. My grandfather's father became endeared to his "step" uncle, the Maharam Shick, and helped him to write his novellae. This same great grandfather would travel to the great Chassidic courts of the region, predominantly of Belz, Tzanz, and Munkacz. He collected stories of many Chassidic masters spanning several generations and compiled them into four anthologies. These works are highly acclaimed in Chassidic circles. My grandfather, toward the end of his life, had these anthologies reprinted into their last available publication.

My mother's mother was born in 1911 in Romania to a well-established devoutly Orthodox family. Like many others, her father could sense the hostile winds that were blowing ever stronger in Eastern Europe. This sense was forcibly knocked into him one day when he was traveling on a train. Some gentiles proceeded to bully him and the incident culminated with his being physically pushed off of the train. You might say that this push landed him in the United States.

He arrived in America with his eldest daughter sometime in the 1920s and was lucky enough to find employment immediately in a sweat shop owned by a Jewish relative. What's more, there was an understanding with this relative employer that he would not be compelled to work on Shabbat.

Sure enough, the first Friday of his employment came around and approximately one hour before sundown he got up from his workstation and prepared to leave. The employer approached him and inquired as to where he was going.

My great grandfather responded, "It is getting close to Shabbat and I must go. We agreed that I will not be forced to work on Shabbat."

The employer responded, "I will honor my agreement but I will not allow you to leave one minute before sundown."

My great grandfather was dumbstruck but he felt that he was in no position to challenge the employer. He continued working until the onset of Shabbat at which point he stopped. Having nowhere to go, he remained in the shop all through the Shabbat. That evening, he lay down on a cutting table and cried all night long. He had received his "hazing" but he stood strong. He never did violate the Shabbat.

Excerpt 3 – The general description of my upbringing

As I intimated, there was nothing overtly chareidi about my upbringing. For the most part, I was brought up to be just like everyone else. Except for Passover, we didn't maintain any chareidi kashrut stringencies, so we could eat indiscriminately in anybody else's house as long as they "kept kosher." Of course, "kosher" still meant kosher by conventional Orthodox Jewish standards. There was a problem here in that we were indoctrinated that we "keep kosher" and that "kosher" meant x, y, and z. Period. We were not taught that "others" might have a more diluted, less demanding interpretation of what kosher meant, nor that our kosher might fall short of another Jew's more meticulous standards. There is only one kosher. Ergo, in a child's perception, anyone who claims to keep kosher is claiming to keep the same (one and only) kosher that he keeps. Needless to say, this caused a number of sticky incidents both when I happily partook of the fare offered in the home of one whose standards didn't meet the accepted norms, as well as being somewhat embarrassed, on some rare occasions, when my standards were more liberal than those of my peers (in some cases, relatives).

The same applied to what we wore. The fifties and sixties was an era wherein, even in the most Orthodox of families, women could be seen wearing slacks and short sleeve tops. I already noted that only the few and the brave covered their hair. Many men would not wear kipot in public or at work, were not "always" wearing *tzitzit*, and certainly never wore them externally. Our family fit into this mold. Yes, I was brought up to wear a kipa and *tzitzit*, but, in terms of general manner of dress, anything goes. In my upbringing, there did not exist a uniquely Orthodox style of dress. Even then, we were quite aware that the Chassidim, the *yeshivaleit*, and the *alter europaisha* (old Europeans) maintained the styles that are now heralded as chareidi, but that was for people who lived in such communities (predominantly on the East Coast), and just was not the vogue in Rainbow Beach. Why should we not be like most everyone else?

Still and all, there were certain areas of observance in which we outshone our peers. I already mentioned that our Passover observance was exemplary. My father would always "import" a full eight days' worth of hand *Shmura* matzah from New York (as expensive then as it is now) and we would not eat matzah that came into contact with water – what is known as *gebrochs*. My father, who used to listen to the cantorial records of Joseph Rosenblatt and Moshe Stern served as the cantor for the High Holidays. One more thing. My mother says that we were just about the only family in the neighborhood who observed the Halacha of immersing new vessels in a *mikveh* (ritual pool) before their first use. The problem was that although there was a mikveh in Rainbow Beach, it was generally only open to women on appointment. My father couldn't get to it under normal circumstances. Not a big problem – there was a large city park at the edge of the neighborhood that had an adequate lagoon. On one occasion, my mother bought a new kitchen knife and sent my father to the park to immerse it. My father went to the park and crouched at the edge of the lagoon and proceeded to immerse the knife. Along comes a policeman and sees this fellow dipping a large knife in and out of the lagoon. Boy, did my father have some explaining to do.

Such were my formative years in Rainbow Beach. I would venture to say that my father's personal standards were of a higher caliber than the prevalent socio-religious standards of the Rainbow Beach community, yet, he seemed satisfied that my ideals should conform to the local norms. Shabbat was for socializing and playing chess, ping-pong, and, in the summer, croquet in the back yard. We frequently had guests at the Shabbat table, sometimes neighboring families, often Orthodox students from the nearby colleges. At the table, everything under the sun was discussed; everything except the weekly Torah portion. The television went on the minute after *havdalah* and went off the next Friday at candle lighting. Sunday was designated for recreation. We almost always went some-where, to the beach, a museum, an amusement park, or just visiting. Afternoon and evening services were overlooked. Aside from meat, kosher was everything that wasn't known to be unkosher. We were Jewish in the synagogue, at the table, and for half of the school day. The rest of the time we were middle class Americans like all others. We woke up each day with *Modeh Ani* and went to bed at night with *Kriyat Shema*, but what took place in between was anybody's guess. There was nothing that couldn't be read, nothing that couldn't be watched, and no decent activity that couldn't be experienced. My father may have had some kind of a threshold for himself, but if so, he never shared it with us. The vestiges of chareidiism were kept behind a glass door in a curio, there to be seen but not to be handled, as if they were liable to be damaged for lack of knowing how to use them.

The engine may have been running – ***but the transmission failed.***

Excerpt 4 – Clarence Darrow at the age of 8

Fast forward to third grade. That was a banner year for me because Maccabee Hebrew Day School did not begin teaching *Chumash* until third grade. Moreover, for some inexplicable reason, they began *Chumash* study at the third Torah portion, *Lech Lecha*, thus ignoring the two preceding portions, *Bereishit,* which discusses Creation, and *Noah,* which discusses the Great Flood. Now, I did know about the Great Flood, because, at summer day camp at the JCC, we used to sing a Christian song about the flood called *Rise and Shine,*[1] but I knew scant little about Creation. The irony is that, as a precocious little kid, with unlimited access to Life and Time magazines, Walt Disney, World Book Encyclopedia, etc., I had seen plenty of evolution diagrams, you know, where there is a lineup of about ten phases of a creature beginning as a chimpanzee and ending up as Stephen Jay Gould. As this "reality" was that which was fed to me by the environment, and, to this point, stood unopposed, I understood this phenomenon to be a proven and undisputed fact. What I am trying to point out here is that, as a nice FFB Orthodox Jewish boy from Natwich, currently an avowed chareidi, I had "discovered" evolution *before I knew anything about Creation.* First impressions count. So much so that, one Sunday morning some considerable time later, my father, who must have noticed this omission, sat down with me and opened a *Chumash* to Genesis 1:1 and initiated me to the wonders of Creation. About midway through the lesson I looked up at him and asked, "Do you really believe in all this?" I am not sure if the expression on his face meant "What have you been reading?" or "Is this really my kid?" or "Where did I go wrong?" or "What have I been paying tuition for?" but all he said was, "Of course I believe it." I do not recall how my own mindset developed on this issue. I reckon that I probably concluded "If Daddy believes that this is how it was, then I suppose that I ought to believe it, too." The trauma of the event was not that I would have to shift gears, but rather, this is what initiated me to the fact that there was more than one set of gears to shift to. To this point I was not aware that religious people and irreligious people do not share beliefs on fundamental issues.

Excerpt 5 – One of a few catalytic events that propelled me into the ranks of the chareidi world

As summer approached, so did the awaited influences. The first of which may seem to be slight and insignificant and it stands to show that the impact of a casual statement cannot be measured. This was the phase of life where my friends were becoming bar-mitzvah and the invitations came my way. In the spring of seventh grade, the older half of the class

---

[1] One stanza ran: The animals came in twosies, twosies, twosies/ The animals came in twosies, twosies, twosies/ Elephants and kangaroosies, roosies/ Children of the Lord.

ushered in the bar-mitzvah era and one of the first was that of David K.

David K. hailed from one of the more solid Orthodox families of the mainstream community in Hammerstone Hills. I had actually first met David at the Bnei Akiva summer camp that was so popular. I believe that his father is a Natwich native, born and raised Orthodox (no small feat), and had attended the local yeshiva (we are talking 1940s and 50s). Typical of Natwich, he wore a hat on Shabbat and his wife did not cover her hair. The family was well placed in the community and members of HaPoel Mizrachi. For the most part they were much like us, albeit a teeny bit more modern (at least my dad is European!)

The bar-mitzvah was a Sunday brunch in a local synagogue. As was stylish then, David's sister, Lillian, was introduced at the dais to "propose the toast." Today, we chareidim call this "offering *divrei bracha* (words of blessing)." I don't recall much of the brief speech but I could not get out of my mind what she said at the end: "So, David, our bracha to you is that you should grow to be a real *Talmid Chacham…*"

Alarms went off in my head. "So they think he should be a Talmid Chacham, huh? How is he going to become a Talmid Chacham? Bnei Akiva in Natwich is not in the business of producing Talmid Chachams. The local minimum-standard modern Orthodox yeshiva doesn't have much of a track record for producing Talmid Chachams. I'll bet his father doesn't study anything more than a Shabbat afternoon *blatt shiur*. Nobody did then. He'll probably attend the local modern Orthodox yeshiva (which he did), go to college (which he did), become a dentist or something (which he did), get married and buy a nice house in Oak Crest (which he did), send his kids to the pareve school (which, in fact, relocated to Oak Crest), go to a weekly *shiur*, give some *tzedaka* and live happily ever after."

I said to myself that if being a Talmid Chacham is truly an ideal, then you have to mean it when you say it. And if it is truly one's goal, there is only one way to do it – one must travel the roads that lead to it, and, in those days, the road signs were pointing away from Hammerstone Hills.

Excerpt 6 – My true initiation into Chareidi-hood

My bar-mitzvah transpired on Chanuka of eighth grade (*everybody* lights candles on *my* birthday!) and it was not much different than anyone else's. I wore a light blue polyester blend suit with a light yellow dress shirt and tie. On the upper level was my personalized knitted kipa. The idea of wearing a black hat had not been broached (incidentally, in that era, black hats were exceedingly hard to come by in Natwich). We had the regular Shabbat morning service at our synagogue wherein I was the chazzan for *shacharit* (morning service) the complete *baal-koreh* and I delivered my speech (no interruptions). My father had asked the revered Chassidic Rebbe to write a bar-mitzvah speech. When he went to pick it up, he brought me along to his home in Syracuse Park and the Rebbe gave me a blessing which I still had not learned to appreciate. The service was followed by a Shabbat afternoon luncheon in the social hall of a nearby non-Orthodox synagogue. I believe that my sister spoke but she did not wish me to become a true Talmid Chacham.

Three weeks after my bar-mitzvah, it happened. The Belzer Rebbe, then a very young man in his early twenties, was in need of some medical attention, and so, he made a pilgrimage to New York. For his followers in America, this was a monumental event, and my father, who never needs much of an excuse to hop to New York, was not about to be left out. On a whim, he decided to take me along for the ride. I never thought about it until now, but I suspect he may have wanted to ask the Rebbe what to do with me.

The Rebbe was staying in Borough Park, my mother's old stomping grounds. As a tyke, we used to go to New York at least twice a year and stay with my grandparents in Borough Park. These trips typically entailed a Friday shopping excursion along 13th Ave. which always included two highlights: lunch at one of the 13th Ave. Kosher Pizza parlors (non-existent in Natwich) and a brief visit to a prominent hat store which was under the proprietorship of my grandfather's brother. We used to call it Uncle Lipa's hat store. These trips ended shortly after my grandmother passed away and my grandfather remarried and moved to Eretz Israel. Now was the first time in a while that we were spending Shabbat in Brooklyn and, needless to say, we relived our ceremonial Friday excursion. Yes, another slice of pizza with a knish and another visit to the hat store. My father was in the market for a fresh hat, but this time, I piped up: "What do you have in my size?" The goods were displayed, measured, fitted, and priced. Money changed hands and thus commenced the coronation. I was hereby crowned a chareidi.

Back in Natwich, I kind of led a double life. The black hat was only worn on Shabbat and, during the week, I was one of the boys. Nobody dared to wear a black hat in school. The balance of the year was spent keeping up at school while trying to grow up. Of course, we talked incessantly about where we would wind up next year, who might go to the "blackie" yeshivot and who most certainly would not. Most of the boys were going to the middle of the road, more secular minded, low-intensity, politics ridden, local yeshiva. Not a single one was going to the local chareidi yeshiva. As for me, I wanted to leave town. In part, it held a sense of adventure, but, more significantly, in our Lost in Space, Star

Trek, Laverne and Shirley, SNL home, there was not much fertile ground for becoming any kind of a Talmid Chacham and I was determined to at least attempt the Lillian K. route. My parents were not thrilled about sending me out of town but a number of forces converged to seal my destiny: (1) I wanted to go. (2) My mother was disillusioned by the local chareidi yeshiva. (3) My father was disillusioned by the local modern yeshiva (mostly the politics). (4) My Dad's chareidi cronies struck again. This time it was a local fellow named Mr. Adelstein who just happened to push for that same high class yeshiva that my mentor/counselor recommended. He had the clout and pulled the strings. My parents had but one stipulation – that it would not discourage me from going to college after four years of high school. It seems that the powers-that-be managed to convince them of that point. I am not sure if anybody warned them that this yeshiva is a Lakewood affiliate.

Off I went to Blackie yeshiva high school. In due time I went 24/7/365 with the black hat, retired the personalized knitted kipa, and swore off movies. I started learning Yiddish (Lithuanian dialect), the moves, the slang, the who's who and the what's what, Mishna Berura and *mussar* (Jewish ethics). I had arrived!

One other thing. I quickly made up my mind that I was not going to college as long as I could avoid it.

Excerpt 7 – My adventures as a student in the Mirrer Yeshiva

The Mirrer Yeshiva has one great advantage – it is located in the heart of chareidi Jerusalem; and it has one great disadvantage – it is located in the heart of chareidi Jerusalem. From its hallowed halls all that transpires can be seen and heard. One can experience a great deal, but one can get swallowed up in the whirlpool.

The particular year that I attended was one of great turmoil. There were virulent forces wreaking havoc both within and outside of the walls of the yeshiva.

The yeshiva itself was entering a state of transition. Rabbi Shmuelevitz had just passed away the previous year and his son-in-law, the scholarly Reb Nachum, was losing his prolonged battle with a debilitating disease. The intensity of his discourses dwindled and, by midyear, he discontinued them entirely. Rabbi Shmuelevitz's brother-in-law, Rav Beinish, was enmeshed in the administrative challenges of directing a yeshiva that was growing in size as it was shrinking in scholarship. Eventually, the proper adjustments were made but that transitional year was beleaguered by a disquieting vacuum.

Outside of the yeshiva there was just too much going on. That was a time of fierce conflicts between the Jerusalem chareidim and the secular powers. There were two main issues. One was the construction of the Ramot Road (Sderot Golda Meir) that would serve as an alternate route to Tel Aviv. This road effectively bisected the then burgeoning neighborhoods of Ezrat Torah and Unsdorf from Sanhedria Murchevet and Ramot with two repercussions – it prevented the chareidi neighborhoods from merging and it ushered in a tremendous influx of vehicular traffic on Shabbat that flowed through this chareidi enclave. What made it truly evil was that the municipality, under Teddy Kollek, had approved plans to build a major sports and recreation center just beyond Sanhedria Murchevet (where the Har Hotzvim industrial park was eventually built). This is analogous to building a disco next door to an old-age home. There is no question that it was intentionally done to disrupt and "hopefully" drive away the chareidi residents of the area.

The second issue was the despicable government policy of involuntary autopsies performed on the deceased. These issues prompted some of the more restless residents of the area to take to the streets for *hafganot* (anti-government protests). Left alone, these hafganot would have been a mere annoyance to the local inhabitants and would most likely have died out. Somehow, the government, in its constant throes of paranoid self-aggrandizement and infinite wisdom, felt it prudent to send a gang of equally restless violent thugs wearing Border Patrol uniforms to confront the protesters. This understandably resulted in unwarranted arrests and injuries, often of people who were not actively involved in the protests, and these shows of brutality provided impetus for more protests.

The truth is that before I came, my American Rosh Yeshiva told me that I was not coming here primarily to study. I was coming here to grow, and grow I did. For certain, it was a very eventful year and every event had a powerful impact on me. In this environment I was able to see close-up the Israeli's love for his country. I was able to see close-up the chareidi's love for Torah and mitzvot. These are the things that I came to see. But there was one other thing that I saw close-up, something that I would have preferred not to see. I was able to see close-up the Israeli's hatred for the chareidi.

When did I see it? For the most part, it was evident from the constant *hafganot* and the fascist-style treatment that fueled them. I already wrote that these confrontations yielded casualties and fomented more confrontations. To some extent they were unavoidable because the authorities

would grant no voice to the chareidim. The chareidim had no other avenue to make themselves heard. Still, whether their cause was just or
unjust, it is one thing when chareidim abandon the study hall and take to
the streets. In such a case, they are waging battle with the "rulers of the
streets." For the moment at hand, they are combatants on enemy turf and
by the rules of warfare, the "rulers of the streets" have a right to vanquish
their "enemies." It is quite another matter when the "rulers of the streets"
take the battles away from the streets and into the study halls. In that
case, they are not there to confront active combatants, they are there to
vanquish sedentary Jews.

This occurred twice. One event was the famous Toldot Aharon pogrom that occurred on Saturday night March 7, 1981. The Toldot Aharon
faction represents the most uncompromising element among the chareidim.
Their headquarters is an imposing citadel that is located literally a "stone's
throw" away from Yeshivat Mir. Members of their group are always among
those who would take part in the *hafganot* but they were certainly not the
only participants and, perhaps, not even a clear majority. It is likewise
true that not every Toldot Aharon follower is a hot-headed fanatic. The
authorities, however, do not wish to be bothered with these petty details.
They hate chareidim the same way as the anti-semitic non-Jew hates the
Jew – indiscriminately. To the anti-semite, every Jew is a street urchin
and every street urchin is a Jew. To the boorish secular Israeli, every
mafgin (demonstrator) is a Toldot Aharon and every Toldot Aharon is a
mafgin.

As winter ebbed,[2] the issues of the Ramot road and the planned developments resurfaced. On the Shabbat of March 6 and 7 the demonstrators surged out and assumed battle stations in full force. There is no indication that anything extraordinary occurred out in "the field." For both
the demonstrators and whatever police were on hand, it was a typical day
at the office. Nobody knew that the police had other plans.

That evening, as the Motzaei Shabbat evening services were wind-
ing down, approximately 300 police officers fell upon the Toldot Aharon
synagogue in Meah Shearim. First, they shot it up with tear gas. Subsequently, they stormed the facility and overturned tables and chairs, broke
the windows, tore off the curtain from the Holy Ark (the worshippers
claim that they attempted to break into the Ark but that it was securely
locked), tore *tallitot* (prayer shawls) and destroyed prayerbooks and other
religious books. They beat up as many people as they could lay their
hands on and dragged off young and old in paddy wagons. Though there

---

[2] This, combined with the fact that in the chareidi-yeshiva world, Adar I is the
most restless month of the year!

had been demonstrations earlier in the day, they were long finished. They had no way of positively associating the individuals that they attacked, beat and arrested, with any who may have earlier participated in the demonstrations. This entire "aktion" was, at the time and place that it occurred, totally unprovoked and, aside from being an exercise in totalitarian intimidation, it served no strategic purpose.

We at Mir were hearing about it as it was going on. It sounded exciting (that year, what wasn't?). Imagine, a true to life pogrom right here in Meah Shearim! And it's being carried out by the Jewish government police, then under the command of Minister of Interior (and Police) Dr. Yosef Burg of the National Religious Party! A number of students went over to see for themselves. I thought better of it. Three of the students, all Americans, were arrested. The next day, I went down there to survey the scene. It can only be described as a "holy mess." The scent of the tear gas was still lingering. Outside of the building there were countless shards of broken glass, some of it was wire reinforced glass from the front door. I picked up a few pieces as a memento of the turbulence of my Israeli experience. I have them stashed somewhere to this day.

The campaign of intimidation was not restricted to Toldot Aharon, which brings us to the second incident.[3] This was certainly not nearly as dramatic as the Toldot Aharon pogrom but, for me, it was much closer to home.

In the wake of this campaign of intimidation there were bands of Border Patrol personnel[4] that patrolled the streets of Meah Shearim and Bais Yisroel (the neighborhood of Yeshivat Mir) looking for trouble. They had a very broad definition of what constituted "trouble." It transpired one evening that I was in the study hall (actually studying) sometime around ten o'clock. In that era, the study hall was relatively underpopulated at night because the married students were entitled to stay at home and many of the unmarried students went to study at the homes of the married ones. Evidently, a small group of the yeshiva boys were overly restless (see footnote 2 above) and were entertaining themselves on the

---

[3] I have no recollection as to whether this occurred chronologically before or after the Toldot Aharon incident. Whichever, it was in the same general vicinity of time.

[4] Nowadays, the Border Patrol is known as the Yassam Brigade. It should be noted that the ethnic makeup of the Border Patrol force was not primarily Israeli Jews but rather pro-Israel Druze mercenaries. These people were not "from the students of our Patriarch Abraham" and they were renowned for their brutality. We can "judge favorably" that an all-Jewish force, even if totally secular, might have been a tad more gentle and reverent of a religious sanctuary. Unfortunately, recent events in Gaza and Amona have undermined this assumption.

roof of the building. At some point, as a Border Patrol jeep passed by the yeshiva building, one particularly hot-headed and heavy-handed hooligan (we are all blessed with characters such as these – and I certainly do not condone these activities) thought it might be hospitable to offer the nice Border Patrol fellows a drink. So he tossed a bottle at their jeep. As hard as he could. Okay, so the bottle was empty - must have been an oversight. The boys also made a point to convey warm greetings commending their professed affiliations to the German National Socialist party. At first, it appeared that the National Socialists were being anti-social as the jeep simply drove on. Not so.

Ten minutes later it came back – with three more jeeps.

Now, about twenty Border Patrol thugs were lined up in front of the yeshiva with billy clubs and crash helmets, and they were clearly on the warpath. The boys on the roof were unfazed. They just showered them with more hospitality in the form of more [empty] drink bottles accompanied with cheery accolades acknowledging their Aryan practices. I and a number of others were congregating at the windows of the main study hall watching the drama unfold and planning a defense. We took stock of our supplies. They had crash helmets and billy clubs. We had portable wrought iron lecterns crowned with a thick slab of dense plywood – and we knew how to use them. The entrances to the building consisted of narrow doorways at the street level. On the upper story, directly above the doorways, there were transom-like windows just big enough for a lectern. We weren't too bad off: we had the weaponry, higher ground, and we probably had more men – assuming there were some in the dorm rooms and other assorted nooks and crannies. They quickly determined that it would not be wise for them to storm the building (legend had it that this had occurred at some similar previous occasion culminating with some Border Patrol personnel storming the nearest emergency room). Thus, they attempted the conventional tear gas maneuver. They loaded two or three launchers, aimed for the arched multi-paned windows of the study hall, and fired. I am not sure if any of them even hit the windows but they all bounced back toward the aggressors. As they were forced to change position, one of them must have realized that it was past their bed-time and they decided to call off the standoff and retreat for the night. The next day, one of the students (American, as were most of the dormers) recovered the spent tear gas canister. It was manufactured in Pennsylvania. The thought of the Jewish government using American tear gas to harass American Torah students in Israel[5] was enough

---

[5] From an economic standpoint alone, the contribution that American yeshiva and seminary students (of all stripes) have generated for the Israeli economy

to make me cry.

Excerpt 8 – The great and lengthy *shidduch* (courtship) story

My return to Natwich was fast approaching and I needed to be prepared. There was one thing that I could take for granted: by the time that I got back to Natwich, my parents would be plotting my next move. It was logical to assume that they would press for some program of *Torah im derch eretz* (Torah study supplemented with worldly endeavors) but from the state of affairs in America as well as the rhetoric within our household, the odds were that such a program would evolve into *derech eretz ulahy im Torah* (worldly endeavors *possibly* supplemented with some Torah study). Of course, for me this was a sticky situation. The degree of chareidi that I had achieved was the result of an uphill battle, but I had reached new heights and I wanted to stay there. Yet, I was now an adult and, as the saying goes, we must "wake up and smell the coffee." I had already been blessed with more years of full time study than I had anticipated and my parents, although reluctant, had still been supportive. Should I still insist on full time study? How far should I "push the envelope?" How far *could* I push the envelope? How far am I permitted to push the envelope?

One is certainly not permitted to oppose one's parents without the sanction of a qualified Halachic authority, and so, about two weeks before my departure from the Holy Land, I sought out the preeminent Torah authority in Israel, Rabbi Yaakov Kanievsky, ZT"L, the Steipler Gaon.

Speaking of pushing envelopes, this is exactly what one needed to do to communicate with the great Gaon. He was hearing impaired so one could not converse with him. One needed to jot down his request on a slip of paper (very commonly the back of an envelope) and present it to him to read and respond. Before I arrived at his quarters, I stopped at the dorm room of a friend of mine in the Ponovezh Yeshiva[6], and there, I took a ruled sheet of 5 x 7 inch notepad paper and meticulously wrote down some words of background, my predicament, and my request that he give me a blessing for success. All this I wrote with great care weighing every word. This took the better part of an hour and the writing covered both sides of the page. At the very end of the note was an added request for a

---

over the past six decades most likely exceeds all of the foreign aid money that this nation has received from the U.S. It is amazing, though not surprising, how underappreciated this is.

[6] This friend was none other than my friend Sruly who is discussed in the "Fallout" chapter in this book.

blessing to readily find a suitable mate.

Armed with my masterpiece of prose, I headed toward Rashbam St. and joined the line of petitioners. My turn came up in due time and I entered his small study, took a seat, and presented him with my note. Initially, he was reluctant to read the entire page. Instead, he put the note aside and it was he who pushed the envelope. He literally pushed a torn envelope to me, handed me a pen and said, "Just write here the synopsis." So much for my hour of meticulous script. Now, I had to condense it all into one line within the next 30 seconds as he looked on (and with a sizable crowd waiting outside) – an exercise in humility, to say the least.

I picked up the pen and hurriedly wrote: "I am an American yeshiva boy who is returning to the US and I am standing at the crossroads of Torah and *derech eretz* and I seek your blessing for success."

The Steipler Gaon asked me a number of questions and I tried to answer them as best I could. In some cases, I was able to point at something that I had written on the original note that would indicate an answer. In the course of this question and answer session, almost all of the points on my note were addressed. All this time he was reading me the riot act: "What do you have to go back to America for? And what do you need with American *parnassah* (livelihood)? It's all *sam hamavet* (poison). What do you mean that you will ask advice from your Rosh Yeshivas in America because they know you better? What do they know? You should go to Lakewood and study tractate *Chullin* and be a Rabbi. If you need to work, you should learn to be an electrician so you will work a few hours a day and study for the rest…"

I was getting an earful and there was nothing wrong with my hearing. Toward the end of this tongue-lashing I meekly pointed to the last line of the note, the request for a blessing for a suitable mate. Thereupon, he looked squarely at me, raised his hand with his index finger pointing skyward, raised his voice and exclaimed, "***Hashem yishlach lecha zivug poh ba'aretz*** (G-d will send you a mate here in this Land)!"

Whoa!!

I was stunned! Here I was counting the minutes to my departure from Eretz Israel and the Gaon tells me that my mate is here in the Land. Not exactly what I expected to hear. What did he mean? Was this a blessing or a curse? I was too put off to even think of asking him what he meant. Anyway, I couldn't – it wasn't on my note sheet. Yet, as do all chareidim, I fervently believed that the words of a *tzaddik* are approved of in Heaven.[7] In some way they will come to pass. Still, it is not my place, duty, or ability to determine how. I must follow a logical game-plan and logic

---

[7] T.B. Moed Katan 18a; Job 22:28

dictated that the next move was to return to America.

One move that I had already factored into the game-plan was that I would stop off in New York and consult with my American Roshei Yeshiva (who knew enough) and other personal coaches before I returned to Natwich. They all pretty much rubber-stamped my preference that I should enlist in Lakewood Yeshiva, get married as soon as possible, study a bit more, join the diamond business, get rich, send them lots of money, and live happily ever after. This was actually a very plausible plan because, even in the past years, I had spent a good deal of my meager vacation time hanging out in my father's office helping out and learning the ropes (and the four C's). I only needed to sell the plan to the folks at headquarters.

As it turned out, thank G-d, they bought the plan with minimal, albeit palpable, resistance. After all, I was the oldest boy and I was named after my father's father. My father, the Holocaust survivor, and the only surviving male of his family was (besides being a bit of a softie) at least as anxious as I was to see me married and he knew that the East Coast was where it's at and that Lakewood was where it's done. He was also relatively satisfied with my command of the four C's even though he didn't think that I could even sell a book of matches to a smoker, so, for the time being, the plan was a go.

I wound up spending five years in Lakewood, all of them single. Except for the emotional roller-coaster ride that goes with trying to get hitched, they were wonderful years.

Three noteworthy events occurred during my initial year. The first was that Lakewood Yeshiva organized a group of sterling Kollel fellows to establish a community Kollel in my neighborhood in Natwich. I was thrilled. The yeshiva held a gala *seudat preida* (parting ceremony) and, although I was just a face in the crowd and I was totally unacquainted with the parting fellows, I felt very special as being virtually the only one who was not only on the *tzeitchem l'shalom* (bon voyage) "committee" but was simultaneously on the *boachem l'shalom* (welcoming) "committee." Although the town of Natwich could boast a respectable representation at Lakewood Yeshiva, I would say that no more than five students were from Hammerstone Hills. My inner thoughts were, "It's about time. Where were you guys seven years ago when I needed you?" In any case, I did readily forge a strong connection to that Kollel and was associated with it at various levels over the next sixteen years.

The second noteworthy event was the sudden illness and subsequent passing of the Rosh Yeshiva, HaRav Shneur Kotler, ZT"L. This tragedy plunged the yeshiva into a transitional phase similar to the one that I experienced in Eretz Israel. I was wondering if I was walking under a black cloud.

The third noteworthy event was that I began dating. This did not occur until close to the end of that year (I suppose that I kept a low profile and nobody really noticed me until then)[8]. Thus began a gut-wrenching saga of ups and downs that was to drag on for more than four years. Four and a half years of incessant phone calls, car rentals, day long excursions, hotel lounges and judgments rendered either by me or against me. I maintained a moderate rate of about ten introductions per year – you do the math. The first one dumped me after one date; the second one liked me a lot so we went out five times until it dawned on me that I was more impressed with myself than I was with her; the sixth one stole my heart and dropped me suddenly; the next one was a victim of rebound syndrome; and so it went, ad nauseam. Some were non-starters, others had seemed promising but, after more than a year, nothing was headed for the finish line – and the words of the Steipler Gaon constantly haunted me.

I couldn't get it out of my head. On the first encounter with every new prospect I would ask them if and when they had previously been to Eretz Israel. Almost all had visited at least once, most had recently returned from a year in seminary, one was born there, and one had gone with her family to settle when she was small, but they had needed to return (that particular one was very promising in its own right and I thought there would be results, but she abruptly called it off).

In the spring of 1984, two years down the road, one of my roommates became engaged to a girl from London. This was the era of People Express and Virgin Atlantic cheapo trans-Atlantic flights and it was the height of Ronald Reagan's power economy when the US dollar was pulverizing most European (and all Israeli) currencies and anyone with a few dollars in his pocket could conquer the world. Consequently, I took advantage of this economic boom to attend my roommate's wedding, which took place in early July, and from there, I hopped a cheap charter to Eretz Israel. Perhaps, with G-d's help, the "sea would split" as I made my way back to the Land of the Steipler Gaon's promise. Before I set out to Eretz Israel I journeyed to Manchester where I dug up some cousins among the Belzer Chassidim. In Manchester, I had an audience with the Manchester Rav, HaRav Yehuda Zeev Segal, ZT"L. I told him my background and the story with the Steipler Gaon. He advised me to return to the Steipler Gaon and request a blessing for a match but not to mention the earlier statement. Upon, arriving in Eretz Israel, I did exactly as the Manchester Rav advised and returned to the Steipler with a request for a (no strings attached) blessing. This I received. It was my last audience with the Steipler Gaon.

---

[8] The famous Lakewood freezer was not yet in operation in those years.

To get the most for my money, I also sought out the blessing of the Rebbe of Ger (the Lev Simcha). I received a blessing and an orange. At least from the orange I received instant gratification. To cover all my bases, I sought out the blessing of the Sephardic Mekubal Rabbi Yitzchok Keduri. My older sister, 26 and similarly single, was also vacationing in Eretz Israel that summer (I knew she was there but hadn't a clue where to find her. She had no idea that I came. I managed to track her down through a "miraculous" hunch) and we went together on a Galilee tour featuring a stop at the tomb of Rabbi Yehonatan ben Uziel.

After four uneventful weeks in Eretz Israel (no sea-splitting), I returned to the US armed with a pocketful of blessings and a stomach-full of oranges; back to Lakewood, where my (former) roommate was setting up a home and I was promoted to senior member of my dorm room. Another complete year passed. I ate copious oranges and drank numerous l'chaim's but none of them were my own. By now, my father was growing justifiably impatient and the strain was beginning to take a toll on my Torah study.

That summer, my father insisted that I take a course on computer programming and I was only too happy to comply. I signed up for the computer programming course at Agudath Israel's Cope Vocational Institute, then located in Borough Park, Brooklyn. I didn't take the full six month course because I wanted to be back at the yeshiva for the holy month of Ellul, but, in the six weeks that I attended, I completed the Introduction to Computers and BASIC Programming Language courses with flying colors. There were other Lakewood students taking the course but I was one of only two unmarried ones. It seems that some of the ladies who do the administrative work at Cope Vocational Institute are on the lookout for overripe single Lakewood boys who do very well on computer courses, and before I knew it, two ladies, a Mrs. H. and a Mrs. N., cornered me and coerced me to fill out a questionnaire that somehow didn't relate to job placement.

Summer passed and fall arrived and, with it, began my fifth year of full time Torah study at Beth Medrash Govoha of Lakewood, New Jersey. I continued meeting new prospects (fueled, in part, by the efforts of the benevolent ladies of Cope Institute), continued drawing blanks, and continued being haunted. I also continued showing up to the study hall but it wasn't with the same energy. I passed my 26th birthday and I felt that I was outgrowing the unmarried faction at Lakewood Yeshiva. I was also becoming more cynical, world-wise, and thick skinned. I started telling the matchmakers that I didn't think that I should be meeting a prospect that was younger than 21. The study suffered so much that, that winter, I took off a month and a half to assist my father in the diamond office during the busy season and I remained in Natwich until after the wedding of my third sister, the first wedding in the family. She had gone to study in Michlala Girl's College in Jerusalem and stayed on for the extended program. There, she was introduced to a British yeshiva student (quite chareidi) and all went smoothly. They were to marry in Natwich and settle in Jerusalem. Eventually, I returned to Lakewood but I didn't have a morning study partner. I was clearly burning out.

That Passover, while back in Natwich, my father told me point blank, "Enough is enough! It's time to start working." This was the moment I dreaded. Though such would be a veritable death sentence for my aspiration of spending at least a few years as a married Kollel fellow, I knew it was the reality. I told him that I agreed with him thoroughly. We decided that I would return to Lakewood for the summer session, but that I would be open to finding a job in the Diamond District in New York.

About five weeks later, in early June, my father called me at the yeshiva and instructed me to go to the Manhattan Diamond District, locate a specific address and office, and to introduce myself to "Eddie." I did precisely as instructed and met with Eddie. Without much fanfare, the gist of the conversation led directly to "when can you start?" The American diamond industry maintains a traditional summer break that spans the first two weeks of July. I replied that I could report to work immediately after the traditional summer break, which, in 1986, fell on Monday, July 14. This would enable me to just about finish out the summer session at the yeshiva and to organize my affairs. It would also buy me about six more weeks to remain a "learning boy," albeit a transitional specimen with at least one foot out the door. Perhaps the sea would miraculously split and the "decree" could be annulled. There was not much room for optimism, as, if nothing materialized when I was clearly "labeled" and in my prime, what should I expect to happen while I was some kind of a past due learning/working hybrid? Besides, I was still on American soil.

Well, man disposes and G-d proposes (do I have that backwards?).

Before anything else, I promptly contacted my Rosh Yeshiva/mentor/coach to hear his opinion as to if I should accept this "sinister decree." I commented that this whole incident seemed a bit surreal to me, "For four and a half years I have been hunting for a wife with no success, and now, I only pretend that I am looking for a job and it falls right into my lap!" His response was (as I expected), "This matter has emerged from G-d.[9] Go with *haztlacha* (success)."

Okay. It's sealed. I'm outta here. But, not so fast; I'm not a "working"

---

[9] Genesis 24:50

guy for another six weeks. In the meantime I'm a – I'm a – ...what am I?

Thank G-d for matchmakers that can't seem to retain some trivial details (I believe they call this *selective amnesia*)!

During the last week of June (I think it was Wednesday night), Mrs. N. from the Cope Institute ladies' auxiliary contacted me. It seems that her husband's cousin's daughter, one Miss Devora M., who had just recently completed the ritual post-high school year at a seminary in Eretz Israel, had returned to New York and stepped off the plane that very morning. Would I be interested in meeting her?

"Has she gotten over her jet lag?"

"She's ready."

"Has she gone out at all yet?" (Experience has told me that it is not beneficial to be somebody's "first one.")

"Yes, she has." (This was true – one guy, one date.)

"How old is she?" (Mrs. N. knew all about my age preferences.)

"Nineteen and a half."

"Sounds a bit young."

"Won't hurt." (Not now, but maybe when I take off my hat and reveal the receding hairline she'll wise up.)

"What kind of boy does she want?"

"She prefers a learning boy." (Understatement.) "But I think this will work." (Well, if it doesn't, I know that I am going to work.)

"You know that I am leaving the yeshiva in two weeks."

"We'll worry about it then."

"Okay. Give me the details."

I did a quick preliminary check through the "grapevine" and got back to Mrs. N. the following day:

"Look, she's a bit young and she's fresh off the plane. I've got half a foot in and a foot-and-a-half out. I am not optimistic. On the other hand, I am going to Natwich next Wednesday (for a week-long buffer period) and I already have dropped my study partners so my time is flexible until then. If she is willing to go out this very Sunday (it's now Thursday) I'll take you up. If not, not."

A little bit later I got the message, "Call her tomorrow. You're on."

"You told her that I'm going to Natwich on Wednesday?"

"Not yet."

"You told her that I'm leaving Lakewood two weeks from Monday?"

"Slipped my mind."

Selective amnesia.

We met on Sunday. Needless to say, it was one of the more pleasurable first dates that I had had in some time.

At one point I inquired as to when is her birthday. She said it just happens to be this coming week.

"So you're going to be twenty?"

"No, I am going to be nineteen."

Selective amnesia. It seems that nineteen and a half really meant half way to nineteen. I would be twenty-seven in December. All the reruns she sees on television I saw on the first run. She was freshly back from her banner year in Eretz Israel and was charged with an enthusiasm that I had long forsaken. (Actually, my "enthusiasm" was extinguished by the tear gas five years back.) I could feel the age difference.

I asked her if she had ever been to Eretz Israel before this year. She said that she had gone on one previous trip. An aunt and uncle (with four girl cousins) had been spending a Sabbatical year in Eretz Israel concurrent to her eighth grade. She spent the year salting away her baby-sitting money and, by year's end, she had enough put away to buy herself a ticket to Eretz Israel and to pay a visit to her normally-close-but-currently-distant relatives. I asked her what year that was. She repeated that it was after eighth grade.

"So that would be 1981, wouldn't it?"

"I suppose so."

"How long did you spend?"

"About a month."

"What month was it?"

"What do you mean?"

"What part of the summer did you go?"

"It was right after school. The beginning of the summer."

"So, that would be July?"

"That's right."

"So, you spent most of July of 1981 in Eretz Israel?"

"Yeah. Why is all this important?"

"Just curious."

I was a bit more than curious. The Steipler Gaon told me in July of 1981 that "G-d will send me a match here in this Land" and this not yet nineteen year old fledgling was right there in Eretz Israel at the time thanks to a steady demand for her babysitting services. This was a new one! Nevertheless, I am not one to be influenced by omens. This was merely a first date and there was much ground to cover. For the moment, this was merely a coincidence. This Steipler issue had to be kept on the sidelines, and it goes without saying, she was not to be let in onto this unsubstantiated augury. It was much too premature. Now, it just so happened that I was very positively impressed by this young, enthusiastic prospect and I was thoroughly enjoying the date. That was just another coincidence.

The next morning, I admonished the matchmaker for "misrepresenting" the girl's age and speculated that it might present a bit of a "generation gap" but I admitted that I had a very good time and I would like to squeeze in another date before my upcoming furlough. I couldn't afford to waste any of my remaining "Lakewood boy" time. At this point, I had no idea what her thoughts were.

Later that day, I placed a call to my father. We spoke about my upcoming visit to Natwich and other issues related to the impending "transition." I also commented that I had just started seeing a new girl. I remarked that I really liked the date I had with her but that I am concerned that she is so very young.

My father, who has a knack for being able to see the larger picture, had a prophetic response: "She vill get older!"

Couldn't argue with that.

We saw each other on Tuesday night and, on this date, she started to lay out her cards. She very much wants to go back to Eretz Israel. In fact, she grabbed one of only four available slots to work the following year as a dormitory counselor at the seminary that she was attending so that she could join a more advanced study program in Eretz Israel. When she was accepted for the post, she conceded to the director that she expects that she is going to start dating, and asked him if it is fair for her to hold the coveted spot – what if she goes so far as to get engaged? His response was: "It's an occupational hazard." So her plan is to go back to Israel if she doesn't get engaged. And even if she does, she would like to live in Eretz Israel and her husband should study all day long and he can be a Kollel head or maybe the Rabbi of a synagogue (déjà vu the Steipler)...

It all sounded good to me because I actually wanted a girl who wanted to marry a Rosh Kollel. The problem was that, despite all my years of studying, I really wasn't planning to be a Rosh Kollel (or a pulpit Rabbi). My erudition was respectable but certainly not at that level. Moreover, I hadn't been raised to be a Rabbi or Rosh Kollel. My immediate plans were to get a good wife and to go back to Natwich and sell diamonds. I would study during the evenings and on Sundays and, hopefully, we would have sons that we could raise to be Rosh Kollels. Anyway, as she was telling me all this, it was obvious that she hadn't an inkling that I was planning on leaving yeshiva in another 13 days. I was not about to lay out my cards. She had four Kings and I had a pair of Jokers. I had to bluff.

I indeed went to Natwich the next day and spent a week. I only called her once, to maintain contact and to arrange a date for the day following my return. This would be the Thursday before the fateful Monday the 14th. I didn't want to call her more than once; I wanted to give her space and let her think.

The dreaded Thursday arrived. This was to be the Date of Reckoning. Like with Moses at three months, I could no longer "hide the baby." Tonight, I would have to tell her that I am about to leave the yeshiva. I certainly harbored feelings that if this courtship goes the distance, I might be able to forfeit the job and return to yeshiva for a stint at Kollel, but that could only be considered once the plate is broken, and no plates are going to break by Monday. I knew that my interest in her was well founded due to my vast experience and her openness. I knew where she stands and that it concurs with my personal aims. At the same time, I also knew that (1) she is not yet aware of my position, (2) my position does not concur with her personal aspirations, and (3) she is about to find out all of this. Of course, such a thing need not be a stress point for people who have been seeing each other for a substantial amount of time and have developed a strong rapport. But such was not our case. Here I am at 26-plus with a 19-year-old who has almost no dating experience; we now know each other all of twelve days – eight of which found me out of town; we have shared all of two meetings. Most people would call this a fresh, unhardened, fragile relationship; not the ideal time to spring surprises. But, ready or not...

After the date warmed up and we were comfortably sipping our Cokes, I opened the subject. I told her that as of this Monday, I am to begin a job at the Diamond District in Manhattan. I saw her face fall like the South Tower on 9/11. She asked me: why? I explained to her that I am no longer one of the younger single students in Lakewood and that I feel that I am outgrowing the unmarried population. I spent five years gleaning what the yeshiva had to offer me, but it is clear that one cannot remain indefinitely in one setting. There reaches a point where it becomes counterproductive. I went on to say that in the capacity of a married Kollel fellow, the outlook would be different, but that is not currently the case and I cannot alter the game plan based on anything but the "facts on the ground."

For both of us, we were in that awkward twilight zone that most couples must transverse – where the situation looks like it is headed for the desired outcome but it is certainly not close enough to the finish line. The parties discuss serious issues that speculate on commitments that nobody is ready to make. I could only say, "If I (not we) was to get engaged, I could then modify the game plan." I could not afford to display conclusive feelings as long as I could not predict how she would respond to this new development. For her to accept this revelation and continue on meant that she is accepting a prospect that is not exactly what she prefers. We call this "settling." I knew (better than she) that she is young enough, idealistic enough, and marriageable enough to have no need to settle. Not yet, at least. And this thought was most "unsettling."

She was clearly crestfallen and "thrown for a loop," but she maintained a positive disposition. As the dialogue continued I could almost sense in her words the message, "So why don't you propose to me right now and we can break a plate before Monday and you can go right back to yeshiva?" Even though I could sense that she felt that way right now, what concerned me was if she would still feel the same way tomorrow. I brought her home and told her that I realize that she has a good deal to think about. "If you want me to call you after Shabbat, I will call you, but if you prefer to stay in touch through the matchmaker (usually for the purpose of softening the axe-blow) then that is what we'll do." She just said, "You can call me."

The fish was in the net.

"Next Monday" waits for no man and, sure enough, it found me with attaché case (oversized lunch box) in hand doing battle with the MTA panhandlers and 47th Street hawkers. By day's end, my left index finger was charlie-horsed from pressing elevator buttons. That week, we invested two more dates, much of which were dedicated to the task of reassuring her that these current developments were merely responses to undesirable circumstances and did not reflect my true aspirations. I am still expected to make an effort to salvage some Kollel time. This much I considered to be a no-lose situation regardless of what ultimately emerges, so I had no problem with it. Furthermore, her ambition of eventually settling in Eretz Israel is not to be disregarded and must remain an open item on the agenda. To this it was easy to say that I say my *ani maamins* on most days and that all Orthodox Jews aspire to eventually settle in Eretz Israel, yours truly no less. After all, I was brought up as a Zionist, wasn't I? She said she wasn't thinking such long term. I assured her that we would monitor events and "take things as they come." We were both thinking in terms of letting the issue come up for review on a Sabbatical basis. For me this meant once every seven years. For her, it meant once every seven days.

In the yeshiva world we say that engagements are a marvel unto themselves. Overnight, it can transform a person from *ahn elter bochur* (an old bachelor) to a *yunger mahn* (a young husband). In any event, I suddenly found myself in a mirror predicament from that of three weeks previous. Then, I was a yeshiva boy with a foot-and-a-half out the door. Now, I am a working man with half a foot back in. My relationship with Devora was taking hold, but the cement at my new job had not yet begun to set. Should I stay, or not?

Some positions were a foregone conclusion. Devora's vote was an emphatic Nay. My parents were just as emphatic with their Yay. That was a fierce deadlock. She held the heartstrings and they held the purse strings. Devora's parents overtly abstained but they seemed to lean toward the Yay vote – it pays to be on good terms with the new *mechutanim* (in-laws). As for me, it was obvious that I needed to follow the directive of Rabban Gamliel: *Make for yourself a mentor and remove yourself from doubt.*[10]

I placed a separate call to each of my former Roshei Yeshiva. They both offered me the identical advice: Keep the job. Another close friend, a Gerrer Chassid who was working in the diamond business, explained it to me in plain English: It is better to work and be married to a girl who wants you to study than to study and be married to a girl who wants you to work.

Excerpt 9 – Our "Kotel Riot" adventure

They say that the easy-going years of newlywedness can be stretched until about the birth of the third child whereupon the first begins school, expenses mount, schedules are tight and travel becomes cumbersome. In October of 1990 with our third child en route, we knew that we were at the threshold of this phase and so we invested in another holiday excursion to Eretz Israel, this time for Sukkot. We expected this to be our last opportunity for the foreseeable future. Once again we were guests of my sister and brother-in-law but this time, for our first time ever, the venue was Har Nof. It's a bit of a strange neighborhood where you walk into a building at one altitude and walk out at another, but the apartments were nice. In any event, it was a most pleasant and relatively uneventful excursion except for one incident.

On the second intermediate day of the holiday, true to our role as religious tourists, we dressed up the two kids and hopped the Number 2 bus to the Western Wall for *Birkat Kohanim*. I had already prayed in the neighborhood and so we only attended the second round of Birkat Kohanim that takes place during the *Mussaf* service. As soon as the ritual ended we regrouped and headed up the back left stairway into the Jewish Quarter in search of some place to grab a breakfast. We located one shop with a suitable *sukka* and we ordered something to eat. Presently we heard a series of loud popping noises, which, at first, did not register in my mind until Devora screamed out, "Hey! They're shooting over there!" I walked a few paces to where I could see the Kotel. In so doing, I was

---

[10] Pirkei Avot 1:16

almost bowled over by throngs of soldiers who were rushing toward the scene. All I could see were the figures of some people running along the top of the Wall in a crouched position and some plumes of smoke. Suddenly, baby Yaakov began to sneeze continuously as the scent of tear gas drifted into the *Rova* (Jewish Quarter). I tried to move down toward the Kotel to see what was happening but I couldn't prevail against a wall of civilians that were rushing up away from it. That turned out to be as close as I got to the infamous and blatantly miraculous Kotel riot of Sukkot 5751.

It seems that some of the local talent among the Ishmaelites were aware that the second intermediate day of the holiday draws a considerable crowd of Jewish worshippers to the Wailing Wall. To the rabble rousers it looked like this was a great opportunity to rouse some rabble and release some rubble. And so, they prepared a few barrels full of large rocks and other refuse (I was told that this included an old discarded refrigerator) which they planned to bombard upon the unsuspecting crowd and thus to inflict as much damage as possible. How neighborly! Apparently, their formidable "intelligence" service was unaware of exactly why so many people come, and for some Heavenly ordained reason, they scheduled their onslaught for about 11:00 which was approximately a half hour *after* the ceremony ended; when the bulk of the crowd had left the Wall and the remainder were not nearly as densely packed as they had been just a few minutes earlier. Miraculously, the initial falling projectiles didn't hit anybody and all who had been in harm's way were able to quickly relocate. Within moments, the only Jews within striking range were all wearing green uniforms and carrying M-16s and Uzis. Quite unfortunately for the Ishmaeli attackers, these green clad men were a bit short on rubber bullets and all they had was live ammunition. No less than 17 of our East Jerusalem cousins had to spend the rest of the day in the morgue. Thank G-d, not one Jewish worshipper was seriously hurt (to my recollection, there was only one who was hurt at all). The international media seemed to be quite disconcerted by the imbalance of these casualty figures and, to nobody's surprise, the Israeli government took a lot of heat. My guess is that this was one of the factors that led to Oslo, an agreement that was designed to level the playing field so that (Heaven forefend) some Jews also make it onto the casualty list.

One thing that greatly disturbed us in the aftermath of this incident was a headline that appeared in a major American newspaper in reference to the joyous dancing at the Western Wall that is always a part of the Simchat Torah celebration: *Jews Dance at the Site of the Killings*.

No news is good news!

Excerpt 10 – The Aliya story (some of it, at least)

Finally, in 1996, the two children's bedrooms were filled to capacity, we had three K-8 plus one nursery school tuitions with two on deck, and my *chavruta* and I were approaching the final chapter of tractate Chullin. Our firstborn was eight years old and was approaching what is known as the aliya "danger zone." After all my stalling, I knew quite seriously that we were facing a window of opportunity that would only shrink.

In August of that year, I undertook another business trip and, this time, I truly did come with more than one order of business. Through the assistance of my Bnei Brak brother-in-law, I merited an audience with Rabbi Chaim Kanievsky, Shlit"a. I told him that I was an American businessman from Natwich with a growing family and my wife was on my case to settle in Eretz Israel *me'az hayita l'frau*.[11] He responded by quoting a Mishna in tractate Ketubot[12]: "All [spouses] can demand immigration to Eretz Israel but not all [spouses] can demand emigration. This applies equally to the husbands and to the wives." He did not seem interested in discussing details such as livelihood prospects, ages of children, or related issues. I thought it would be wise to get a second opinion from one whom I could converse with at length, in my native tongue. I approached Rabbi Chaim Pinchas Scheinberg, Shlit"a and presented the issue. He didn't seem to be too interested in particulars either; he merely said that "I am pro Eretz Israel." I asked him whether I needed to be concerned about the prospects for a livelihood and he said that if I made sure to distribute a respectable amount of *tzedaka* (charity) I should not be concerned. So much for lengthy conversations. To make one final stab at a dissenting vote, I approached the Rebbe of Ger, Shlit"a. No dice. He did nothing more than wish me *hatzlacha* (success). The bout had gone 15 rounds and Devora won by a 3-0 decision. Despite this, there was one permanent member of the [job] security council who retained veto power – Dad.

My father had always been aware of my wife's pro-Israel inclinations so it was no surprise to him when I told him that we actually wanted to go. My father asked me what my plans were. I told him that I thought the company could benefit from an Israeli-based buying office. I was hoping that I could establish an efficient pipeline to ensure a continuous supply of merchandise – some of which can be quite scarce – and thus

---

[11] Pronounced *l'froy* meaning "ever since she was a wife." Play on words from Exodus 9:24 *me'az hayita l'goy* which means "ever since it was a nation." In the real verse, it is referring to a plague. Here, it is not – is that right, dear?

[12] Talmud Bavli Ketubot 111a

help the company to grow. He said that he had enough business and he didn't need the company to grow, especially if I left his office in Natwich. He also said that there were so many suppliers that parade to our office where he can buy with "home field advantage" that there was no true advantage to having an overseas buyer. His message was that I was not to depend on his operation to artificially sustain mine. I had to be viable on my own. Regardless, he offered me his blessing and total support to make the move, including that he would not take me off the company payroll for the short term.

I must admit, I know few people (none, actually) who have been offered such a deal. As the wellspring of excuses had run completely dry, we made our way to the local Aliya office.

Appendix B
Articles

Item 1:

Original text of Mark Twain's (Samuel Langhorne Clemens) essay about the Jews that was modified for the Preface of this book

Note – This item is the conclusion of a lengthy essay entitled "Concerning the Jews" by Mark Twain. It was originally printed in Harper's Magazine in March of 1898.

If the statistics are right, the Jews constitute but ONE PERCENT of the human race. It suggests a nebulous dim puff of star dust lost in the blaze of the Milky Way. Properly the Jew ought to be hardly heard of; but he is heard of always has been heard of. He is as prominent on the planet as any other people, and his commercial importance is extravagantly out of proportion to the smallness of his bulk. His contribution to the world's list of great names in literature, science, art, music, finance, medicine, and abstruse learning are also way out of proportion to the weakness of his numbers.

He has made a marvelous fight in this world, in all ages; and has done it with his hands tied behind him. He could be vain of himself, and be excused for it. The Egyptian, the Babylonian, and the Persian rose filled the planet with sound and splendor, then faded away to dream-stuff and passed away; the Greek and the Roman followed and made a vast noise, and they are gone; other people have sprung up and held their torch high for a time, but it burned out, and they sit in the twilight now or have vanished. The Jew saw them all, beat them all, and is now what he always was, exhibiting no decadence, no infirmities of age, no weakening of his parts, no showing of his energies, no dulling of his alert and aggressive mind. All things are mortal but the Jew; all other forces pass, but he remains. What is the secret of his immortality?

Item 2:

Full text of Elliot Jager's column about the Rambam (Maimonides) that is referenced in Chapter 4 (page 112)

Return of the Rambam

By ELLIOT JAGER

Jerusalem Post - Dec. 26, 2004 - 23:14 - Updated Dec. 27, 2004 - 10:41 (reprinted with permission)

Moses Maimonides, known as the Rambam – for Rebbe Moshe Ben Maimon – died in December 1204, but he's never been more in vogue.

To mark the 800th anniversary of his death, a dozen major academic conferences worldwide have dealt with his legacy.

The Jewish National and University Library at Givat Ram has just opened an exhibition of Rambam manuscripts and first editions. The Destiny Foundation, headed by Rabbi Berl Wein, the plain-speaking but deep-thinking historian and theologian, has just released a valuable and entertaining animated documentary.

And settler leaders have cited the Rambam in their battle against disengagement.

My first Rambam experience took place when I was a teenager working as a shipping clerk at Beigelisen's Lower East Side book store. The *Guide for the Perplexed* caught my eye. I purchased it for 20% off its $3.50 cover price using my employee discount (I was the only employee).

The blurb on the back cautioned it was aimed at "scholars" puzzled by the conflict between religion, science, and philosophy.

Unfortunately, the Guide was way over my head; it sat mostly untouched until last week, when my interest was piqued by watching Wein's DVD Rambam – The Story of Maimonides, in which Leonard Nimoy (Mr. Spock) plays the voice of Rambam.

As the film shows, Rambam, born in 1135, was forced to flee Spain when its relatively tolerant Muslim rulers were defeated by the puritanical Islamist Almohads. The Maimon family went first to Fez, then to the Muslim-controlled Holy Land, and eventually to Egypt.

There Rambam became a palace physician and official head of the Jewish community (in 1177). And he remained an astonishingly prolific theologian.

Still perplexed after all these years, I was inspired by the film to take another crack at understanding the sage. Here's what I've learned so far: The Rambam was an elitist, an intellectual, and a pragmatist.

As an enlightened, self-sacrificing elitist, he felt a weighty responsibility to serve the community. This noblesse oblige forced him to lose precious study time.

His attitude toward the unenlightened masses: They should be allowed to embrace certain popular – but spiritually meaningless – religious rituals and dogmas without which their faith might be shattered and their observance undermined.

Our religious, political, and business elites wouldn't know what to make of the Rambam's selfless behavior. They'd probably think him a chump; a frier.

As an intellectual, the Rambam argued – *a la* Donald Rumsfeld – that it was easier to identify what God wasn't than what He was. I can just hear him saying: "There are things we know, things we don't know, things we know we don't know, and things we don't know we don't know."

My crash course also told me that, for the Rambam: (1) the Creator isn't a figure who micro-manages whether or not you stub your toe getting out of bed in the morning; (2) God preserves the cosmos, not the individual; and (3) Judaism emphasizes intellect over ecstasy.

Still, each stream of Judaism claims him. Within Orthodoxy he's appropriated by everyone from the Lithuanian mitnagdim to Lubavitch.

If the Rambam were alive today, I pressed Rabbi Wein, where would he feel most comfortable?

"He'd be hardal – ultra-Orthodox national-religious."

Perhaps. What's clear is that the Rambam would be uncomfortable with the more insular Orthodox sects because he argued that to better understand God, one has to study science and philosophy.

The Reform movement claims the Rambam because he rejected Scriptural literalism, embraced rationalism, championed religious liberalism, and repudiated superstition.

For its part, the Masorti movement values the Rambam for his cautious halachic innovations. Rabbi Louis Jacobs wrote approvingly that "Maimonides' struggle for a rational approach to Judaism is evident on practically every page of his writings."

But Rambam's rigid "Thirteen Principles of the Faith" – albeit written at the start of his career and open to interpretation – are nevertheless problematic for Conservatives.

Jacobs: "In matters of faith, the more correct approach is not to ask what Maimonides said 800 years ago, but what a teacher with his intellectual integrity would say if he were alive today."

What about Rambam's politics? Would his pragmatism in dealing with the Muslims of his day extend to an accommodation with the Palestinian Arabs? Would he acquiesce in a withdrawal from parts of the Land of Israel?

Speaking to Arutz 7 last week, Rabbi Yisrael Ariel invoked Maimonides in defending the right of soldiers to refuse to carry out disengagement-related orders.

"Maimonides wrote... that if the king makes a decree to nullify a Torah commandment, he must not be listened to, because... [it] contradicts those of the Master's..."

But the late Yeshayahu Leibowitz, a vehement anti-settlement theologian, claimed that the state delineated by Maimonides (and invoked by Ariel) "never existed, and never will exist within the framework of historical reality."

Plainly, the scope of the Rambam's writings open them up to opposing interpretations. Who knows what the sage meant when he said, "Great is peace, as the whole Torah was given in order to promote peace in the world."

I'll go out on a limb and say that if Prime Minister Ariel Sharon could convince the Rambam that disengagement is best for the commonwealth, the sage would agree to withdrawal even if some individuals were hurt by it.

But since Sharon has bulldozed rather than barnstormed for his plan, my hunch is the Rambam would remain agnostic on disengagement.

Hebrew University Professor Avi Ravitzky told me that for the Rambam, the Land per se is not the highest value. What Jews need is sufficient room to pursue a Torah way of life. This yardstick is what should determine borders.

I asked Ravitsky if he agreed with Wein that the Rambam would affiliate with today's Orthodox. "In terms of observance? Definitely.

"In terms of his thinking, the Rambam was, well... the Rambam. He's beyond labels."

Item 3:

Full text of article by Naomi Ragen that is referenced in Chapter 9 (page 221)

Note – This item originally appeared in the Jerusalem Report on September 14, 1998. Currently, it is accessible at Naomi Ragen's web site - http://www.naomiragen.com/Articles/Handwriting.htm (reprinted with permission)

Handwriting on the Wall

By NAOMI RAGEN ©

One recent Friday night, someone spray-painted the words "Death to Dosim "(slang for observant Jews) on the outside wall of my synagogue in Ramot, Jerusalem. They wrote it in Hebrew, in four-foot high black letters, opposite the entrance to Nachshon Hall, named in honor of Nachshon Waxman, the soldier kidnapped and murdered by Hamas terrorists only three years ago.

"Stupid kids" my own teenagers shrugged when they saw the graffiti.

Probably. But I keep thinking about the hand that wrote those words and who it might have belonged to. Was it someone who knew that Nachshon's parents would be sure to read it as they entered the synagogue that Shabbat morning? Did they realize that that Shabbat, in Nachshon Hall, we would be celebrating the bar-mitzvah of Dov Kalmanovich's son, the same Dov Kalmanovich who was one of the intifada's first victims, whose entire face was burned away by an enemy who wished him dead because he was a Jew and an Israeli?

What could have brought another Jew and an Israeli, growing up in his own country, to deface a Jewish house of worship and to wish its occupants dead?

I thought about it. Perhaps it was someone who had seen ultra-Orthodox Jews throwing stones at cars traveling on nearby Bar Ilan road one Sabbath. Perhaps it was someone who'd watched bearded, black-suited Jews on TV ignoring the siren for Israel's fallen during Memorial Day, or who had read endless newspaper articles about how the ultra-Orthodox were receiving army exemptions, subsidized rentals, preferred mortgages, and educational stipends despite the fact that they burn the flag of the country in which they live and spit in the faces of those whose pockets they empty with such cynical arrogance, for that is the picture our television and newspapers paint, based unfortunately on the awful reality.

I, of course, and my family, as well as the Waxman family, and the Kalmanovich family, are not guilty of any of those crimes. We serve in the army with pride. We support the State with our taxes and pay our bank mortgages, and our children's unsubsidized college tuition. We deplore the disgusting manipulations of corrupt, self-serving "religious" politicians who callously use our G-d and His holy Torah, to siphon off funds desperately needed for the unemployed, the handicapped, social and educational programs, handing them over to those perpetuating a parasitical lifestyle that is as far from Torah values as it is possible to imagine.

But how could the "stupid kid" who wrote those hateful words know that? After all, we don't raise our voices in protest when religious extremists achieve yet another victory against the State and its well being. We don't say out loud what many of us believe, that the greatest tragedy for the Jewish people in the land of Israel is the fact that there is an intermingling of synagogue and state. We don't say loud enough: "One nation, one draft" and those who won't serve, and won't work, and won't pay taxes, can leave and try their luck siphoning off funds from the welfare offices in Williamsburg. We don't object that the National Religious Party is out there with all the rest, its hand outstretched to get its share, its political agenda geared to its own narrow constituency's interests, and the Torah, and G-d, and justice and the public good be damned.

Of course, that doesn't mean that the idiot who wrote those hateful words should be looked at with a forgiving eye. If he's an adult I would tell him to understand that he has now joined a unique group which includes Hitler and his brownshirts, Chimelnetzki, and others of that ilk. If he's still a child, then I turn to his parents and blame them for raising a Jewish child in the land of Israel without a single Jewish value that would prevent him from desecrating all that is most precious to us as a people.

And to all the so-called self-appointed "guardians of our faith" who think that their arrogant disdain for the great majority of the people of

Israel can go on forever, I would say read the handwriting on the wall, for in great part, it is the fruit of your labor. And to all those Jews who speak at home of "Dosim" as one disgusting entity that includes every Jew keeping faith with his heritage, I would say – here, look at what you've done, created a little homegrown anti-Semite. And for myself, and others like me, who deplore the excesses of the religious right but do nothing publicly to prevent them, I say, we can no longer avoid seeing the handwriting on the wall, for it's our wall they're writing on.

Appendix C
Glossary

Glossary

Aliya	Immigration to Eretz Israel
Assiah	Deed; Undertaking (active)
Baal Koreh	Person designated to read from the Torah scroll at synagogue services.
Baal Teshuva (BT)	Formerly non-observant Jew who has returned to a life of observance
Baalebatishe	Working class
Beit midrash	Study hall
Bekesha	The long (usually black) over-garments favored by the Chassidim
Birkat Kohanim	Special blessing that the kohanim (priests) confer to the populace during the morning services in Eretz Israel
[Camp] Bracha	[Camp of] a blessed (successful) existence
[Camp] Kelala	[Camp of] a cursed (happenstance prone) existence
Chavruta	Study partner
Cheder	Primary school for chareidi children
Chillul Hashem	Desecration of G-d's name. See the end of Chapter 6 (page 171).
Cholov Yisrael	Milk that is produced under the supervision of orthodox Jews

Chumash	Any or all of the Five Books of Moses
Daf Yomi	Popular world-wide Talmud study program that is predicated on covering one folio of Talmud every single day. In this program, the entire Babylonian Talmud is completed every 7 ½ years.
Derech	Literally: Road or path. Usage: Path of traditional observance
Eimah Yeteirah	Excessive domination. The stuff "control freaks" are made of.
Einikle	Grandchild; descendant
Eruv	Halachic mechanism for transforming a non-permissible zone into a permissible zone regarding transporting objects on Shabbat. Typically consists of a physical enclosure.
FFB	**F**rum **F**rom **B**irth – Raised as an observant Jew
Gebrochs	Broken particles of matzah (or matzah meal) that have come in contact with water. A widely accepted stringency among many Ashkenazic Jews, predominantly those from Chassidic backgrounds, forbids the consumption of gebrochs on Passover.
Geniza	Burial service for Jewish religious texts that are damaged, worn, or otherwise unneeded.
Goldene medina	Golden State. A Yiddish euphemism for all of America, not just California.
Hakhel	Literally: Assemble. Special ceremony that oc curred once in seven years during the Temple era when all Jews were required to assemble at the Temple and hear the king read the book of Deuteronomy.
Hashgacha	Rabbinic supervision
Hashkafa	Religious ideology

Havdala	Special blessing made over wine at the conclusion of the Shabbat or festivals to allow us to engage in mundane activities
Heimishe	Home style
Hesder yeshiva	Israeli yeshiva affiliated with the National Religious movement that combines Torah study with IDF Army service.
Kedoshim	Saintly people
Kibud av v'em	[The commandment to] honor one's father and mother
Kiddush	Sanctification blessings that are recited over a cup of wine to usher in the Shabbat or a Jewish festival.
Kiddush Hashem	Sactification of G-d's name. See the end of Chapter 6 (page 171).
Kipa (pl. Kipot)	Yarmulka; skullcap
Kitzur Shulchan Aruch	Abridged version of the Code of Jewish Law written by Rabbi Shlomo Gantzfried in the 19th century
Kollel	Chareidi fellowship system for married scholars wherein the scholars receive stipends for intensive Torah study.
Lulav	Palm branch – one of four plant species that are brandished on Sukkot
Megillah	Parchment scroll that contains the story of Esther that we read on Purim
Mehadrin	Meticulous
Mezuzah	Parchment containing two paragraphs of the Shema that we affix to our doorposts
Mikveh (pl. Mikvaot)	Jewish ritual pool

Minyan	Jewish prayer group requiring a quorum of ten adult males
Mitnaged	Literally: opponent. East European Ashkenazi Jew who does not conform to Chassidic rituals
Mitzvah	Religious commandment
Modeh ani	One line declaration of gratitude to G-d for restoring our souls that we recite each morning the moment we awaken.
Mohel	Expert in ritual circumcision
Motzaei Shabbat	Saturday night
Mt. Neverest	Tongue-in-cheek expression for the ultimate goal of a Jew according to Rabbi Pinchas ben Yair and Rabbi Moshe Chaim Luzzato. This is to emulate G-d to the extent that one is able to revive the dead – thereupon, one can live for eternity and "never rest".
Natwich	**N**orth **A**merican **T**own **W**ith **I**ntegrated **C**ommunity of **H**ebrews
Navi	The books of the Prophets.
NCOJ	Non-Chareidi Orthodox Jew. This is defined as a mitzvah observant Jew who who does not meet the definition of chareidi as defined in this book. One is not automatically an NCOJ merely because he does not wish to consider himself chareidi.
Oht	Sign of our devotion to G-d
OTD	Off the Derech – straying from the path of traditional observance
Peyot	Ear locks
QOF chareidi	**Q**uaker **O**ats/**F**agin chareidi Explained in Chapter 3 (page 70).
Rosh Chodesh	New moon. First day of a new month on the Jewish lunar calendar.

Shalom Bayit	Marital harmony
Shamor/Shemira	Observance (passive)
Sharav	Heat wave
Shatnez	Mixture of wool and linen that the Torah forbids us to wear
Shavuot	Jewish festival that falls on the 6th and 7th of Sivan (late May or early June) and is the anniversary of the revelation at Mt. Sinai and the transmission of the Ten Commandments. There is a custom to stay awake and study throughout the night, hence, the "all nighter".
Shel yad	The portion of the phylacteries that is worn on the arm.
Sheva Berachot	Ceremony of reciting seven blessings for a bride and groom at the wedding and after festive meals over the course of the first week of marriage.
Shiur; Blatt Shiur	Shiur is a Torah lesson; A Blatt shiur (page lesson) is a Talmud lesson which is aimed more at covering material on a superficial level than in-depth study.
Shlit"a	Acronym for **Sh**eyichye **L**'Chaim **T**ovim **A**rukim – May he live many long and good years
Shmitta	The Sabbatical year when all planting and harvesting is forbidden.
Shmura matzah	Matzah prepared from wheat that has been guarded from moisture from the time it was reaped. The Seder matzot must be of this quality as long as such wheat is available.
Shochet	Expert in ritual slaughter
Shteibel	Small one-room synagogue, usually located in a private residence.
Shtreimel	Round fur hats worn by many married Chassidim on Shabbat, festivals, and important occasions.

Shulchan Aruch Code of Jewish Law written by Rabbi Joseph Karo in the 16th century

Simcha Joyous event such as a wedding, bar mitzvah, or circumcision ceremony

Sukka Booth (Tabernacle)

T'chelet Ancient blue dye that is prescribed in the Torah as a component of the *tzitzit*. There are plausible claims that the genuine dye has been rediscovered but this is not universally accepted by chareidi sages.

Talmid Chacham Learned scholar

Tefillin Phylacteries. A specific group of passages from the Torah that are encased in small black leather boxes and are worn on the head and one arm during morning prayer services.

Tzaddik Saintly individual

Tzedaka Charity

Tzitzit Ritual fringe tied onto four cornered garments

$Xd_{20}Lv_{26}D_6$ Exodus 20, Leviticus 26, Deuteronomy 6 – the "molecular composition" of the chareidim

Zachor/Zechira Commemoration (active)

ZT"L Acronym for **Z**echer **T**zaddik **L**'Bracha; the Hebrew version of OB"M – Of Blessed Memory